LEABHARLANN CHONTAE ROSCOMAIN

This book should be returned not later than the last date shown below. It may be renewed if not requested by another borrower.

Books are on loan for 14 days from the date of issue.

DATE DUE	DATE DUE	DATE DUE	DATE DUE
2 9 OCT 2002			
28. JAN 05			
30. MAY 06.			
04. OCT 06. 18. OCT 07.			
.OV 07			
29. NOV 07			

BEEN
THERE,
DONE
THAT

EDDIE FISHER

with David Fisher

BEEN THERE, DONE THAT

HUTCHINSON
LONDON

First published in the United Kingdom in 1999 by Hutchinson

The Random House Group Limited
20 Vauxhall Bridge Road, London SW1V 2SA

Random House Australia (Pty) Limited
20 Alfred Street, Milsons Point, Sydney,
New South Wales 2061, Australia

Random House New Zealand Limited
18 Poland Road, Glenfield
Auckland 10, New Zealand

Random House South Africa (Pty) Limited
Endulini, 5a Jubilee Road, Parktown 2193, South Africa

The Random House Group Limited Reg. No. 954009
www.randomhouse.co.uk

A CIP catalogue record for this book is available
from the British Library

Papers used by Random House
are natural, recyclable products made from wood grown in
sustainable forests. The manufacturing processes conform to
the environmental regulations of the country of origin

ISBN 0 09 179371 8

Printed and bound in Great Britain by
Biddles Ltd, Guildford and King's Lynn

For Betty

The only wife I've ever had,

and the most beautiful woman

in the world.

CHAPTER ONE

My name is Eddie Fisher, and I'm a singer.

When I was a small child—I couldn't have been more than three or four years old—I opened my mouth and this beautiful sound came out and, for me, the world was changed forever. Everything that has happened in my life, the fame I've enjoyed, the fortunes I've earned, the marriages, the affairs, the scandals, even my drug addictions, *everything* I owe to the fact that when I opened my mouth this sound, this music, came out. I didn't have to work at it; I didn't even have to practice. It was there, it was always there, and once I thought it would be there forever.

That gift in my throat made me feel like a king—and caused people to treat me like one. It made me a star, one of the most successful singers in American history. Sometimes it all seems so hard to believe, I had more consecutive hit records than the Beatles or Elvis Presley, I had 65,000 fan clubs and the most widely broadcast program on television and radio. That sound took me from the streets of Philadelphia to the White House; Harry Truman loved me, Ike loved me, Jack Kennedy and I shared drugs and women, and it transformed me from a shy little boy into a man who attracted the most famous and desirable women in the world.

And it was that sound, a clean, smooth, lyric baritone, that put me at the center of one of the most widely publicized love affairs. . .affair? The word *affair* doesn't even begin to describe what it was. It was a storm, a maelstrom of passion and betrayal. For almost five years, my life was detailed in the headlines. It was the greatest media frenzy of the time, the first great Hollywood love story of post-war America. It was the harbinger of what was to come years later, the beginning of attack journalism, the birth of the paparazzi. I remember one night in Rome, when my wife, Elizabeth Taylor, was about to begin filming *Cleopatra*, then the most expensive movie ever made. We turned on the outdoor lights at our villa and found photographers climbing over the walls. We were besieged. They even came to our door disguised as priests.

At the height of my career, I found myself in the middle of two of the most publicized love triangles of the twentieth century. Me, "Sonny Boy," the skinny Jewish kid from the streets of Philadelphia, and all because I had this gift, an incredible, powerful sound.

I was born in Philadelphia in 1928, the fourth of seven children. Supposedly there were already eleven girls in the hospital nursery when I was born. Because I was the only boy, the nurses made a big fuss over me. Some of them had recently seen the great Al Jolson's latest movie, *The Singing Fool*, so they sang me to sleep with a line from a song in that film, "Climb upon my knee, Sonny Boy." So to my family I was always Sonny Boy, or Sonny. That never changed. Even when I was married to the most beautiful movie star in the world, when I was earning $40,000 a week singing in Las Vegas, spending time with Frank Sinatra and Rocky Marciano, when I had songs at the top of the charts, none of that mattered; to my family I was still Sonny Boy. But as things turned out, it probably would have been more appropriate just to call me the Singing Fool.

One of my most famous songs was "Oh! My Papa." It was a huge hit. When my father came to see me perform I'd look at him lovingly and sing it: "Oh, my Papa, to me you are so wonderful." Yeah, wonderful. I wasn't much of an actor. One year the *Harvard Lampoon* voted me the worst actor of the year, an honor I had truly earned. But when I looked at my father lovingly and sang that song, that was the best acting of my career. My father was mad at his life. He worked hard and had nothing to show for it, so he took it out on his family, especially my mother and my oldest brother, Sid. My father was a nasty, abusive man, a tyrant. I never saw him hit my mother, though my brothers and sisters insisted he did. But I know I saw him hit my brother. I'm not sure that really mattered, because the verbal abuse was just as bad. I'll never forget the sound that came out of his mouth: loud and shrill and nasty. There was nothing nice about it. It was a sound that seemed strong enough to drill right through the walls. When he started yelling, I'd be so embarrassed I'd run and close the windows and hope that no one would hear him. When I finally left home, my little sister, Eileen, became the window closer. The only thing my mother ever wanted from my father was a divorce, and as soon as her children were old enough, she left him.

My parents were part of the massive wave of Russian Jews who came to America around the turn of the century to escape the poverty and the pogroms of Eastern Europe. My father, Joe, was thirteen years old when he immigrated. My father's family name was Tisch or Fisch, but it became Fisher when he landed in America and got his papers. My father's family never accepted my mother and never had too much to do with us until I became famous. Then they would come to the night-clubs and proudly sit right in the front. I was told they felt that my mother's family was too poor. Too poor? Maybe the big difference was that the Fishers' house had a porch. The only time I ever heard the Fishers say anything kind about my mother was in the limousine on the way to her funeral.

When they married, my mother was fifteen years old, my father almost eighteen. They were just kids. My father was an intelligent man, and he had been educated in Russia. He loved to read, he loved history; it was real life that gave him problems. Both of them had been forced to drop out of school to help support their families, so they got married and had their own family they couldn't support. My father never really had a chance. I suppose that's why I always felt so sorry for him.

The 1929 stock market crash and the Great Depression barely affected my family. We had nothing to start with, so we had nothing to lose. My father worked in leather factories long before the unions created decent working conditions. These places were hot and dirty and the pay was terrible, but nobody dared complain. People like my father, immigrants with little formal education and limited technical skills, were happy to have any job. I remember going with him to work one day. Although he never said anything to me, I think he wanted me to see for myself what his life was all about. At that time he was making leather suitcases. The "factory" was a sweatshop; it was dark and filthy and dangerous. People didn't matter, production did; how many pieces a day. I couldn't believe how hard he worked, how much muscle it took to make a cheap suitcase. I didn't vow that day that I would never work in a place like that, nothing dramatic like that, because that possibility never occurred to me. I had been born with magic in my throat, I was going to be a singer. There was never a day that I doubted that.

In 1934 my father was in a terrible automobile accident. The driver collided with an ice-delivery truck and was killed, and my father was badly hurt. For several weeks it looked like he was going to die. But he lived and collected almost $5,000 in insurance. That was a fortune, and for just a little while, we were rich. Imagine that, a car wreck was the best opportunity my father ever had. He used the money to open Fisher's Delicatessen. Most of the family worked there. My father wore a clean white apron and ran the place, the children stocked the shelves and cleaned up, my mother cooked the meats and made the potato salad. It was the only time in my childhood that I remember my father being happy. But it didn't last very long. We didn't know how to run a grocery store, and even my mother's wonderful potato salad wasn't enough to keep us in business. It only took us about a year to lose the entire insurance settlement.

After that, my father peddled fruits and vegetables from the back of an old LaSalle or Packard. He took out the back seat and drove down to the wholesale market on the docks and bought leftover peaches and tomatoes and whatever else was in season. Every penny had to count. He'd empty the boxes of strawberries and then refill them, putting the rotten ones on the bottom so they wouldn't be seen, then squeeze the corners of the boxes so it would take fewer berries to fill them. He'd use every trick to make a few pennies. I was so embarrassed; I hated him for making me feel dishonest.

My brother Sol and I would fill baskets from the back seat then walk through the alleys between the buildings, singing as loudly as we could to attract attention. We sang the songs of produce peddlers: "Sound, ripe tomatoes here, ten cents a quarter peck . . ." Housewives would lower their baskets from their windows; we'd fill them with whatever we had, and they'd give us a few pennies. I was a skinny little kid and, supposedly, these women would see me and feel so sorry for me that they would put food in their baskets for me when they lowered them. Years later, after I'd become a big star, after I was able to afford to go to Hong Kong and buy 140 silk suits, 185 monogrammed silk shirts, and 50 pair of silk pajamas, after I was able to give a forty-carat diamond bracelet to Elizabeth, this was the story my mother most enjoyed telling reporters.

We lived surrounded by poverty. Our neighbors were just like us, Jewish immigrants struggling to survive. But even in that world I still felt like everybody else was rich and we were poor. To my mother's great shame, we had to go on "the dole"—we had to accept welfare several times: seventeen dollars and fifty cents a week. For food and used clothing we had to go to the distribution center set up in an abandoned railroad station. My mother was so embarrassed that the neighbors would know that we were "on relief" that she would put a pillow in the baby carriage, cover it with a net, and make me wheel it to the welfare center. Then she'd fill the carriage with flour and potatoes and whatever they gave us, cover it again, and I would wheel it home. I always pushed the carriage through the rear alleys so no one would see us.

There were many times we couldn't pay the rent, so at night we would pack the few pieces of furniture we had and our ragged clothes, and move someplace where the landlord didn't know we were broke. The place I remember most of all was a tiny house with two bedrooms and one bathroom. I slept in a bed with my two brothers. There was only enough hot water for one bath, so we'd fill the tub and all nine of us would use the same water. The toilet flushed only once, then it couldn't be used for a long time. It was tough, very tough. When I was fourteen years old I began staying with the family of a man named Skipper Dawes, who had discovered me and put me on radio. His house was warm in the winter and dry when it rained, and it had a real shower, but the thing that most amazed me was that his toilets refilled with water after being flushed. I used to go into the bathroom just to flush the toilet several times.

I never had a piece of new clothing. Everything was either a hand-me-down or something we got from the welfare. When I wore holes in the soles of my shoes, I'd cut out cardboard soles and use them as inserts. I usually had two cardboard patches in my shoes and two spares in my pocket. The cardboard did not work very well in the winter, when the snow would soak right through to my feet, so when I walked in the snow or rain I would pull down my socks and fold it over to cover the holes.

My mother did her best to make sure her children were clean, but I always felt dirty. No matter how much we washed, no matter how hard she tried, we lived with dirt and bugs. There were bugs on everything—on our clothes, in the beds—they were inescapable. We would squeeze them with our fingers, so our sheets were always spotted with dried bug blood. On occasion we would take our mattresses outside and put burning newspapers under them, because everybody in the neighborhood knew that was an effective means of getting rid of bedbugs.

Somehow, though, somehow I knew that I was going to get out of that world, and I knew that my voice was going to take me out of it. My mother believed that. She and my grandmother, my *bubba*, did everything to make it possible for me. Their dream was that I would be a successful singer and take the whole family out of the poverty.

My *bubba* was the first person to encourage me. When I was two or three years old, she would sing old Jewish folk songs to me and the next day I'd sing them back to her, word for word. Who knows where something like that comes from? "Watch," she told my parents, "this one is going to be something special."

I was a very shy little boy and I didn't like to draw attention to myself. So when company came to the house, I'd run upstairs and hide under the bed because I knew my mother was going to make me stand on a chair and sing "The Good Ship Lollipop."

But eventually I discovered that my voice set me apart from everybody else. It was the one thing I could do better than anyone else. When I sang, people stopped what they were doing to listen, they made me feel so very special. When I was still a small child I was singing in the synagogue. I was seven or eight years old and I was singing duets in Hebrew with the cantor. You're not supposed to applaud in the temple, but when I sang, the congregation applauded. Oh, I loved that sound, that feeling of being appreciated. Once I figured out that I had this gift, I wouldn't stop singing. They couldn't get me to stop.

I never had a singing lesson, so I never learned anything about technique. My technique was that I opened my mouth and let it out. I was born in tune. I didn't know flats or sharps, and I couldn't read music. I just opened my mouth and sang. I was small, but I had a big voice. I had a wonderful tone. Even as a child my voice filled the whole room. People were always amazed that such a big sound came out of such a small person. I learned how to sing by listening to other people singing. My grandparents had a wind-up Victrola and I'd listen to Enrico Caruso singing. He was the only professional singer I ever heard. And I'd listen to the cantor in the synagogue and the radio, and whatever I heard I could repeat. I'd hear a song once, twice at most, and I would know it.

My mother bought an upright piano for forty dollars. Now where she got forty dollars I will never know. I do know there were many things a lot more important than an old upright piano that she could have used the money for. But that was for me, that was an investment in my future. She did her best to teach me to sing. She wasn't very musical, she could barely play that piano, but she would play all the Jewish songs and I would stand next to her and sing them.

When I was almost five years old my sister Miriam's choir was chosen to sing in a talent contest at a Valentine's Day party. I went with her to a rehearsal and sang along with her. Sang along? I practically drowned out the choir. The choir leader turned to me and asked, "Was that you making that noise?"

Noise? "I was just singing," I explained.

He asked me to sing another song. Maybe I sang "Animal Crackers in my Soup," or one of my *bubba*'s folk songs, but whatever it was, when I finished he told Miriam I could come to the party with her and participate in the contest. "He should wear a white suit," he suggested.

My mother made a white suit for me; she sewed me a pair of short pants and a white shirt, and from somewhere she got me a pair of white shoes. I felt so good that night; I felt clean. I guess that was the first time

I felt the love of an audience. It was an extraordinary feeling. I didn't want to get off that little stage. I won first prize, a big cake—the first thing I ever earned with my sound.

After that my mother entered me in every amateur contest she heard about and I usually won. I won the contests at schools and at the movie theaters. Eventually I tied for first place with a violin player in the biggest amateur contest of all, *Arthur Godfrey's Talent Scouts.*

My mother wasn't a stage mother, she never had to push me onstage to sing. I craved the response that I got when I sang for an audience. I wanted to perform more than anything else in the world, and she made sure I got that opportunity. Years later she would sit adoringly in the front row at nightclubs and concerts all over the country and I would sing "My Yiddishe Mama" for her. That was my love song for her.

My talent made me feel special. Even as a small child I knew that the rules that applied to other children didn't apply to me. I could get away with things my brothers and sisters could not. I wasn't a good student in school, but no one seemed troubled by that, since I had that voice. Only once in my childhood did my mother ever hit me. When I was ten years old my teacher sent a note home to my mother asking her to come to the school the next day, a Friday. "What is this, Sonny?" my mother wondered.

I didn't know—but I knew it couldn't be good. The next afternoon my mother met with my teacher. During this meeting my teacher complained about my attitude. I was completely out of control. I did whatever I wanted to do when I wanted to do it. When I wanted to go to the boys' room, she explained, instead of raising my hand and asking permission, I just got up and walked out of the room. When I was told to do something I often refused, telling her I didn't have to, I didn't want to. I would not listen to anybody. And I was only ten years old.

After this meeting my mother took me into the cloakroom and slapped me across the face. I was stunned. How could she hit me? How could she hit someone with a voice like mine? A singer is supposed to have special privileges. "What's that for?" I asked.

"Three-quarters of it is to bring you back to earth," she said angrily. "Just because you sing nice don't you think you're better than anyone else 'cause you're not, and you never will be. And the rest of it is because you pull me away from the house when I need to prepare for Sabbath!"

When my teacher told my mother she shouldn't have slapped me, my mother replied proudly, "All my children were brought up to be nice. If you ever have a problem again with him, I'll be right here to help you."

My talent did not impress my father. Maybe he was jealous that I was able to escape the streets that had trapped him. He never did a thing to help me. In fact, he tried to discourage me. When I was a teenager he got me a job in a pants factory, putting new pants in order. I quit after the first week and wouldn't go back. He was furious, screaming at me that if I didn't go back I'd end up being a bum. "So," I screamed right back at him, "I'll be a bum." By that time I didn't care what he thought. I had stopped paying any attention to him.

I think my success confused him. When I was fifteen years old I was earning more than he did. That must have made him feel like a failure. I always felt he hated me for it, but then I found out that he would stand on the corner of Broad and Market Streets giving away pocket-sized color photographs of me.

He didn't want me to be in show business. It was a world he didn't understand and didn't like. His dream for me was that I would become a cantor, that I would sing in the synagogue. We fought about that many times. The only time I ever saw him respond to my singing was in temple. As I sang with the cantor one Saturday morning I looked at him and he was crying. He tried to hide it—he bowed his head so I couldn't see his face—but he was crying. Neither of us ever mentioned it.

I was always aware that I was Jewish, every minute of my life I was aware that I was Jewish, but I was never religious. I learned all the prayers, I could sing them in Hebrew, but I didn't accept any of the religious teachings. I was much more a cultural Jew. I felt like I belonged to a very special club and I was proud of that. I knew that I was a member of the same religion as Al Jolson and Eddie Cantor, and I wanted to be just like them.. . .show-business Jews. I did not want to be like my father, who went to shul every Friday night and kept all the holidays and prayed and still became an embittered man.

We lived in ethnically mixed neighborhoods in Philadelphia; some Jews, Italians, Irish, but no blacks, and at times every boy there had to defend his background. I was never confronted with real anti-Semitism, just other kids making stupid remarks that I never took very seriously. I got into my share of fights over anti-Semitic remarks, but the truth is that I was never really bothered by them. And my parents never talked about their lives in Eastern Europe; it was as if that part of their lives never really happened. Even after the war, when we started to learn the details of the Holocaust, they never discussed it. If any members of my family died or suffered in the Holocaust—and I can't imagine that they didn't—I never knew about it. Everything else in my life was secondary to my singing career. There was nothing, *nothing*, that was going to get in my way, and that included my religion. One of the best-known anti-Semites in show business was Arthur Godfrey, the host of radio's most important amateur talent contest. Godfrey owned the Kenilworth Hotel in Florida, which supposedly had a sign in front that read NO DOGS OR JEWS ALLOWED. But when I got the opportunity to appear on *Talent Scouts*, I leaped at it. I didn't care that Godfrey wouldn't let me in his hotel as long as let me sing on his radio show.

The irony of that, of course, is that the audience who embraced me first were the Jews. I was the universal Jewish son. . .the handsome, polite young boy with the big smile and the beautiful voice. I was the nice Jewish boy they all wanted their daughters to marry, the Jewish Sinatra. When I sang the Kol Nidre in perfect Hebrew, oy, they *kvelled* for me, *kvelled*. And when I sang "Oh! My Papa," it was so beautiful even the goyim cried.

I got my first big break at Grossinger's Hotel in the Catskill Mountains, the "Borscht Belt," or "Jewish Alps," as they were known. Eddie Cantor was the godfather of my career and Jennie Grossinger, everybody's Jewish mother, was the godmother. An economically powerful Jewish middle class emerged after World War II, most of them the first-generation American-born children of European immigrants, and I was one of the first big Jewish stars. I was the new American Jew, who spoke without an accent like our parents and grandparents, who didn't even look too Jewish. So when I married a *shiksa*, when I married Debbie Reynolds, it was all right because—well, because we were both adorable, and following strict religious dogma wasn't the most important part of being Jewish. But when Elizabeth Taylor converted to Judaism and I married her, well, as my mother often said when trying to describe something wonderful, *words can't express.*

I started singing professionally when I was twelve years old. The only thing that surprised me about that was that it had taken so long. There just was never any doubt in my mind that I was going to be a star. I remember earlier that year I'd spent my life savings to buy a ticket for the first live show I ever attended, Frank Sinatra performing at the Earle Theater. After the show I joined the large crowd waiting outside for him. I just wanted to get as close as possible to him. But just before he came outside, his bodyguards started pushing people around like they were animals. I was appalled. This was Frank Sinatra. How could he treat his fans that way? As I watched, I really did vow to myself that when I became as big a star as Sinatra, I'd never treat *my* fans that way.

I made my debut on a local Philadelphia radio station, WFIL, appearing on a children's program called *When I Grow Up*. Anyone who didn't grow up listening to radio just can't imagine the impact it had on our lives. As much as the introduction of television and computers changed society, they don't begin to compare with the importance of radio. Radio connected all the towns and cities in America for the first time. It allowed us to know what was happening in the world within hours instead of days; it made it possible for us to hear, live, the legendary entertainers we'd only read about. The radio was the most important piece of furniture in most houses; the living room furniture was arranged so people could sit around the room and look at it. Every night my father would sit next to our radio, the only thing of value he owned, and listen to the news in Yiddish. The world came into my house through that device. So the opportunity to actually sing on the radio, where my parents and friends could hear me was—well, words can't express.

Officially, Skipper Dawes was the "educational director" of WFIL, but in fact he was a producer, writer, director, and talent scout. Skipper would go around to all the local schools auditioning kids for his radio shows. When he came to my school, Thomas Junior High School, I was actually too shy to audition for him. I don't know why, I'd been a soloist in the synagogue for years, I wasn't shy about singing for my family or friends, but I just wouldn't audition for him. I don't think I even told my mother about it. But when Skipper Dawes invited one of the girls in my class, a singer named Ida Schwartz, to come down to the station for a second audition, she dragged me along with her.

We went there after school. At the station she introduced me to him, then told him I sang a little too. I'm sure he smiled—when I think of him I always see a big smile on his face—and asked me to sing. I loved moments like that, when I was about to sing for someone who had never heard me, because I knew that when I opened my mouth and this big voice came out of my little body, they would be just blown away. I didn't have much of a repertoire so I sang "The Army Air Corps Song," "Off we go, into the wild blue yonder, flying high, into the sky. . . ."

That moment marked the end of Ida Schwartz's singing career. Three hours later I was singing on the radio. I didn't even have time to be nervous. My family and my friends gathered around the radio set and listened. My mother was thrilled; my father said nothing about it at all.

Skipper Dawes must have spent years listening to perky children singing "On the Good Ship Lollipop" before I walked into his studio. After I'd sung only a few bars, I think he realized that I had a special talent. Right after the show he asked me to appear regularly on *The Magic Lady Supper Club*, probably the most popular kids' show on Philadelphia radio.

The Magic Lady was a fifteen-minute show broadcast three times a week. After the regular performers on the show had sung a few songs, the Magic Lady would appear and take us all to the "mysterious kingdom of Natar!" or "Tip Top Mountain," where we would just barely survive some sort of danger and then, just before the show ended, find ourselves in an even more precarious situation. It was an old-fashioned radio cliffhanger for kids, and it was very popular. My character was the appropriately named Boney, and my best friends, Joey Foreman and Bernie Rich, played Slick and Cough Drop. Skipper wrote all the scripts. Even then I wasn't much of an actor, but I could read my lines well enough to impress an audience of twelve-year-olds. I didn't enjoy acting, I was a singer, and all I really wanted to do was sing.

Skipper didn't pay us to appear on the show, although when he found out I had to walk several miles to get to the studio because I couldn't afford the trolley fare, he began paying me two trolley tokens per show. I didn't care about the money; just the chance to be on the radio was payment enough. In my neighborhood I became a star. I was on the radio. Everybody knew who I was. When I'd come home after a broadcast people would look at me differently, treat me with respect. I'd go down to Joey Foreman's parents' candy store and the other kids would know who I was. I felt like a prince, like a king.

I was very conscious of my new status. For several weeks Joey Foreman and I sold hot dogs and soda during football games at Franklin

Field, but one on Saturday afternoon someone from the neighborhood recognized me. I got so embarrassed I hid under the stands until the game ended. I never went back. My family needed the money, and I probably made four or five dollars for the day, but it just wasn't worth it to me. I was a singer, a crooner, in those days, not a hot dog vendor.

Magic Lady was so popular that its sponsor, the Lit Brothers Department Store, which was right across the street from Gimbel's, hired Skipper to create a Saturday night show on which I would be the master of ceremonies. So I became the host and star of the *Junior Music Hall*. Joey Foreman was my announcer. Because as Eddie Fisher I was usually left hanging over a cliff on *Magic Lady*, Skipper decided I should use a different name on *Junior Music Hall*. So for a short period of time I performed as Sonny Edwards, Sonny for Sonny Boy, the Edwards for Edwin, my real name. I don't know who we were trying to fool—I mean everybody recognized my voice—but it seemed like the professional thing to do. And I knew I was a professional radio performer because Skipper was finally paying me.

At the height of my success on WFIL, I was making twenty-five dollars a week. In addition, Skipper wrote jingles for our sponsors and paid me ten dollars to record them. "Beneficial Savings Fund makes saving money lots of fun"; ten dollars! "Take a six and add an 'o,' to make it six-oh-six. You get a square deal at Square Deal Furniture six oh six oh six oh six oh, downtown at sixth and Mar-ket Streeeeeet!": ten dollars! The money didn't matter, but what I was doing meant everything. I was living in heaven. My father took the money from me as soon as I got home and gave me maybe fifteen cents for spending money. Throughout my entire career the money I earned never meant anything to me. I learned how to spend thousands of dollars as quickly as I spent that fifteen cents. I always thought there would be more.

After *Magic Lady* and *Junior Music* were firmly established, I became the host of *Teen Time*, a Saturday afternoon show sponsored by Breyers ice cream. Skipper Dawes wrote our theme song, "Teen Time"; "Let's get together 'cause it's Teen Time/No matter whether you're a sweet young thing or old as the hills/Teen Time's always loaded with thrills. So get in the groove now, 'cause things are gonna start to move now."

By the time I was fifteen years old I had three shows on the air. I was a star in Philadelphia. I was singing on the radio six days a week. My picture appeared in advertisements on the fronts of trolley cars, and the newspapers reported that by the time the trolley reached the end of the line my picture was covered with lipstick. That was all pretty exciting stuff. Once my career began I lost all interest in school. Not that I had all that much to begin with. I was never a particularly good student; school just didn't seem relevant to me. The teacher I remember most of all was Mrs. Munser, who taught Spanish. And I remember her because she gave me a passing grade when I deserved to fail. Later she committed suicide. But I really disliked most of my other teachers. I took German because the teacher was a bass in the synagogue choir, but even that didn't help me. I started cutting classes to hang out at the radio station. And in the middle of my senior year of high school I dropped out. My parents accepted it; it was not at all unusual for the children of poor immigrants to quit school to help support their family.

Besides, Skipper Dawes was giving me a much better education than I would have gotten in high school. Skipper was a very decent man. He never tried to push me. Instead he offered suggestions. When I read my lines, for example, he'd gently correct my pronunciation and inflection. He didn't tell me I had to do it his way, he didn't make me feel like an uneducated kid from the streets, he simply pointed out to me how beautiful words could sound when pronounced correctly. Initially he limited his advice to helping me with my singing and my acting, but once I learned to trust him, he began to teach me about everything else in my life.

I was a product of the streets. I wasn't just rough around the edges, I was nothing but edges. I'd never been taught anything about hygiene or grooming. It wasn't that my mother didn't care, but with seven kids and no money there was only so much she could teach me. I didn't know how to brush my teeth properly after every meal or comb my hair; I'd never even owned a handkerchief. Skipper never made me feel dirty or inferior, he just showed me the proper way to take care of myself. He made me understand that if I intended to be a professional singer, my appearance was just as important as my voice. You're a nice-looking young man, he told me, you should take advantage of that. When I showed up at the studio with dirty hands and greased-down hair, he gave me soap and a comb and sent me into the rest room to clean up. He knew I couldn't afford new clothes, but he showed me how to take care of the clothes that I had.

I cleaned up pretty good—even I could see that when I looked in the mirror. I never thought of myself as handsome, but when my face was washed and my thick, dark hair was combed and I smiled, I could understand why the girls thought I was "cute."

After I'd been working with Skipper for almost two years he invited me to his home in the suburbs, in Swarthmore, to meet his wife and his two sons. I remember that I slept in my own bed—for one of the first times in my life I'd had my own bed with clean sheets. I remember the feeling of those clean sheets. I remember that when Mrs. Dawes opened the window in my room, fresh, cool air blew in. And I remember that at night Mrs. Dawes tucked me in bed. I guess most of all that's what I remember, that tenderness.

I don't know if I had ever really understood what it meant to be poor. I had no basis for comparison. But after spending time at Skipper Dawes' house I knew that this was the kind of life I wanted to have, that I was going to have, no matter what I had to do to get it. I didn't want to be poor anymore, and I didn't want my mother and father to be poor. And I knew that my voice was my only way out.

It was also at the radio station that I had my first real encounters with girls. Now, even before I started working there I was aware of girls. I knew that they had some sort of mysterious power over me that I didn't understand. Just about everything I knew about men and women I'd learned from Joey Foreman and my brother's two-by-fours, little illustrated books that showed characters like Popeye having sex with Olive Oyl. The only things I learned about relationships from watching my parents was that they involved a lot of screaming and unhappiness; the only advice my father ever gave me was that I should never fall in love with a *shiksa*, a girl who wasn't Jewish.

Never fall in love with a *shiksa*. The secret of happiness. I paid no more attention to my father's advice about love than I did anything else. In my lifetime I had relationships with so many of the most beautiful, desirable, and famous women in the world, not just Elizabeth and Connie Stevens and Debbie Reynolds, but sex symbols like Kim Novak and Mamie Van Doren; classic beauties like Marlene Dietrich, who advised me never to marry an actress, and Merle Oberon; movie stars like Ann-Margret and Angie Dickinson, Stefanie Powers, and Sue Lyon, who wanted to compare my sexual prowess with Richard Burton's; singers like Abbe Lane, Michelle Phillips and Dinah Shore, even women of controversy like Judith Exner, who also had long-lasting affairs with my friend, the Mafia boss Sam Giancana and President Kennedy, and Pam Turnure, Jackie Kennedy's press secretary. There were models and Play-boy Playmates and New York showgirls, Las Vegas chorus girls and beauty queens. I didn't even have to pursue them; gorgeous women were constantly coming on to me. Men used to hang around with me just to get my cast-offs.

Until my marriage to Elizabeth, my singing career was more important than the pursuit of romance, but after that. . .after that women became my addiction. Women became more important than my career. I know now that if I had worked as hard on my career as I did on the pursuit of women, my life would have been very different. I chased romance my whole life. I think Sammy Cahn and Julie Stein must have been thinking about me when they wrote "I fall in love too easily and I fall in love too fast/I fall in love too terribly hard for love to ever last."

It's a beautiful lyric, but it's less beautiful when it so accurately de-scribes your life.

I didn't start out that way. If anyone who knew me when I was fifteen years old were told then that Eddie Fisher would eventually be in the middle of one of the biggest romantic scandals of the twentieth century, they'd still be laughing. That little skinny guy? With the pompadour? I was so innocent. As a teenager I would run away from girls. On *Magic Lady* I worked with a beautiful fourteen-year-old named Marion Hol-lingsworth. She was very mature; she already had all the right parts in the all the right places. And she was a *shiksa*, which made her really an exotic woman. I had a big crush on her. I was completely infatuated. So whenever I was around her I got very nervous. I got scared. She actually pursued me. One night, I remember, Skipper had a party for the cast at his house. She followed me outside—and I ran away from her. I wanted to kiss her, but I was just too frightened. I wouldn't dream of doing something like that with a nice girl like Marion Hollingsworth.

I lost my virginity to a prostitute when I was fifteen years old. Joey Foreman's uncle had decided it was time that Joey and I were initiated into this particular wonder of the world and took us to an apartment on North Broad Street. I'd heard of places like this, but I never would have dared go there by myself. Two women were waiting there for us. I couldn't tell just by looking, but I assumed they weren't Jewish. It was well known that Jewish girls didn't let guys do things like that. To be honest, about all I really remember about these women is that they didn't look anything at all like Olive Oyl in the two-by-fours.

That was the first time in my life I saw a woman completely naked. And I liked it. I mean, I didn't know what to do about it, but I liked it a lot. One of these women took me by the hand and led me into a bedroom. I think the thing that most amazed me was how normal everybody acted, as if having sex was something people did every day. I didn't have the slightest idea how to do it, but she taught me everything I needed to know. I was a quick learner, probably a little quicker than I would have liked. Joey Foreman always swore that I came out of that room singing "Ah, sweet mystery of life, at last I've found thee."

Most of the women I've really been attracted to in my life were not Jewish. Or at least, like Elizabeth, they didn't start out that way. I'm certain any good psychologist could explain the reasons for that. A good place to start would be with my mother, who was constantly telling me, "Marry a nice Jewish girl. Like your sisters." Now, there was an arousing thought.

People don't believe me when I tell them how shy I was with girls as a teenager. But it's absolutely true. When I was sixteen, for example, Joey Foreman and I both had a real crush on Angelina Costellano, the soprano on the *Prime Time Junior Music Hall*. Angel Eyes, we called her. Joey was heartbroken when she confessed that she loved me more than him. One night I took her to a wedding and when she sat on my lap I got an erection. I sat perfectly still, terrified she would notice. I figured if I didn't move, and if I didn't think about the fact that this beautiful young woman with a perfect body was sitting on my lap, it would go away in—maybe a month. That was the entire extent of my sex life that year.

The girls loved me. We had a girl chorus on *Teen Time*, the Choru-lines. They were all younger than me, they all had nice voices, and all of them had a crush on me. Why not? I was cute. With Skipper's guidance, my hands were clean and I was nicely dressed, I was a nice person, and I had this voice. When I looked directly into a young girl's eyes and started singing a love song. . .Well, I learned very early in life how seductive that could be. But I never took advantage of it. I'm sure I could have had many relationships if I had chosen to, but the truth is that I just didn't have time for women. Let me repeat that, because it's the last time you'll see that sentence: *I just didn't have time for women.*

My singing career was the only thing that mattered to me. I had become a teenage celebrity in Philadelphia. In addition to starring on *Magic Lady* and *Teen Time*, I had become the host of the hour-long *Prime Time Junior Music Hall*, which was being broadcast from the Delancey Street Theater in front of a live audience. I had to conduct interviews, which I didn't like to do. I was too nervous, afraid people wouldn't like me. But when I sang. . .when I sang all my fears disappeared. A smile came on my face. I sang straight from my heart and a beautiful sound came out.

I was surrounded by people who kept telling me how wonderful I was, that I had a beautiful voice, that I was going to be a big star. I got about as much positive reinforcement as it was possible to get. When I was sixteen years old I got one ticket to Perry Como's *Chesterfield Show* and took the train to New York City to see the broadcast.

I worshiped Perry Como. Long before I met him I just knew that in addition to being a magnificent crooner, he had to be a very good person. Everybody knew he had been trained as a professional barber, a working man, but had found success as one of America's most popular singers. Later, after I got to know him, I found out that he was even better than I had hoped. He was the best of them all.

Here's how much respect I had for Perry Como: When I trying to romance a woman, I played his records. What finer tribute could I ever pay to him?

His fifteen-minute show made me *kvell*. He was smooth, he was brilliant. I mean, I knew that someday I was going to be in his category, but he was very impressive. After the show he sang a few songs for the studio audience, then asked if anyone would like to sing a song. Where I got the courage to raise my hand I will never know. But that was the impact Perry Como had on me. "I'll sing, Perry," I leaped out of my seat and shouted, "I'll sing." I sang one of his hits, "Prisoner of Love." That was a perfect song for my voice at that point: it was right in my range. Of course the lyrics were well beyond my experience—but eventually I caught up!

Like every other audience who had heard me sing, when I opened my mouth and this big sound came out, first they were surprised and then they were dazzled. As the applause died down, Perry asked me to sing a second song. I didn't hesitate, singing Bing Crosby's hit, "Wrap Your Troubles in Dreams." I was great. I destroyed, I killed. When I finished Perry looked at me, maybe he put his hand on my shoulder, and smiled. And he said, "Well, I guess I'm going to have to start sharpening up my barber tools."

After working with Skipper Dawes for four years at WFIL, I was getting very frustrated. I was all ready to be a star, but nothing was happening. I was not yet seventeen years old, but I felt like my career was passing me by. I was shocked when the ABC radio network, the Blue Network as it was known, gave Skipper his own show and he didn't hire me. He used the Chorulines on it, but not me. I blamed that on one of the program directors, a real anti-Semite whose mistress became the soloist, and I was terribly disappointed. Everybody around me was going national, but I was stuck in Philadelphia.

In 1946, Eddie Cantor came to Philadelphia to promote his new movie. At that time Eddie Cantor was one of the biggest and most beloved stars in show business. He was a great entertainer, a comedian who could sing and dance and act. He was a star of radio, movies, and the Ziegfeld Follies, bigger than Jolson. He was known for his humanitarian gestures and his long marriage. Eddie and Ida Cantor might have been America's best-known married couple, and a lot of his humor was based on their loving marriage and their five daughters—their five *unmarried* daughters. Eddie Cantor was also known for discovering talented young people and giving them the chance for stardom. So when Eddie Cantor came to Philadelphia, Skipper told me Eddie was going to visit the station to talk about his movie, and while he was there he was going to listen to me sing. I was positive that was going to be my big break.

Cantor arrived at the radio station, posed for some newspaper photographs with his well-known "banjo eyes" bulging, said a few nice words about his new movie, and then left, complaining that he had a temperature. He was too sick to spend three minutes listening to me sing? Even if you're dying you can wait three minutes. I can't begin to explain how much that hurt. Until that day just about all my dreams had come true. I was singing on the radio, and my biggest dream of all was to be discovered by Eddie Cantor. I had come so close. Cantor had actually come to Philadelphia, and he was supposed to listen to me sing. Then I just knew, I *knew*, that he would make me his newest discovery and overnight I would become a star. Instead, I had to get up the next morning and go back to work at the same local shows I'd been doing for years. Hanging from all those cliffs was killing me.

The music business in the 1940s was completely different than it is today. Las Vegas was a small city in the desert, and there was no such thing as television or even stereo. The big money for a singer was made by selling "singles," records with one song on each side; getting that record played on jukeboxes; by performing with a big band and, occasionally, doing live shows in big theaters like New York's Paramount. Songwriters and music publishers made money by selling sheet music, the music and lyrics of popular songs, enabling people to play them at home.

After Skipper got his network show, the song pluggers, the people whose job it was to convince singers to record certain songs or get radio producers to play certain records on their shows, started coming to see him. Skipper convinced one of these guys, a man named Lester Sacks, who ran Sinatra Songs, a subsidiary of one of the major music publishing companies, to listen to me sing. Skipper had written a little audition piece for me called "Just a Kid Who Loves to Sing," a takeoff on Sinatra, Como, and Crosby, that allowed me to show off my range. "Just because my hair is sorta curly," it began, " 'cause I'm underweight as you can see/Some folks think I'm copying Sinatra/but Sinatra's even skinnier than me!/When I'm compared to Perry Como, I just take another Bromo/I'm just a kid who loves to sing."

Lester took my audition tape—it was actually on acetate—back to New York and played it for other song pluggers and band leader Buddy Morrow. Morrow was putting together a new band and needed a male singer. I think he figured what I lacked in experience I made up for in good looks. The girls might like me, and the girls brought in their boyfriends. So he hired me for seventy-five dollars a week.

A week later the Buddy Morrow Orchestra opened at the Blue Room of the Lincoln Hotel, just off Times Square in the heart of New York City, New York. Maybe it wasn't Tommy Dorsey or Harry James, but it was a big band in New York City and I was the male vocalist. I had packed my one bag, promised my mother I'd be careful, and left Philadelphia. My brothers and sisters were all very excited for me. This wasn't local radio; I was going into show business. I don't remember if my father even wished me luck.

I lasted three nights with Buddy Morrow. I had never sung with a big band, and I didn't know how to read sheet music; I couldn't even keep time. He paid me thirty dollars and fired me. Fortunately, Charlie Ventura, who had been in Gene Krupa's band and was trying to make a go of it on his own, heard me my second night and offered me a job singing with his dance band at the Boston Post Lodge in Larchmont, New York. It wasn't just off Times Square, it wasn't even Manhattan, but it was a well-known dance hall, and, most importantly, it meant I didn't have to go back to Philadelphia.

I was really just a scared kid with natural talent. I was a high-school dropout with desire and confidence; now my desire was as strong as ever, but my confidence was shaky. An old press bio written after I'd become a star refers to my job with Charlie Ventura's band as "a nightclub engagement." The kind of fame I enjoyed not only changed my future, it also changed my past. On paper, my past was a lot more exciting than I remember it being. I lasted almost four weeks with Charlie Ventura— and I hated every minute of it. I got to sing one song, then I sat down and the singer sang one song, then I got up and sang. When the band appeared on network radio I was allowed to sing one song. It was the most boring job I'd ever had. I learned quickly that I had no interest in being a band singer. I wanted to be a star.

One night a man named Manny Mangel, whose brother managed the Ventura band, heard me sing. Manny Mangel was a steward at the Copacabana, the most famous nightclub in the world. In the 1940s the Copa was the epitome of sophistication and elegance. Fine dining, a performance by one of the biggest stars in show business, a world-class dance band, and a floor show featuring gorgeous chorus girls. Manny told me that Monte Proser, the legendary owner of the Copa, was looking for a male singer for a spot in the show, and offered to get me an audition. I was six weeks out of Philadelphia. I'd been fired by one orchestra leader and was about to lose my second job. Chances that I'd get this incredibly desirable job seemed pretty slim. But I had confidence, and that sound. I always had that sound.

More than 200 male singers auditioned for the job. Skipper Dawes came up from Philly to play the piano for me. The room was empty, chairs were upside down on tables, and Monte Proser was sitting by himself way in the back. I did my whole audition routine and when I finished, he offered me a job. "Is a hundred twenty-five dollars a week enough?" he asked. One hundred twenty-five dollars a week to sing at the Copa! Was that enough? Was Jolson Jewish? I was so excited I didn't know how to respond. I didn't know whether to simply say yes or fall on my knees and kiss his highly polished shoes. I was ready to start that night. But then Proser asked me how old I was.

"Seventeen," I told him. But I looked younger.

"That's a problem," Proser said. New York City cabaret regulations prohibited anyone younger than eighteen from performing in a club where liquor was served. And believe me, a lot of liquor was served at the Copa. Proser offered me a job as a production singer the following September, after my eighteenth birthday. Then he sent me over to see a friend of his named Milton Blackstone. That was the day my career really began.

Milton Blackstone had a theatrical advertising agency on West Fifty-seventh Street. It's difficult to describe exactly what it was that Milton did, except that everybody in show business seemed to love him. Particularly the important newspaper columnists, people like Walter Winchell, Louis Sobel, and Leonard Lyons. Milton made the things happen that people needed to happen. He fixed problems, he found jobs for people, and he handled the advertising for most of the important nightclubs, cafés, and hotels in New York, places like the Copa and Lou Walter's Latin Quarter. He was also the promotional genius who transformed the Catskills from a sleepy region in upstate New York known for its numerous small boardinghouses and tuberculosis sanitariums, a place where people went to escape the oppressive heat of the New York City summer and where Jews, in particular, went because they were not welcome in many other clubs and hotels, into one of the most popular resorts in America.

In the mid-1930s Milton convinced welterweight boxing champion

Barney Ross to train for a championship bout at Grossinger's. When newspaper columnists went there to report from Ross's training camp, Milton made sure they were treated very well. So they wrote nice things about Grossinger's, particularly about the woman who ran the place, Jennie Grossinger. Other boxers began training there, more reporters came, and Grossinger's became famous. After the war, Grossinger's became *the* place to go in the Catskills for the new, affluent Jewish middle class.

In those days the big resort hotels had resident theatrical groups, performers who lived there all summer and put on the nightly shows for the guests. Shelley Winters, for example, was on the staff at Grossinger's. It was only after the war, when hotels like the Nevele and Brown's began competing with Grossinger's, that Jennie insisted on hiring big-name entertainers. Jennie Grossinger and Milton Blackstone made Grossinger's a world-famous hotel. As Milton's advertising line correctly proclaimed, "Grossinger's has everything," and important people from every walk of life spent time there.

Milton was about my father's age, but he had all the personal warmth my father lacked. After we'd spoken for a few minutes he offered me a summer job at Grossinger's, at thirty-five dollars a week, plus room and board, to sing with the dance band.

At the time it didn't seem like much of a job. It was just a way of spending the few months until I was old enough to sing at the Copa. I'd get some more experience, I'd learn a little more about singing with a band, and I'd have a nice time. But I figured that my career would really begin when I returned to New York in September.

Skipper Dawes drove me to Grossinger's. We would never work together again. Eventually Skipper would become the producer of band leader Paul Whiteman's radio and television shows. He was the first person in my life, besides my mother, to encourage me, to help me. He'd taught me just about everything he knew. He made me believe I had a special talent.

But no one, not Skipper, not my mother, and even with all my self-confidence not even me, could possibly have imagined what was about to happen.

CHAPTER TWO

I was bigger than the Beatles. Bigger than Elvis. Hotter than Sinatra. Every song I recorded turned to gold. Every appearance I made sold out. Fan magazines reported every move I made. I enjoyed the kind of super-stardom few people have ever known. I was the Coca-Cola Kid—I signed what at that time was probably the biggest endorsement deal in history. Practically the first time I appeared on television it was as host of my own twice-weekly show. President Eisenhower asked me to sing for him. Princess Margaret flirted with me. I didn't think it was possible to get any bigger.

Then I started dating Debbie Reynolds. And everything I had previously experienced turned out to be just the beginning.

Stardom didn't actually happen overnight. It took about three years.

I spent that first summer at Grossinger's sharing a room with the house rabbi, the tennis pro, and a six-foot-six-inch basketball player, and singing to the music of the Eddie Ashman Band in the Terrace Room. The primary thing I learned that summer was never share a small room with a large athlete. And after hearing the tennis pro snoring, I knew what the rabbi was praying for.

I made my debut as the male production singer at the Copa in early October. I will never forget *Variety*'s review: "Proser determined he'd help keep [money in his checking account] by paying no supporting act over $300. . .And he's accomplished that. . .by demonstrating his eye for new, young talent. There's nothing any boite operator need hang his head about in the warbling of Eddie Fisher and Annie Rooney or the terping of Ronnie & Ray and Olga Suarez [All New Acts]." Maybe it wasn't a rave, but at least I was warbling rather than terping.

I sang three songs a show as the chorus line, eight gorgeous young girls, paraded around the stage, three shows a night. The headliner was comedian Joe E. Lewis, the King of the Nightclubs who was known as much for singing humorous songs like "Sam, You Made the Pants Too Long" as he was for his drinking and his sexual prowess. By the third show every night he was completely drunk, but he never missed a show or forgot a lyric.

It was a terrible job. I wore a bolero jacket and pink scarf and sang silly love songs to Annie Rooney as the chorus girls did their dance numbers in revealing costumes. I use the word *dance* very loosely here. Basically, they showed up. I was singing my heart out and nobody paid the slightest attention to me. I didn't care, I loved every single minute of it. I was performing at the Copa.

Years earlier, New York City's blue laws prohibited performances on Sundays. To get around that, Sunday night would be Celebrity Night at the Winter Garden Theater on Broadway. The greatest performers in show business would stand up—right in the audience—and sing and tell some jokes. It wasn't organized, it was simply very talented people performing for each other. Nobody knew who was going to perform, although the Winter Garden was known as Al Jolson's theater so he was usually the last act to go on. Even after the blue laws were modified these celebrity nights remained a show-business tradition. And on some Sunday nights at the Copa, after the third show, big stars would give impromptu performances.

Everybody loved Joe E. Lewis, and one Sunday night after I'd been working at the Copa for about three months all the big stars who were in New York showed up to pay tribute to him. That was some night. I sat on the steps leading up to my small dressing room watching as Frank Sinatra, Eddy Duchin, Johnny Green, Jackie Gleason, Vic Damone, and other people performed. And then, about five o'clock in the morning, right in the middle of all this incredible talent, Joe E. Lewis walked out on the stage dead drunk—he'd been drinking all night—and said, "Okay, now I'm gonna give you a kid that's gonna cut 'em all."

". . .a kid that's gonna cut 'em all." If I close my eyes I can still hear him saying that. It was a complete surprise. The Copa girls, most of whom were older than I was and treated me like a little brother, pushed me out on that stage. And I sang. Oh, did I sing. I sang the medley Skipper Dawes had arranged for me, and I sang it better than I'd ever done it before. I stopped the show cold. I owned the stage that night. I was eighteen years old and I had them all—Sinatra, Gleason, Damone, everybody in that place—on their feet cheering for me. Sinatra did a mock swoon, clasping his hands over his heart and sighing, "Ohhh, Eddie." When I came offstage the Copa girls surrounded me and started crying. I was so happy I started crying too.

Even now, even considering everything that happened after that, I think that was the most exciting night of my life. That was the first time I touched stardom.

The next day Jack Entratter, a bouncer at the club who later became the front man for some of Frank Sinatra's involvements, came to see me. "Frank Costello wants to manage you," he said. Frank Costello, who ran one of New York's five Mafia families, was the real owner of the Copa. I'd never met him, although I had often seen him sitting in the shadows. At that time I don't think I knew enough to be intimidated. Who knew how completely organized crime controlled certain areas of show business? I thought talent was all that mattered. I told Entratter that I already had a management agreement with Skipper Dawes.

"Go and tear it up," he told me.

I was very polite, but I turned him down. Maybe Frank Costello was really serious about it, but more likely it was just a passing whim, because if he had wanted it to happen it would've happened. But I never heard another word about it. When I finally met him he didn't even mention it.

George Evans, the press agent who made Sinatra by paying teenage girls a dollar each to stand outside and scream for him, also wanted to manage me. Those were the days when I was so innocent I believed contracts were supposed to be honored.

I knew Skipper Dawes couldn't really help me. I wanted Milton Blackstone to be my manager, but he turned me down. He already represented too many clients, he explained politely; he just didn't have the time to manage an unknown, even an unknown with talent.

Monte Proser wanted me to stay at the Copa as the male singer when Joe E. Lewis's engagement ended, he even offered me a raise, but I turned him down. Imagine that, me turning down the Copa. Who did I think I was, Eddie Fisher?

I didn't know any better. What I lacked in experience I made up for in poor judgment. I thought I was ready to go off on my own and be a star. I had the voice, but I didn't understand that I didn't have the personality or experience to support it. It was a little incongruous to hear this beautiful baritone coming from this kind of gawky kid. When I got onstage I just opened my mouth and sang. I had no style, no stage presence at all. I had to grow into my voice.

That took more than two years and a lot of disappointments. Two years doesn't seem like such a long time now, but to a kid it was an eternity. I took any job I could get. I did whatever I had to do to survive. When I got top billing in one seedy nightclub, "direct from the Copacabana in New York City!" and no one came to see Eddie Fisher, I agreed to change my name to Dickie White. Fortunately, no one came to see Dickie White, either.

I was desperate for a job, any job that involved singing. Like a lot of young singers I hung out in the office of the music publishers in Tin Pan Alley, the Brill Building at 1619 Broadway. When they found a new song that they thought might interest a *real* singer, like Dinah Shore or Jo Stafford, they'd pay me ten dollars to "put it down on wax," to record it. Then I'd go to Dinah's office, or Herb Jeffries' or Buddy Clarke's office and sing it for them. Herb Jeffries flipped over me when I sang the classic

"When Flamingos Fly" for him, and for Buddy Clarke I demonstrated "Spring in December, Winter in May." I was a "song plugger." My job was to sing a song so convincingly that someone else would immediately want to record it. If I really sold a song, no one would ever hear my version of it again.

Lester Sacks' brother, Manny, who ran Columbia Records, liked me a lot. Manny was one of the greatest human beings in the world. But he was always busy. He had Como, he had Sinatra, and he had. . .Fisher? They were big stars, I was trying to earn money to eat. "Oh, don't worry, Eddie," he'd tell me, "you're gonna make so much money you're going to throw it away." He did get me my first legitimate recording job. He paid me fifty dollars to sing a chorus with the two Marlin Sisters, accompanied by an organ, on their million-selling record, "You Can't Be True, Dear." The only thing I remember about that recording session is that for some long-forgotten reason I sang the chorus barefoot.

One job I did not get was a role in a Broadway show titled *As the Girls Go,* being produced by a man named Mike Todd. Mike Todd. Within a few years Mike Todd would become my best friend, my idol. Calling Mike Todd a producer doesn't begin to describe him. He was a showman. An entertainer. He had more ideas in a day than most people have in a lifetime, and he had the courage to try to make them happen. He was too big for Broadway. He produced his first show at the Chicago World's Fair. *The Flame Dance* featured a beautiful girl dressed as a moth— everything Mike did featured at least one beautiful girl—and a prop candle. At the climax of the show the moth "flew" into the candle and her asbestos wings caught fire—and she stepped safely out of the costume to a huge ovation.

He used the money he made from that to produce his first show, *Bring on the Dames,* starring Pete the Personality Penguin. The money he made producing a peep show for children, entitled *Kute Kris Kringle*—kids looking through a small slit in a department-store window saw a live Santa Claus about two inches tall making toys at his workbench—he invested in *The Hot Mikado,* which featured more pretty girls, a volcano that actually erupted, a pair of golden shoes that danced by themselves, and a mammoth waterfall of soapsuds. Mike Todd's *Hot Mikado* was a big hit at the 1939 World's Fair in New York.

A peep show for kids. I don't think anybody except Mike Todd would have thought about doing that and then actually go out and do it. I auditioned for him at the Winter Garden. He sat way in the back of the darkened theater making out with his wife, the movie star Joan Blondell. I sang my heart out for him; I did eight choruses of "April Showers." "Let me hear you again," he'd yell up to me when I finished. I knew I had very little chance of getting the part; it required some dancing and I couldn't dance a step. Eventually Jack Cassidy got it and played it on Broadway.

At the end of the audition Mike Todd called me over. Taking the cigar out of his mouth, he smiled like he owned the world and told me, "I like ya, kid. You got a good voice. Now go home and come back and see me again when you're a little older."

I was getting by. I did a week in Boston at the RKO Keith, a movie and a show, two weeks with Eleanor Powell at the Town Casino in Buffalo. I made my debut at the famed Paramount Theater in New York City, where only a couple of years earlier girls had fainted in the aisles when Frank Sinatra performed. Truthfully, I didn't actually perform *in* the show; I was the Paramount's first "recessional singer"—I sang the title song from Edward G. Robinson's movie *The Night Has a Thousand Eyes* as people left the theater. This was another great job: Every night a thousand people walked out on me. I saw more behinds in two weeks than the biggest coward in the army sees in a lifetime. I even toured with a theatrical version of the hit radio show *Stop the Music!* I would sing the first few notes and the instant a contestant thought he recognized the song I was singing, he rang a bell and I stopped. I went three months without singing more than eight bars of any song.

I ate mostly at automats and shared walk-up apartments. For a brief time I lived on West Fifty-second street—"Reefer Street," as it was better known—with a pimp who would wake me up in the middle of the night and make me take a walk when one of his girls needed my bed for an hour. Singing was easy for me; it was surviving that was tough.

After kicking around for two years I realized I couldn't live on the memory of one night at the Copa and hope. Finally I went home. I don't know what I planned to do. It probably would sound dramatic to say I was ready to go to my father and ask him if he could get me that job in the pants factory, but I never reached that point. My mother reminded me that Milton Blackstone had told me to call him if I needed help. I didn't want to call him. I'd asked him to manage my career and he'd turned me down. I was going to punish him by not asking him to save my career. But I was out of options.

Milton Blackstone offered me my old job at Grossinger's. I didn't look forward to going back, I'd already spent two summers there and did not see the advantage of spending another summer in the Catskills. But it was a job, and it included room and board, and at that time it was the best offer I had.

I was very popular at Grossinger's. I wasn't exactly the lounge singer—they didn't have a lounge—I was just included in the package. In addition to free tennis, golf, and water sports, guests got the music of Eddie Fisher. The young women really liked me. And their mothers, their Jewish mothers, loved me. When I was singing people would stop dancing and gather in front of the bandstand, the biggest compliment a performer could receive at Grossinger's. And I was getting better. I was more comfortable onstage. Until that summer I'd rarely spoken between songs. I had no little patter. I was too shy. But the atmosphere at Grossinger's was so supportive I gained confidence. I even began to kid around in my act.

And after three summers there, Jennie had made me feel like part of the extended Grossinger family. Eventually she would become almost as close to me as my mother. I loved Jennie and I know she loved me. She was a warm, wonderful woman, one of the few people in the world I ever really confided in. I married Debbie Reynolds in her daughter Elaine's home. When Elizabeth and I needed privacy we went to Grossinger's. When I needed a safe place when my world fell apart, I went to Grossinger's. When I looked at Jennie's face I saw a saint. In all the years I knew her, the only person about whom I ever heard her say a harsh word was her husband, Harry. Her marriage was not a particularly good one. Listen to me, the expert on good marriages. It only took me a lifetime to find one. But marriage was really secondary to Jennie; her real love was the hotel, even more than her real family.

One the many things I admired about Jennie is that she never lost her love of learning. She was always taking courses, always studying something. Even when she became older and frail she was busy taking piano lessons and Spanish lessons, and she continually encouraged me to do the same thing. The very first gift she gave me was a dictionary. And sometime later she gave me the book *Six Who Changed the World*, pointing out that all six of those people were Jewish.

The other thing Grossinger's offered was the chance for me to be discovered. Again. At some point during the summer most of the important Jewish celebrities and agents and producers came to Grossinger's. It was a big status symbol, sort of like the Jewish hajj. The first summer I was there, for example, John Garfield came up for a few days to look for girls. John Garfield was then one of the biggest movie stars, the star of the classic boxing movie *Body and Soul*. Every Jewish boy knew that John Garfield was really Julie Garfinkle and wanted to be a tough guy just like him. My friends Joey Foreman and Bernie Rich and I followed him around like he was God. But when he left, chances were an even bigger star would show up.

For the Labor Day weekend in 1949 Jennie had booked Eddie Cantor, probably the most popular performer in the Catskills. Cantor was there to raise money for the new state of Israel. While Cantor's own career was starting to slide, he still had the power to turn an unknown into a star. Milton Blackstone told me that Cantor would listen to me sing while he was at Grossinger's, but I hadn't forgotten that he had been too busy to hear me at WFIL. I didn't want to be that disappointed ever again.

At Milton's insistence, Cantor came to the afternoon band rehearsal. He was polite, but he certainly didn't seem to be impressed with me. But that night he changed my life. I was taking my bows after finishing my second number when Eddie Cantor came out from the wings. He raised his hand to stop the applause, then put his arm around my shoulders and said, "This kid, and I never saw him before, sings better than anyone I've heard in years, and I've heard them all. This boy isn't a crooner, he's a singer. In my opinion I think he is destined to become the most important singer of popular songs in America." The audience cheered. I was stunned. I couldn't believe this was happening to me. Finally. Then he continued, "With five single daughters, I need to take him home with me." He smiled, and asked the audience, "How would you like to see me take him with me on my cross-country tour?" The audience screamed its approval. I just stood there, beaming.

I had been "discovered" again, but this time it was by Eddie Cantor.

It had been completely unexpected. My mother had been in the audience that night to see me, and Jennie brought her up onstage. "Mrs. Fisher," Jennie asked, "how does it feel to have such a successful son?"

My mother put her hand on her chest and replied, as I knew she would, "Words can't express."

Almost fifteen years later, when Cantor was a sick man, he told a columnist that the whole thing had been a publicity stunt. "Milton Blackstone practically shoved him down my throat," Cantor said. "I wasn't impressed by him." If that was true I didn't know anything about it. And even if it was true it didn't matter. We left the following week on a national tour and as soon as Cantor saw the way audiences responded to me, I became his boy. Two years later, as I was leaving to serve in the army, he put his arm around me on national television and said, "I love you like a son."

I grew up on that tour. When we got on the train in New York I was an innocent kid, completely naive. I actually believed the stories I read in the newspapers. I finished the tour in Los Angeles a different person.

I began to realize that Eddie Cantor was not quite as devoted to his wife, Ida, as everyone seemed to believe when he gave his secretary a line in the show. It seemed to me that they spent a lot of time alone in his hotel room rehearsing that one line. Of course, at that point I was still so naive I hadn't figured out what the secretary's real talent was.

I was very disappointed to discover that Eddie Cantor was simply a human being with the same weaknesses as everyone else. The reality that his career was ending made him a very unhappy man, and he took out his anger on some of the other people on that tour. I learned that he had had many affairs, including a longtime relationship with comedienne Joan Davis. If anything existed for publicity, it was his marriage to Ida. She was a lovely, classy lady, and they had long ago made their peace with each other. Their "happy marriage" was the foundation of his public image, and real life was not allowed to intrude on his career. I remember, after he had suffered a serious heart attack and was dying, I went to see him. It was so sad, so very sad. Ida was also sick, and their rooms were at opposite ends of the house. They were as far apart as it was possible to be.

As Cantor's latest "discovery," I received a tremendous amount of publicity on the tour. One day the syndicated columnist Dorothy Kilgallen had written something untrue about me. As I later found out, Kilgallen hated Jews, but in particular she disliked me because she knew I was going to be competition for her favorite escorts, the popular young singers Johnnie Ray and Julius La Rosa. I don't even remember what she wrote, although it had something to do with President Truman's daughter, Margaret. Whatever it was, it was terrible, and it was a complete fabrication. I couldn't believe newspapers would allow columnists to make up a story and print it as fact. I was very upset about it. I was afraid my family and friends might read that and think it was true. But what really surprised me was that no one else was the slightest bit bothered by the fact that a newspaper would print a lie. They told me to ignore it. This is how naive I was: I thought if something was printed in the newspaper it had to be true.

That was an important lesson to learn, because within a few years incredible lies would be written about me. But by that time I was so used to it that I wasn't even bothered by it.

I also learned from Eddie Cantor how to protect my image. While we were in Chicago I went with my cousins to hear the great black actor and singer Paul Robeson speak at a political meeting. It might have been a Communist Party meeting; it was certainly some left-wing organization. I didn't care about communism—I really didn't even understand what it was—but Paul Robeson. . .I'd heard him sing. He had the most magnificent, deep sound, and I wanted to see him. He'd played *Othello* on Broadway; he'd introduced the song "Old Man River." That night I heard him before I saw him. I was sitting in the audience watching the stage when suddenly this big, big voice boomed from the back of the hall, and he continued singing as he walked down the aisle to the stage. It was an incredibly effective entrance. It was unforgettable. So later in my career I would open my shows exactly the same way.

The next morning I told Cantor that I had gone to this meeting. I was still very excited about it. Eddie Cantor was beloved for his humanitarian work; he founded the March of Dimes and he raised tens of millions of dollars for Israel. But when I told him I'd gone to see Paul Robeson, the color drained out of his face. He looked at me like I was out of my mind. "Don't you dare tell anybody else you went to that meeting," he said forcefully. Being seen at a meeting with Robeson, he warned, was more than enough to end my career before it had really begun. He told me I was very lucky that no one had recognized me. Recognized me? No one had ever heard of me. The point Cantor was making was that if I wanted to be a star, I had to make choices consistent with the public image I wanted to project. Perception was more important than reality. Give the public what they want.

Few performers knew how to relate to an audience better than Eddie Cantor. There was a huge crowd at the Coliseum in Chicago for our first show there. It was certainly the biggest audience I'd ever faced and I was very nervous. Just as I was about to go onstage I saw Cantor approaching. I knew he was going to build up my confidence. He was going to remind me that I had real talent, that all I had to do was go out there and sing and they would love me. He put his arm around my shoulders and said, "Don't worry, kid. After I get through introducing you, if you go out there and pee they'll love you."

Now that was real talent.

Early in the tour Eddie Cantor took me out for dinner and asked me to sign a management contract. He offered me $500 a week to work exclusively with him. Five hundred a week in 1949 was a tremendous amount of money. Turning down Frank Costello was one thing, but turning down Eddie Cantor? All Costello had behind him was the Mafia; Cantor had all twelve tribes of Israel. I did what I always did in difficult situations. I called Milton Blackstone. Milton gave me the best advice any manager ever gave his client. "Do what he tells you to do," Milton said, "but don't sign anything."

Cantor accepted my decision gracefully. Whatever his original motives were, eventually he became extremely supportive of me. He put my mouth where his money was. During the tour he introduced me to executives at RCA Victor, who were trying to sign him for their new label, Bluebird Records. Originally Bluebird was supposed to consist of a male singer, a female, and Eddie Cantor. At this meeting Cantor told them, "If you want Eddie Cantor, you have to take Eddie Fisher."

I sang *a cappella* for them right in their office. I blew the doors off the hinges. Halfway through my first song they offered me a contract. I was in the studio a week later, making my first solo record, "My Bolero," and on the flip side "Foolish Tears." With a national tour with Eddie Cantor and my own record being released, I thought I had it made. That record became a collector's item—because so few of them were produced or sold. It made all the impact of a cloud on a windy day. But when Bluebird Records folded, I was the only artist on the label to be picked up by RCA. Eddie Cantor's recording career was over, but mine was just beginning. I made several records for RCA. And while they sold nicely, none of them really qualified as hits. I was doing okay, but I still didn't feel too far away from counting pants.

The tour was a big success. We sold out the biggest theaters in every city: the Hippodrome in Baltimore; the Earle in Philly, where I had stood on the side and watched Sinatra's bodyguards push his fans around; the Askarben in Lincoln, Nebraska, the great Orpheum in Los Angeles. And I finally made the bill at the New York Paramount. By the end of the tour Eddie Cantor and I had become good friends. In Los Angeles he introduced me to all five of his daughters, all five *unmarried* daughters, as well as stars like Bob Hope, George Burns, Jack Benny, and Bing Crosby, and show-business executives who might be able to help me. I got a few bookings on my own, and if he couldn't be there in person to introduce me, he made a recording, which we played on the sound system: "A new boy who is destined to become the most important singer of popular songs in America, Mr. Eddie Fisher!" The exclamation point is mine.

Eddie Cantor had done everything possible for me, for which I would be forever grateful. But it was Milton Blackstone on whom I relied. Milton used to sit at the bar in the Terrace Room at Grossinger's, drinking Cutty Sark on the rocks, just watching me. Milton was very sharp in those days; he didn't miss a thing that was going on around him. But no matter how hard I tried, I couldn't convince him to become my manager. It seemed like everybody else in show business wanted to manage me, and the only person who didn't was the only person I wanted. "Eddie, I don't have time," he insisted. In addition to his advertising agency, Milton owned a brickyard and a shipyard. He had his hands in all kinds of plans and schemes. He never really said no to me, but he wouldn't make a commitment. "We'll talk about it tomorrow," he said. His whole life, whenever there was something he didn't want to do, "We'll talk about it tomorrow."

The Terrace Room was the Copa of Judiasm. It was *the* meeting place for writers and actors, doctors and lawyers, the leaders of the big garment-industry companies. I performed there every night of the week except Sunday. And every night of the week I stopped the show. Seeing Eddie Fisher had become an event. I was a star in the Catskills before anybody east of New Jersey had ever heard of me. One night I was feeling very bold, and with the Terrace Room still vibrating with applause, I rushed right over to Milton and practically begged him to manage my career. "Mr. Blackstone," I asked him, "just give me one day a week." I guess I had finally become more exciting than a brickyard, because he agreed.

Milton was quiet, intense, and efficient. When he decided to do something, nothing stood in his way. And once he made the commitment to be my manager, my career became the sole focus of his attention. Nothing else mattered. When I was doing my television show, for example, Freddie Robbins, who worked on the commercials, loved telling Milton outrageous lies like, "Milton, my mother died this morning," knowing that Milton would reply, "That's nice, how was Eddie's rehearsal?"

In early June 1950, Milton Blackstone got me a shot on Milton Berle's television show. The *Texaco Star Theater* was the most popular show on the air, and "Uncle Miltie" was the biggest star in TV history, even if TV history was only about three years old. When Milton Berle claims he discovered me, he means that the national exposure I received on his show led to my career taking off. Finally.

A few days after that appearance Milton Blackstone called me. He was incredibly excited. Fran Warren, the supporting act for Danny Thomas at Bill Miller's Riviera, had gotten sick and they wanted me to fill in for her. The Riviera, in Fort Lee, New Jersey, was a very popular club. It was just over the George Washington Bridge from Manhattan, and all the important columnists reviewed the shows there. I'd performed there the previous New Year's Eve but made no impact. It was just another in a long string of one-night shows. But now, coming off my success with Milton Berle, I was certain to receive serious attention. The next day I bought my first tuxedo, and that night Eddie Fisher was born.

"A new night club star came into his innings. . .when Eddie Fisher tore the crowded house apart," wrote Louis Sobel. Earl Wilson raved, "Singer Eddie Fisher, who replaced the ailing Fran Warren, is merely wonderful. There's no reason he shouldn't become a big star." "Sensational, to put it mildly," Lee Mortimer reported, "The cash customers cheer and beg for more, indicating the lad is the song find of the year."

Variety, the *New York Times, Time* magazine, every review was spectacular. I killed that night. Killed. The audience wouldn't let me off the stage. I sang and sang and sang. When the orchestra didn't have sheet music, I sang *a cappella*. People stood on their chairs and cheered and screamed. I think the only person in the house who wasn't thrilled for me was Danny Thomas.

At the end of that booking I was a star. Milton Blackstone's phone started ringing and didn't stop for fifteen years. In one night I became the hottest act in show business. Within weeks I was performing before sold-out audiences at the best clubs in the country: the Chez Paree in Chicago, the Mocombo in Los Angeles, Monte Proser's new club in New York City, the Cafe Theater. Every variety show on television wanted me as a guest. I was Walter Winchell's first guest on his new TV show. I was one of the first guests on columnist Ed Sullivan's Sunday night show, *The Toast of the Town*. I *was* the toast of the town. Every dream about success I'd ever had suddenly started coming true. My latest record, "Thinking of You," broke into *Billboard*'s Top 50 list. It was my first hit—and the first of twenty-two consecutive hit records. The next two songs I recorded, "Turn Back the Hands of Time" and "Bring Back the Thrill," immediately shot to the top of the charts. By the end of the year I had been named America's Most Promising New Male Vocalist in *Billboard*'s annual disc-jockey poll, as well as Discovery of the Year and Male Singer of the Year.

All the major motion-picture studios begged me to take a screen test. I began receiving thousands of pieces of fan mail every day, and fan clubs were organized around the country. And certainly among the most satisfying things that happened to me was that the high school from which I hadn't graduated welcomed me back on Eddie Fisher Day, and the city named a street near my parents' house, Eddie Fisher Street.

Eight months after my appearance at the Riviera I played the Paramount, sharing top billing with the DeMarco Sisters and the Russ Case Orchestra. The Paramount offered a movie and a live show, five performances a day. The movie was *Cry Danger*, but I don't think anyone bought a ticket to see that movie. They came to see me.

Few entertainers have ever experienced the kind of adulation I received when I opened at the Paramount. There is no way to describe accurately the feeling of being at the center of that kind of frenzy. Or, as my mother would say, words can't express. Older women wanted to mother me, but the teenagers wanted to marry me. Or at least be close to me. I was the new Sinatra, the *Jewish* Sinatra, one of few entertainers as comfortable singing for a sophisticated nightclub audience as I was performing for the bobby-soxers on the Paramount stage.

Years earlier, Rudy Vallee, singing through his megaphone, had made the young girls swoon, but Frank Sinatra, and then Johnnie Ray, made them faint in the aisles. The media referred to the teenage girls as bobby-soxers because they wore socks that went above their ankles, and long ponytails. And the bobby-soxers turned out by the thousands to scream for me. I could barely hear my own voice, and I knew they couldn't hear me at all. But no one seemed to care. They could hear me sing on records and on the radio, but they had come to the theater to see me, to show me their love.

I probably would have thought it ironic—if I had known then what irony really meant—that my singing had created such a sensation that no one in the audience really wanted to hear me sing. It wasn't anything at all like performing in a nightclub. But the louder they screamed, the more I wanted to sing for them, even knowing they couldn't hear me.

It was thrilling. I loved it more than they did. Savored it. You know what it feels like to stand onstage and control an audience like that? It made me feel like a god. Better than a god. And as intense as it was, I wanted more. Louder. Bigger. More. I just didn't understand how powerful it was, and how dangerous it would be for me.

I was up on the fourth floor of the building with my family looking down on the crowd. Thousands of girls were standing behind barricades on Broadway, waving. I opened the window and leaned out and waved back. I encouraged them to scream louder. And they did. When they started getting out of control, mounted police moved in to maintain order. I remember trying to leave at the end of the day; I got about twenty feet outside the theater and this screaming mob surged toward me. A wave of people threatened to drown me. As much as I loved it, I was also frightened by it. Had they moved forward, these kids would have trampled the people in front of them. Three policemen on horseback got in front of me and started backing up. All I could see was the rear ends of these horses, and I turned and quickly went back inside to safety.

It was that way in every theater I played. The girls would bring box lunches with them and sit through the same show four or five times, screaming during each show. They would wait outside the stage entrance for hours, for hours, knowing they wouldn't get an autograph, just hoping to see me as I got into a limousine.

It took a long time for success to happen so fast. For a while it didn't seem real. I think that I knew it wasn't all a wonderful dream when I recorded a song titled "Anytime." Several weeks later I was driving by myself in Washington, D.C., and I turned on the car radio and heard the song for the first time. When it was done I switched to a second station—just in time to hear the song played again. A few minutes later I heard it on a third station. Three times in no more than ten minutes. I knew it was a smash hit; in fact it was my first million-selling record. I was thrilled, I was going crazy in that car—and I had no one to tell.

It would be more than a decade later before I could simply walk down a street without being mobbed by fans or media. I'd become imprisoned by fame. And at first, it was even more wonderful than my greatest fantasies. At first.

I was paid $5,000 for my week at the Paramount, more money than my father had earned in the best years of his life. But the money was secondary to the fame, the adulation. I really didn't care very much about the money. I had no concept of how much money I was making, except that it was a lot. I gave it away. I gave presents to everyone. My sister wanted an expensive leather jacket; I bought her two of them. Milton Blackstone handled everything; he negotiated the contracts, got the checks, set up bank accounts, and made the investments. One of the very first things I did with my money was buy my family a supermarket. It failed within a year. My family ate more than we sold; they ate everything, they ate the fixtures. I didn't care. I knew that as long as that sound came out of my throat I could make as much money as I ever needed.

I think my incredible success gave my mother the courage to finally leave my father. They had fought so often about money that I thought my money might solve their problem; I tried to force them to get back together by buying them a house and a car, and giving them money each week. I gave them as much as I could afford, but my mother finally had the one thing she wanted that money couldn't buy: her freedom from my father. At that point in my own life I believed that married people should stay together, at least, as my mother had once promised, until all the children were out of the house. I thought any problems could be worked out. That was me, the great marriage counselor.

My father was devastated. He moved in with me for a while, and at night I would hear him crying for her. Over and over he'd ask me, "What did I do so terrible, Sonny Boy, tell me, to deserve this?" What could I really tell him? Your whole life? I began to understand that he had done the best he was able to do. One thing I did know for sure, though: What happened to my mother and father would never happen to me. When I married it would be for love, and forever.

I was so popular I didn't think anything could stop me. All it took was a war. Five years after the end of World War II the North Koreans invaded South Korea and the United States decided to make a stand against communism on the Korean peninsula. The fighting in Korea was never officially declared a war—it was "a police action"—but thousands of American soldiers were dying there. It was a very unpopular war; a lot of World War II veterans were recalled just as they were getting their civilian lives started and they were very bitter about it. I had been too young for World War II, but at twenty-two years old I was just the right age for Korea.

But still, I was stunned when I received my draft notice. How could they do that to me? I wondered. I was Eddie Fisher. I had hits on the *Billboard* charts! How could they stop my career just when everything was starting to pay off? Even Milton Blackstone, Milton who could do anything, could do nothing about it. My departure for the army was a little different from most people's: Before reporting to Fort Devens I recorded several songs to be released while I was in the service, Eddie Cantor dedicated his entire *Colgate Comedy Hour* to me, and my going-away party, sponsored by RCA, was covered by the newspapers. On April 11, 1951, I became Pvt. Edwin Jack Fisher.

I was assigned to the Sixteenth Armored Engineer Battalion and sent to Fort Hood, Texas, for basic training. The rest of the guys in my basic training company came from the deep South, places like Mississippi, Alabama and Tennessee. This was long before television and chains like McDonald's and the Gap had blurred regional lines, and some of my fellow draftees had never even seen a Jew before. In fact, some of them had never even spoken to a northerner. Most of them had never heard of me, they didn't know that I was an entertainer; they just figured I was mighty peculiar. At mail call one guy got two letters, another guy got four; I got 4,500. My mail was delivered to the barracks in potato sacks. I was constantly receiving long-distance telephone calls. Photographers were sneaking around trying to get pictures of me. Eventually I let the guys in my platoon read my mail. They loved it, they went crazy. These letters were all from women. Many of them enclosed photographs, others declared their eternal love for me. Some of these women wanted to have my baby, others were having a baby and wanted me to adopt it. All of them wanted to go out with me.

Under the circumstances there was nothing else I could do: I let the guys in my platoon answer these letters. At night the barracks was like a TV sitcom, with all of us sitting around reading my mail. Some of the guys started corresponding with these woman—one of them actually ended up marrying someone who'd written me a fan letter.

I didn't know what basic training was going to be like for me. Milton had tried his best to make it a little easier, but the army turned down his request for a television set in my barracks. The thing that surprised me most about basic training was how much I enjoyed it. I was treated no differently from anyone else; I did my time on KP and cleaned out the grease traps. I learned that this one was my rifle and that one was my gun, and which one was for shooting and which one was for fun! I turned out to be a terrible shot. About the seventh week of basic we made the traditional twenty-mile march with full pack in the sweltering Texas heat. A lot of guys didn't make it; they had to hop on the back of a truck and get driven in. But I marched every foot of it. By the time I made it my rifle felt like it weighed 400 pounds. I was the last guy in, and my fatigues were caked with sweat, but I made it, I made it. I was really proud of myself. It was like a movie; as I stumbled into camp hundreds of guys were there cheering for me.

I got no special treatment at all. By the end of basic training I was in the best shape of my life. I actually grew muscles. I was healthy, I was tanned, I'd been completely accepted. I remember that we were being paid twenty-one dollars a month, and one day somebody read in the newspaper that I'd just received a royalty check for $365,000. I knew nothing about it. Three hundred and sixty-five thousand? I couldn't even imagine that much money. I hadn't gotten the check, Milton had. The nickel or dime I got for every record added up to a fortune. But instead of being jealous, the guys in my platoon treated it like a joke. They treated me like a king—for about an hour. I'm sure I was the richest guy in the grease traps that night.

About a week before the end of basic I was ordered to report to the United States Army Band at Fort Myers, Virginia. Milton Blackstone had managed to get me assigned as a soloist with the army band. Obviously it made sense. When heavyweight champion Joe Louis was in the army he toured the camps giving boxing exhibitions; I was the most popular male singer in America, so what was I going to do in the army—be an infantryman?

Gen. John J. Pershing had established the U.S. Army Band to assist morale just after World War I, and with most of America's talented young musicians to choose from, it was a very good band. It was one of the best assignments in the army. We had no barracks, so I rented an apartment at the Dorchester on Sixteenth Street in Washington. When we weren't rehearsing or playing, we were on our own. When I wasn't singing with the band, I appeared all over the country at blood drives, bond drives, and recruiting campaigns. People literally gave their blood to see me. See Eddie Fisher and buy war bonds. See Eddie Fisher and join the army and go fight communists. I may have been the first private in the United States Army assigned to appear on television. One day after leaving Fort Hood, as the guys in my platoon were getting ready to ship out to Korea, I was singing on a TV show. In my first eight months with the band I appeared on more than 150 local and network TV and radio programs and made personal appearances everywhere from the Philadelphia Music Festival, in front of 90,000 people, to Carnegie Hall. On the Fourth of July, I sang at the Washington Monument for a crowd estimated at more than a quarter of a million people.

When I entered the service I was afraid that my fans would forget about me. But every song I recorded before my induction, as well as records I made on weekends and furloughs with almost no rehearsal, hit the charts. One week while I was in the army I had six records, six of them, in the Top 50. "Wish You Were Here," a song I really disliked but was forced to record by RCA, became my first number-one hit.

The army didn't miss an opportunity to put me in front of an audience. I didn't mind performing for soldiers and at recruiting rallies and blood drives and at fund-raising events for cancer and polio and muscular dystrophy and numerous other charities, but after a while I found myself singing too often at luncheons and events hosted by senators and congressmen and their wives. It got to be too much for me. I felt like I was being used; I wanted to get out of Washington. But I was making the congressional wives happy, so the army wanted to keep me there. Finally, I got a letter from Korea, from one of the guys in my basic-training platoon. He wrote that the soldiers fighting there felt like they'd been forgotten, and asked me to "come on out and sing for us." I didn't think the army could possibly turn down my request to entertain the fighting troops in Korea.

I had underestimated the power of a senator's wife. My request to go to Korea was rejected. One of the people I'd met in Washington was the largest operator of jukeboxes in the city. As I had become the number-one play on jukeboxes, he loved me. When I explained my problem to him he said, "You want to go to Korea? I'll get you with Truman."

That was when I discovered that the power of a political contributor is greater than that of a senator's wife. I had sung for President Truman, his lovely wife, Bess, and their daughter, Margaret, at several events. I'd been introduced to the President, but we'd never really spoken. Within days I was escorted into the Oval Office to meet him. He rose to greet me, asking, "How's my favorite PFC?" Three years earlier I couldn't get a job, suddenly I was meeting privately with the President of the United States. It was awesome.

I remember that he was standing at the window, his hands clasped behind him, looking out at the perfectly manicured White House lawn. "You know what, Eddie?" he said softly. "I don't know what the hell I'm doing here."

I was shocked. If President Truman didn't know what he was doing there, I certainly wasn't going to be able to help him. I wasn't even sure what I was doing there. I was so nervous my knees were shaking. I had one thought in my mind: I wish my mother could see me, a little Jew boy in the Oval Office with the President. I didn't know anything about politics. I didn't know whether he was a good president or a bad president; he was *the* President. I was this ignorant kid who happened to be born with a sound in his throat. As far as I was concerned, he was a great man. He'd dropped the atom bomb to end the Second World War and bring my brother home. He'd fired General MacArthur. I mean, what could I say to him, "Yes, you do"?

At least he knew what I was doing there. "Eddie," he finally continued, "not only am I going to send you to Korea. . .I'm going to send you all over the world."

I was one of the few soldiers the army did not want to send to Korea. "I have had some difficulty getting these orders issued on him," the commanding general of the Washington, D.C., region wrote, "as many people are reluctant to lose him, even temporarily, from the Washington–New York scene." But as President Truman's "favorite PFC," and perhaps the only PFC he knew, they had no choice.

The flight to Korea took fifty-four hours. It was the first time I'd ever been out of the country, the first time I'd flown over water, and I didn't like it at all. Seats were assigned according to rank, so as the only private on the plane I was as far in the back as it was possible to be and still be on the airplane. It was an awful flight. I had a toothache, I was nauseous because of the turbulence, I was freezing, and I was scared. We flew through the blackest clouds I'd ever seen. I was convinced we were going to crash. But other than that it was a pleasant flight.

I spent forty-six days in Korea and gave seventy-one scheduled performances in front of more than 150,000 United Nations troops, as well as countless other unscheduled performances. The joke was that if I saw two guys in a muddy foxhole I'd jump down there with them and sing "Wish You Were Here." My tour was so successful, the army reported, that I "equaled the response which Betty Hutton received while touring Korea." And admittedly, even with all my new muscles, Betty Hutton was much nicer to look at than me.

Taegu, Korea, was a lot farther than fifty-four hours from the Paramount. As the soldiers there told me, it wasn't much of a war, but it was the only war they had. The whole country was a war zone. I sang in big shows for thousands of troops and for just a few dozen wounded soldiers in hospital wards. I sang on stages and I sang from the backs of trucks, in drenching rainstorms and in tropical heat. I had a little group with me, a tap dancer, an accordion player, and I usually sang between twenty and twenty-five songs. They just put me down somewhere and I started singing.

To create a "stage" for me at night, they'd ring an area with jeeps and turn on their lights. Unfortunately, the lights attracted bugs, millions of bugs, bugs that would eat right through my clothes, the biggest bugs I'd ever seen. Communist bugs. They flew into my nose, my ears, and, when I opened my mouth to sing, right into my mouth. But the shows always went on. Always. And as I later found out, in addition to the bugs, the lights probably attracted North Korean soldiers too.

I spent a lot of time on the front lines. We heard rumors every night that we were going to be overrun by the Chinese. The last instructions we got before going to sleep were where to run when the attack came. I listened, but the truth is I wasn't scared. I felt a sort of invincibility. I felt, they're not going to kill Eddie Fisher now. I'm too big a star to be killed in a war.

But at other times I did get very nervous. Going up the mountain to Chorwon, "Old Baldy," we came under mortar attack and had to dive into trenches. That got my attention. Another night—I don't remember exactly where I was—all of a sudden we heard these strange sounds, and the searchlights began sweeping the area. I was with a captain I knew from Fort Hood and he told me confidently, "Don't worry, Eddie, I got a gun. If I can remember tonight's password we'll be fine." If? Does peeing in my pants qualify as being very nervous?

Everybody tried to be very nice to me. The first day I was there a captain of the military police took me to the local whorehouse, a hut with no running water, two windows without glass, and several filthy mattresses on the floor. Inside were four old Korean women whose teeth had been knocked out so they could more easily provide service. It was all very legal. Hundreds of men, hundreds, were waiting patiently in line. They paid me the nicest possible compliment: They offered me the opportunity to go right to the front of the line.

I declined gracefully. What I should have declined and did not was an offer from the only Jewish general in Korea to show me North Korea from the air—in a helicopter. I agreed to go with him because I didn't want another Jew to think I was a coward. He was a real swashbuckling type, a cowboy. He wore two guns on his hips, like General Patton. There is a Yiddish word to describe a person like this: *putz*. Of course, I was the *schmuck* who went with him. The North Koreans were the enemy. There was absolutely no need to go see them. The only thing North Korea looked like from the air was too close. It was crazy to fly over their territory in 1952, just crazy. And it was even crazier to do it in a helicopter. I had been scared before, but this time I was terrified. I was a singer, not a moving target.

On the flight back to the United States I performed for our troops in Tokyo, the Aleutian Islands and Alaska. It was an extraordinary trip. I really felt like I was doing some good. After spending several weeks in the United States, I toured Europe, doing shows for soldiers stationed in England, Scotland, France, and Germany. I wasn't sorry when my two-year hitch came to an end, and I was very happy to have served. I'd spent two wonderful years in the army, I had even found time to get my high school–equivalency diploma, and when I was discharged on April 10, 1953, I felt like I'd become an adult. And an even bigger star.

Before entering the army I really didn't feel like a star. I'd had only two hit records. But during my two years in the army, about fourteen more records had been released and become big hits, I'd appeared all over the world in front of huge audiences, and I'd become very comfortable onstage. That doesn't mean I wasn't nervous about resuming my career. Two years is a long time. The young girls who had been screaming for me at the Paramount were two years older, and as I knew from my own sisters, the attention span of a teenage girl was probably closer to two hours than two years. I was worried I might have to start over again.

But Milton Blackstone had taken care of everything. The day after I lost my army pay of $94.37 a month, I returned to the Paramount for a special Welcome Home Eddie engagement paying $7,500 a week. I was separated from the army at midnight, my first show at the Paramount was at 11 A.M. I had three hours of rehearsal. The movie was Vincent Price's 3-D classic horror film, *House of Wax*, but I was the only live act. Any doubts I had about my popularity ended as I stood offstage and sang the first four bars, "Whyyyy . . ." I couldn't hear another word for five minutes. Fans stormed the stage. They were screaming, yelling; it was one loud, continuous roar. Girls fainted in the aisles. I didn't even have to sing. Nobody cared, they just wanted to see me. It wasn't a concert, it was an event. At the end of my first show I had to sing twelve encores.

Twelve! I think it was then I began to believe that I was more important than my music.

I had the sound for the times. It was a big sound, and it came from my heart. I didn't try to schmaltz it up, I didn't take any shortcuts. It was real. I was belting. I did five shows a day and I gave everything I had every show. These performances were love affairs; I loved my fans as much as they loved me. And after a few days I started losing my voice. I was singing loudly, trying to be heard above the screams, and my vocal cords were inflamed. It wasn't serious—with rest my voice would come back—but I had three more weeks of shows to do and I didn't want to disappoint anyone. The great songwriter Hugh Martin—he had written many of Judy Garland's hits—was accompanying me on the piano, and he said, "I've got a doctor who'll bring back your voice just like that." He snapped his fingers loudly. At that point I was willing to try anything, so Milton and I took a cab to the office of a Dr. Max Jacobson on East Seventy-second Street.

The office looked more like a chemist's laboratory than a doctor's office and Max looked like—Max. Like a mad scientist, I guess. I remember noticing at our first meeting that his fingernails were filthy, stained with chemicals. He was nothing like any other doctor I'd ever met. He was a German refugee, with big thick glasses, a big thick accent, and a completely commanding personality. Max was in charge of life. Milton and I were escorted into his office and almost immediately he began to mix up some chemicals.

The whole situation made me very uncomfortable, but I was too polite, and maybe too desperate, to leave. Besides, Hugh Martin had told me that Max treated hundreds of very important patients, among them Franklin Roosevelt's secretary, Cecil B. DeMille, Alan Lerner, and Zero Mostel. Directors, producers, even his ex-wife still came to see him for shots, so did editors of *Reader's Digest*, stockbrokers, advertising executives from Madison Avenue, and eventually even Milton Blackstone. Apparently the magic elixirs of Max Jacobson were well known in New York. In fact, as I later learned, many of his patients referred to him affectionately as "Dr. Feelgood."

I could barely speak above a whisper. My throat felt raw. But seconds after Max gave me my first shot, I opened my mouth and started singing loud and clearly, *"Ah sweet mystery of life . . ."*

Thirty-seven years later I stopped.

On April 17, 1953, I became an addict. Of course, that was long before I knew I was taking drugs. Two shots, one in the arm and one in my buttocks, and I had no trouble doing my five performances that day. But the next morning I was exhausted and my voice was gone again. But two more shots, just two shots, and my entire body was energized. I felt terrific. It was like a wave of sunlight passed through my body, rejuvenating my voice. What I did not know was that Max's "vitamin cocktail" was in fact a mix of vitamins, calcium, and methamphetamine—mixed in whatever dose Max thought appropriate. Speed. In those days that stuff was not only legal, but nobody really knew what it was. If I had known I was taking drugs I never would have done it. Never. I was against drugs. I barely drank. It was medicine, wonderful medicine. And Max was a genius.

Max could do anything. The real secret ingredient in Max's medicine was Max. He was funny and very smart and completely convincing. Somehow Max made people believe anything was possible. If you didn't know Max you can't appreciate the quality of his magic. He would make older women feel young again. He would convince the blind that he could make them see. People who suffered from multiple sclerosis came to him by the hundreds. Eventually I became his greatest disciple. We traveled together around the world—I even went with him to the White House where he gave shots to President John Kennedy before extremely important meetings.

Max was shooting the stars. His patients were the biggest movie stars and politicians and multimillionaires. Very important people depended on him. They worshiped him.

Those of us who believed in Max didn't understand the danger. And once we understood it, we didn't believe it. And once we believed it, we didn't care. For a long time we only saw the good things Max did. When the American Medical Association tried to stop him, we rallied behind him. Max made us feel good. And if one shot didn't make us feel good, we'd go back and he'd adjust the dose and the second shot would make us feel better.

Sometimes, though, sometimes I wonder what would have happened if I hadn't lost my voice that day, if I hadn't met Max. Things might have been very different.

For a time I had my own magic. Anything was possible. When I was getting ready to be discharged, Milton had told me that Coca-Cola had offered to sponsor my TV show. My TV show? That's how fast things were happening in my life. I thought he was crazy. Who was going to give a twenty-four-year-old who'd barely appeared on national television his own show? As it turned out, both Coke and Pepsi. Milton and I met with Sonny Werblin, then the head of the giant talent agency Music Corporation of America, at Toots Shors restaurant. MCA controlled all the big bands, and that gave them control of the music business. In one pocket Sonny had the offer from Coke, and in his other pocket was Pepsi's offer. I never knew all the details. I trusted Milton completely, but we accepted Coke's offer of $1,500 a week to do a twice-weekly fifteen-minute program.

Coke Time went on the air on April 17, 1953. It was originally hosted by veteran movie star Don Ameche, who would introduce me and my guests and do all the commercials. He was the kind of mature, sophisticated spokesman that Coke wanted. I was the boy singer. The show required very little rehearsal. We pioneered the use of cue cards and TelePrompTers on *Coke Time*. We had to. I was so busy recording, promoting, and making personal appearances that I didn't even have time to memorize the lyrics of the four songs I sang each show. So the few lines of dialogue I had and the lyrics were printed on cue cards and TelePrompTers and hidden all over the set.

Television was still so new in 1953 that I didn't know enough to be nervous. It turned out that I was a natural—when the director told me to turn to my right I turned to my right. When they told me to stand in the middle of the set, I stood right in the middle of the set. The boom microphone followed me wherever I went. As long as I could follow simple instructions I could be a television star.

Opera star Anna Maria Alberghetti made her American debut on my first show. We made pasta and sang and read all our lines correctly. On my second show I turned the wrong way, away from the camera, and flubbed some lines. It didn't matter. Absolutely nobody cared. Poor Don Ameche. He was a wonderful man who just wanted to do his job, but the audience wouldn't let him. They didn't want to hear him talk, they didn't even want to hear me sing; they just wanted to look at me and scream. After the second or third show the producers stopped the screaming by threatening to eject anyone who yelled out loud. But the Coke executives were just beginning to understand what they got when they hired me.

Within a month Don Ameche was eased out "to do a Broadway show," and I started doing the live commercials. At that time Coke's national spokesman was Irish tenor Morton Downey. But as I became more and more identified with Coke, they began using me in their magazine advertising. Eventually Milton negotiated a deal in which they paid me $1 million a year to replace Downey. That was a million dollars a year in 1953, ten times what President Eisenhower was earning. The most expensive cars were $3,000. Houses were $7,000. They were paying me a million dollars a year to do a TV show, pose for pictures, show up at ballparks and boxing matches, and drink Coke. And I loved Coke. I loved it a lot more for a million dollars, but it had always been my favorite drink. It was an incredible deal. Coke's entire annual advertising budget at that time was $22 million, and they were paying me $1 million. Eventually I became the Coca-Cola Kid; I was so synonymous with Coke that at soda fountains kids would order "Eddie Fishers."

Coke loved me. I remember Bob Woodruff, the president of Coke telling me, "Now son, y'all are a member of the Coca-Cola family." Which probably made me the only Jew in the family. At one point I was so important to them that they offered me the distribution rights to Cuba. They offered me all the Coke in Cuba! Then they offered me half the distribution rights to Atlantic City. Naturally, being an astute businessman, I held out for Florida. I'm still holding out.

Morton Downey was not happy about any of this. His close friend, the syndicated columnist Jack O'Brian, another anti-Semite, hated me for replacing Downey and started writing really nasty things about me. I didn't care. With so many wonderful things happening, I barely noticed. And Morton Downey and I got along. Coke insisted I have him on the show several times a year. One St. Patrick's Day, I remember, I was going to close the show by singing the old Hebrew ballad "Mother McRee."

Kol Nidre I could sing from memory, but "Mother McRee"? The lyrics were written for me on the TelePrompTer. I did the commercial and walked onto the set for the song and waited for the lights to come on so I could read the lyrics. The light did not come on. I stood grinning into the camera, dying. I looked like I was having a heart attack. Suddenly

I saw Morton Downey leaving the studio and I came up with one of the greatest ad libs of my life, "But you know, there's nobody in the world who can sing an Irish song like Morton Downey, and I think it's most appropriate that he sing this final song with me."

He came running back. He was a real trooper and he knew when the spotlight was shining. I sang the entire song staring at his mouth, trying to remember the lyrics.

It was a very basic show. A couple of sets, four songs, exchanged a few lines with my guest, five commercials, and out. One week we had a very pretty nurse on the show to receive a check for $300,000 I'd helped raise at a series of benefits for Long Island hospitals. I introduced her and asked if she was really a nurse. She said quite firmly that she was—because that was the line written for her on the cue cards. Actually she was a model.

In April, I performed at the Paramount and my TV show went on the air, in June I went to England for a two-week engagement at the London Palladium. My return to civilian life had not been very difficult.

I was as big a hit in Europe as I was in the United States. We sold out every show. People waited in line six hours for tickets. This was only a few weeks before the coronation of Queen Elizabeth, and London was just brimming with excitement. I was asked to sing at an important charity event, the red, white, and blue ball. I was thrilled until I arrived at the ball and realized I'd be performing for royalty. I really did get very nervous—but then I received a lovely note from the Queen's younger sister, Princess Margaret, telling me, "Please don't be frightened. I'll be leading the applause."

She requested that I sing my latest hit, "Outside of Heaven." When I introduced the song I looked right at her and said, "This is for someone special." Maybe she blushed—or maybe that was her complexion. When I sang the song, I gave her my most seductive Philadelphia stare.

We were introduced after my performance. She seemed very small for a princess. She was very attractive, with lovely big blue eyes. I know I looked great: I was wearing a beautifully tailored tuxedo, I was in great shape, even my teeth had been capped and were perfect. But no matter how handsome I looked on the outside, inside there was this skinny kid selling fruits and vegetables in the alleys of Philadelphia jumping up and down screaming "Oh boy, oh boy." I didn't know what to say to her.

No one I knew had ever spoken to a real princess before. Trying to start a conversation, I said, "I hear you like American singers."

She stepped back as if there were a spring attached to her back. She looked horrified, as if I was flirting with her. "What?" she snapped.

I *was* flirting with her, but I was doing my best not to let her know I was flirting with her. "I mean," I stammered, "you like their music."

She calmed down and agreed that she did. Then she asked me, "Would you like to dance?" Would I like to dance with an English princess? This was my chance. First a dance, then a walk in the moonlight, then—who knew? England had already had a King Edward, but he hadn't been Jewish. Maybe because I wanted to save the monarchy, but more likely because I was too shy, I responded, "I'm sorry, I don't dance." A photographer took a picture of the two of us at the moment I was turning her down, and the next day it was printed in newspapers around the world.

She asked me if I was staying for the coronation and I told her I would love to. I figured maybe she needed a date. But she didn't invite me. We continued speaking just a little while longer, just the two of us, until one of her aides interrupted. With that, the princess and I shook hands and parted forever. If I'd had just a little more time, England might have had its first Jewish prince.

I did get to spend some time alone with one of the Queen's ladies-in-waiting during that trip. And, as the Brits like to say, that's when I found out what she was waiting for.

I'm not sure it's possible to really comprehend how fast all this happened to me. At the beginning of this chapter I was sharing a room at Grossinger's with a rabbi, a tennis pro, and a basketball player; twenty-eight pages later I'm singing for Princess Margaret in London. I had very little preparation for any of this—I sort of had to make it up as I went along.

And this was really only the beginning. By 1954 I had become the most popular singer in America. Irving Berlin wrote a song just for me that I introduced on *Coke Time*: "When the clouds are not as clear as they used to be/There are salesmen selling fear but they can't scare me." The greatest songwriter in history was writing songs for me. All the movie studios were sending me scripts, practically begging me to do a picture for them; any picture, it didn't matter. I had fan clubs around the world;

I had the entire ninth floor of 221 West Fifty-seventh Street, where people did nothing but answer my fan mail. I had totally eclipsed Frank Sinatra. One afternoon up on the sixth floor at NBC, the elevators opened and a group of teenagers piled out and ran right past Sinatra to get to me; they practically pushed him out of their way. Sinatra recorded the song "I'm Walking Behind You" and it bombed, then three months later Vic Damone recorded it and again it bombed; I recorded it and it went right to number one and became my biggest hit. The songs didn't matter; every record I released immediately became a big hit. I could have made any song a hit, I could have recorded "Felix the Cat Whines" and it would have gone gold. One week on the TV show *The Hit Parade* three of the seven hits they played were my songs, the first time in history that had happened. Manny Sacks showed me the sales figures for RCA's entire roster of singers: I'd sold more records by myself than all their other singers together—including Mario Lanza, Perry Como, and Elvis.

The songs didn't matter. I was too busy making hit records to be concerned about the music. I didn't pay attention to the importance of the music. Among the things that made Sinatra so great was that he cared so much about the songs he sang. Tony Bennett, Perry, Ella Fitzgerald, Nat King Cole, even Bing Crosby, they all cared about creating a legacy, a catalog of songs that meant something. They made an investment in the music. I didn't. I recorded pretty much whatever they put in front of me. They came to me with a song called "Oh, My Papa," and as soon as I heard the lyric I agreed to record it. The sentiment alone was enough to make it a big hit; it was a worldwide hit.

Success came so easily for me that I didn't learn until it was too late how difficult it really is. Once in my life the music mattered more than anything else, and then I met Max and his drugs, and then there was romance. Oh, the women, the beautiful, wonderful women. Maybe it was drugs first and then romance; maybe the romance came first. But eventually the music simply became a means to the drugs and the women.

I had it all once. And I let it get away.

But oh, the women were wonderful.

CHAPTER THREE

It isn't the music that people remember most about me, it's the women. It's Debbie Reynolds and Elizabeth Taylor and Connie Stevens and Ann-Margret and—the list of beautiful women I romanced is a long one. But the woman who changed everything was Elizabeth Taylor. Among them all, she stood alone. To me she was *everything*. And the fact that she was mine was too much for me to believe. That was beyond even my own wildest dreams. We had the kind of love affair that, if you're very lucky, happens once in a lifetime. Once in ten lifetimes.

But long before I knew Elizabeth Taylor I had fallen in love with being in love. And even after everything that happened, I've never lost that feeling. Never.

I don't know exactly when the music stopped being the most important thing in my life. Maybe when I got that first shot from Max Jacobson.

But more likely it was when I began to understand that the most beautiful women in the world were available to me. Not just available, I didn't even have to pursue them. They ran after me. And some of them I let catch me.

That all came as a big surprise. For a long time I didn't see myself as the person the media pictured. I didn't feel like that handsome kid grinning from the cover of countless magazines. Inside, I felt the same way I had way back in Philadelphia: very nervous around pretty girls and thrilled when an attractive woman showed an interest in me.

When I mention the women who pursued me, I don't include my fans. This was the mid-1950s, a decade before "groupies" starting keeping lists of the rock stars they had sex with. Every performer was wary of fans. Occasionally a young girl would sneak into my apartment or dressing room, but I'd get her out of there as quickly as possible. I remember being told very early in my career that a fan had tried to set up Danny Kaye, and his managers had prevented it from happening. It might've ruined his career. And we all knew about the baseball player Eddie Waitkus, who'd been shot by a fan he'd invited up to his hotel room. I never even looked at a fan, I never let a fan into my life. I didn't have to; for a time the whole world was mine.

I really was innocent once. In an article in a fan magazine entitled "If You Had a Date with Eddie Fisher," I wrote—or someone wrote for me—"I'd like my date to be sweet, well-mannered, attractive, bright— all the qualities American men look for in American women." Corny, but absolutely true. At least for a time. And once in my life I found that person. Her name was Joanie Wynne and she was a Copa girl.

The primary qualification for a Copa girl was that she had to be gorgeous. The Copa girls were the epitome of beauty and sophistication. Every man in the world dreamed of dating one of them. Tommy Dorsey married a Copa girl. Jan Murray married an exquisite Copa girl. When I was eighteen years old and just starting out, my dressing room was right next to theirs. I wasn't in heaven—this place was better than that. The girls adopted me, and they took care of me. And as time passed, some of them took better care of me than others. I mean, I was slow and shy at first, I was a scared kid, but when they led I followed. Very quietly I made my way through the line, but I stopped when I reached Joanie Wynne.

She was simply a beautiful person. She was the only virgin in the chorus line and I was practically a virgin, and we fell madly in love with each other. The other girls pushed us together; everybody thought we made a perfect couple. She was a good Scotch-Irish Catholic girl from Sheepshead Bay, Brooklyn. After Joanie and I had been dating for several months I told my mother, "I'm going to marry this girl."

My mother accepted the news very calmly. "Over my dead body you'll marry a shiksa."

In fact, we never seriously considered it. Get married? It took us months and months before we even slept together. Getting married was the last thing on my mind. I couldn't even afford to take her out for dinner to a real restaurant. A big night out was using the quarter slots at the automat. But she never cared. I took her up to Grossinger's for a weekend and bought her a gold bathing suit for ten dollars. I wanted her to have matching gold shoes, but I couldn't afford them, so I paid for one shoe and she paid for the other. She was making more money than I was and she was very generous. When I couldn't afford make-up for my next singing engagement she would buy it for me. For Christmas 1948, she gave me one of the nicest presents I've ever received. She bought me a wire recorder, one of the first personal tape recorders, so I could hear my own voice. It was a big, heavy thing, and it must have cost her several weeks' salary. She lugged it up four flights of stairs to my rented room. The recorder was very nice, but her real present was the investment in my talent.

We dated several months before we decided it was time to make love. We waited that long because both of us were very nervous about having sex. Even after we knew we were going to do "it" we had to find a place where we could be alone. I was renting a back bedroom from a trumpet player in the Copa band and his wife for ten dollars a month. The room didn't even have a door. But finally one afternoon, when the trumpet player and his wife were out, we started making love. We fumbled around for a few minutes and then, just as we reached that perfect moment we'd been waiting for, the trumpet player and his wife came home.

The wife started screaming at us. We were sinners! We were going to go to hell! We were so scared we thought we were going there directly from my ten-dollar-a-month apartment. Joanie was mortified and I felt terrible. Sex! With an exclamation point! Caught! We thought they were going to report us to the police. We spent the rest of that afternoon just talking about how this might affect our future, until we went to work that night.

Eventually Joanie Wynne and I rented a four-dollar-a-night room at the Lincoln Hotel and consummated our relationship. It was heavenly. It was so exciting. I fell in love that night—I loved sex. After that I couldn't get enough of her. I wanted to have sex with her all the time

When Joanie's mother found out we were doing "it," she accepted the news as calmly as my mother. She called me every day to ask, "When you are going to marry my daughter?"

Maybe I should have married her. But we just drifted apart. She was the first woman who really broke my heart. After we'd been dating on and off a few years, she was working at the Beverly Club, a mob-owned gambling joint in Kentucky. I called her there and I was told she was playing golf with an orchestra leader named Nat Brandwynne. Nat Brandwynne! I knew Nat Brandwynne; he had a big-time reputation with the women. I also knew his big secret—he wore a toupee. I knew right away that if she was playing golf with him she was probably sleeping with him. I felt so awful. Terrible. When I finally got her on the phone I really wanted to hurt her, so I said the very worst thing I could think of at that moment: "How could you sleep with a bald-headed guy!"

It was while I was still in pain from breaking up with Joanie that I discovered that sex without real love was just—terrific. After finishing the coast-to-coast tour with Eddie Cantor I was doing four shows a day at the Orpheum Theater in downtown Los Angeles. I spent a lot of time at Cantor's house, but sometimes I just liked to walk around by myself. I loved Hollywood—I felt like I was walking on hallowed ground. One day I walked by this small theater on Las Palmas and Hollywood Boulevard that was presenting a new play by Jean-Paul Sartre, *The Respectful Prostitute*. I'd heard of Sartre and thanks to Joey Foreman's uncle I knew about prostitutes, so I went in to see it. While I don't remember the performance, I do remember the star.

After the performance, as I had been taught was proper by Eddie Cantor, I went backstage to congratulate the cast. I met the actress who had played the prostitute and we were instantly attracted to each other. I don't remember which once of us asked the other for dinner, but I suspect she asked me because in those days I doubt I would have had the courage to ask her out. She drove us up to Carmel. After a lovely dinner we checked into the Captain's Table Motel. I was thrilled. I was with a very attractive older woman, the star of the show, and she was pursuing me. The night was perfect for romance.

But when we took off our clothes I saw that her back was badly scarred. Long, deep scars. And I lost all interest in her. I tried to be a gentleman, but I wanted the night to be over. Still, the sex was very nice; the physical parts of it were great. I learned that I didn't really have to be in love with the woman I was with to enjoy sex. But being in love—even just for the night—made it so wonderful, so much more enjoyable. And I fell in love so easily.

It took me a long time to get started with the women. But once I got started I couldn't stop. As I discovered, I had a very big libido. Beauty made me crazy. I spent my life in pursuit of perfection. And I was very fortunate to find the one perfect woman—many times. Romance dominated my life, and that was the biggest mistake I ever made.

I didn't have to try very hard to overcome my natural shyness. As an attractive, rising young star in show business I found that I was a very desireable commodity. Beautiful, famous women pursued me. Joan Crawford put her arms around me and wanted to take me home. I ran. Edith Piaf, the legendary French chanteuse, whispered in my ear that we should leave together. I ran. When I was married to Debbie Reynolds, Zsa Zsa Gabor wouldn't leave me alone. "Why are you married to Debbie Reynolds?" she'd ask in front of whoever was standing there. "You should be with someone like me, someone who can make you a man." Zsa Zsa would come to my show every night and make a big entrance just before I went on. It got to be very embarrassing. "Come to my bungalow after the show, I'll make a man of you." I just laughed, and I ran. Hedy Lamarr made a big pass at me. Lee Strasberg sent me to the legendary acting teacher Stella Adler for a lesson, she ended up chasing me around the room, and that was the end of my acting lesson. Lucille Ball came on to me. . .if I wasn't attracted to the person I ran.

Fortunately, I was attracted to a lot of women. There are a lot of beautiful women in show business. I got very spoiled early in my life, I got hooked on movie stars and starlets. The first actress I ever dated was named Wanda Hendricks. Our first date was arranged by her studio. We were together once and had a lovely time, but Milton Blackstone told me not to see her again. "She only wants to be with you because of who you are. She knows she'll get publicity by dating you." And I listened to him as if Milton Blackstone knew something about women.

For a time I wondered if women were attracted to me because I was a star or because I was simply an attractive man. I'd always ask myself; Does she like me because I'm a famous singer and if she goes out with me her picture will be in newspapers and magazines, or because I was a poor kid with good manners from Philadelphia? Now there's a silly question, the truth is that it didn't matter. The famous singer was the poor kid from Philly. So I didn't care if the women I dated got publicity out of our relationship as long as I was also enjoying myself.

And I did enjoy myself. A banquet of beautiful woman had been set before me. Of course, Milton did everything possible to control me. Milton wanted me to remain true to the entire American public. I remember how he warned me to stay away from Terry Moore, who was a starlet when we dated. Dated? We went out several times but we "dated" only once—that was in the front seat of a car in the middle of New York City. As it turned out, Milton was probably right about Terry Moore. Years later Terry claimed to have been secretly married to Howard Hughes. I don't know if that's true or not, but I remember she told me that when she was married to the college football star Glenn Davis, he caught her in bed with Howard Hughes, and Davis beat Hughes so badly that he was hospitalized for three weeks.

In those days women were not supposed to enjoy sex as much as men. Supposedly, they did "it" to please men, and if the man wasn't serious about the woman, he was condemned for "taking advantage of her." With my success came the realization that that wasn't completely true. There were women who enjoyed being with men and didn't need the promise of an engagement ring. Or at least a dinner with photographers at the Brown Derby. The English actress Joan Collins, for example, had a reputation for liking men. I met her one night against the wall of Dean Martin's swimming pool. Marlon Brando was there, Dean, and several other people, and we were all naked and screaming and having a wonderful party. Until the neighbors called the police. That was pretty much the extent of my relationship with her and I think we both enjoyed the quality time we spent together.

I make it sound so easy, so simple. And it was. But I learned very rapidly that the most important erogenous zone is the mind. As long as I live I'll turn my head to look at a beautiful face or a beautiful body, but if I didn't connect with a woman mentally I couldn't be there. When I was with Elizabeth Taylor her figure was far from perfect and at times she was overweight, but to me she was always the most beautiful woman I'd ever known. We connected completely on so many levels.

I learned the importance of some sort of mental connection from a gorgeous young woman named Joan Olander. When Monte Proser left the Copa to open Cafe Theater he booked Jackie Gleason and Josephine Baker for opening night, but they both wanted the big dressing room so neither one showed up. I was Always Available Eddie, so just before I left to go into the army I filled in for the opening. Joan Olander was a gorgeous eighteen-year-old chorus girl. She had a perfect figure. Better than perfect. I was told she'd been married and divorced at fifteen, and had been dating former heavyweight champion Jack Dempsey since she was sixteen. Joan was gorgeous. We made a very cute couple. She fell in love with me and told Dempsey, but what was he going to do about it? He was married. Every time we went out she insisted we go to places where we would be seen; she was desperate for attention. I thought the whole thing was ridiculous, and I knew she was using me, but. . .Joan was gorgeous. She was the last woman I slept with before I was inducted.

Two years later, as I was getting ready to come home from Korea, I asked a general if I could make a phone call to the States. That was not an easy connection to make—most soldiers calling from the Far East literally had to take a number and wait a day or more for their turn—but I assured the general that this was very important. Maybe he thought I was calling my mother. I called Joan Olander and told her I was coming home: "Get a room at the Beverly Hills Hotel."

The plane I was on lost an engine coming in to Fairbanks, Alaska. In Korea I had flown on anything that could get into the air, I'd flown with pilots in training, if the Wright Brothers had been in Korea I would have flown with them, but I'd never been as terrified as I was on that flight to Alaska. So even after being without a woman for almost two years, with one of the most beautiful women I'd ever seen waiting for me in a bed at the Beverly Hills Hotel, I took the train to Los Angeles. By the time

I reached the hotel I could barely contain my anticipation.

By then Joan Olander had changed her name to Mamie Van Doren, but nothing else had changed. Five minutes after I got there we were in bed having sex. And when we were done I couldn't wait to get away from her. Once the touching was over there was absolutely nothing there. The only level on which we connected was physical and, believe me, I was shocked when I realized that that wasn't enough. I mean, Jo—Mamie was gorgeous. Obviously, being with her was still a lot better than reading the dirty comic books I found in the bottom of my brother's drawer, but it still left me feeling unfulfilled.

We went out several times after that and the things that had not bothered me at all before we slept together suddenly became extremely irritating. For example, she was always looking past me for the cameras. At the famed Mocombo restaurant one evening I refused to have my picture taken with her, but I didn't hesitate to be photographed with the great actor Edward G. Robinson. She was furious. She told me "You can just kiss my lily-white ass," then marched out of the place by herself.

Mamie was gorgeous, but Edward G. Robinson was a Jew and spoke Yiddish.

The greatest of all pickup lines, as I learned years later, was probably, "I'll have my plane pick you up." But in those days I didn't have any special lines, I didn't have any technique. I had a natural gift for conversation. And if a woman responded to me, it was because the chemistry between us was right. But I also treated women with respect. I loved the ceremony of a seduction. I loved taking a beautiful woman to dinner and entertaining her, I loved the conversation. I loved the challenge and the chase, but most of all, I loved the winning.

In the chase I used every weapon at my disposal. One week my guest on *Coke Time* was singer Jane Morgan. Although she was an American, she had become famous singing in French in Europe. She was a gorgeous blond and the moment I met her, I knew I was destined to be with her. But, just to help destiny, I had the director get a tiger-skin rug for her number. I flirted with her from the moment I met her and we ended up in bed together. It was wonderful, glorious. "You know, everybody's talking about you," she said.

I was flattered. The word was that I was getting a reputation as a real ladies' man. "So, what are they saying?" I asked.

She started laughing, then told me, "All of my gay boys think you're gay."

I sat up. "What?" Me, homosexual? I insisted she call one of her gay friends right then. As soon as he got on the phone I yelled at him, "I am *not* a homosexual!"

Not that I didn't have opportunities. Early in my career I was approached by a lot of different men. At first I was so naive I didn't understand I was being solicited. I thought these guys were just being friendly. Even when I realized they were flirting with me I was very polite. I brushed them off as nicely as possible. When I was performing at the London Palladium, Noel Coward showed up regularly to see my show. Then he invited me to his theater and showed me how to control an audience. "You must always keep a curtain between you and the audience," he explained. "You are the entertainer and you must never let the audience forget that."

I don't think Noel Coward had any concept of bobby-soxers. In England the teenagers sat respectfully in the gallery and never approached the stage. Noel Coward was used to the more polite British audiences. I knew there were many things he could teach me, but it was obvious that his interest in me was more than professional. Years later when we crossed the Atlantic together on the *Queen Elizabeth* he would show up in the steam room every day when I was getting a massage. Looking at me lying on my stomach, covered only by towel, he asked, politely, "Just let me pat you once, dear boy. Just let me touch it a little."

That's when I told him, politely, about the curtain I kept between me and other men.

A beautiful body or a beautiful face wasn't enough to make a woman attractive to me. I used to hang out with Marilyn Monroe, for example, yet I was never attracted to her. As physically beautiful as she was, the drinking and the pills made her ugly. One night Elizabeth and I went to the Sands Hotel to celebrate Kirk and Ann Douglas's seventh wedding anniversary. We were sitting with Dean and Jeanie Martin. I sang a special parody Sammy Cahn had written, and I think Dean did something, then Frank Sinatra, who was there with Marilyn, got up to sing. I don't know whether Marilyn was drunk or stoned, but she was slobbering all over herself. When Frank started singing she started banging on the stage floor. I saw Frank make a simple gesture toward her, and guards appeared immediately and practically dragged Marilyn out of the room. She was embarrassing. I saw her like that so many times.

Jayne Mansfield was even worse. There were a lot of men who would have given everything they owned to spend one night with Jayne Mansfield. But they were the men who didn't know her. She had a beautiful figure, but she was a nasty drunk. Her husband, Mickey Hargitay, was a good guy, but he was in a tough spot with her. He liked to drink too, but she made him a lot crazier than all the booze. I think I knew them before I really understood how a woman could destroy the man who loves her, before Elizabeth, and I couldn't understand why he stayed with her. People used to say she was dumb, but she was smart enough to know that all she had was her body and she used it. She was a big flirt, she was jealous of other women, and she was constantly instigating fights.

In a Los Angeles restaurant one night she insisted I sit at her table. Mickey hadn't gotten there yet. Next thing I knew a fight was about to start and all I wanted to do was get out of there before it started. I went outside just as Mickey came roaring up to the place in his car. I threw my arms around him and warned him, "She's looking to start a fight. You'd better do something."

"Don't worry about it," he said. Mickey was a big guy, former Mr. Universe. "I'll take care of it. I love you." Then he ran in to fight for her honor.

Her honor? She had about as much honor as she did talent.

What attracted me most to a woman, I guess, was her essence. Her persona. Obviously I loved beautiful women, but I walked away from a lot of them once I spent even a little time with them. I don't really know how to define that attraction, but I recognized it when I found it. It didn't have much to do with physical appearance or even age, because I was often attracted to older women. Jane Morgan was almost forty, for example, when we were together. Dinah Shore was at least ten years older than I was. We had been close friends for years—we were both Jewish singers with our own shows—when we finally spent a night together. I'd always thought she was a very sexy lady, but I thought so from a distance. One night she invited me to her house for a party, and after a wonderful evening of good food and singing around the piano, going into her bedroom seemed the most natural thing in the world. I remember that on her dressing table was a photograph of Manny Sacks, who'd introduced us. I knew the picture very well because I had the same one in my house; it had been taken on Eddie Fisher Day at Grossinger's, when all the songwriters were invited for a golf tournament. The only difference between Dinah's photo and mine is that I had been cut out of the framed picture in her bedroom. Dinah was a wonderful, intelligent, very sexy lady.

But the older woman to whom I was the most attracted was Marlene Dietrich. I never knew nor cared how much older than me she was; Marlene Dietrich was ageless.

She was probably even older than my mother when we met, but she was beautiful. She was Dietrich. She was a star. Some people tried to convince me that she was an old woman, but I would tell them she was a young girl. In private few celebrities are equal to their public image, but Marlene Dietrich, just like the image she created in films like *The Blue Angel,* was the most sensuous woman I've ever known.

I saw Marlene for the first time while I was playing the London Palladium. She was doing one show a night at the Ritz. I became infatuated with her when she made the most provocative entrance I've ever seen onstage, walking dramatically down a spiral staircase wearing a transparent gown. I was mightily impressed and wanted very much to meet her. But I did not go backstage to congratulate her after her performance. This was the legendary Marlene Dietrich, I was a pop singer. I was intimidated by her.

She did a wonderful nightclub act. It wasn't her talent as much as the force of her personality that captivated the audience. Her presence dominated a room. Noel Coward believed a performer should keep a curtain between themselves and the audience, Marlene Dietrich seduced her audience.

I met her briefly at a dinner party columnist Leonard Lyons gave to introduce Marlene to Adlai Stevenson. Apparently Marlene had heard Stevenson speak and wanted to meet him. Maybe she was attracted to him—who knows? But whatever her feelings were before this party, it was obvious to everyone there that she quickly lost interest. I've always suspected she thought Stevenson was gay. He was a wise man, but in person there was something quite unappealing about him. He had absolutely no charisma.

My date for dinner was Margaret Truman, the former's president's daughter. Leonard Lyons had fixed us up. But I wound up that night with Honey Warren, the daughter of Supreme Court Chief Justice Earl Warren. We dated several times after that and she traveled with me to several concert appearances. But what I remember most about that night was standing on the side just watching Marlene move about the room with such incredible confidence and grace.

Marlene Dietrich actually picked me up. She came to see me at Bill Miller's Riviera the night it was closing to be replaced by a highway. It was a memorable evening and the audience responded. After my first show she invited me to her table. She was putting together a new act, she explained, and asked me for suggestions. Now, the truth is that she didn't need any advice from me. As she later told me, "I was singing in the cabarets before you were born." But she knew how to make me feel important. I introduced her to the talented young songwriter I'd discovered, Jerry Ross, the nephew of a friend of mine from Grossinger's, and his writing partner Dick Adler. I was taking them around to music publishers, and eventually they would write the great Broadway shows *Pajama Game* and *Damn Yankees*. Several days later she called to thank me and invited me for dinner.

To have been seduced by Marlene Dietrich is to have been taught how to make love by the expert. Marlene was my teacher, but her great skill was that she never made me feel like her student. In her Park Avenue apartment she created a perfect environment for romance. We ate dinner by candlelight as music played softly in the background. Afterwards we sat together and spoke of our lives. She was so easy to talk to I found myself revealing things to her that I would not have told anyone else. Eventually she led me into her bedroom; if the living areas were designed for romance, her bedroom had been made for sex. Everything about it was just right, from the intimate lighting to the carved mirrors on the ceiling.

Marlene's daughter, Maria Riva, wrote that her mother had "bedded" me. But I know that I meant more than that. I was more than a conquest for her. She told me that she once had been deeply in love with a German singer, Richard Talber, and she often compared me to him. There was a time in our relationship when she would have done anything for me. But just by being with me she was already doing exactly what I wanted.

As a lover she was incredible. Incredible. Her great skill was making me believe I really knew what I was doing. She made me feel so at ease, so comfortable, I couldn't make a wrong move. With Mamie Van Doren and so many others sex was all physical, but with Marlene it was much more; it was an emotional connection, a means of communicating on another level. I've had that experience with very few women in my life. With Elizabeth certainly, and with my wife Betty Lin, but the first time was with Marlene.

I knew of her legendary reputation; I knew she had been with men from Gen. George Patton to Gary Cooper, and I also knew she had been with as many women as men. She loved men and she loved women, but whoever she was with, she was the queen.

We saw each other often, and we always ended up in her bedroom. And as much as I loved the sex, just being with her was thrilling. She was not afraid of life, and lived it to the fullest extent. I don't think my mother knew I was seeing Marlene Dietrich. If she had she would have objected. Objected? If she had been unhappy when I was seeing Joanie Wynne, just imagine how she would have reacted when she found out her Sonny Boy was dating Marlene Dietrich. To the rest of the world Marlene was one of the great women, but to my mother she was a *shiksa*. One of the great *shiksas* in the world maybe, but still a *shiksa*. She still had hopes that I would end up with a nice Jewish girl like my sisters. But those friends of mine who knew about this relationship tried to talk me out of it. She was too old for me, they insisted. At times even she brought up the difference in our ages. But it made no difference to me. We made our own world and in that world she was a young girl. No one else could possibly know how wonderful it was to be in that world.

So I paid no attention to anyone else's opinion—except Milton Blackstone. My affair with Marlene had been very quiet. There was never a word about it in the press. But after several weeks I thought it was time for us to appear together in public, so I invited her to accompany me to Rocky Marciano's defense of his heavyweight title at the Polo Grounds. I'd met Rocky when he was training at Grossinger's. At times I'd even run with him in the morning, and we'd become close friends. A Rocky Marciano heavyweight championship fight was a major event, and I was aware that reporters and photographers from around the world would be there.

I think it would be unfair to describe Milton Blackstone's reaction when I told him I was taking Marlene to the fight as apoplectic. No, I think it was much worse than that. Milton was always overly cautious with me and my activities, always concerned about building a positive public image. It was Milton who arranged my endless charitable appearances, Milton who arranged my triumphant tour of Korea while I was in the army, Milton who introduced me to important people like Cardinal Spellman, Milton who made the deal that turned me into the Coca-Cola Kid. At first he was very good for me, and I listened to him, but I didn't know when to stop. It was also Milton, for example, who didn't want me to be "too Jewish" because, incredible as it seems, a lot of people didn't know I was Jewish. Many people thought I was Italian. It was Milton who convinced me to turn down an invitation I truly wanted to accept to accompany New York's Francis Cardinal Spellman on his Christmas trip to Korea. I wanted to go back to Korea, and I thought the symbolism of a Jew and the most powerful Roman Catholic clergyman in America making this trip together during the holiday season would be wonderful. But Milton convinced me not to go, telling me that the rabbis would not approve of it. I've always been very sorry I didn't make that trip.

But not nearly as sorry as I was that I listened to him about taking Marlene to the Marciano fight. Milton usually was pretty subtle; he guided me rather than tried to control me. Not this time. "If you take her to that fight your career will be over," he said flatly. Not ruined, it will be over.

I didn't understand his reasoning, but I accepted it. By that point I had become so dependent on Milton I didn't feel I had a choice. I called Marlene and explained the situation to her. She understood; she was Marlene Dietrich. I went to the fight alone, feeling like a real coward. Although we spoke on the phone after that night, that was the end of our love affair. But she must have had good feelings about me, because later she tried to fix me up with her daughter.

While I was ashamed of my behavior, I didn't have any time for regrets. I was too busy living my greatest fantasies. I was the most popular singer in America, bigger than Sinatra, bigger than Como, and my career was continuing to grow. President Eisenhower, making a nationally televised speech from a charity dinner at the Astor Hotel, interrupted the tightly scheduled program to ask me to sing Irving Berlin's "Count Your Blessings," which I'd done for him before the show went on the air. "Count Your Blessings" became Berlin's last big hit. Irving Berlin, perhaps the greatest songwriter in history, let *me* dig through a foot locker filled with his unpublished songs to see if there was anything I was interested in recording. He even wrote a song especially for me called "I'm Not Afraid," which I introduced on *Coke Time* literally three hours after he'd finished writing it. All the legendary songwriters wanted me to record their songs: Cole Porter, Julie Stein, Sammy Cahn, Richard Rodgers and Oscar Hammerstein. When I was performing at the Empire Room in the Waldorf, Oscar came to see me every night for three weeks.

One night I stopped by a studio just to watch my idol, Perry Como, working on a record. Only a few years earlier I'd come out of the audience after his program to sing a song, and now I was more popular than he was. On the spur of the moment, Manny Sacks decided Perry and I should record a duet. The producers taught me two songs and Perry and I recorded "Maybe," and "Watermelon Weather." Within weeks it became a big hit record.

For me, anything seemed possible. I wasn't just a pop singer, I was becoming an industry. I was generating money for everyone with whom I came in contact, so whatever I said I wanted, no matter how outrageous it was, people took me seriously. I used to give people impossible challenges. Once, I remember, I told my friend Julie Chester, a music publisher, "I want to talk to Edward Teller."

Edward Teller was one of the greatest scientists in the world; he had been instrumental in the development of both the atom bomb and nuclear bomb. "I could get him on the phone for you," Julie Chester said.

Sure enough, I'm rehearsing in my house one day when Julie came rushing in and said breathlessly, "I got him on the phone."

"Tell him to call back," I said. Eventually I spoke to him. But I didn't have anything to say. What was I going to tell the man who helped invent the most powerful and potentially destructive weapons in history? Don't do it again? Instead I said, "There's something I have to talk to you about that's very important. Are you going to be in Los Angeles anytime soon?"

"I am," Teller said, "but tell me, what is it you want to talk to me about?"

"Well," I continued, improvising, "it's something so important I can't tell you on the phone. I have to see you alone and in person."

"I'm sorry," he said, "but I'm terribly harassed and hurried . . ." That bothered me. No one should harass the man who invented the hydrogen bomb! We never met.

For a time it was like the world was my magic lantern. All I had to do was make a wish and somebody tried to make it come true. Which is how I came to meet Debbie Reynolds.

Debbie Reynolds was better known than Edward Teller. And certainly much cuter. In fact, Debbie Reynolds was probably the most famous virgin in America! In 1954 she was one of the most popular female stars in motion pictures. I fell in love with her while I was in Korea—along with about a million other GIs. One night I was sitting in a tent. It was pouring outside, and we were watching Gene Kelly, Donald O'Connor, and Debbie Reynolds dancing through a storm in *Singin' in the Rain*. And on that sheet that was hung in the front of the tent she looked like a dream. She was too good to be true. Only later did I find out how accurate that impression was. Watching that movie, I think it was impossible not to fall for her. I told myself that as soon as I got back to the States, I was going to date her.

I fell in love with the adorable character created by a movie studio. I fell for the image. Me, who had learned long ago the difference between image and reality. What got into me? Now that's the question I should have asked Edward Teller.

Philip Roth wrote in *Portnoy's Complaint*, his classic novel of a Jew coming to grips—many times—with his sexuality, "I too wanted to be the boyfriend of Debbie Reynolds—it's the Eddie Fisher in me coming out, that's all, the longing in all us swarthy Jewboys for those bland blond exotics called shiksas." While I never considered Debbie Reynolds to be exotic, she certainly portrayed the All-American girl; she was the cheerleader, the Girl Scout. She was so innocent that supposedly in high school she wore sweaters embroidered with the initials N. N.—meaning "nonnecker." Maybe that image was what originally appealed to me so much. And she certainly was pretty. Whatever it was, at first I was greatly attracted to her.

I'd met her once very briefly. In 1951, I had performed with the U.S. Army Band for wounded soldiers at Walter Reed Hospital in Washington, D.C. Debbie had also performed that day, singing the gimmick song

"Abba Dabba Honeymoon" from her picture *Two Weeks With Love*. I remember standing in the wings watching her, watching this cute little girl singing and tap dancing. She impressed me, apparently a lot more than I impressed her. Debbie's mother, Maxene, claimed that when we were introduced I looked so young that she had wondered, What is a sixteen-year-old boy doing in an army uniform? I don't remember what Debbie and I said to each other that day, but I was probably too shy to flirt with her.

I was formally introduced to her in June 1954. It wasn't exactly a match made in heaven—it was actually made in a publicity office. All the movie studios were after me to do a film for them. Paramount offered me the role of a singing cowboy in the film called *Red Garters*. I could have been the first Jewish singing cowboy. What was I going to sing, "Oh My Papoose"? Jeff Chandler called and wanted me to do a cowboy picture with him titled *Centerstage*. "You gotta do this picture with me, kid," he said.

"I can't play a cowboy," I told him, "I'm Jewish."

"That doesn't matter," he insisted. "I'm Jewish and I play a cowboy."

"I can't," I repeated. "How do I play a Jewish cowboy? Ride my horse from right to left?"

MGM wanted me for the musical remake of the gangster film *Dead End*. It was ridiculous; I knew I couldn't act. I couldn't even act like I could act. But the studios didn't care. They were in the business of making money, not great movies. As they did several years later with Elvis, they just wanted to put me in any piece of *dreck* that my fans would pay to see.

Producer Joe Pasternak wanted me to star in his picture *The Ambassador's Daughter*, so I went out to meet him at MGM. After showing me around the lot, he took me to the set of the movie *Athena*, where Debbie Reynolds was waiting to meet me. This was a very carefully arranged spontaneous meeting. The studios encouraged me to date their stars—and starlets—because everything I did generated publicity.

A year earlier, I'd responded honestly to a question from a fan magazine that the Hollywood star I'd most like to meet was Debbie Reynolds. As Debbie's mother, Maxene later told the media, Debbie just happened to be in her dressing room practicing her harp when Joe Pasternak and I stopped by. Practicing her *harp*? Now there's publicity symbolism. But the fact is that I didn't care if it had been carefully scheduled to happen spontaneously, the moment she opened the door of her trailer I was smitten. She was twenty-two years old and absolutely adorable. She was a fantasy in every way. And as I looked into her lovely eyes, it was impossible to imagine how much I would grow to dislike her. After those first few innocent minutes, it was downhill for the next forty-five years.

I wanted to go out with her. I knew her reputation for purity, but I didn't care. I was looking for something more than sex. I was looking for a real relationship. I guess I was looking for the warm, loving relationship my parents never had. And all the Debbie Reynolds movies I saw made me believe she was the kind of old-fashioned girl with whom I might find happiness.

I got her phone number from disc jockey Johnny Grant. When I called, Maxene answered the phone. "Hello," I said. "Is Debbie there please?"

Maxene was the guardian of the family jewel. "Who's calling?" she asked. That was the nicest thing she ever said to me.

"This is Eddie Fisher," I said pleasantly.

As I later heard the story, Maxene had often watched my television show and thought I was very attractive. So when I identified myself she didn't believe I was really me. "Eddie Fisher?" she responded. "Sure, and I'm Lucille Ball."

Eventually I convinced her that I was me and she allowed me to speak to Debbie. We got along very nicely on the telephone and I began calling her regularly from New York. When I returned to Los Angeles to play the Cocoanut Grove, I asked her to be my date for my opening. She immediately accepted the invitation. When I hung up the phone that night I felt that warm tingle of anticipation. I was really looking forward to spending time with her.

We went out for the first time the night before, to a party at Dinah Shore's house. We sat at a table with Jerry Lewis and Jack and Mary Benny and had a wonderful time. I didn't know anything about her, which helped enormously. I found her to be very interesting. She was just so natural, so sweet; I had never realized what a wonderful actress she was.

Opening night at the Cocoanut Grove she sat with Mike Todd, with whom I'd become very close friends, and the actress Evelyn Keyes. I was a big hit. The only thing that prevented the night from being perfect was the fact that I had accidentally made two dates.

These things happen. While visiting MGM I'd also invited the beautiful actress Pier Angeli to my opening. Although we'd never met before, she assumed I was asking her to be my date. And if I hadn't met Debbie, that probably was my intention. These two women were close friends, and both of them thought they were with me. Unfortunately, they were seated at adjacent tables. This was like the plot of a bad movie, the kind of movie the studios wanted me to make.

When I sat down with Debbie before the show, Pier believed she had been rejected. She ran out of the club, crying hysterically. I felt terrible, and I ran right after her. When I caught her she handed me a gold chain with half a coin on it, telling me, "When you find the other half of this, you'll find love."

I knew then that I was in Hollywood. No one back in Philadelphia said things like that. I really did feel very bad. I hadn't meant to hurt her. I drove her home and raced back to the club in time to make my opening-night entrance. I kept that half of a coin for a long time, then misplaced it. It didn't matter—by then I'd already been married three times. The last thing I needed was more love.

Debbie sat through my two shows, then we went to a party in my honor. I felt wonderful. I felt like Debbie and I were a good match. I was so happy that night that I danced with both Debbie and Evelyn Keyes, and I never danced. I had turned down Princess Margaret, but I danced with Debbie. At the end of the evening I drove her to the small, unpretentious house she shared with her parents, and gently kissed her good night. After the Copa girls and the French chanteuse and Marlene with her mirrors on the ceiling, there was something sweet and innocent about being with Debbie.

We saw each other almost every night after that. As I had learned from Mike Todd, I started sending her flowers after every date. After our third date I gave her a small pearl-and-diamond bracelet. Then I gave her a diamond necklace, and a LaCoultre wristwatch—one of only three made in this design—with a very small face surrounded by larger diamonds. I gave her a boudoir clock with my photograph in the back; I gave her a miniature white poodle we named Rocky and, as any gentleman in my situation would have done, I gave her a personal soft-drink dispensing machine. As the months passed, the gifts got larger and larger: For Christmas I gave her a fire-engine-red Thunderbird convertible. And flowers, endless flowers. I don't remember how much any of the gifts cost. It didn't matter. I was earning money in piles, and I couldn't spend it as fast as I was earning it.

Debbie and I were like two young kids. In fact, we weren't just like two kids, we *were* two kids. As sophisticated as we looked, at least as I looked (Maxene was still making Debbie's dresses), we were both immature. Our success in show business at such a young age had insulated us from having to grow up. In fact, the image we were selling to our fans was that we were young and innocent. And that was almost true. Neither one of us had ever had a real loving relationship. Debbie had dated Robert Wagner on and off for more than a year, but she still claimed to be a virgin. And the closest I had ever come to a commitment was buying one gold shoe for Joanie Wynne.

We spent most of the six weeks I was in Los Angeles together. It was easy to fall in love. We did all the things that I never had a chance to do as a teenager. We went water skiing at Lake Arrowhead. We went to amusement parks. We went to the best restaurants and most exclusive parties. One day down in the tiny cellar of her house she put on a whole show just for Joey Foreman and me. She plunked her teeth, she tap danced, and she did a great imitation of me with my Coca-Cola bottle, mouthing the words to my hit "Lady of Spain."

I knew I was falling in love with her because I read it every day in the newspapers. Our romance fulfilled the highest standards of journalism: We sold copies. Our romance was the biggest story in Hollywood. The leading gossip columnist, Louella Parsons—I called her "Mom"—anointed us America's Sweethearts. *Time* magazine wrote that we were "the entertainment world's most refreshing romance." One month I think we were on the cover of five national magazines. The newspapers reported every one of our dates. People loved the concept of Debbie and Eddie, and because we were the subject of so much positive publicity MGM encouraged our relationship and Coke supported it. It was like being class couple of America's high school.

After we'd dated for a few weeks the media started speculating about when we were going to get engaged. Engaged? Married? Maybe it was my life, but it was their story. And our marriage would sell a lot of their magazines. Admittedly I enjoyed the publicity; at that point I didn't know any better. And Debbie? Debbie loved it. She craved it. Needed it. Whatever negative feelings I have about Debbie, I've never met anyone who worked harder at her career. And our romance was important to *her* career. She'd made eleven movies by the time we met, but she had never experienced anything like the attention she got for dating me. Photographers camped outside her house waiting for her to come out. Her picture appeared in the newspapers just about every day. The gossip columnists wrote about her. Her telephone never stopped ringing. Our few dates had transformed her from a popular actress into a major celebrity.

She gave the media whatever they wanted. She happily posed for all the pictures and did all the interviews. After we'd been dating only three months she told a columnist that after we were married we would live in Hollywood, co-star in pictures, have six children, keep our marriage private, and never be apart. "We want privacy," she confided to a reporter for the largest newspaper syndicate in the country, "but if the photographers want to shoot pictures of the house when we move in, all right. We'd pose for them outside the home."

I really was falling in love with her. But even more, I think, I was falling in love with the concept of being in love. We were having so much fun together that we were able to overlook the fact that we had absolutely nothing in common. We could hardly have been less suitable for each other. I had grown up on the streets of Philadelphia, and Debbie Reynolds had been born Mary Frances Reynolds on April Fools' Day in El Paso, Texas. A month before she had been born, she told me, carbon monoxide fumes from an old gas heater had almost killed her mother. "That's why I need so much sleep," she explained. "I was gassed before I was born."

I was a Jew; she was raised in the Church of Nazarene, a fundamentalist Christian group. Her grandfather had been a lay preacher and she'd grown up attending tent revival meetings in dusty Texas fields. Everything was forbidden: dancing, singing, movies—a deacon had warned her that she was damned when she signed with Warner Brothers—and certainly sex. Dating a Jew was probably so unthinkable they didn't even list that one. Debbie told me once that she didn't know what a Jew was when she'd moved to California. As it turned out religion was never a problem with us; by the time we met neither one of us was very religious. But we were the products of our religious upbringing and we came from totally different cultures.

Our personalities were as different as our backgrounds. I was naturally shy; Debbie was an extrovert. She was always on, always performing; even when we were alone she was role-playing. I don't think she ever knew the difference. While we were dating she told a fan magazine, "Some of my friends have said, 'But you and Eddie are so different, so opposite.' He knows that I'm not showing off, that I don't even stop to think what I'm doing; I'm just enjoying myself. Some fellows get embarrassed. They're so concerned with what people will think, but that's because they don't join in the fun and Eddie does."

What initially was cute to me eventually became embarrassing. No matter where we were, what we were doing, if somebody got a laugh or sang a song, Debbie would always try to top them. It was compulsive behavior. I was always sort of laid-back. I didn't have to always be the focus of attention, but Debbie needed to be in the spotlight. Not that she wasn't good at it—sometimes. Just after we were married, I remember, we were in Las Vegas during Passover and we went to a show-business seder with all the great comedians. I was the youngest Jew present, so in keeping with tradition I asked the four questions. Jackie Leonard did something. Milton Berle did his thing. Joe E. Lewis told a story. It was quite a group. And finally, with absolutely perfect timing, Debbie stood up and said, "And now I'd like to say a few words on behalf of Jesus Christ . . ."

She put the best comedians in Las Vegas right on the floor with that line. She could do that at times. But she worked so hard at everything, at dancing and singing and acting, that she just didn't know how to stop. So eventually her whole life became one long performance.

The one thing we did have in common was childhood poverty. Her father, a wonderful man named Ray Reynolds, had been a carpenter on the railroad but often had been laid off during the Depression. For a time her family, eleven people including her older brother, grandparents, and relatives, lived in a one-bedroom house. They moved to Burbank, California, not far from the Warner Brothers studios, when she was eight. She grew up intending to be a gym teacher, but when she was sixteen she won the Miss Burbank beauty contest, wearing a bathing suit with a hole in it and doing an imitation of Betty Hutton singing "My Little Horse Ran Away." A talent scout from Warners spotted her in the contest and arranged a screen test. A year later she was performing in musicals. When her option at Warner Brothers expired, MGM signed her. It was Louis B. Mayer who put her in *Singin' in the Rain*, which I saw in a tent in Korea and fell in love with her.

The media was correct: We did make a cute couple. It was all very nice and simple; I loved being with her, she loved being with me, the media loved us being together, and we loved the media attention. Debbie and I spent a lot of time together, although we were rarely alone. We did just about everything together—everything except sex. In the 1950s in America, sex was a four-letter word. Nobody talked about it. Television programs and movies followed "the three-legged rule," which stipulated that if a man and a woman were in a horizontal position at least one foot had to be touching the floor. "Good girls" still didn't have sex until they were married. And Debbie was a very good girl. For a while, at least. And I was willing to put up with it. For a while, at least.

With Debbie, the anticipation turned out to be the most exciting aspect of sex. There was a lot of heavy petting, a lot of panting. I certainly wanted to make love with her. She had a great figure and she was incredibly sexy to me—and she remained that way right up until the first time we had sex. Debbie has always claimed she was a virgin when we married. That I know is not true, because I was there long before our marriage.

I remember sleeping with Debbie in her house one night and we heard her parents talking, and Debbie told me that she was sure her mother and father no longer had sex. I had never actually thought about my parents' sexual relationship, so I was surprised to hear her speak with such certainty. What I didn't realize was when she told me that she was actually telling me our future.

I don't think Debbie ever really enjoyed having sex with me. She was just not a sensual person. I don't remember where we made love for the first time. It might have been the Essex House in New York. Or maybe in the little pool house behind the house in which she lived with her parents, the house she'd built with her royalties from her hit song "Abba Dabba Honeymoon." We'd been dating for a while and we were in love.

I didn't force her into anything, although maybe I pushed a little. And while I suspect she was afraid of doing it, there was a tremendous attraction between us. What I do remember was that the sex was terrible. We were like two robots. There was no tenderness, no shared excitement or joy. Just a great feeling of relief that we'd finally gotten *that* over with. There was certainly no sense that we were communicating on another level. It was completely physical and it didn't feel that great. The fantasy that I'd held on to since the night she had danced into my head in Korea ended that night.

That was not how I remembered sex with Joanie or Joan or Marlene or even Princess Margaret's lady-in-waiting, who couldn't wait. Sex with Debbie was about as exciting as a December afternoon in London. I knew it had to get better because it couldn't get any worse. After that, the only thing that made it exciting was that we had to sneak around. When we went to London, for example, Maxene came with us as our chaperone. Remember chaperones? We'd have to figure out how to get away from her mother, never an easy thing to do, but it made it much more of a challenge. The anticipation, the challenge, was always better than the actual sex. The worst part of the sex was the sex.

The media—and her mother—wanted us to get married. We weren't so sure. We talked about it a lot and eventually it just seemed inevitable, like something we had to do, if just to get everybody to stop talking about it. Our relationship was completely out of our control. America wanted us to get married. The fact that both of us questioned whether or not it would work was buried under the media speculation about when we were going to be married.

There were at least two times when I really was in love with her. Once was when Ed Sullivan was on vacation and I hosted his Sunday night program. Part of the job was introducing the celebrities in the audience. I introduced Debbie, and the audience gave her a big ovation and she stood up and waved to me, and the camera focused on her. I saw her on the monitor and she looked gorgeous. She looked so innocent and happy; she looked like the girl I wanted to be in love with.

The second time I was hosting my show from the Hollywood Bowl in Los Angeles. The night before, I'd been in New York for my friend Rocky Marciano's fight with Ezzard Charles. In the middle of the fight I'd had to leave to catch the red-eye flight to California so I could rehearse my show the next morning. I waited until the last possible moment, but just as I was walking out Rocky got knocked down for the first time in his career. I had to leave with him struggling to get off the canvas. When I got on the plane I didn't know what had happened in the fight. I begged the pilots to find out who'd won. Finally they told me that Rocky had gotten up and knocked out Charles. It was a great flight.

On my show the next night my guests were Louis Armstrong, Peggy Lee, Lily Pons, and André Kostelanetz. In the middle of the show, Rocky Marciano surprised me. These were the great days of live TV, and it was not at all unusual for unscheduled and unexpected guests to suddenly walk out onstage. After the fight Rocky had gone to a plastic surgeon to have his nose patched and then flew to California for this surprise. He'd come directly from the airport to the studio. He was accompanied by his manager, Al Weil. Weil lifted my arm and Rocky's arm and proclaimed, "Two champs!"

Then Rocky told me in front of America, "I had the fight of my life last night and I got a big hit. But you, you got one right to the heart." There's nothing like heavyweight poetry. And again the camera focused on Debbie. I looked at her and I knew why I had fallen in love with her.

I'm sure there were other times when I loved her. I just don't remember them. It's so much easier to remember the times I hated her—there were so many of them.

Just about everybody close to me warned me not to marry her. Milton Blackstone encouraged our relationship because of the publicity it generated, but he never believed I would actually marry her. He hated Debbie; he knew exactly what kind of person she was. I wasn't ready for marriage, he told me, and certainly not to her. The executives at Coke were slightly less diplomatic. They told me bluntly that I was "married" to them and warned that marrying Debbie might jeopardize my contract with them. They were very firm about it. Another one of my closest friends, a song publisher named Marvin Cane, told me at the wedding, "Eddie, this is crazy. The car's outside with the motor running. Let's just get the fuck outta here before you make this mistake."

It seemed like everybody in the world, except the media and Debbie's mother, was against this. At a party one night Humphrey Bogart looked at Debbie and me and blurted out, "You two kids will never make it." Frank Sinatra and I had formed a music publishing company; he took

Debbie out for lunch on the set of a movie they were making and tried to talk her out of it. Eddie Cantor called Debbie the Iron Butterfly and told me I was crazy to even consider marrying her. Mike Todd was against it, affectionately telling me, "You little Jew bastard, you marry her, I'll kill you." I did a command performance for Queen Elizabeth and Prince Philip in Blackpool, the first time in history a command performance had been held outside London, and as I went through the receiving line after the show Prince Philip shook my hand and said softly, "You're not really going to marry that girl, are you?" Even *Star* magazine wrote, "Eddie will make a wonderful husband. . .but not now."

My mother—my mother just wanted me to be happy. "Whatever, Sonny Boy," she said. And Dr. Max Jacobson? Max just wanted to give Debbie one of his shots. He didn't even know what was wrong with her, but he was confident he could cure it.

I don't know why I finally decided to marry her. Certainly I had strong feelings for her, and I know she loved me. Maybe I realized that marrying her was the only way to get out of this situation. So finally, the same week that Joe DiMaggio and Marilyn Monroe announced their separation, Debbie and I announced our engagement.

Milton Blackstone took the news very well. He spent the next three days locked inside a hotel room with his head wrapped in cold towels.

CHAPTER FOUR

Several years ago I took my mother to the wedding of my daughter, Carrie, to Paul Simon in his apartment on Central Park West. Somehow they had forgotten to invite her, but I took her as my escort. It was a lovely affair. It was the first time in years I'd seen Debbie. My mother was sitting in the living room like a beautiful queen, and just about everyone there paid homage to her. Finally, Debbie came over to us. "Mama-la," she said, kissing her. Then she told me, "You go away, we women have to talk."

Believe me, getting away from Debbie has always made me happy. So while they sat whispering to each other I mingled with the other guests. At one point Carrie saw what was going on and suggested, "Why don't you get back with Deb? She's still got great tits." Carrie's always had a wonderful sense of humor. It was quite a day, *Saturday Night Live* with the family. Eventually my mother signaled me to come over. "Sonny Boy," she said, "let's go home."

As we went downstairs in the elevator she was unusually quiet. I could see she was very upset. Finally she said softly, "Sonny Boy, Debbie has cancer."

"What?" I said, and then I almost burst out laughing. "Mom, when I married her thirty years ago she told me the same thing about her mother. Don't worry about it—both of them are fine."

My mother refused to believe me. "But she told me with tears in her eyes. How could it be? She was so sad."

Whatever I said, I knew my mother was going to worry about Debbie. "Listen, Mom. I'm gonna call Debbie's mother," I promised. I found out she was in Colorado and phoned her there.

"Maxene, this is Eddie."

This time she didn't respond "And I'm Lucille Ball." As we hadn't really spoken in decades, I assume she was surprised to hear from me. "Oh," she said, "and to what do I owe this call? You never called me for anything your whole life."

"I just want to see how everybody is," I said. When she told me she was fine I asked about Debbie's father. "And how's Hoss? How's his health?"

Unfortunately, that very good man had Alzheimer's. But his general health was fine.

Maxene must have thought I was crazy. "And Debbie, how's she feeling?"

"Strong as a horse," she said.

I never asked her directly if Debbie had cancer. That answer was obvious. When I told my mother about this conversation, she still had difficulty believing me. "But Sonny Boy, we had this big discussion. She told me."

People do not believe me when I tell this story. They think I must have made it up. I didn't. That's Debbie. I didn't understand her when we were married, and I don't understand her today. I've made a lot of mistakes in my life. I've done so many stupid things: I've been a drug addict, the world's worst father, I wasn't such a great husband. I admit it all, I admit everything. So when I criticize Debbie Reynolds I'm not claiming that I was perfect and she caused all our problems. I know what I did wrong. But not Debbie. Debbie's whole life has been an act. The studios created this wholesome image for her and she's spent her whole life playing that role. She's been very good at it, great at it, but it's an act.

When I left Debbie for Elizabeth Taylor, for example, she should have won an Academy Award for her portrayal of the wronged woman. She insisted to reporters that we were a loving couple until Elizabeth came along and broke up our happy home. She told them, "It seems unbelievable to say you can live happily with a man and not know he doesn't love you." She didn't know I wasn't in love with her? Perhaps the fact that we were living apart, hadn't slept together in months, and had been to a lawyer a year earlier to work out a divorce agreement might have given her a clue that I didn't love her. The only reason we were still together was that she had become pregnant with our son, Todd. In fact, she announced that fact to me right after we'd come back to the house after finalizing our divorce.

Everything Debbie ever did was planned to protect her image. I remember that when my relationship with Elizabeth first became public Debbie met reporters and photographers with her hair in pigtails and a diaper pin stuck in her blouse. A diaper pin. I never saw a diaper pin in her blouse as long as we were together. The truth is that our life together was a sham for the media. I think that if it wasn't for all that publicity, our marriage probably would have lasted a week.

Her whole life revolved around her career. She's managed to sustain a career since the early 1950s. I have great respect for that. I certainly wasn't able to do it. But doing that required incredible dedication. Nothing was allowed to get in her way. When we used to fight, which we did often, she would remind me, "Do you realize you're married to one of MGM's greatest properties?" She was completely driven. Carrie told me once when she was still a little girl, "We're not allowed to call Mommy when she's on the set. Not even in an emergency."

Long before we were married I began to understand that the image I had fallen in love with was not the person I knew. Knowing that, why did I marry her? Why didn't I just walk away? I think there is only one possible answer to the question: I don't have the slightest idea.

I was living in a dream world. No matter what I did, somehow my career kept growing and my life got better and better. The country wanted us to get engaged, I read that in *Life*, and I was a patriotic American. People I didn't know were continually telling me how lucky I was to have a girl like Debbie. Of course, this was still a time when people believed in movie stars.

I don't think I fully appreciated the fact that getting engaged meant that one day I would have to marry her. Appropriately, Eddie and Ida Cantor threw us a lovely engagement party at the Beverly Hills Hotel attended by 400 guests, forty-five photographers, and at least as many reporters. Debbie was beautiful, happily showing off the seven-carat diamond ring I'd given her. It wasn't so much a big party as much as a Hollywood photo opportunity. We spent more time posing for those photographers than enjoying the party. It seemed like each one of the photographers wanted a picture of the happy couple kissing, and we dutifully gave them what they wanted. In contrast, when Elizabeth and I were married and the photographers asked us to kiss for their cameras, she told them, "We're saving that for ourselves." Georgie Jessel offered the most memorable toast at the party: "I only hope that you will be as happy as I might have been on several occasions."

We set our wedding date for the following June. That seemed to be a long time in the future, enough time for me to figure out if I really wanted to marry her or not. Debbie and I made a lot of plans; originally we were going to get married at the Beverly Hills Hotel. Then we decided that wasn't big enough, so we moved it to the Cocoanut Grove. Debbie even paid to have the invitations printed, as her brother complained to reporters, but fortunately never mailed them because we changed plans again. We were going to elope and just get it over with. Then we changed them again: a small wedding followed by a reception at her house. Most people might have figured out that the fact we couldn't agree on where to get married was an indication that we weren't sure we should get married. At least one of us wasn't sure.

I continued doing my TV show in New York and she was making movies in Hollywood, so we spent a lot of time apart. In April we went to England for the royal command performance in which I sang "A Man Chases a Girl"—and from offstage Debbie responded, "Until she catches him." Finally, I could no longer postpone a decision. So I postponed the wedding. At the dedication of a high school in Grosse Point, Michigan, we announced that the wedding had been moved back several weeks. Career demands, we explained. I had to fulfill previously arranged club engagements. Or I had to work on my TV show. Meetings. I figured this could go on as long as I could make up excuses. To save herself some embarrassment, Debbie went to Korea to entertain the soldiers.

Debbie was furious. She blamed Milton Blackstone. "I want a man, not a puppet," She told gossip columnist Sheilah Graham. She told gossip columnist Jack O'Brian that my desire to move my TV show to Hollywood had been blocked by Milton. Her brother claimed that Milton was putting pressure on Debbie to renounce her church and embrace Judaism. It was ridiculous, all of it. Milton didn't have anything to do with it. He was as ambivalent as I was, but he didn't want to be responsible for any decision except where I performed and how much I got paid.

I met with Jack O'Brian in his car. O'Brian was another columnist who hated me because I was Jewish, because I'd taken the $300,000 a year Coca-Cola job away from his friend Morton Downey, and because Milton hadn't given him a big Christmas present. When I insisted that Milton had absolutely nothing to do with my problems with Debbie and told him to leave poor Milton alone, he warned me, "Okay, but from now on it's you and me."

Oh, that was a big threat. What did I care? Jack O'Brian was going to hurt Eddie Fisher? Who did he think he was?

Like a lot of other young couples, as Debbie and I got closer to committing ourselves to spending the rest of our lives together—people actually thought that way in the 1950s—we grew farther and farther apart. Maxene once said, "Debbie is an arguer by nature. Never agrees with anyone." I began to see that side of her more and more. We couldn't agree about anything. We fought all the time. It certainly wasn't all her fault. I know how frustrating my ambivalence must have been for her. I was never sure if she really loved me or just loved being at the center of this tidal wave of publicity, but there was never a moment when she didn't want to marry me. The amazing thing was that at times I still loved her, when I still saw something attractive and enticing about her.

People say that you never forget your wedding day. They're right. Believe me, I've tried. Milton finally decided that my relationship with Debbie had gone too far for us not to get married. In 1955, singers who wanted to maintain their popularity did not leave the girl next door at the altar. What had happened in our relationship was simple: Instead of Debbie becoming more of a real person, I'd been incorporated into the image. The media continued to feature us as the ideal young couple, and rather than objecting I went along with it. We were so cute that we didn't have fights, we had "spats." We were so popular that the day Disneyland opened, Walt Disney invited Debbie and me to ride down Main Street with him. Maybe we should have gotten married that day; we could have done it in Fantasyland. I suppose I could have walked away from the whole thing. There would have been some damage to my career, but I would have recovered. I just didn't have the courage to do that. I had to marry her. It wasn't so much an old-fashioned shotgun wedding as it was a flashbulb wedding. Maybe it was much more of a business decision than an expression of love.

We decided to get married at Grossinger's on Sunday, September 25, 1955. "We" meaning Milton and I. Debbie willingly went along with it. Debbie was so anxious to get married that I suspect she would have gone along with just about anything I suggested. Disneyland; home plate at Yankee Stadium; as long as we were finally getting married she wouldn't have minded anything. Jennie Grossinger was delighted to host my marriage. And Max was thrilled to give us the necessary blood test—although Debbie insisted that his nurse actually draw her blood. I don't really remember, but I can't imagine that Max didn't also give me a good boost while I was in his office. I certainly needed it. The ceremony was to be held in the brand-new home of Jennie's daughter, Elaine Grossinger Etess.

We tried to keep it secret, inviting only our families and closest friends. The wedding came together so fast we didn't have time to make proper preparations. Or change our minds. The first problem came when Debbie's mother borrowed a gown from MGM, but Debbie forget to bring matching shoes with her. All the shoe stores in the nearby town of Liberty were closed on Sunday. Elaine had to convince the owner of a local shoe store to open because "Debbie Reynolds didn't have any shoes to wear at her wedding."

The second problem was my fault. When we'd set the date I'd forgotten it was Yom Kippur, the Day of Atonement, the holiest of the Jewish holidays. It was the day when Jews prayed for forgiveness for all their sins. Many Jews would have considered marrying a *shiksa* on Yom Kippur a sin. How could I ask forgiveness for getting married on Yom Kippur when I was so busy getting married on Yom Kippur? I had to choose between God and Debbie Reynolds. When I explained to Debbie that we had to postpone the wedding one day, until sundown Monday when the holiday ended, she thought I was canceling again. She flipped out. Screaming, crying, she was totally out of control. God probably would have taken the news better that I was marrying Debbie. "You're upset," I said. No I didn't. I just explained the situation to her.

We spent the night before the wedding in separate rooms in the Milton Berle cottage. It was a typical night before the wedding. Everybody was calm: Debbie was in her room fainting and I was in my room with friends, still trying to decide whether to stay or run for my single life.

Once again, Milton Blackstone was the voice of reason. "A lot of people get married without loving each other," he told me. "It's too late to change your mind." Ah, sweet mystery of love.

There were about fifty people at the wedding. Fittingly, my divorced parents watched from opposite sides of the room. Milton served as my best man. Debbie's very close friend, Jeanette Johnson, who had become the gym teacher Debbie once dreamed of being, was her maid of honor. "I'm as nervous as a wet hen," the judge conducting the ceremony told reporters. The judge was nervous? Imagine what was going on in my mind. It was reported that "Fisher's voice nearly broke when he whispered the final, 'I do.'" Sure. I probably should have said "I do?"

Debbie was as beautiful as a bride should be on her wedding day. As I looked at her I really did hope that our marriage might work. Our six-tiered wedding cake was five feet high and three feet wide. Milton, caught up in the excitement of the moment, told reporters, "I've never seen two happier people."

Our marriage was very successful, for at least the first several hours. Unfortunately, by the time the morning newspapers printed photographs of me feeding Debbie a piece of our wedding cake and reported how happy we were together, I was miserable. We spent our first night together in a small farmhouse near the hotel. And when we were finally alone, and I looked at her, there was basically only one thought in my mind: I did?

I got up early Tuesday morning and went for a long walk. Then I began running. I didn't know where I was going. It was like I was in the middle of a nightmare, but it was my life. I panicked. I ran until I just couldn't run anymore. I think I was finally beginning to understand that while I was one of the most popular entertainers in the world, that almost anything I wanted to happen would happen, I had no control over my own life. I went where Milton told me to go, I sang the songs RCA wanted me to sing, I married Debbie Reynolds because. . .To this day I still don't know why.

Just like any other newlywed couple, we spent the first days of our honeymoon at a Coca-Cola bottlers' convention in Atlanta. I broadcast my TV show from there, then Debbie and I appeared before an audience of Coke bottlers and employees. They welcomed us warmly and Debbie, with that big, warm, adorable smile, thanked them graciously. "I don't drink Coke," she told them. "It's bad for your teeth. I drink milk."

Who needs a million dollars a year just for doing a little TV show? The room was absolutely silent. Then, fortunately, people started laughing. For that instant I'd forgotten that none of those people knew the real Debbie. They thought she was kidding. Being cute. That's how good a comedienne she was; people laughed when she was being serious. I laughed loudest.

Back in New York we went to Yankee Stadium to see the Yankees playing the Dodgers in the World Series. When it was announced that we were in the ballpark, we received as loud an ovation as any of the players. Then we took the train to South Bend, Indiana, where I appeared at the launch of a new television station that was carrying my show. And finally we went to Independence, Missouri, to visit former President Truman and his wife, Bess. If either one of them knew that I'd abandoned their daughter at a party and gone home with Honey Warren, they were too polite to mention it. The nicest part about being with Harry and Bess Truman is that they really seemed to be in love with each other.

It was a wonderful week. But at the end of it I was still married.

We never actually had a conversation about trying to make it work. I think we both tried, but we just didn't belong together. After spending the first several months of our marriage living in my apartment in the Essex House, when Debbie had to return to Hollywood to star in *The Catered Affair* with Bette Davis, I went with her. Milton did not want me to go, maybe because he knew that this move was the beginning of the end of our friendship and business relationship. The move made a nice story for the media: the loving husband moving across the country to be with his loving wife. But that was no more true than anything else written about us. The truth was that I had wanted to move to Hollywood for several years. I wanted to be a movie star, but Coke had insisted I do my show from New York. After my marriage, Coke had little choice. The company certainly did not want to be accused of keeping America's most popular lovebirds 3,000 miles apart.

Hollywood seemed the natural place for me to be. I was the most popular male singer in America, I was a big television star, I was married to a movie star, I wanted to make movies. It seemed like everybody in the entertainment industry wanted to be in Hollywood: Sinatra had moved there, Dean Martin, the talent agencies were moving their headquarters out there, CBS was building a new broadcasting facility. Even Van Cliburn, the classical pianist who became famous as the first American to win the Soviet Union's prestigious Tchaikovsky Piano Competition, told me the three things he wanted most in life were a house in California, a career in motion pictures, and the opportunity to meet Elizabeth Taylor.

We rented the house in the Pacific Palisades that had once belonged to Norma Shearer and Irving Thalberg, the "boy wonder" producer. My movie career did not exactly take off as rapidly as I had hoped it would. Many years later I remember going to see *Star Wars* and watching in awe as Carrie created the character of Princess Leia. I like to believe she inherited at least a little of her intelligence and wit from me, and she has a special kind of niceness that I hope came from me, but I can't take any credit for her acting ability. Anyone who has ever seen me act knows that I couldn't have been the source of that aspect of her talent. The only acting I had ever done was co-starring with former child star Margaret O'Brien in a televised version of *Romeo and Juliet*. I actually gave Margaret O'Brien her first TV kiss. About my performance I think it's accurate to say that I was to acting what Laurence Olivier was to pop music.

I would describe myself as an enthusiastic actor. I thought I could learn how to act. I watched many of the great actors and it just didn't look that hard. As I later learned, though, their ability to make it look that way is what made them great actors. But when I saw a singer like

Sinatra become a successful actor I believed, that given the right part and the right direction, I could become at least adequate.

What I lacked in talent I made up for in ambition. I didn't want to do a silly musical; I wanted to do a meaningful motion picture. I should have listened to Perry Como. He made one movie in which he sang "Hubba, Hubba, Hello Jack" in a barbershop. He hated the process. Years later I owned the rights to the Lerner and Loewe musical *Paint Your Wagon* and I wanted Perry Como to star in it. He had absolutely no interest in the part. "Eddie," he told me, "why would I want to sit in a studio waiting to come on and read four lines when I could be out playing golf?"

Anyone who has ever seen me play golf knows I'm a better actor than a golfer. For a while there was a big rumor that I was going to star in the remake of Jolson's *The Jazz Singer*. That was the first full-length movie with sound. It was the story of a poor Jewish boy whose father wanted him to be a cantor but instead he went into show business. I seemed like a natural choice. I had been discovered by Jolson's contemporary, Eddie Cantor, I certainly was Jewish, and I had the big singing voice necessary for the part. But I knew I couldn't handle that role. I was too young to be believable. Instead Danny Thomas got the part and I thought he was brilliant.

I almost got a role in Marlon Brando's *The Young Lions*, a powerful war picture. That was a role I really wanted. But Dean Martin got it instead of me. The screenwriter promised me a part in his next picture, but the day after *The Young Lions* opened, he dropped dead of a heart attack.

The movie I really wanted to do was Budd Schulberg's *What Makes Sammy Run?* I had several meetings with Lew Wasserman, then the president of MCA, the talent agency that represented me. I wanted to play the lead, an aggressive producer named Sammy Glick, maybe the ultimate Jewish hustler. I knew a lot of real Sammy Glicks and I felt confident that was a character I could play. Wasserman decided Sammy Glick was "too Jewish, too negative." He hated the concept and did not want the picture made. I think he decided it was bad for the Jews.

Milton Blackstone was absolutely no help. He knew the Catskills, not Hollywood. He knew nothing at all about the movie business. I didn't need exposure, I didn't want to make a musical, I wanted to do something that would help me create a new image. I wanted to be an actor, not a pop singer just walking through a silly movie. Instead, MCA convinced me to co-star with Debbie in a musical for RKO titled *Bundle of Joy*.

NO *BUNDLE OF JOY* the *New York Times* headlined its review when the film opened. Believe me, they were being kind. The movie was terrible. I was terrible. This was an idea that didn't even seem like a good idea at the time. It was precisely the type of film I didn't want to make. It was simply a means of exploiting all the publicity surrounding our marriage. But everybody convinced me it was a great deal. We should have filmed the deal, not the script. It was an updated remake of a wonderful David Niven and Ginger Rogers film entitled *Bachelor Mother*. It's the story of a single woman who finds a baby and pretends it's hers in order to keep her job at a department store, where she falls in love with the son of the owner of the store. When originally made in 1939 the concept of a single woman pretending to be a mother was so risqué the studio had to fight the censors to keep the title, but our script suffered from an abundance of cuteness. It was so relentlessly sweet it made you sick. In one scene, for example, I was supposedly reading to Debbie from a baby-care book. "Take a spoonful of food, place on a piece of gauze, and rub gently into the navel." After which Debbie took the book and discovered I was misreading it. Instead of "food," I should have said "warm oil"!

Warm oil Get it? That was the big joke. This was a light comedy that wasn't funny.

I owned 65 percent of the film and Howard Hughes owned the remaining 35 percent. At that point I think MGM was paying Debbie $1,250 a week. I paid her $150,000 to make the movie. I tried hard to make the picture even slightly better, but all RKO cared about was getting it made as fast and as cheaply as possible. I was long past being naive, but even I was surprised to see how little the studio cared about quality. I felt they had absolutely no respect for the audience; they were so certain our fans would pay to see Debbie and me being cute together that there was no need to waste money on things like a decent script or nice sets. The money they didn't spend on good sets they also didn't spend on good costumes or good musical arrangements.

Every song sounded the same; I wanted to take out six of the eight songs in the film. "There's too much music in the film," I said. I pleaded with them. Maybe they realized that taking out some of the songs meant putting in more of the brilliantly written dialogue. Fortune cookies were better written. My friend Joey Foreman was promised a supporting role, but the studio hired someone else. I desperately wanted to change the title. I wanted to title it *Always*, after the Irving Berlin song that had become one of my biggest hits. In fact, I called my very close personal friend Irving Berlin from my table at the Ambassador Hotel, where I was having lunch with Marlo Thomas and another starlet. "Irving," I said, playing the role of important producer. "I think I'd like to use the title *Always* for the picture I'm making with Debbie."

"That's wonderful," my very close personal friend Irving Berlin responded, "It'll cost you half a million dollars."

Actually it wouldn't have mattered if Berlin had given us permission to use the title. The head of the studio, Bill Dozier, refused to even consider changing the name of the picture because "we've already spent sixty-five thousand promoting it."

I had looked forward for so long to acting in a movie, and when I finally got the opportunity I hated every minute of it. Every second. Every line. I owned 65 percent of the movie and I was embarrassed to be in it. Here's how bad the entire situation was: The best thing about it was Debbie.

Professionally, I have always admired Debbie Reynolds. It was while we were working together making this movie that I learned what a hard worker she was, what a perfectionist. Debbie worked harder than anyone else on the set. She would rehearse until everyone else was exhausted, and then work some more. I never knew anyone who had so much energy and was not a patient of Max Jacobson. Debbie and I actually lived in a little cottage at the studio while we were making the picture to save time going back and forth. So after shooting all day we would go back to our cottage and rehearse our scenes for the next day. She would work with me on my insipid lines, trying to squeeze some sort of emotion out of me.

Debbie was life's cheerleader. When she committed herself to a project, even a project as obviously terrible as *Bundle of Joy*, she did everything she could to ensure its success. I learned just before we started shooting that Debbie was pregnant with our first child. The child was scheduled to be born two months after we finished shooting, one month before the picture was scheduled to be released. Believe me, the RKO publicity department could not have planned it more perfectly. Instead of a birth announcement, the day after Carrie was born RKO bought a full-page advertisement for theater owners promising that *Bundle of Joy* would be the greatest holiday gift they had ever received. What could possibly be a better way to promote a Debbie and Eddie film about a baby than Debbie and Eddie having a baby of our own to help promote the film? Now, did Debbie plan it that way or was it just a fortunate coincidence? Truthfully, I think it was a coincidence.

But even being pregnant didn't slow down Debbie. When she was seven months pregnant she insisted on doing elaborate dance numbers. The male dancers were tossing her over their shoulders, throwing her around. "Are you crazy?" I shouted at her. "How can you do that?"

Nothing stopped her. Nothing. And I guess she knew what she was doing, because in October 1956, Carrie was born perfectly healthy. Both Carrie and Todd were gorgeous, perfect babies. They looked like a little prince and princess. I was a very big help at both of their births. Both times I fainted. I was so—overwhelmed that the doctor who delivered them had to drive me home from the hospital.

Bundle of Joy premiered in December. The studio made us attend premieres in both Los Angeles and New York. Making this picture was difficult enough, watching it twice was torture. At the Capitol Theater in New York I stood outside, and as my friends walked out and bumped into me they had to invent excuses as to why they were leaving. The excuses were better than the picture. Georgie Jessel had a radio interview; Jackie Robinson had a baseball meeting. My mother stayed for the entire picture. She loved it—she thought I was wonderful. They should have used that in the ads: "Eddie's mother loved it!" Instead, the reviews were uniform: "Eddie Fisher," wrote *Time*, "no actor, has a pleasant voice and Debbie Reynolds has a pleasant face." The *New York Times* called it "sadly deficient entertainment. . .an obvious and witless re-work of a plot that has gray hairs, and its music and dancing are depressingly lacking in class." The movie was a failure in every way. So my motion-picture debut was not the success I had once imagined.

Ironically, this was probably the only period of our marriage during which Debbie and I were happy together. Debbie loved being pregnant. She just blossomed. But she also liked the incredible publicity that came with the birth of our first child. The newspapers and magazines could not get enough photographs. We were on the cover of every fan magazine. First it was me and Debbie, then me and Debbie and Carrie. With the movie and the baby and the publicity and our careers, there was so much going on around us that we didn't have time not to get along with each other.

That period didn't last very long, though. What was the real problem between us? Debbie and I were just very different people. The things that made me happy were not things she seemed to enjoy. I could never really figure out what was going on in her mind, what her aim was, what she expected. She seemed to have some sort of Master Plan about our life, but I never figured out what it was. I've been asked often what I learned from that marriage. That's simple: Don't marry Debbie Reynolds.

We were one of Hollywood's glamour couples, and we led a very exciting life. It seemed like we were always over at Jerry Lewis's house on Amalfi Drive, or Frank's place, or we'd go to the racetrack with Mike Todd and Elizabeth Taylor. We'd have dinner with Jackie and Rachel Robinson, the Sam Goldwyns, Jack Warners; spend time with Ernie Kovacs and Edie Adams, Tony Curtis and Janet Leigh, Bill Holden, Gary Cooper and his wife. We were regulars on the A-list party scene. I'd stand around the piano with people I admired, like Judy Garland and Ethel Merman, and we'd sing all night. Celebrities were constantly dropping by our house. Debbie and I both enjoyed it. But it was rarely quite as wonderful as it seemed to be when I read about it later.

By this time I'd learned to accept the fact that much of what was printed in the newspapers and magazines wasn't true. Not just about Debbie and me, but about every celebrity. A lot of it was the creation of imaginative public-relations people and studio publicists and agents and even columnists and reporters. Having the legendary Bette Davis over for dinner, for example, might sound glamorous, but the reality was that I couldn't wait for her to leave. Debbie and Bette Davis had become friends while making *The Catered Affair* and Bette began hanging around our house. But the Bette Davis I knew wasn't the great actress with whom I'd become enamored watching her movies back in Philadelphia; no, this person was a washed-out, ugly drunk who would sit there making drool eyes at me while talking to Debbie. And while the life that Debbie and I were leading might have seemed thrilling to everyone reading about us, in fact the problems we faced were exactly the same problems most married couples have to deal with: getting along with your spouse's friends, money, in-laws, career demands, and sex.

What made Eddie run? Everything. We would fight about everything, even the way we would fight. Debbie was constantly complaining that I was always in "a mood," that I was always sitting by myself out by the pool. That was true. I just couldn't bear to listen to her complain, so I would walk away. As Debbie's mother told a reporter, "Debbie sometimes makes him very angry and he clams up! The more she raises sand, the quieter he gets."

Debbie didn't like my friends or my lifestyle and, after a while, I don't think she liked me very much. She didn't seem to welcome anybody who came from my side of the hill. She rarely made my oldest friends, Joey and Bernie, Lenny Gaines, feel comfortable in our house. If I was having a good time with my friends she would do anything to break it up. One night, a few weeks after Carrie was born, I had several friends over for a poker game. Dean Martin was there, and Rory Calhoun, George Gobel, and some producers. I liked poker, I liked to gamble, and I could afford it. She was up in her bedroom and she kept calling me over the intercom, "Eddieeeee, Eddieee . . ." I spent the night running up and down the stairs. She didn't feel well, she complained, she had an infection and she insisted on showing me. What do you want me to do, I asked her, you want to go back to the hospital? Back downstairs. Ten minutes later, "Eddieeee! Eddieee!" That whine just cut right through me. "I don't feel well." What can I do for you? This went on all night long. Every ten minutes. Over and over. What was really bothering her was that I was having fun with friends and she wasn't included.

We finally decided to end the game, went into the bar and found a sheepskin wine bladder and started passing it around. As far as I was concerned I wasn't using drugs at that time—I was on Max—and I was never much of a drinker. I was the only one who wasn't already drunk when we went *into* the bar. But I caught up with them. An hour later I walked them outside to say good night. Dean was so drunk he was throwing up and Gobel was leaning on him for support. I thought it was very funny until I went back inside. That's when the room started spinning. I'd never seen the decor move so fast. This was the first time in my life I'd been drunk, and I barely made it to the toilet. I hated the feeling, hated it. I was throwing up wine and it looked like blood and it really scared me. The only positive thing about being that drunk was that I couldn't hear Debbie complaining.

The biggest fights we had were about money. Now the primary difference between us and most couples who fight about money is that we had a lot of it. We were millionaires. We could easily afford anything we wanted to buy. I was earning much more than she was—in addition to my salary from Coke my royalty checks were considerable—but I didn't mind Debbie spending it. What I did mind was the way she spent it. Debbie loved buying antiques, and she knew what she was buying. But we'd go shopping for music boxes, for example, and somehow end up buying expensive staircases that had to be shipped across the country. I wouldn't have even minded that—we could afford antique staircases— but I objected to the fact that she economized on less important things— like clothing and food.

I may be the first husband in history to complain that his wife didn't spend enough money on clothing. Maybe because I was embarrassed by the used clothes I had to wear as a child, clothes have always been important to me. I've spent a fortune on clothes for myself and the women in my life. I love the feeling of being well dressed, and I love to be with someone who dresses well. That wasn't Debbie. She was a movie star and she was still wearing dresses her mother had made for her. I ended up buying her wardrobe for her.

I will never forget the night I told her Lenny Gaines was staying for dinner. She sighed, and told me we only had two steaks. Two steaks? The house was big enough for a herd of cattle to live in style, particularly if they liked antique staircases, and we only had two steaks? I just never understood things like that.

The biggest fight we ever had was about money. After we were married, my accountants wanted us to file a joint income-tax return. That's the most normal thing in the world for a married couple to do. It would have saved us about $300,000 in taxes. But she refused to sign the return. Her business manager had advised her to file an individual tax return, she explained, so that if anything happened to me she wouldn't be responsible for my debts. I was furious. Sometimes Debbie had no connection to the real world. *We* would save $300,000—but *she* didn't want to take the risk. This wasn't an investment in cattle futures, this was a simple exercise in bookkeeping. I cursed at her; I think I called her a "stupid bitch." And in return, she slapped me across the face.

It was a much better scene than anything from *Bundle of Joy*. The fact that she hit me didn't change the way I felt about her in the slightest. By that point I hated her so much I could barely look at her. I used to leave the house praying for a miracle—that by the time I got home she would have disappeared.

Ah, love.

Many years later Debbie was still complaining that her husbands spent all her money. The worst offender was her second husband, Harry Karl. I knew Harry, whose family made a fortune in the shoe business. Not a happy man. Once, I remember, one of the few times I went over to Debbie's house to see Carrie and Todd, I ended up sitting with Harry. He began by telling me that he was a wonderful husband and father, and somehow changed the subject to his former wife, Marie McDonald. She was known as "the body," which was an accurate description. He started telling me about their sex life together. "She was the best," he said, "Why else would I still be giving her thirty thousand dollars a month?"

Maybe he was trying to impress me. But the fact that he was confiding in me was sad. I felt very sorry for him. I didn't tell Harry how well I knew Marie McDonald's body. Marie and I had been together on one of Bob Hope's Christmas tours to military bases and after the tour had stayed together in Paris for a couple of days.

Harry had his problems. In addition to a gambling addiction, he apparently spent a lot of money on women. But I don't quite understand how *he* could have stolen *her* money. Together they spent tens of millions of dollars. They had a new house on the beach, a big house in Beverly Hills, and they drove around in a Rolls-Royce. They went through a lot of money—and I don't think Debbie ever earned enough money to support that kind of lavish lifestyle.

I got off easy. All it cost me was a million dollars and a lifetime of being insulted. It still seems like a good deal.

The normal in-law problems we might have had were aggravated by the fact that Debbie's mother, Maxene, was also managing her career. I didn't like Maxene and Maxene didn't like me. Normally I would say that the only thing I have against the city of El Paso, Texas, is that Maxene Reynolds came from there; but that's too small. It doesn't really begin to express my feelings. The only thing I have against the entire state of Texas is that Maxene Reynolds came from there. She was an incredibly pushy woman; she had something to say about everything. She would have gotten in between our sex organs if she could have. Oh, now there's a horrible thought.

Debbie lived with her parents until we were married, wore the clothes her mother made for her, and did whatever her mother told her to do. Maxene was a shrewd woman. Nothing mattered to her but Debbie's career. I think she understood far more than her daughter how advantageous to Debbie's career our marriage would be, and so she really pushed it. Sometimes I felt that the real heavyweights in my marriage were Maxene and I, and we were battling over Debbie. But I had no chance. Debbie was absolutely loyal to her mother.

I think of myself as a happy pessimist. I tend to look at things from a negative point of view, although I generally manage to find something positive in a situation. But Maxene was perhaps the most negative person I'd ever known. She constantly found fault with everybody and everything, and was always making nasty remarks about people. She made Milton Blackstone seem, to use a favorite expression of my father's, like a regular comedian. To me, Maxene was the human equivalent of chalk scratching on a blackboard. And maybe the nicest thing I could say about Debbie was that she wasn't nearly as awful as her mother.

I always felt sorry for Debbie's father, Ray Reynolds. He was a wonderful man. He just sat in his chair and minded his own business. As much as I despised having Maxene around the house, I loved it when he came over. I'd have to beg him to come; I'd have to invent things that had to be done that he might find interesting. He was a very good chess player and on occasion I would beat him—which means I was a good chess player. I learned enough about chess from him to beat the great chess-playing bandleader Artie Shaw at chess, and nobody beat Artie Shaw in chess—except me. Debbie's father understood his wife and his daughter, and he gave me the best advice about dealing with them that I ever got: He'd wave his hand and tell me, "Just go off by yourself somewhere. Just get away from them."

And then there were the problems Debbie and I had with sex. Actually, that's not true. We didn't have many problems because we didn't have sex. Debbie's sexual appeal on the screen was based on her wholesome image. She was the ultimate good girl. The sexiest thing about her was that she didn't look sexy, which men naturally found to be incredibly sexy. She was the antithesis of sex, the sexually elusive high-school cheerleader every guy on the football team wanted to sleep with, the mountain of innocence. Mount Virgin. The real challenge was getting to the summit. Debbie understood that; she encouraged it, happily played that role. Debbie has always been incredibly smart about her career. I always believed Debbie thought of sex in a dispassionate way, as a commodity to be used to attract an audience, not at all as something physical to be enjoyed. She certainly knew how to use it for that purpose.

When Debbie and I were married, other men were constantly reminding me that I was luckiest guy in the world because every night I got into bed with Debbie Reynolds. Some people still believe that. Those people refuse to accept the fact that the Debbie Reynolds they saw up on the big screen was a fictional character.

Debbie had a perfect figure when we were married. Physically she really was every bit as attractive in real life as she was on the screen. But after our babies were born she lost that figure, and she did nothing—either on the inside or outside—to make herself attractive to me. Compared to Elizabeth, well, there is no comparison. Elizabeth did not have a great figure either. At times during our marriage she gained considerable weight. I saw all that, I saw every imperfection, but when I was with her all I saw was her beauty. Whatever Elizabeth actually looked like, she made me see a queen.

What was missing from my marriage to Debbie was sexual passion. After we were married Debbie just wasn't very interested in sex. She didn't seem to enjoy it very much. Now, I've heard all the rumors about Debbie's sexuality. And before I heard them about Debbie I'd heard the same kind of rumors about myself. I remember Jane Morgan telling me—and this was while we were making love—that all her gay friends thought I was a homosexual. Eventually just about every performer becomes the subject of rumors concerning his or her sex life, drug usage, money problems, and such. Actually, that sounds like the story of my life. In fact, being the subject of rumors is one way of knowing you're successful. And there certainly has been speculation about Debbie's sexual proclivity. Many years ago Debbie told the host of a TV show that I intended

to write that she was anti-Semitic and gay. "In answer to the first accusation," she said, "I was married for seven years to a Jew, Harry Karl,
and that should take care of that. As for being gay, I have never been
gay nor have I ever had a gay relationship."

The truth is that the truth is none of my business. It hasn't been for
a long time. And Debbie, like everyone else, is entitled to her privacy.
But I do get asked about it. People are always curious about the private
lives of stars. I think the best answer is to quote the great radio character
Baron Munchausen, who was known for telling the most unbelievable
stories and when challenged replied, "Vus you dere, Sharlie?" As far as
the rumors about Debbie's private life, I vusn't dere. And even when I
was there, I didn't want to be there.

For a long time our marriage was a charade for the media. My job was
being half of the happy couple. Believe me, I played my role of the loving
husband very well. I posed for all the pictures, I said all the right things,
and I made all the appropriate public appearances with Debbie and our
baby. I felt like a hypocrite. I was leading the same kind of phony life
that I'd found so unappealing when Eddie Cantor was doing it, but by
then I had learned how much of show business was simply show. Some
reporters and columnists knew the truth, but nobody cared. Happiness
sold magazines. So if being the happy couple sold magazines and movies
and records, Debbie and I would be the happy couple. There was an
unspoken agreement in show business between the celebrities and the
media that as long as the celebrities played by the media's rules, the
media would perpetuate the myth.

The only magazine that did not play by those rules was a monthly
called *Confidential*. It was the 1950s version of the supermarket tabloids.
When Debbie was pregnant with Carrie, *Confidential* ran a cover story
titled "Eddie Fisher and the Three Chippies." According to this story I
had been at a party in a Detroit hotel room with baseball players from
the Detroit Tigers and had had sex with three "luscious lassies. . .a
blond, a brunette and a redhead." Supposedly I was such an incredible
lover that one of the satiated girls sighed, "Boy, I'd support this guy
forever if he'd let me."

Now there's a dilemma: What was I going to do, sue *Confidential* and
be forced to prove I wasn't a great lover? I was in that hotel room with
members of the Detroit Tigers and the three women, but I did not have

sex with any of the women. I stayed faithful to Debbie for a long time, till after Carrie was born. I had many opportunities, but as long as I felt our marriage had a chance of surviving, I didn't want to cheat on her. It was only after it became obvious Debbie and I couldn't stay married that I began a series of affairs.

There was no single event that marked the real end of our marriage. I didn't stomp out angrily one day and never come back. There just came a time when I could barely stand to be alone with her. We were wrong for each other. I knew I had to get away from her.

In early 1957 I was the headliner at the opening of the new Tropicana Hotel in Las Vegas. In less than a decade Las Vegas had grown from a small oasis in the desert into a mecca of neon lights, gambling, and beautiful girls. It had become *the* destination for high rollers from everywhere in the world, an American Monte Carlo. Organized crime built it, with the help of entertainers like Sinatra, and owned it. And the Tropicana was the newest and glitziest hotel. Mike Todd had once warned me against playing Vegas, but that was one of the few times I didn't listen to him. Vegas was the center of the action, and it was where I wanted to be.

The Tropicana hired the prettiest girls in Vegas and paid them double what the other girls on the Strip, as the row of hotels and casinos was known, were making. And they were gorgeous, just absolutely gorgeous. Let me put it this way, one of the less attractive Tropicana girls had just been Miss Australia. The Tropicana chorus line made the Copa girls seem like the minor leagues. Their choreography consisted basically of wearing as little as possible, and they did it very well. While I performed they would dance in a circle around me wearing a pearl in their navels. The most difficult part of my act was watching what was whirling around me and remembering my act.

Debbie came to Las Vegas with Carrie for my opening. At one show, I remember, I put Carrie, who was six months old, on my lap and sang to her. During another performance Debbie surprised me by putting on one of the huge headdresses the chorus girls wore and joining the chorus line. There were eight tall, gorgeous girls and Debbie, just a little over five feet. Debbie was the one wearing the gold lamé top. Maybe it was funny, and the audience certainly appreciated it, but I was beyond finding anything she did amusing. To me, this was just another example of

Debbie's desperate need to be the focus of attention. I didn't like it when Debbie did it, and I didn't like it several years later when Elizabeth put on a waitress's outfit and created a furor during my act by dropping a tray of dishes. Call it ego or pride, professionalism, or maybe it was my own need to be the focus of attention, but I was furious with Debbie for doing it.

After Debbie returned to California I fell in love with an eighteen-year-old Tropicana girl named Pat Shean. Like so many of the women in my life, she was the most beautiful girl I had ever seen. At least for the several months we were together. It began very innocently. At the end of my show I would tease some of the girls onstage; it was part of my act. But then one night as I sang "Oh! My Papa" I turned and saw her standing in the wings, watching me. I smiled at her and she smiled back. Well, I knew what that smile meant. From that moment she would stand there during every performance, night after night, show after show, and eventually we got together.

I didn't know when our affair began that she belonged to Bing Crosby. Many of the Tropicana girls were "on scholarship," as we called it. Another one of them was dating Jackie Gleason. I knew that she belonged to Gleason because she told me her fantasy was to call him from my dressing room while giving me oral sex. I turned her down. I don't remember why. Maybe I just didn't want to cheat on the girl with whom I was cheating on my wife.

My love affair with Pat Shean had absolutely nothing to do with Bing, although the fact that she was with Bing and wanted to be with me probably made her even more appealing. I mean, this was the great Bing Crosby, a man I'd grown up practically idolizing, and his girlfriend preferred to be with me. Bing Crosby was one of the legendary womanizers in Hollywood. I suspect he knew about it, I know he really disliked me, but I didn't care. Bing Crosby was another person who was nothing at all like his wonderful public image. He certainly could sing, he had a great sound, but he was a cruel bastard. I remember flying from Casablanca to Paris with his son, Gary Crosby. Gary got very drunk and started telling me some of the things his father had done to him and his brothers. "That cocksucker," he said, "I could slit his throat. . .slit his jugular vein and suck his blood out." That's the way his son felt about him. I think that says everything. So I didn't mind at all having a grand affair with his girlfriend.

I was very lucky Debbie never found out about Pat Shean. Pat lived in a motor home not far from the hotel. We usually spent the night there, making love and searching for the pearl that kept falling out of her navel. She was the shyest girl with whom I'd ever made love, if it's possible to be a shy nude showgirl. One night I left her trailer about five o'clock in the morning to go back to the Tropicana. I was driving a black Cadillac convertible I had given to Milton Blackstone as a present. I hadn't gone more than a few yards when a car slammed into the Cadillac from behind, sending me careening across the road into another car. The Cadillac flipped over. I just sat there, stunned. The Cadillac was totaled. It looked like the whole car had collapsed, except around the driver's seat. The woman who had hit me from behind had crashed into a tree and broken her nose and several teeth, the man with whom I'd collided was bleeding from a deep cut on his head. And me? Not a scratch. The accident was so bad that the police took me inside the Tropicana and made me drink two brandies to calm down. That was the first time I'd ever heard of the police making the driver of a car that had been in an accident have a drink. That was Vegas.

I was so lucky, lucky to be alive and lucky that Pat Shean had not been with me, because I don't think anyone sitting in the passenger seat could have survived that crash. Once I realized she was safe, I realized how close I had come to disaster. If she had been in the car, even if she hadn't been badly hurt, that would have been the end of my marriage and probably the end of my career. Thirty years later a movie star could survive getting caught having oral sex with a prostitute in a car, or picking up a transsexual, but not in 1957. A sex scandal would have been the end of it for me, particularly for me. Cheating on Debbie Reynolds? Cheating on America's Sweetheart? If I had been caught my father couldn't have even gotten me back my old job in the pants factory.

I called Debbie immediately. I didn't want her hearing about the accident on the news. I told her I was returning to the Tropicana after watching another performer when I'd been in an accident and the police made me have several drinks. Las Vegas is one of the few places in the world where that story is completely credible.

When I finished my eight-week run in Las Vegas I rented an apartment for Pat Shean in Hollywood. She expected me to leave Debbie and marry her. I was always a very honest cheater. "We're not getting married," I told her. "I can't even get out of this one."

When she gave me the ultimatum—Marry me or the affair is over—there was nothing I could do about it. Eventually she married Bing's son Dennis, which certainly brought her relationship with Bing full circle. And Bing? He was so upset about my affair with his girlfriend that several months later, when Jerry Lewis was appearing on my show, he stunned Jerry and me by walking onstage totally unannounced with Jerry's former partner, Dean Martin. It was the first time Martin and Lewis had been together in public since they had broken up their act. Crosby never said a word to me about Pat Shean. Hey, that's show business.

That wasn't the only affair I had when married to Debbie, but it was the one that mattered. Once I started cheating on Debbie, I didn't stop. I even had an affair with one of Debbie's closest friends. She was a beautiful woman whom I had always believed to be gay. One afternoon when Debbie was out of town she came over to the house and proved that I was wrong. All afternoon and all night she proved I was wrong.

I don't think Debbie had any affairs while we were married, although once she tried to make me jealous by telling me that Sinatra had asked her to go away with him for a weekend. Sure he did. I knew Debbie too well to ever believe that. Debbie Reynolds was not Frank Sinatra's type.

We were together in magazine covers only. Just as my mother had felt towards my father, the only thing I ever wanted from Debbie was a divorce, and for a long time she refused to give it to me. We both knew it was inevitable. At least I knew we both knew it was inevitable, but Debbie persisted in believing we could save our marriage. I suggested she see a psychiatrist, hoping he might be able to make her understand that our marriage was done. She insisted we go together. I didn't want to go—I didn't need a psychiatrist, I needed a divorce—but finally we went to see him together.

He buried her. After hearing from both of us he asked to see me alone. While Debbie waited outside, he asked me, "What is this fixation she has with money and property?" Boom, he hit it right on the head. When she came back into the room he confronted her with that. I think she was really hurt. She started crying. I know I'm not perfect at life, I've been very good at not being good, but I've always admitted it. I see the reality of my life. But Debbie never believed there was anything wrong with her. Everything that was wrong between us was my fault. Confronted with the opinion of this psychiatrist, she broke down. And she refused to see him again.

I don't know exactly what finally caused Debbie to agree to a divorce, but over time she changed, and we began discussing the dissolution of our marriage. Maybe she had gained the security she needed from the success of her career. As my career had leveled off to simple stardom— no one could sustain the success I had enjoyed—hers was in its ascendancy. In 1956 Coca-Cola had canceled all national advertising— including my television show—after a bitter dispute with its bottlers over the introduction of a "family-sized" bottle. Although Chesterfield cigarettes hired me to host the hour-long *Chesterfield Supper Club*, the Coca-Cola Kid was done forever. The innocent kid with the big smile and a bottle of Coke had been replaced by a sophisticated man with his ever-present cigarette. I had to learn how to fake smoking cigarettes to do the five commercials. My records were still selling, but my teenage audience had grown up and young singers like Elvis Presley had taken my place. My nightclub appearances and occasional concerts were still extremely successful, but my meteoric rise had evolved into a comfortable stardom.

Debbie's hard work had paid off with movie stardom—and a huge hit record, *Tammy*. Debbie always believed I was jealous of her success in the music business, but that has never been true. I was never in competition with her, and I knew her success would make the divorce easier. Although we knew our fans would be surprised and probably disappointed when we announced our separation, both our careers were so well established that it would have little long-term affect. The question became working out the financial details of the divorce and the timing of the announcement.

Mike Todd and Elizabeth Taylor had rented a $20,000 a month villa at Cap Ferret, in the south of France, to celebrate the opening of *Around the World in 80 Days* in Europe, and invited me to meet them there. I loved spending time with them, just loved it. Their relationship was always fun and games and laughs and fighting and making up. When I was with them I knew what was missing in my marriage. Everything. So I arranged to play the Palladium in London, then meet them in France. Against my wishes, Debbie insisted on joining us. Mike Todd and Debbie

Reynolds were about as opposite as it is possible to be; Mike was a wildman, capable of saying anything to anyone, capable of doing the most outrageous things. He just didn't care what other people thought of him. Debbie was prim and proper. Mike and Elizabeth—and admittedly me too—used to poke fun at her righteous attitudes. Debbie's presence just seemed to put a damper on fun. She knew how we all felt about her, so probably for moral protection, Debbie arranged to meet her friend Jeanette Johnson in Spain.

The villa was magnificent. It was like a movie set. It overlooked the Mediterranean, had a beautiful pool, and was a short drive from the casinos of Monte Carlo. People like David Niven, William Holden, and Gary Cooper would come over in the afternoon for a swim. As much as I love women, I loved being with men like that. I was thrilled; I was like a little boy who got to play with his heroes.

Late one night Mike decided that he and I should drive to Monte Carlo to gamble. Elizabeth was pregnant and didn't want to be left alone. Mike told her solemnly, "We're just gonna go down there for forty minutes. We'll be back in an hour." There was no chance of that. It took forty minutes just to get these. Mike couldn't kill five minutes in an hour.

Elizabeth was furious. "You go," she warned, "and if you're not back in an hour the bedroom door'll be locked."

"We'll be right back, baby," he practically swore. "Please don't lock the door." Debbie had nothing to say about it. Several hours later, as we drove back to the villa, he explained to me that Elizabeth often made threats like that but never really meant them. And as he knocked on the bedroom door pleading with her to let him in, he repeated that she never really meant those things. Believe me, wherever Mike is right now, he's still pounding on that door to get in. And probably still insisting to anyone listening to him that she really doesn't mean it.

It was August and it was hot and sensuous and there were all these beautiful women around and everybody looked great and felt wonderful and one night I had a couple of drinks and I just couldn't help myself, I made love to my wife. Imagine that. Our relationship was so bad I have to justify having sex with my wife. But it was one of the most wonderful nights of our entire marriage. It was the night our son Todd was conceived.

After several weeks in Cap Ferret, Debbie met Jeanette in Spain and

I went to Israel with my piano player. This was 1956, and modern Israel was still being carved out of the desert. They treated me like King David. I was King Eddie. They took me all over the country, showed me all the historic sites. I performed at the Sea of Galilee, the same place Leonard Bernstein gave his historic concerts, for 600 recently arrived Hungarian Jews. They were being protected by one Irish soldier with an old M-1 rifle. These immigrants were surrounded by Arab states dedicated to the destruction of Israel, and their entire army was one soldier. But their spirit was so incredible that they probably believed the Arabs were out-gunned. We had no piano, so my piano player played the accordion. It was a memorable evening.

I performed at several nightclubs in Tel Aviv. One night a beautiful young actress named Dalia Lavi unsuccessfully tried to sneak in to see me perform. I found out about that several years later when we met in Hollywood. At that time I invited her to come with me to Temple Israel to hear me sing the Kol Nidre. Now there's another one of the greatest pickup lines of all time: "Come hear me sing the Kol Nidre."

The Jewish girls I met in Israel were nothing at all like the Jewish girls I knew in America. Besides the fact that they carried guns. There was something incredibly appealing about their confidence, which bordered on arrogance. Maybe because these women lived under the threat of death, they just weren't afraid to express their passion. I had a brief affair with a young soldier. I remember she had the most beautiful soft olive skin. She was a close friend of Moshe Dayan's daughter, who was also a soldier. Whoever thought I would fall for a girl in uniform? The other woman with whom I had an affair in Israel was a private secretary to Israeli founder David Ben-Gurion. That relationship lasted a little longer and was more meaningful. She was older than me and once had been very close to Danny Kaye. She was a terrific person, and Ben-Gurion, one of the founding fathers of Israel, depended on her.

If I could have told my mother about these women she would have been very proud of me. Not only was I finally dating nice Jewish girls, I was dating a personal assistant to one of the legendary Jewish figures in history. But I couldn't tell my mother; while Debbie and I had agreed to divorce, we were still married in the eyes of the media. I didn't feel I was cheating on her, though. As far as I was concerned, we were divorced. All that was missing were the details.

By the time I got back to Hollywood, Debbie had moved my belongings into the guest room. I know she still hoped for a reconciliation, but I was excited about going forward with my life. We went to see my attorney, Mickey Rudin, to work out the details. We agreed on just about everything, from child support for Carrie to the division of our property. Debbie got the antique staircase we had bought in Mobile, Alabama, just after we married; I got my freedom. She got the house; I got my freedom. Whatever she wanted, it didn't matter to me; I got my freedom. We even drafted a statement for the media. It was all set, done.

The moment we got home I started packing. I was going to move into a hotel. Debbie followed me into the room and after a long, uncomfortable silence, announced, "I'm with child."

I stopped packing. I turned and looked at her, shaking my head in disbelief. "What did you say?" I stammered.

With an anxious half-smile on her face, she told me, "I'm pregnant."

CHAPTER FIVE

Nothing in my life could have prepared me for my love affair with Elizabeth Taylor. Never, never did I dream that I would be at the center of one of the greatest scandals of the century. And certainly not at the center of two of them. But none of it would have happened if Mike Todd had lived. If Mike had lived, everything would have been so different.

Mike Todd. Dames and low comedians, he used to say, that was his business. But that was just Mike Todd creating an image for himself. I loved Mike Todd. He was my idol, the one man I admired more than anyone I'd ever known. The person I most wanted to be like. Mike made every day an adventure and squeezed as much living out of life as anyone I've ever known. He had the guts to be the person most of us, myself included, only fantasize about being. I never saw him take a step back. He was a rogue and a gambler and a dreamer, a promoter and a perfectionist; he was a man of great taste and outrageous demeanor, the ultimate showman. The con man with a heart of gold. Okay, so maybe it started out being somebody else's gold heart, and even if nobody quite knew how it got there, it ended up in Mike. There never has been anyone quite like him. I think I enjoyed his life more than my own.

His greatest creation was Mike Todd. The name on his birth certificate—and his tombstone—was Avrom Hirsh Goldbogen, the son of an Orthodox rabbi. I never knew where the name Mike Todd came from, but I guess he felt you couldn't put the name Avrom Hirsh Goldbogen up in lights. "Avron Hirsh Goldbogen presents Elizabeth Taylor" doesn't sound just right. But "Mike Todd presents . . ." was okay. He was at least fifty-three years old when he died in a plane crash; the media wrote that he was only forty-eight because he'd changed his birth certificate. He didn't want to be fifty-three so he made himself forty-eight. That was pure Avrom Hirsh Goldbogen.

I met him in Palm Beach, Florida, in 1951, while I was on tour for the army. Milton Blackstone told me Mike was staying by himself at the home of *New York Journal-American* publisher Walter Young and might be looking for some company. Milton thought Mike Todd could teach me about show business. I called him there and, in his own shy way, he told me, "Hey, you little Jew bastard, get your ass over here."

I actually knew quite a bit about Mike Todd before I met him. In 1948, when I was just starting out, I'd been on the same bill with his third wife, Joan Blondell, at the RKO Keith in Boston. A lot of people believe she was the real love of his life. I could understand that. As Mike would say, she was a great dame. She was doing a semi-strip. She never actually took off anything revealing, but like Mike she was great at creating the illusion. I helped her, pulled a thread, caught a skirt. Almost every night we'd sit in her dressing room and she would sip champagne and tell me about her lovers. Dick Powell, her former husband, was still calling her all the time, and Mike was always around. At that time nobody knew who Mike Todd was. His headlines were still in the future; she was the star in their marriage. But she would tell me how supremely confident he was, how absolutely nothing seemed to slow him down. She made him sound like some sort of larger-than-life character.

And within minutes of finally meeting him it was obvious she hadn't been exaggerating. As soon as I got to Walter Young's house Mike told me we were going to the beach. When we got there he pushed some sand together to make a stage and started his ballyhoo, "Step right up, ladies and gentlemen. Eddie Fisher is going to sing his biggest hits for you. Step right over here . . ." laughing the whole time. Hawking his product. I think that was probably a pretty good metaphor for Mike Todd: building a stage out of sand.

From the day we met until the day he died he was my best friend. I was the star, but he ran our show. I was his gopher. I was his straight man. He used me every way he could, but I loved being used by him. "Make way for Eddie Fisher." It was so much fun. When I met him he wasn't really doing very much of anything but selling his dreams. He was going to make a movie of Arturo Toscanini's life. He was going to bring the La Scala Opera Company to the United States. He was going to revolutionize the movie business with some kind of new screening system, Cinerama, and a pure Mike Todd gimmick that allowed the audience to smell the things they saw on the screen called Smell-O-Vision. He was going to make a movie of *War and Peace*. Every day there were new ideas.

Mike was big with the girls. Women loved him, and he loved them right back. He was always surrounded by women. Give him five minutes alone with a woman and she would do anything for him. A lot of the financing for his projects came from women he charmed into sharing his dreams. Whatever he was selling that particular day, they were buying. I heard him make his pitch for *80 Days* maybe a hundred times: "There's never been anything like it in the history of the movies, the greatest wonders of the world like no one has ever seen them," and each time he made it sound as fresh and exciting as if he were devising it at that moment. I think he was with all his leading ladies, including Gypsy Rose Lee, and a lot of them hated him for leaving them. By the time we became friends he and Joan Blondell had divorced and he was living with the actress Evelyn Keyes, who had been one of Scarlett O'Hara's sisters in *Gone With the Wind* and had starred in *The Jolson Story*. The fact that he was living with somebody barely slowed down his social life. "Eddie," he'd say with a big smile and a cigar hanging out of his mouth, "c'mon, let's go out and get us some broads." Once I caught him with three women in his house; one in his bed, one in the shower, the third in the swimming pool, while he was running between them, laughing, trying to keep them apart. I remember going to a party at his house for Edward R. Murrow and discovering that Marlene Dietrich was the host. This was long after my affair with her, and she was very sweet to me. "Mike," I said, "what are you doing with Marlene?"

He shrugged. "Nothing, kid, she's just hosting this thing for me."

I went into his bedroom and found her clothes hanging in his closet. I knew I had him. "What are you holding out on me?" I asked him. "You're with her, aren't you?"

"Me?" He was laughing, always laughing. "Nah, she's just hosting a party."

Mike convinced people he was so tough that he never had to show how tough he really was. He was tough in his mind, he acted tough and he spoke tough, and that was enough to make people think he was a tough guy. That was a big part of his act. It was that self-confidence, that bravado, that attracted the ladies, and the ladies attracted the investors. Inside he was a softy. We were flying from Los Angeles to New York one night on a TWA flight that had sleeping berths. We could only get one berth and he insisted that I use it. "I'm gonna be up all night playing gin," he explained. But later that night he climbed into the berth and slept opposite me. All night long, though, when he thought I was asleep, he kept covering me up, making sure I was covered by the blanket.

The more I got to know him, the more I wanted to be just like him. When we became friends I knew almost nothing about the way the world really works, and then there was Mike Todd, in the back room oiling the springs. I tried to copy him from the tips of his shoes to the way he combed his hair. Mike ordered custom-made socks by the gross from Sulka—doesn't everybody order 144 pairs of socks at the same time?— so I had my socks custom-made. Clothes were important to him because they were an essential part of his image. You look rich, you feel rich, you act rich, people believe you're rich, they're willing to trust you with their money. Broadway producer George White wore a brand-new shirt every day at a time when custom-made shirts cost fifty dollars each. He never wore the same shirt twice. Everybody knew he was rich so they wanted to invest in his shows. In fact he was wearing Arrow shirts at a dollar apiece—but, as Mike pointed out, he only wore each shirt once.

I learned the real value of money from him. He loved to tell people, "I've been broke but I've never been poor." To him that meant that a lack of funds was a temporary condition that shouldn't be allowed to interfere with his usual lavish spending. He was a big gambler, he lost Del Mar racetrack in a card game. He lost $250,000 to Darryl Zanuck on one hand and they never spoke a word again. I don't know where he got the $5 million he needed to make *Around the World in 80 Days*. I don't think anybody did. That's about $100 million today, and he raised it a little bit here, took from this pocket, sold a piece of this business, *hondled* a little with the studio, borrowed, begged, convinced actors to work for promises, but somehow got it made. One day he called me at the studio where I was rehearsing my Chesterfield show and said, "I need half a million to finish the picture. Call Manny Sacks and see if he's interested."

Manny Sacks was then David Sarnoff's top lieutenant at RCA. "Eddie, that's a lot of money," Manny said responsibly. "I have to have a board meeting to get that kind of money."

When I reported that to Mike he told me, "I can finish it for a quarter million. Call him back and tell him all I need is two hundred and fifty thousand."

I loved being in the middle of one of Mike's schemes. As far as he was concerned, being asked to loan him money was a compliment. It meant that he trusted you enough to give you this opportunity. But Manny had the same answer: He had to call a meeting. Eventually Mike got the money he needed from Bill Paley, who owned CBS. Who knows how many millions that investment eventually returned for Paley?

He spent money on that picture as if it was his own. The picture was never intended to go into general release in two thousand theaters. *Around the World in 80 Days* wasn't just a motion picture, it was a "spectacular." Mike treated it like a show; it played in only one theater in each city, tickets were sold on a reserved-seat basis, it even had an intermission. Rather than giving theater owners a piece of his business, he "four-walled" it, meaning he rented the theater and owned the box-office receipts. In fact, he owned everything in the theater except the popcorn—and the popcorn eventually became the subject of a lawsuit between Mike and Harold Mirisch. The night before it opened in New York he was so deeply in debt he couldn't make the rent, and I had to give him a certified check for $25,000 so he could open the doors in the morning. But the word had gotten around that he was in financial trouble.

I was in a hotel room with Mike and Elizabeth Taylor and Mike Todd Jr. when Otis Chandler of the Los Angeles Times Corporation called and offered to buy 75 percent of the picture for $25 million or 50 percent of the picture for $15 million. Either deal was enough to get Mike out of debt and guarantee a profit. If the picture was a big success he'd make less money, but in exchange he'd have the security of knowing before it opened that he was going to make money. Holding his hand over the phone, he asked, "What do you think?" Any sane person would have leaped at the offer, but this was Mike Todd.

"Take it," I said.

"Yeah, take it," his son agreed.

Elizabeth was against it. "Okay," Mike decided, looking at me, "majority rules. You guys lose." He turned down the offer. Money was freedom for Mike. It allowed him to make his own decisions, and there wasn't enough money in the world for him to sell that right.

Around the World in 80 Days turned out to be his greatest professional achievement. It's hard to even write down the title without humming the title song. "Around the world, I searched for you/I traveled on, when hope was gone/da da dada, da da dada, da da daaaa da da." Mike was an old-fashioned producer; he made every decision from changes in the script to the sound level in the Rivoli Theater on opening night. And I lived every minute of it with him.

It really is a spectacular picture. It's got everything: fifty major stars, 60,000 extras, 75,000 costumes, elephants, hot-air balloons, David Niven, Shirley MacLaine, and it was shot in thirteen countries in a process Mike created and co-owned called Todd-AO. He created the word *cameo*, meaning a brief appearance, and convinced stars like Sinatra, Dietrich, Ava Gardner, Buster Keaton, Charles Boyer, Noel Coward, Ronald Coleman, and even Edward R. Murrow to work for much less than their usual fees. Nobody but Mike Todd could convince Edward R. Murrow to be in his picture. Sinatra got a new Thunderbird for maybe one day's work, but just having him in the picture was worth millions of dollars in publicity. By the time Mike was done just about every star in Hollywood wanted to do a cameo.

Marilyn Monroe wanted to appear in the movie so badly that she auditioned privately for him—but he turned her down. I was there, in a triplex apartment at 715 Park Avenue. They went into a room, where she read lines for him. The whole audition took five minutes. He knew the value of putting her in the picture, but he just wouldn't compromise his vision. At least he didn't make her sing the same lyric all afternoon, as he had once done to me. But when he threw a nationally televised first-anniversary party for the film in Madison Square Garden, Marilyn was one of his celebrity guests.

Part of Mike Todd's genius as a producer was that he knew what he didn't know. And his ego never stopped him from asking people he respected for advice. The director of the film was Michael Anderson, but Mike was looking over Anderson's shoulder every shot. He spent close to a million dollars filming the crossing-the-Atlantic scene and he wasn't satisfied with it. So he invited some of his friends, the greatest directors in Hollywood, Billy Wilder, William Wyler, John Huston, George Stevens, and Fred Zinnemann, to look at the footage. These were directorial cameos. And he'd listen to their advice. They told him the scene looked phony, that he had to redo it. It was a million-dollar problem. It probably wouldn't have made any difference in the success of the movie, but Mike insisted that he had to reshoot it. He borrowed another half million to do it.

He also knew when *not* to listen. For example, after watching Mike make it look so easy I became convinced I could be a producer too. I had my own cigar. One day, after watching Shirley MacLaine singing in the dailies, I waved my cigar in the air and told him as if I knew what I was talking about, "Mike, you gotta get rid of her. That squeaky voice of hers is killing the picture."

"Eddie, I can't get rid of her," he explained. "She's everywhere in the film."

"But you've got to do something. She's got the worst voice I've ever heard. She doesn't sing, she screeches."

"Maybe you're right," he decided. "Maybe I will have her voice dubbed."

I'm still waiting.

He did let me record the title song, though. As soon as I heard it I told him I wanted exclusive rights to record it. "I can't do that, Eddie," he said. "Crosby's doing it, Sinatra, Nat Cole wants to do it . . ." Ten great singers had already committed to record it.

"Mike, I'm first," I insisted.

So one night Mike made the entire eighty-two-piece orchestra sit there holding their instruments for two hours until I'd done my *facockata* Chesterfield show and rushed over to the studio to cut the record. Mine was the first version of the song to be released. Mike also wanted me to do a cameo in the film, but my *Bundle of Joy* contract with Howard Hughes stipulated that I make my first appearance onscreen in that picture, so I couldn't do it. But when Hughes also prohibited Mike from using my version of the song on the soundtrack, I was irate. I knew how good that song was—it eventually won an Academy Award—and to give it up to appear in this bundle of crap just made me furious. There was nothing I could about it. Eventually Mike and I sort of got around that contract by using my version of the song as walk-in walk-out music, the music theaters played before and after the film as the audience entered and left, and I sang it on television as often as possible.

Even though this was Mike's first picture—as it turned out, his only picture—and he had sold or mortgaged just about everything he owned to get it done, he was remarkably calm the night it opened in New York City in October 1956. I sat with him in the very back of the Rivoli Theater and we personally operated the sound system, raising and lowering the volume as if controlling the sound on a television set. It was an invitation-only black-tie premiere, so he knew many of the people in the audience. In the middle of the picture he noticed that a woman across the aisle had fallen asleep. Falling asleep at the premiere of his movie! I thought Mike was going to put a fist through her. He growled at her until she opened her eyes, and when she saw Mike glaring at her she immediately sat up straight and almost went into shock. For the rest of the evening she sat rigid, continually glancing at him as if worried what he might do if she closed her eyes again.

When the film ended Mike just about stood in the aisle with his arms crossed defiantly, daring people to leave before the final credits ran. When he saw Walter Winchell, whom I knew very well, trying to walk out, he made me run over to stop him from leaving. The reviews were incredible, better than even Mike would have written. Well, maybe better than anyone except Mike would have written. *Around the World in 80 Days* was a huge international hit, eventually winning the Academy Award as Best Picture of 1956. Just as much as the peep shows he once put on at the World's Fair, in every possible way it was a Mike Todd production.

His courtship of Elizabeth Taylor was no less a spectacular production. I don't think any two people fit together so perfectly as Mike and Elizabeth Taylor, although for a time I believed Elizabeth and I did. When they met in 1956, she was already the most famous movie actress—and considered by many people to be one of the most beautiful women—in the world. In other words, perfect for him. The ultimate trophy.

I had met her briefly several years earlier at a party hosted by Merv Griffin and Roddy McDowall in the apartment they shared in the Dakota. She spent most of the evening sitting in a corner with her close friend Montgomery Clift. I know we were introduced, although the only thing I remember about that night was being awestruck by her extraordinary beauty. I mean, by that point I had been around a lot of beautiful women, but I'd never met anyone like her. I fell in love with her that night. I can still close my eyes and see her sitting in that corner.

She was recently divorced from her first husband, Nicky Hilton, but I was much too shy to pursue her. She was out of my range, I thought, out of my league. I saw her one other time, maybe a year later. I was visiting the MGM lot and she walked past me without acknowledging me. She was upset about something—she was in some kind of snit—but she was just as beautiful as I remembered her. There are major events in my life about which I have absolutely no memory, and then there are moments of absolutely no significance that never disappear. Elizabeth Taylor in the great beauty of her youth, sitting in a corner, throwing back her head and laughing, and Elizabeth striding purposefully across the MGM lot are two indelible moments.

By the time Mike met Elizabeth she had been married to the actor Michael Wilding for about five years. It was her second marriage; her first, to Nicky Hilton, had lasted less than a year. When Elizabeth and Michael Wilding were married in 1952, a reporter had written, "The bride wore a dove gray suit, the groom wore an air of surprise." Michael Wilding had been compared to the young David Niven and had been given a big push by the studio, but he never really became a big star. They had two children, but there were all kinds of rumors in Hollywood about his sexuality. In fact, after I had been married to Elizabeth, the gossip columnist Hedda Hopper, who had often written nasty things about me, invited me to her house one afternoon, served me a glass of champagne, and told me, "I want you to testify for me that Michael Wilding is a homosexual."

Apparently she had written that he was gay and he was suing her for libel. I said, "I don't know if Michael Wilding is a homosexual." When I told her that I wouldn't testify for her, her face clenched up and she just about took back my glass of champagne. If she hadn't liked me before that day, after that she really hated me.

Perhaps more than anything else, the trait that Mike and Elizabeth had in common was that when they saw something they wanted, they pursued it relentlessly. They knew what they wanted, they went after it obsessively, they didn't let anything get in their way, and almost inevitably they got it. Sometimes they acted with all the subtlety of Sherman's army marching through Georgia. And from the day Mike Todd met Elizabeth Taylor, he was going to have her.

They met on Mike's rented yacht. Elizabeth's marriage to Michael Wilding was just about done, and she was secretly dating the assistant director of *Around the World in 80 Days*. Elizabeth got around with the men. Mike invited that AD, Elizabeth, Michael Wilding, and several other friends to join him and Evelyn Keyes on his rented yacht to watch the shooting of one of the final scenes. That was some weekend cruise. Elizabeth and her husband were breaking up, her boyfriend was there, Mike and Evelyn were having their own problems, and Mike was eventually going to steal Elizabeth from her boyfriend. Shakespeare couldn't have put together a more complex cast of characters.

I wasn't there when Mike and Elizabeth met, but that meeting affected just about every day of the rest of my life. I can just imagine Mike's reaction when he saw her. He probably took his cigar out of his mouth and smiled, knowing his life was about to become even more interesting. And Elizabeth? She was so used to having men fawn over her that she probably didn't even notice his interest.

A week later Mike invited Debbie and me to a small barbecue at his house in the Hollywood Hills. Elizabeth was there with Michael Wilding. David Niven, and his wife were there. Shelley Winters claims she was there, but if she was she must have been hiding in the bushes. Mike was even more gregarious than usual, and I noticed he lavished a lot of attention on Elizabeth. It was pretty obvious what was happening. I couldn't believe his *chutzpah*, acting that way right in front of Evelyn Keyes and Michael Wilding.

At the end of the evening Mike walked Debbie and me to our car. He had this big smile on his face, and he was trying to communicate something to me that he didn't want Debbie to know. Finally it clicked. "You're in love," I said, "you little Jew bastard."

He admitted it to me the next day. "You tell Evelyn?" I asked. I didn't particularly like Evelyn. I thought she was too tough, but she was a very smart woman and had been good for him. She'd made several important contributions to the movie and now, when it was just about done, he intended to end their relationship.

"Not yet," he said. "I'll give her a million bucks and send her to South America. You think that's okay, Eddie?" I don't know what happened to that million dollars, but he did send her to Venezuela, ostensibly to see if theaters in Caracas could be equipped with Todd-AO projectors to show the movie. But the fact is that Evelyn was gone the moment he met Elizabeth; as always it was just a matter of working out the details.

A week later Mike told Elizabeth that they were going to be married. As Elizabeth liked to tell the story, she was relaxing at MGM when this madman grabbed her arm and directed her down several corridors into an empty office. He sat her down on a couch, pulled up a chair, and launched into a half-hour speech telling her that he was in love with her and that they were destined for each other. When you're with me, he told her, you're with me all the way. He never bothered asking her how she felt—he had already made that decision for her. That sounds like pure Mike Todd. He sold his love with the same intensity he sold his productions. A lot of people thought he was a sophisticated con man, but Mike never said a word he didn't believe, at least while he was saying it.

That was precisely the kind of approach Elizabeth would have found irresistible. She was stronger than most of the men she knew, and she was always in control of her relationships. Most men were intimidated by her beauty, her success, and her reputation, but not Mike. She'd never met anyone like Mike. Even the fact that she was married didn't slow him down. Within a couple of weeks Elizabeth officially announced her separation from Michael Wilding.

Mike and Elizabeth were crazy about each other in a way only crazy people can be. Neither of them lived by the normal rules of society. Their behavior was outrageous, and they didn't care what anybody else thought. Mike called her "My fat little Jewish broad, Lizzie Schwartzkoff," or he would tell her in front of a group of friends, "Soon as I finish my dinner, I'm gonna fuck you." In the middle of a small dinner party he offered Elizabeth the ultimate compliment: "Any minute this dame spends outta bed is completely wasted." Sometimes he would just reach over and grab her breasts or stick his hand under her dress. I know they loved to shock people, particularly Debbie, Debala, as Elizabeth would jokingly refer to her. "Where's Debala? You lucky stiff." Debbie was just mortified by their behavior and, knowing that, Mike and Elizabeth would be even more blatant.

Mike was so happy. Before he'd met Elizabeth, I was his front man. He'd blast his way through crowds or into restaurants yelling, "Make way for Eddie Fisher. Eddie Fisher coming through." But being with Elizabeth gave him real power. He used her as he had used me, and we both loved him for it. I was one of only a few thousand people he would confide in. He used to tell me everything about their relationship. Everything. Things I really didn't need to know. Once when he was in Hawaii, for example, meeting with the Kaiser people about building Todd-AO theaters, he told me that he and Elizabeth would have phone sex. That was the first time he'd ever done that and he loved it, so naturally he couldn't wait to tell me all about it.

Both of them were very physical people. They liked to touch each other all the time. But they also used to hit each other. I know that sounds terrible, and I'm not defending Mike, but the hitting was part of their relationship, and it was always a prelude to sex. Maybe it was a means of releasing their passion, I don't know, but I had never seen anything like it. I still believed the way to impress a woman was soft music and flowers.

I was staying at the Beverly Hills Hotel one night because Debbie and I were fighting, as usual, when Mike called and asked me to meet him at producer Harold Mirisch's house. They were in the middle of a high-stakes card game and Elizabeth was bored. "Come over and talk to her," he ordered. "Tell her how great I am."

Well, Mike was great, and I did as ordered. I never got tired of talking about him. Elizabeth and I drank champagne and played gin while we waited for Mike. Every once in a while he'd come into the room and give her a kiss and tell her his card game was almost done. They were going to drive to Palm Springs later that night, and sometime after midnight he told us to go to her house to pick up her clothes.

He told us. He didn't ask, he didn't suggest—he told us. I was one of the biggest stars in the world. I could fill any room, sing anywhere, but when Mike told me to do something, I did it. We were close friends, but we were only as equal as he wanted us to be. That was acceptable to me. I know I found things in him that I never saw in my father, and I know he thought of me as his son. So Elizabeth and I drove to her house. She was still living in the same house with Michael Wilding, but it was as if he didn't exist. He lived in a small room, and nobody ever mentioned his name. As she collected her belongings we drank some brandy and talked some more and opened another bottle of brandy and before we knew it, it was three-thirty in the morning. When I looked at my watch and realized how late it was, I knew we had a problem. "I think we'd better call Mike," I said.

He'd left Mirisch's house an hour earlier. He was home, and he was furious. Livid. She had done the worst thing a woman could do to him. By not returning to Mirisch's house and not calling, she had embarrassed him in front of his friends. He screamed at her, "You're not gonna fucking step all over me like you stepped on everybody in your whole life."

He was out of control. She wanted me to listen to him cursing at her, so I put my head next to hers. I was cheek to cheek with the most desirable woman in the world. Her hair, I remember, was kinky. Oh, I heard every word, but I couldn't concentrate. I was overwhelmed by the scent of her. It was extraordinary. It was as if I were breathing in her essence. It was heaven. Absolute heaven. It was. . .my feelings were all jumbled up. For an instant I'd almost forgotten that this was my best friend's woman. I didn't want to feel that way, but I couldn't help myself. It took me a couple of seconds to regain my composure, but I couldn't look at her. I couldn't look at her for a long, long time.

Mike finally hung up the phone. I called him back. Elizabeth was hysterical and I was going to be the peacemaker. "Stay out of this, Eddie," he told me. "I just hope you had a good time."

I didn't even know what he meant by that. He couldn't possibly have thought that Elizabeth and I. . .That wasn't possible and he knew it. "Mike, listen," I started. "I'm bringing her—"

"Don't you bring her here," he said, sounding serious. He really didn't want to see her.

Elizabeth went to pack her bag. She was terribly upset. Ten minutes passed, twenty, a half hour. I called her, no answer. I started getting anxious. She had really been upset. I called her again, and again she didn't answer. I was getting worried. I didn't know what she was capable of doing. I started sweating. The thought of suicide. . .I dismissed it. This was just a lovers' quarrel. The bathroom door was closed. Locked, I guessed. I grabbed the handle and started to throw my weight against it—and I burst into her bathroom. She was sitting in front of her mirror, applying her makeup. She turned and smiled at me. "I'm almost ready," she said.

On the drive to Mike's house I spilled a glass of brandy on my clothes. I started worrying that Debbie would find out and think I was out with Elizabeth. Normally I wouldn't have been concerned about Debbie's feelings since we were practically living apart, but I didn't want anyone even to think Elizabeth and I were together. I was totally innocent, except maybe for a thought or two in my mind, so I felt guilty.

The first thing I saw when we got to Mike's house was a policeman standing at his front door. Oh no, I thought, now *he's* committed suicide. When you were with those two, those were the kinds of thoughts you had. I made Elizabeth stay in the car as I spoke to the police officer. "What's the problem?" I asked.

"There's been a disturbance down the hill," he explained. "We're just checking the neighborhood."

Mike answered the door dressed in his white silk pajamas, trying to muss up his hair as if he'd been sleeping. But I noticed the pajamas didn't have a wrinkle in them. "I got Elizabeth with me," I told him.

"Bring her in." He left the door opened and walked away. I went back to the car and got Elizabeth and her Yorkshire terrier and we went inside. By that time she was drunk, and it was obvious she was afraid of him.

"Don't leave me," she said.

I was staying for Elizabeth, I was leaving for Mike. I didn't know what to do. Mike solved that problem for me. Bam! he smacked her. "What'd I tell you—" he yelled at her. Bam! All I saw was the bare bottoms of her feet as he dragged her into his bedroom.

She called me the next morning. "Oh, he hit me, he hit me. I need to get to sleep and I can't. What should I do? Should I take a sleeping pill?" Take a sleeping pill, I told her. A half hour later she called me again: "I still can't sleep." Sure, Elizabeth, take another sleeping pill.

I could never get used to the fact that she tolerated being hit, that maybe she even needed it to respect a man. Nicky Hilton kicked her in the stomach when she was pregnant. And with Burton, they could have sold tickets to their bouts. He beat her up so badly when they were making *Cleopatra* that they had to close the set for several weeks to allow her bruises to heal. She hit me all the time too, and tried to goad me into hitting her back. I wouldn't do it. "Go ahead," I'd tell her. "Hit me, but I'm not gonna hit you." After she smacked me six or seven times I turned my body and told her, "Now try this side." She'd force me to pin her down to stop her, and inevitably that led to sex.

Debbie and I spent a lot of time with Mike and Elizabeth. We went to the racetrack, nightclubs, to shows, dinners. We traveled to Mexico, France, New York, and believe me it wasn't because they were so in love with Debbie. Elizabeth and Debbie knew each other from the studio, and they were almost exactly the same age, chronologically, although they were completely different movie types. Elizabeth was the ultimate femme fatale while Debbie was the eternal ingenue, so they never competed for parts. They certainly weren't friends. In fact, Elizabeth didn't like Debbie very much. She couldn't bear Debbie's righteous attitude. She and Mike were always making some sort of remark like "Oh, you had to bring her, huh?" We were always putting her on or trying to find some way of getting rid of her. It wasn't that Debbie was always so wrong and we were so right, but we were like kids. We were having fun, and she brought all the joy of a parent to our party.

Debbie knew how we all felt. She was particularly proud of her participation in the Girl Scouts—there were endless publicity pictures taken of Debbie in front of a tent, Debbie involved in some scouting activity—and she recalled that Elizabeth had once said despairingly, "When are you gonna get over being a Girl Scout?"

To which Debbie replied defiantly, "Never. I like being a Girl Scout." When Elizabeth countered that she would never want to be a Scout, Debbie pointed out, "You wouldn't be allowed in the troop anyway."

Finally Elizabeth told her, "Nobody can be a Girl Scout forever, Debbie."

Hearing that, I can imagine Debbie stood up and said proudly, "Why not? Two dollars a year and you can be a Girl Scout forever!"

The Marines used to say there were no cowards on the beaches; well, there were no Girl Scouts in the Las Vegas casinos or the nightclubs where I performed. And the last thing Mike and Elizabeth and I wanted was a Girl Scout to correct our table manners.

Because Elizabeth and I both loved Mike, we became close friends. Elizabeth was incapable of being alone, so when Mike was busy I became her second choice. I was enchanted by her, in a best-friend-of-her-husband's sort of way. Nothing ever happened between us, less than nothing. We'd sit and drink champagne and talk for hours, often at her house. I got to know Michael Wilding, a very nice man, and I felt sorry for him. She paid no attention to him at all. He'd drink all day and he suffered from epilepsy so he had to take Seconal. In addition to his being drunk and drowsy from the pills, his career was not going well and he was just about broke. It appeared to me that his kids even pretty much ignored him. He was so sad, so terribly sad. I was convinced that his love for Elizabeth had just about destroyed him. I sympathized with him, but in a distant, detached way. I was confident that I would never allow a woman to have that kind of power over me.

Elizabeth revealed the most intimate details of her life to me. I became her father confessor. She'd grown up living two parallel lives: the very public movie queen and the very private woman. And they were two different people. On the screen she was the epitome of femininity, a woman of grace and beauty; in private she was tough and raunchy. She could drink and pop pills and curse as well as any man I'd ever met. Of her movie-star image, only her legendary beauty was real. And in those days she was as beautiful without any makeup at all as she was after spending hours in front of her mirror.

For someone who had spent most of her life being a public figure, the public actually had little idea what she was really like. She was a woman who loved men as much as they loved her and was not shy about it. "I think sex is absolutely gorgeous," she once said, and it was obvious she enjoyed telling both Mike and me about her romantic experiences. Maybe she thought she was shocking me. Some of the things she revealed did surprise me, though.

She told me that she'd had an affair with Frank Sinatra while she was married to Wilding. According to Elizabeth, she wanted to divorce Wilding and marry Sinatra, so she called him as asked him to marry her, but he didn't want any part of that.

Then she won her Oscar for her performance in *Butterfield 8*. After the ceremony she was holding court in our bungalow at the Beverly Hills Hotel. Everybody in Hollywood came there to congratulate her, all the actors and directors and writers, and she allowed them in one at a time. Finally Sinatra showed up. I was all ready for a big scene; I thought this was going to be one of those great moments of payback. Instead she welcomed him and spent more time with him than with people she genuinely liked, people like John Wayne. Elizabeth was an incredibly complicated woman, but I've never known anyone who was more honest about her feelings.

Several years later, when Elizabeth and I were involved in a court fight, my good buddy Sinatra called and said, "Why don't you lay off Liz?"

I laughed at that. "Oh, come on, Frank," I said. "You know Elizabeth almost as well as I do." He knew exactly what I meant by that and backed off. End of conversation.

Of all her other affairs, those that surprised me most were with Rock Hudson and Montgomery Clift. No matter what people believe about Rock Hudson and Montgomery Clift, I'm sure she slept with both of them. The fact that they were homosexuals wouldn't have bothered her at all; in fact I think she was in love with both of them. This was a different time, and AIDS didn't exist. One night we were at the Crescendo, a club in Los Angeles, watching Rock Hudson holding hands with Johnny Mathis, and she shook her head and sighed, "To think that I had . . ."

Another night we were with Monty Clift and a priest who was the cousin of a friend of ours. By dessert the priest was playing with Monty under the table. It was so outrageous it actually reminded me a little of

Mike Todd. Elizabeth didn't care what Monty did because she was crazy about him; if he had been as interested in women as she was in him, who knows what would have happened.

I liked him too, but he was deeply, deeply troubled. When I was with him I could almost feel impending doom. There was a storm in his eyes. It seemed like he was always either drunk or on some sort of pills. When Elizabeth was making *Suddenly, Last Summer* and we were living in a London hotel suite, Monty would visit us and get very drunk or stoned and sit on the ledge of the terrace, maybe a few inches from falling to his death. I stood close to him, ready to grab him if he leaned back too far. That was my lasting image of Montgomery Clift, always wobbling a few inches from death. The terrible car accident he had leaving Elizabeth's house one night disfigured him, but long before that he was struggling with life.

Monty Clift gave me my second acting lesson. When Elizabeth forced the producers to give me a part in *Butterfield 8*, Monty volunteered to help me with my lines. We were living at the Park Lane Hotel and Monty arrived promptly at nine o'clock in the morning. I handed him my script to look over and went inside to change clothes. A few minutes later I smelled smoke and ran back: Monty had passed out and his cigarette had set the script on fire in his hands. At my first acting lesson Stella Adler chased me around the room; at my second lesson Monty Clift set fire to my script. Acting was certainly a tough profession for me.

Elizabeth loved telling me bawdy stories. When Michael Wilding was making a picture with Victor Mature, for example, she was sleeping with Victor Mature. They had to devise ways of meeting secretly, which she described in hilarious detail. Years later, when we were married and she was having her affair with Richard Burton in Rome, I thought about that story as I walked around the grounds of our house trying to figure out how Burton was going to sneak in. At that point her stories no longer seemed so hilarious to me.

I know she never cheated on Mike Todd—even with her husband— and as far as I know he was completely faithful to her. They found what they needed in each other: Mike was a showman and Elizabeth was the greatest showpiece in the country. He was the only person I ever knew who loved the camera more than she did, and marrying the most photographed movie star in the world gained him attention he could never have achieved on his own. Wherever they went, the photographers followed. And in Mike, Elizabeth finally found the man who could dominate her.

Mike and Elizabeth announced their engagement at the New York premiere of the movie, which guaranteed even more publicity. The engagement ring was exactly 29.7 carats because, Mike was quoted as saying, "thirty carats would be vulgar and in bad taste." That's a great press agent's line. Mike would have never objected to vulgarity—as long as it was great vulgarity. The ring cost him $92,000, but it generated a million dollars' worth of press.

It was the best time of Mike's life. *Around the World in 80 Days* was a smash hit and he was engaged to a woman he loved. He showered her with gifts, with flowers and diamonds and emeralds, rubies, sapphires, and fur coats; he rented an airplane, a yacht, and three houses. Who knows where the money to pay for all of this came from. I know he was deeply in debt and revenues from the movie were only just beginning to trickle in, but he never stopped. He bought several paintings from Aly Khan's collection, including a Monet, a Utrillo, and a Degas, admitting, "People in Hollywood think I'm crazy paying that much for pictures that don't even move." He bought a Rolls-Royce Silver Cloud. He bought gowns from the most expensive designers. He and Elizabeth were perfect for each other: He loved giving, she loved getting. Even Elizabeth, who knew luxury, was impressed. The only thing that prevented them from being married was the fact that she already was married, but when she became pregnant in December, Mike knew they couldn't wait too much longer. A few years later, having a baby out of wedlock became a sort of antistatus symbol, at least that's what I told myself when Connie Stevens gave birth to our beautiful daughter, Joely, but this was still Dwight Eisenhower's 1950s. Churches were still issuing lists of movies parishioners were advised not to see. While Elizabeth might have enjoyed the scandal of having a child by one man while married to another, it would have had tremendous professional repercussions for both herself and Mike. And as outrageous as they enjoyed being in private, both of their careers were dependent on the ticket-buying public. I doubt Mike ever forgot that. He wanted to get married as quickly as possible.

Michael Wilding agreed to a Mexican divorce, and at the end of January 1957 we all went to Acapulco for the wedding. It was a typical Mike Todd production: It took place in a cliff-top hacienda, with lavish Mex-

ican food, strolling violinists, thousands of imported white gladioli and
orchids, pounds of caviar, gallons of champagne. I was Mike's American
best man, the great Mexican comedian Cantinflas was his Mexican best
man, and Debbie was Elizabeth's matron of honor. Her primary qualification for that honor was that she was there. One happy couple getting
married, one unhappy couple on the verge of a divorce. When we got
back to Hollywood I started looking for a place to live by myself.

The party went on through most of the night. The next morning Mike
brought me into their bedroom, like a sultan bringing me into his tent.
Elizabeth was lying on the bed, barely covered by a very short nightgown.
Every part of her body was visible, more even than I wanted to see. But
Mike wanted me to see her. He was just showing his best friend his
greatest treasure. And Elizabeth was completely at ease with me standing
there; she didn't even attempt to cover up. To me, this was Mike's way
of bonding with me, his way of proving how close we were.

Around the World in 80 Days was opening around the world. It took
David Niven and his faithful sidekick, Cantinflas, less time to navigate
the globe in a balloon than it did Mike Todd to open his movie. Of course
there was less money in it for them. The London premiere was even
bigger than the opening in New York. Mike had the British press magnate
Lord Beaverbrook in his hip pocket, so the picture was front-page news,
back-page news, and featured in the middle. At a party in the Dorchester
I met Laurence Olivier and his wife, Vivien Leigh. I'd always thought of
them as this gorgeous couple, madly in love with each other. That was
what I'd read in the newspapers. That night they weren't even talking to
each other. They could barely look at each other. I had to laugh at that;
I'd believed the stories I'd read about their loving relationship just as
completely as other people believed stories about my wonderful marriage
to my beloved Debbie. Prince Aly Khan was there with his mistress,
Ralph Richardson was there, and John Gielgud. In those days I admired
the classically trained British actors with their deep, *deep* mellifluous
voices and their carefully rehearsed spontaneous intensity.

Mike had rented the Battersea Gardens amusement park and invited
2,000 guests, among them Michael Wilding, who met the woman he
would marry after Elizabeth that night. As always, I did as many television and radio appearances as possible to hype the movie. I was a foot
soldier in his campaign to make *80 Days* the most popular movie of all

time. "Go over there and tell 'em how fucking great it is, you little Jew bastard," Mike would instruct me. It was fun, such incredible fun. We were a great team, Mike and I and Elizabeth.

On August 6, 1957, Elizabeth gave birth by caesarean section to Elizabeth Frances Todd. "Liza" was premature, weighing under five pounds, and barely survived. It was not an easy birth. Elizabeth had had painful back surgery several months earlier. Her back problems forced her to take painkillers, lots and lots of very strong painkillers, and her health was not good. Doctors told her afterwards that having another child would put her own life in jeopardy, so she had her fallopian tubes tied to prevent another pregnancy.

Mike was ecstatic at Liza's birth. He told reporters that he was considering buying the Taj Mahal as a present for Elizabeth, even though the plumbing was bad. He decided to brighten her New York City hospital room with the Monet's he'd bought from Aly Khan. As we drove to the hospital, our taxi had to stop suddenly and a sharp edge put a big hole in the painting. Mike was very upset, not that this valuable painting had been damaged, but because he didn't want to hang damaged goods in Elizabeth's room.

In February 1958, Debbie gave birth to our son. Once again, I fainted at the birth. I wanted to name him after Mike, so I gave him the option, Michael or Todd. So my son was named Todd Emanuel, the Emanuel in honor of Manny Sacks, who had been so supportive early in my career. I didn't see how I could leave Debbie and our two babies—the negative publicity would have destroyed me. So we made peace with each other. I don't know if Debbie knew about the other women, but she never said a word. We moved into a larger house, with a swimming pool bordered by a low retaining wall; we bought a new station wagon; we bought new furniture. Somehow, when I wasn't paying attention, my life with Debbie had replicated the marriage of Eddie and Ida Cantor. And who knows, we might have even stayed together for years. But three weeks after my beautiful son's birth our lives were shattered.

Mike was always searching for something new and bigger and better and more spectacular than anything he'd previously done. To celebrate the first anniversary of the picture running in New York, he decided to throw a black-tie party for 18,000 invited guests—at Madison Square Garden. Somehow he convinced CBS to pay *him* to televise what was nothing more than one long commercial for his movie. Then he convinced manufactures to donate 14,000 prizes—everything from a Cessna to ivory chopsticks to give away. He even convinced Sir Cedric Hardwicke to ride an elephant into the Garden. He served a ton of baked beans, 10,000 egg rolls, and 15,000 doughnuts and hot dogs. As it turned out, no one had ever seen anything like it—it was one of the biggest disasters of his career.

The party raged completely out of control. Waiters ended up selling bottles of champagne, formally dressed guests were throwing food at each other as well as at the Philadelphia Mummers marching band, the guests stole the door prizes and battled over souvenirs. Eventually the frustrated guests started fighting with each other, causing them to slip on the ice cream dropped on the floor. I watched the debacle with Mike and Elizabeth. They were both drunk and Mike was moaning, "What they hell are they doing? They're ruining me! The whole thing's wrong." Elizabeth was crying.

I loved it. Maybe because I'd talked Mike into putting one of my best friends, Lenny Gaines, in charge of the whole thing, but I remember telling him supportively as we watched this debacle, "No, Mike, it's not that bad." Compared to what, my marriage? I might have even described the whole event as "colorful." As a party it was a shambles, a mess. But as a TV show it was a great success. It got one of the highest ratings of the year, which translated into great exposure for the movie. And in a sense it might have even added to his reputation as a great showman: Even when one of his projects failed, it failed on a legendary scale.

My own career was sailing so smoothly on a calm ocean that I didn't realize that the rudder had fallen off. I enjoyed playing a role in Mike's success so much that I wasn't paying enough attention to my own professional life. Television was growing up very rapidly, and it was changing. People consider the 1950s the "golden age of television drama," but it was also the time of the variety show. Perry Como, Bob Hope, and Dinah Shore hosted shows. Dean Martin had a new variety show. Jimmy Durante had frequent variety specials. Ed Sullivan's Sunday night *Toast of the Town* was the archetypal variety show. Steve Allen had a show, Jackie Gleason had a variety show. It seemed like we had more hosts than guests.

So the same guests were endlessly recycled, and then the hosts began exchanging guest appearances on other hosts' shows. Eventually these shows became interchangeable; there was no semblance of originality or spontaneity. At the beginning of the 1957–58 season MCA, the giant talent agency that controlled both the performers and the sponsors, decided I should co-host an hour variety show with taciturn comedian Lonesome George Gobel. I loved George, but I hated the idea. George Gobel was a very funny man, the problem was that we were both very low-key performers. But because MCA represented both of us, as well as most of the major talent in the business, they pretty much dictated what we would do. The format of the show required both of us to sing and do some comedy. Believe me, more people laughed at his singing than at my attempts at comedy. It didn't work at all. And Gobel could sort of talk his way through a song.

After thirteen weeks they figured it out and we began alternating as hosts, occasionally exchanging guest appearances. But what bothered me most about the whole episode was that I had no one to fight for me. Milton Blackstone was the expert on the Catskills and the nightclub world, but he knew even less than I did about television or the movie industry or Las Vegas. We were still legally partners in my career and he would send me long, typewritten memos critiquing my performances, but I had stopped listening to his advice. I was making all the decisions about my career, and I really didn't know what I was doing. After spending so much time with Mike I knew how to act like I had all the answers, but I had neither the experience nor the knowledge to make the right decisions. Everything had gone so easily for me in the past that I just sort of assumed that it would continue. So I made a lot of wrong decisions about my career, and I made some enemies because of the way I made those decisions. In those days it was easy for me to believe I knew everything. I had to get a lot smarter to understand how much I didn't know. I paid absolutely no attention to the only lesson I should have learned from Debbie: To have a career you have to work at it—and work at it.

Still, everything would have been different if Mike had lived.

The success of *Around the World in 80 Days* had made Mike a major player in the movie business and he had plans, big plans. Mike never had a small plan in his life. He announced that Elizabeth was going to star in *Don Quixote*, with John Huston as Quixote and Mickey Rooney as Sancho Panza, and supposedly Mike hired Picasso to do a drawing for the initial advertising campaign. He announced that he was going to hire units of the Soviet army for a spectacular production of *War and Peace*—he even took Elizabeth to Russia and called me from the Kremlin to complain that Khrushchev wouldn't meet with him—but when he learned the Russian army was not for rent, he announced that Elizabeth would star as *Anna Karenina*. He was still perfecting his Todd-AO process, and forty years later it's still the best projection system, better than Cinerama, CinemaScope, or VistaVision. One day he was showing me the different types of screening systems—he'd worked with Lowell Thomas on the development of Cinerama before Todd-AO—and I was overwhelmed. He took his cigar out of his mouth and told me, "Eddie, all this is nothing. I've got nine more processes . . ."

If he had lived. Mike had rented a twin-engine Lockheed Lodestar and renamed it the *Lucky Liz*, which Elizabeth had decorated for him. I'd flown on the plane only once. In late December 1957, Mike and Elizabeth and Debbie and I were flying to Palm Springs to celebrate Christmas and New Year's Eve. But as the pilots began preparing for the landing, they announced we were coming into Las Vegas.

Maybe Mike had planned it, but he acted surprised. "Las Vegas?" he said. "We wanted to go to Palm Springs." But as long as we were in Vegas, Mike decided we would stay for the night. We spent the night in the casino. At six o'clock in the morning, I remember, we were playing roulette and our pilots were watching us. They were drinking brandy. They had been up all night and they had been drinking all night. And at nine o'clock in the morning they took off on another flight. That made me feel very uncomfortable.

I tried to convince Mike to hire another pilot I knew, but when Mike went to find him he was out of the country. Mike liked his pilots and he trusted them.

In March 1958, Mike was to be roasted by the New York Friars Club, who had named him Showman of the Year. Sammy Cahn had written risqué lyrics to *Around the World in 80 Days* that I planned to sing at the dinner. Mike wanted me to fly with him to New York on the *Lucky Liz*, but I had to go to Greensboro, North Carolina, to film a commercial for Chesterfield. "You take the plane," he insisted. "I'll meet you in New York."

"You take it," I insisted, "How else you gonna get there?" I could never talk Mike out of anything, but this time I talked him out of it.

Mike couldn't get anybody to fly with him. That must have made him crazy, eight hours on an airplane with nobody to talk to or play cards with. Elizabeth was sick. She was filming *Cat on a Hot Tin Roof* on a very tight shooting schedule at MGM and had a temperature of about 102 degrees. Her doctor told her if she went to New York she might not be well enough to work when she returned, so she stayed home. Mike invited Joe Mankiewicz, Kirk Douglas, Elizabeth's agent Kurt Frings, entertainment journalists Vernon Scott and Mike Bacon, publicist Warren Cowen, and Richard Brooks, who was directing Elizabeth in *Cat on a Hot Tin Roof*. Jack Benny told me Mike wanted him to fly with him. Joe E. Lewis told me Mike called him. Over the years so many people have told me they were supposed to be with Mike on that airplane. Finally Art Cohn, who was working with Mike on his autobiography, decided to go with him. They took off from Burbank Airport in a violent thunderstorm.

I took a commercial flight to New York and checked into the Essex House. I was watching television with my press agent, Jim Mahoney, and several other friends when it was announced that Mike's plane had crashed into the mountains of New Mexico. I just sat there. "Everybody out," Mahoney ordered. "Leave him alone." I went into the bedroom, sat down on the bed, and started crying. I really couldn't believe it. I couldn't believe Mike would allow that to happen. That was the first time in my life I had to deal with the death of someone I really cared about. Mike wasn't my father, he wasn't my brother; he was the best friend I ever had. I was devastated, absolutely devastated.

I didn't know what to do. The one person whose advice I needed was dead. I just sort of reacted. I spoke to Debbie on the phone. She wanted to go to their house and I told her to stay away. This was my job and I didn't want to share it with her. I didn't want to share anything with her, even a tragedy. But she went over there anyway and brought Elizabeth's children home with her to our house.

I flew back to Los Angeles immediately. I didn't even go home. I went right to Mike's—to Elizabeth's house. It was surrounded by police and private security guards, reporters, and photographers, friends, and relatives, neighbors, and curiosity seekers. People I'd never seen before in my life were walking in and out of the house as if they owned it. One of the first people I saw was Elizabeth's doctor, Rex Kennemar. Minutes after I got there Elizabeth came walking down the long steps dressed in a transparent nightgown, completely oblivious to all the people in the house. The look on her face was one of total disorientation. She was so distraught and so medicated she was in a different reality. She walked right past me without even a glimmer of recognition. Several minutes later, as she went back upstairs, she finally noticed me. "Please, Eddie." she said. "Come tomorrow so we can talk. I can't . . ."

I don't have a lot of memories of the next few days. They passed. I remember bits and pieces of things. I remember being in the middle of perfectly lucid conversations with Elizabeth and an instant later she would be crying hysterically. I remember her alternating between blaming herself for allowing him to go and screaming that she should have been on the plane with him, that she should be dead, that she wanted to be dead.

I flew with her to Chicago for Mike's funeral on a TWA DC-7 provided by Howard Hughes. Debbie stayed in Los Angeles with Elizabeth's children. Mike Todd's funeral had all the solemnity of one of his premieres, but without the meticulous planning. A tent had been erected around the gravesite to shield the service from spectators, and the police put up barricades to keep away everyone except invited mourners. Hundreds, maybe thousands of people were at the cemetery when we arrived. They were sitting on headstones, picnicking on the grass. Some of them even brought their children. The graveside ceremony was brief, but we could hear the spectators shouting, demanding that Elizabeth make an appearance. Everybody wanted to see the grieving widow.

Even though Elizabeth was still in her twenties, she had already been through a lifetime's worth of unique experiences, but nothing like this. None of us, not me, not any of our friends, had ever experienced anything as unexpected and as devastating as this. Mike was the lion in all of our lives, our leader, and without him we just sort of moved along.

My mother was absolutely right, trying to describe the emptiness. . . well, *words can't express.*

There was a closed coffin, but I knew it was more for show than anything else. The plane had exploded on impact and whatever remains were found couldn't be identified. This was decades before DNA identification was available. The only items recovered from the wreckage were Mike's wedding ring and some platinum cuff links I'd given him. After the service Elizabeth asked for a few minutes alone at Mike's grave. When she came out of the tent the spectators broke through the barricades and besieged her. Mike Todd Jr., Dr. Kennemar and I surrounded her, and fought through to the crowd to our limousine. People jumped on the hood of the car, held cameras against the windows and took pictures, screamed her name. It was bizarre, unbelievable. These people weren't mourning Mike; they were desperate for some connection to celebrity. For them this was a big show, with big stars, and it was free. Although I hated them, I couldn't blame them. Mike had spent every minute of his life trying to be noticed, and his death and funeral were front-page news on just about every newspaper in America. Georgie Jessel summed up Mike's life when he said that Mike had gone from being a sideshow barker at the Chicago World's Fair to the man who could tell Picasso, "Wrap up those pictures. They'll make a nice present for Elizabeth."

When we returned to Los Angeles, I was really frightened for Elizabeth. I knew the depth of their relationship, I knew how much they had loved each other. Maybe I wondered for a few minutes, Who replaces Mike in her life? But I knew the answer to that one: He was irreplaceable. And knowing that behind her sophisticated facade there was a very vulnerable little girl, a little girl with a highly developed sense of drama, I began to worry that Elizabeth might try to commit suicide.

During the next few weeks I spent a great deal of time with Elizabeth. Maybe not as much as people like Dick Hanley, Mike's secretary, who was an absolute rock, and her close friend Sydney Guilaroff, and Arthur Loew Jr., whom she adored, and Rex Kennemar, but I was there almost every day. I began to believe I could play an important role in her recovery. I thought I was consoling her, but in fact we were consoling each other. She received thousands of letters and telegrams from all over the world, and we would sit up in her bedroom and I would read these letters aloud to her. Many of the people who wrote hadn't liked Mike very much when he was alive, but in these letters they sweetened their relationship.

The thought of having a love affair with Elizabeth never entered my mind. Never. Even those times when we were alone in her bedroom, I never saw her as a beautiful, desirable woman. She was my best friend's widow; she was my friend.

After several weeks she went back to work on *Cat on a Hot Tin Roof*. Getting back into a routine was part of the healing process. For a few hours each day, at least, she had to focus on something besides Mike's death. She was tremendous. She really earned her second Academy Award nomination—no one ever said that Elizabeth Taylor was not a great actress.

The routines of daily life helped both of us survive Mike's death. Gradually Elizabeth began spending time with other men, not dating exactly, but being with them. I felt like I was her brother or her father, that I was supposed to take care of her. And I did care deeply about her. I understood that she needed the company of a man, I knew that, but when I realized she was spending a lot of time with Arthur Loew, Jr., a wealthy bachelor, I found myself becoming possessive of her, and maybe a little jealous. I did what I could to break up that relationship, encouraging her to spend more time with Mike Todd Jr. I guess I was falling in love with her but I wouldn't admit it, even to myself. I was married, unhappy but married, and I knew that Elizabeth Taylor was not going to fall in love with me. Not Eddie Fisher. Not even in my fantasies did she fall in love with me. It was just too ridiculous. So I continued to believe that was I was protecting her out of friendship, out of my loyalty to Mike.

About six months after Mike's death I was scheduled to open an eight-week engagement at the Tropicana Hotel in Las Vegas. Several days before my opening Elizabeth decided she was going to come. I was thrilled. Absolutely thrilled. This was her first public appearance since Mike's death, her reentry into the world. I felt honored that she chose my opening.

Opening-night audiences are usually packed with friends and relatives and dedicated fans. When I announced that Elizabeth was in the room that night—as if anybody hadn't noticed her entrance—the audience greeted her with affection. She was the beautiful survivor of a tragedy, the young widow left with an infant, the queen of show business. Everybody loved Elizabeth Taylor. It was a highly emotional moment for everyone in that room.

Afterwards she came back to my dressing room. Sammy Davis Jr. was in the middle of the picture-taking stage of his life, and he carried a camera everywhere and snapped everything. He took a photograph of Elizabeth with me and had it enlarged, then put it in a heart-shaped silver frame. The Rat Pack, Sinatra and Dean Martin, Peter Lawford, Joey Bishop, and Sammy, were well known for their outrageous behavior, but they often did things in a subtle way. In this photograph Elizabeth and I are just looking at each other and smiling, but people who didn't know better would swear we'd been in love forever, that there was no Mike Todd, no Debbie Reynolds, just the two of us. Putting the photograph in a heart-shaped frame was Sammy's way of saying that he knew love when he saw it.

Later, as we celebrated my opening in the Tropicana lounge, Elizabeth told me that she still had trouble getting to sleep. Well, I had the answer for that sitting at our table, Dr. Max Jacobson. Eventually, I took Max up to her suite and he gave her a shot, a mild sedative. It relaxed her but didn't put her to sleep, so while my celebration was going on downstairs I sat quietly with her. We just talked for most of the night. Two friends.

She returned to Hollywood the next day. But at about four the next morning, after I'd finished my second show, she called me. I seem to recall that I was still in my dressing room, but I may have been back in my suite at the hotel. I wasn't surprised. I figured she was having difficulty sleeping and needed a friend to talk to, and knew I'd be wide awake. I don't remember much of our conversation except that she said emphatically, "When you get back, we have to talk. I want to see you."

I assumed she meant she wanted to talk about Mike. Which demonstrates how little I understand women.

CHAPTER SIX

I've seen what love can do to a man. I remember Robert Wagner, inconsolable, bursting into my bungalow in hysterics when he found out Natalie Wood was having an affair with Warren Beatty. He was so in love with her, so desperately in love, his heart was just broken. There was no way to comfort him. I remember William Holden crying like a baby as he pleaded on the phone with Cappucine, "Please come back to me. I'll die without you." William Holden was a broken man. I remember Frank Sinatra putting his arm around my shoulders on the *Eddie Cantor Show*, exposing the thin cuts on his wrist he made when supposedly he'd tried to commit suicide over Ava Gardner—the one woman in his life he couldn't control.

So I knew what could happen when a man really loves a woman. I just didn't think it could happen to me.

I finished my engagement at the Tropicana and got home in time for a surprise thirtieth-birthday party Debbie had planned for me at Mike Romanoff's restaurant. The only surprise was how many people knew about it, including me. Debbie had reserved the seat next to me for Elizabeth. Debbie moved in mysterious ways, but Elizabeth never showed up. I hadn't spoken to her since that night she'd called me in Las Vegas, and I was looking forward to seeing her. I was very disappointed. In the middle of the party she phoned to apologize. "Eddie, I'm sorry I didn't come. I have my period and I just feel awful."

I'd spent enough time with her to recognize the slur in her voice. "That's baloney," I said. I really did say things like that. "You don't have your period. You've got a hangover."

She burst out laughing. "Can you come by the house tomorrow?" she asked. "I've got something of Mike's I want you to have. I'll be out by the pool."

Endless songs have been written about the way love begins, but I don't know of any of them that got it right. The moment you fall in love, really fall in love, your life is forever divided into the time before that moment and the rest of your life.

I've never known when Elizabeth decided she was in love with me. But I know, as surely as I've known anything in my life, that it was all planned. That she knew exactly what she was doing. When I got to her house, the door was open. I called her name and she didn't answer. I walked through the house to the pool, into the greatest scene of my life. She was sitting by the pool, wearing a flesh-colored bathing suit. Liza was playing between her legs, and there was a glass of wine next to her. I came through the doors onto the deck and she turned toward me.

We were in love. Not a word was spoken, but I knew I had just started the rest of my life. One look, our eyes met, and the feeling that ran through my body. . .I'd never felt anything like it before, but somehow I knew, this is what love feels like.

My birthday present was a gold money clip she had given to Mike. On it was engraved a phrase I'd heard him use so often: *I've been broke many times, but I've never been poor.*

"Would you like to go for a drive?" I asked. I drove toward Malibu.

She was holding Liza in her arms. I wanted to take her hand. I wanted to know for certain that she was feeling the same thing I was feeling, but I hesitated. I felt like the high-school kid sitting in the movie theater with the prettiest girl in class, trying to get up enough courage to put his arm around her. Finally I reached over and took her hand. She squeezed my hand gently.

We drove in silence for several minutes. I didn't even dare look at her. A million thoughts were spinning in my head. Finally I said softly, "I'm going to marry you."

She looked at me. "When?"

"Soon," I said. "As soon as possible."

If they had written dialogue like this for *Bundle of Joy*, that picture would have been a success. We drove past Malibu until we found a deserted stretch of the beach. As Liza played in the sand I held Elizabeth in my arms for the first time. We kissed. It was a gentle kiss, a sweet kiss. It had nothing to do with sex, it was love. It was all heart and soul. We knew it was right. My head was pounding, my heart was pounding. It was maddening. For the first time in my life I understood the meaning of all the love songs I'd been singing.

There was never a question in my mind that I would leave Debbie as soon as possible. Our marriage had been over in everything but fact for a long time, and now I had the reason to end it.

Over the next few weeks Elizabeth and I spent every possible moment together. We made up excuses to get together for lunch and dinner and meetings. I was thrilled just to sit next to her, just to feel her body next to mine. Our relationship was so sweet. We didn't have sex for a long time and the passion inside both of us was growing and growing and growing. We were bursting with love. But no one seemed to notice. I was amazed. It seemed impossible to me that anyone could fail to see this crazy attraction.

Somehow Debbie didn't see it. How that was possible I will never understand. The three of us spent a lot of time together. We even went to the premiere of *Cat on a Hot Tin Roof* together, and Elizabeth was just outrageous. She really didn't seem to care if we were caught. She was fierce; she wanted to let the rest of the world go to hell. Elizabeth lived by her own rule: She wants what she wants when she wants it. If we were in a restaurant or at a party she would follow me from room to room, just waiting for us to be alone for an instant, and then she would throw herself at me. At a restaurant one night, with Debbie sitting on the other side of me, she took my hand and put it under her dress. At a party another night she grabbed my hand and put it on one of her breasts. When I left she would beg me to stay or demand to know when we would be together again. Weeks passed and we still hadn't made love. I don't know why; maybe sex was the threshold beyond which there would be no turning back. But for a time, both of us were very happy playing this game.

Believe me, I was probably more surprised that Elizabeth was this crazy about me than the rest of the country would be when they found out about us. I'd never even considered the possibility of a romantic relationship with Elizabeth. I'd always felt she was beyond me, definitely out of my league. In my mind I'd put her on a pedestal, and the fact that the most desirable woman I'd ever known was pursuing me, pursuing me relentlessly—well, I knew what it was to have my greatest fantasy come true.

I think, if it were up to her, she would have just told Debbie, "Leave the house." But it wasn't up to her. As far as the public knew, Debbie and I were blissfully happy with our two young children. We were still "America's Sweethearts." I had to figure out how to announce to the world that I was leaving sweet little Debbie for my best friend's widow without destroying Elizabeth's and my careers.

I was insanely—and secretly—in love with her. I would have done anything to please her, anything except admit the truth publicly. At one time, for example, Van Cilburn was staying with Debbie and me. He'd sit at my piano, playing sonatas, playing complete symphonies, some of the most beautiful music ever written, for at least six hours every day. Friends of mine had had brand-new stereo systems installed, but I had the greatest pianist in the world, live. Occasionally he would take a brief rest, and when he did, he'd put an inner tube around his waist and paddle around the swimming pool. He'd previously told me that one of his dreams was to meet Elizabeth, so I had this wonderful idea: I would have the greatest pianist in the world put on a private concert for her. Now appearing in the role of Mike Todd: Eddie Fisher.

Van Cilburn was a very eccentric guy. He had performed in the greatest concert halls in the world; he had played for world leaders, yet when I asked him to play for Elizabeth he told me that he couldn't do it. "I don't have my piano," he explained.

"I'll get you any piano you want," I said.

He shook his head, "Eddie, you can't get a grand piano in this house. There's no way."

"I'll break down a wall if I have to."

He agreed. I didn't actually have to remove a wall, but I did have to take out several windows and frames to get the piano into the house. I told Debbie that Van Cilburn wanted to meet Elizabeth, and that it would be a good way to get her out of her house. It would cheer her up.

After dinner the four of us moved into the living room and Van Cliburn performed for us. He played for almost two hours, played from a place in his soul that I had never known existed. Occasionally Elizabeth and I would make eye contact and my heart would start pounding. I wanted to be with her so much. Listening to that beautiful music, looking at that beautiful woman. . .it was one of the most glorious nights of my life. When Van Cliburn finished he was completely exhausted—his clothes were dripping wet. He had given to Elizabeth the greatest gift he could bestow: every last ounce of his talent.

At the end of the evening I opened the front door—and I was stunned. Hundreds of people—it seemed like the entire population of Beverly Hills—were sitting on the lawn or standing in the street. They'd been there for hours, listening silently to this concert. The house was open to the swimming pool, so they were able to hear quite well. When Van Cliburn appeared in the doorway, they started cheering. He received a standing ovation from the neighborhood. I felt so good inside. I'd produced a memorable evening. Elizabeth was impressed, which was all that mattered to me. It was exactly the kind of thing that only Mike could have done.

We didn't make love for a long time. I don't know why. We wanted to all the time, but I just felt we shouldn't. I sort of liked the anticipation. Anticipation is a very underrated emotion. I much preferred later than sooner. I liked the concept of sustaining love without sex. Well, at least I liked it for a while.

In late August, Elizabeth was going to Europe for a brief vacation, but I insisted she change her plans and meet me in New York. I lied to Debbie, told her that my sponsor, Chesterfield, wanted me there for meetings. But since our whole life together was a bigger lie, deceiving her didn't bother me at all. I checked into the Essex House; Elizabeth was staying at the Plaza. I don't know who we thought we were fooling. When I got to the Plaza, Elizabeth told her secretary to leave for the evening. As soon as we were alone I held her in my arms and began kissing her. "When are we going to make love?" she asked.

I was very cool. "Tonight," I said. But the night came very fast.

It had been worth waiting a lifetime for Elizabeth. It was so much more than a wonderful physical experience, so much more than anything I'd ever experienced. Even that first time we made love it was as if we had been together forever. Elizabeth in reality was far more than Elizabeth in my fantasies. She was a sexual being, a woman who loved sex, who loved being sexual. She was so much more than the sexual image created for her by the studio. She was uninhibited, wild, free, so totally free with her body. We couldn't get enough of each other. There had been other women with whom the physical sex had been great; other women I lusted after, and there was Debbie, but until that night I had absolutely no idea what it was like to make love to a woman with whom I was deeply in love. Elizabeth changed everything in my life.

We spend our lives hearing about love and talking about it and reading about it and looking for it, but until I was with Elizabeth I had no idea how wonderful, how all-consuming, it could be. If I had known that first night we spent together how our love was going to help destroy my career and, for a time, my life, if I had known how much pain my love for Elizabeth was going to bring me, I still wouldn't have hesitated. Whatever happened between us, it was worth it.

We spent the next day just walking around New York. I guess I finally accepted the fact that we would have to go public. I just didn't want to hide my love for her anymore. We went to the Central Park Zoo; we kissed on Fifth Avenue. And nobody paid any attention to us at all. Nobody seemed even to notice us. I thought I had to be in heaven. The most famous actress in America and one of the most famous singers kissing in the street, and nobody noticed us.

It was difficult for me to accept the fact that this woman, this extraordinary woman, this incredibly smart, sexy, sophisticated woman, was crazy about me. She made me feel wonderful about myself. Back at the Plaza that night we were making love when Cary Grant called Elizabeth.

As I listened in on an extension, he told her about this amazing drug he'd discovered and he wanted her to take it with him. I don't remember if he said it or not, but later we found out it was LSD. Elizabeth turned him down, turned down Cary Grant for this kid from Philly.

We knew we had to tell Debbie. I didn't want her finding out from reporters. The story Debbie has often told was that she suspected I was with Elizabeth and phoned me at the Plaza at two o'clock in the morning. Knowing that I would avoid her call, she pretended to be Dean Martin. Completely fooled by this brilliant deception, I answered the phone. Oh, she was clever.

Except it didn't happen that way. As I remember it, I called Debbie. And I told her bluntly, "I'm with Elizabeth in New York and we're in love."

Debbie surprised me with her response. She was very calm. She said, "We'll talk about it when you get home." Talk about it! I'd just told her I was in love with another woman and she reacted as if I'd told her I'd be home a little late for dinner. It was like I was in the middle of an episode of *Father Knows Best*. Talk about it! She didn't scream or yell. It was as if she was completely detached from reality. But when I hung up that phone, I felt free.

Elizabeth and I started appearing together in public, although always with other people. We spent the Labor Day weekend at Grossinger's. Supposedly I was there to cut a ribbon, opening a new swimming pool, but we stayed together in Jennie Grossinger's home. Exactly nine years earlier Eddie Cantor had discovered me right there and started my career. We returned to New York and spent a week going to the theater and the best nightclubs, famous places like the Blue Angel, Ed Wynne's Harwyn, Quo Vadis, the Embers, the Colony. We thought we were being circumspect. We were always careful to leave separately. At the Blue Angel, for example, Eva Marie Saint helped us sneak out the back way— and we got away with it. Well, we got away with it except for that one photographer from *Life* magazine, who took pictures that ran worldwide. The truth is that our secret was out. Everything we did was reported in the gossip columns. Leonard Lyons reported that Elizabeth and I were inseparable. Winchell wrote that we were madly in love and that I was going to divorce Debbie. The telephones started ringing endlessly, photographers waited in front of the hotel and the clubs for a picture of us together. Naturally I did the right thing under the circumstances: I denied everything. Elizabeth was my friend, I protested, I'm just a friendly escort. Debbie is fine, home with the kids. Smile, smile.

Of course the only person who believed any of it was Debbie. Either that or she was a complete phony. I had originally been scheduled to return from New York the Tuesday after Labor Day. At seven that morning she went to the airport to greet me. Just she and a few reporters. Doesn't every wife greet her husband at the airport with reporters and photographers to record the homecoming? The fact that we'd only spoken once, when I'd told her I was in love with another woman, didn't stop her from waiting lovingly at the airport. And when one of the arriving passengers asked her what she was doing there, she replied, "Oh, I came to meet you."

A week later Elizabeth and I returned to Los Angeles on separate planes. When she landed she was besieged by reporters, who begged her to say something, say anything. "Hello," she said.

My plane landed at three-thirty in the morning. After spending the rest of the night at my friend Joey Foreman's apartment, Joey and I went to see Debbie the next morning. The entire front lawn of the house was staked out with reporters. It looked like there were hundreds of them. Until that moment I don't think I quite realized the impact this story would have. Maybe because I knew the truth of my marriage, I sometimes forgot that as far as the public was concerned, Debbie and I and the kids were still a big, happy family. Our divorce was going to come as a real surprise.

To avoid the reporters I sneaked into the house through the back door. As soon as I got inside I was struck by the beautiful aroma of. . .lima bean soup. Debbie was in the kitchen cooking lima bean soup. She was trying to save our marriage by cooking my favorite meal. Believe me, even the prospect of lima beans was not enough to make me stay with Debbie.

When I walked into the kitchen and she saw me, she asked, "Is it true?"

"Of course it's true, Debbie," I said.

"Are you staying?" she asked.

"No. I'm going."

Then she very neatly laid down the fork she'd been holding and went completely out of her mind. She sat down on the floor and started pounding the marble tiles, screaming and yelling, crying. The reporters standing outside could hear her screaming almost as clearly as the neighbors had heard Van Cilburn. "Debbie," I said to her, "you've got to get control of yourself."

"Control? Control?" She ran upstairs and locked herself in the bathroom. I thought she was going to try to commit suicide. Of course I always thought women were trying to commit suicide. I remember there were a lot of people coming in and out of the house. . .press agents, friends, studio representatives. Every once in a while Debbie would come downstairs to scream at me. "You should know better! It doesn't look good to behave that way! It doesn't look good to have stories like this in the papers. You never see stories like this about me!" I just sat there listening, taking it. I didn't know what else to do.

At one point I went out and told the reporters, "We're having a misunderstanding. We hope to work it out. We have nothing further to say." I don't know why I did that. Maybe I thought they would all decide, Oh, well, we might as well go home, and leave. Instead they started shouting questions at me. I retreated back into the house.

There is no course that prepares you to deal with situations like this one. And even if there was, I was a high-school dropout. I was making it up as I went along.

The next few days were a blur. Debbie decided we needed to see a marriage counselor. She pleaded with me to go with her. I knew it was a complete waste of time, but I agreed to go. It would have done just as much good to go see Frank Sinatra. She scheduled an appointment with a doctor at UCLA, but the problem was getting out of the house. She didn't want to face the mob of reporters waiting in front, so she decided we would climb over the brick wall in the backyard, where her friend Camille Williams would meet us and drive us away.

So there I was, thirty years old, escaping from Beverly Hills. We made our getaway. As we sprinted around the swimming pool, the reporters spotted us and started chasing us. I boosted her to the top of the wall, then she gave me a hand to help me up. We made it over the wall and ran barefoot across the neighbor's yard. The neighbor's two dogs started chasing us, barking, trailed by a pack of reporters, screaming. Waiting for us in a car was, according to reporters, "a sparsely dressed brunette" who said she was "Camille from Burbank." This was the worst escape in history.

I sat in the marriage counselor's office and listened for fifty minutes. I didn't say one word. Debbie rattled on, but the more she said the more obvious it became that our marriage was over. At the end of the session the therapist leveled with Debbie, telling her, "Your husband has left you. He's in love with another woman, and he says he is going to marry her. Now, what do you want him to do?"

Debbie had no answers. At that moment I felt so sorry for her. And maybe that was the very last time in my life I did feel sorry for her.

Camille was waiting for us when we got out of the doctor's office. But her car wouldn't start. The battery was as dead as our marriage. So Debbie and I got out of the car and pushed it down the street into a gas station. It seemed like every reporter in America was camped out on our front lawn waiting for a few words, and when we really needed help, there was no one around.

When we got back to the house I told the reporters we'd been to a doctor because "she's nervous about something." And then I lied, without even being asked: "I do not love Miss Taylor and she does not love me."

That session with the counselor convinced Debbie our marriage was over. We met with her attorney that afternoon, who announced to reporters, "A separation exists between Eddie and Debbie" The media treated it like a major news event. It's difficult today, when every single aspect of a celebrity's life is revealed to the public, when homemade sex videos of stars are available on the Internet, to understand the impact of this announcement. But in the 1950s, America was just beginning to change, and people still held tightly to the traditional values of family and country. Divorces were still relatively rare. Unhappily married people stayed together for their children. So the unexpected breakup of our seemingly loving marriage shook that bedrock. People believed in Debbie and me. I think they saw us as representative of the young couples who were beginning to shape America's future.

And as it turned out that's exactly what we were.

Debbie played the role of the jilted wife brilliantly. Appearing for photographers with diaper pins in her blouse, in case anyone might forget she was a mother, she told reporters, "It seems unbelievable to say that you can live happily with a man and not know that he doesn't love you. But that, as God is my witness, is the truth.

"We had marital differences in the beginning as most couples do, but for the past one and a half years, I had truly believed that we had found our happiness. I know I had.

"I now realize when you are deeply in love how blind one can be. Obviously, I was. I will endeavor to use all my strength to survive and understand for the benefit of my two children."

I didn't know what she was talking about. The fact that a year earlier we'd worked out the details of a divorce might have hinted that I didn't love her. Or the fact that we no longer had sex. I understood she was playing her role. But as I read her statement I began to hate her.

It was inevitable that Elizabeth Taylor would be blamed for the breakup of our marriage. She played the role of the beautiful temptress so well in movies that people easily confused it with real life. In her own defense she said, "You can't break up a happy marriage. Debbie and Eddie's never has been."

Later she added, "What am I supposed to do, ask him to go back to her and try? He can't. If he did they'd destroy each other."

It didn't make any difference what she said. Six months earlier the nation had mourned with the beautiful young widow. Now, suddenly, she was accused of being a home-wrecker. The same reporters who had written lovingly about her when Mike died turned on her. Gossip columnist Hedda Hopper, who was supposedly her friend, reported that Elizabeth had responded to criticism about entering a relationship only months after Mike's death by telling her, "Mike is dead and I'm alive."

Mike is dead and I'm alive. Even after everything that happened between Elizabeth and me and that Welsh actor named Burton, just thinking about that quote makes me furious. I was no longer the naive kid I'd been only a few years earlier. I knew what certain reporters would do for a story, but this one even surprised me. In fact, what Elizabeth really said was, "You know how much I loved Mike. I loved him more than my life. But Mike is dead now and I'm alive and the one person who would want me to try and live and be happy is Mike." That's not "Mike is dead and I'm alive."

But that was just the beginning. This became, as one columnist wrote, "the most discussed marriage since the Duke of Windsor married Mrs.

Wallis Simpson." This was the soap opera of the 1950s. A romance that defied the rules of society! I was a married man. My best friend had been dead less than six months and I was sleeping with his widow. It had everything the print media needed to sell copies: the innocent wife, the beautiful vixen and the. . .what? I didn't exactly know how to describe my role. The unfaithful husband? The disloyal friend who seduced a vulnerable widow? The man who would give up his loving family to pursue true love? I knew there was going to be negative public reaction, but I never dreamed we would be subjected to such unrelenting and vicious attacks. But that's what sold newspapers.

For a time we averaged about 7,000 nasty letters a week, from furious housewives to Ku Klux Klan chapter presidents. We received voodoo dolls with pins stuck in them. Newspapers reported that TV viewers considered me immoral and refused to let me into their living rooms. The ratings for my Chesterfield show, never great, fell rapidly, and former fans organized an "Eddie-Liz boycott." When Steve Allen announced that I was going to be a guest on his show, the audience booed. TV audiences don't boo dictators, but me they booed. Columnists wrote that my career was already over, pointing out that I hadn't had a hit record in several years, the one movie I'd made had flopped, and my TV show was not a big hit. And my pal Jack O'Brian pointed out, "Eddie never was too intellectually bright." It seemed like the whole world was against us. Day after day it got worse. I became the worst husband in the world. Even years later, after President Kennedy had been assassinated, Jackie Kennedy told a reporter, "Anyone who is against me will look like a rat—unless I run off with Eddie Fisher." And Debbie continued grieving as publicly as possible, although at times she told columnists that she didn't blame me, she blamed Elizabeth for stealing me away, or she blamed Sinatra and Dean Martin for corrupting me with their drinking and gambling. She made it clear that she would welcome me back, explaining how lucky I was "to be loved by two women." And she posed forlornly for various magazines, including one photo with the kids and a dog, which was captioned, "Can't Daddy be with us all the time?" Meanwhile, she continued to work, starring in the ironically named movie, *The Mating Game*. A second movie she had planned to make, *How Good Girls Get Married*, did not go into production.

The favorable and sympathetic publicity was wonderful for Debbie's career, and within a year her annual income had soared from less than $75,000 to almost $1 million. As an aging ingenue she was having difficulty finding suitable roles, but as the center of all those headlines she became a very bankable actress.

One of the few actresses in Hollywood doing better than Debbie was Elizabeth. The publicity didn't hurt her career, either. *Cat on a Hot Tin Roof*, which was released about a month after our affair became public, was a big hit. She was second to Glenn Ford—with whom Debbie was co-starring in *The Gazebo*—as the leading box-office attraction. And she was nominated for an Academy Award as Best Actress.

Only my career was damaged. But I didn't care. I wasn't worried about my career. I figured that as long as that sound still came out of my throat I'd figure out how to earn a living. The only thing in the world that mattered to me was Elizabeth.

I wanted to marry Elizabeth, but Debbie told reporters that she didn't believe in quick divorces, that she wanted to give me a chance to come to my senses. Well, I had come to my senses; that's why I'd finally left her. Would I have left Debbie if Elizabeth and I hadn't fallen in love? Absolutely, but probably not at that time. I was already leading an independent life and until there was a reason to divorce Debbie, I probably would have stayed with her and our children. Knowing me as well I do now, there is no doubt that if it hadn't been Elizabeth someone else would have provided the reason for me to leave.

In those days unmarried people who lived together "lived in sin." Or, as in our case, Beverly Hills. At first we lived secretly in the Beverly Hills home of Elizabeth's agent, Kurt Frings, and his wife, Ketti. We spent most of our time in a small room up several flights of stairs in which Ketti did her writing. The room didn't even have real beds. But that was our "love nest," our "womb with a view." Reporters were practically living in front of the Fringes' home. To avoid the media we had to sneak in and out, usually lying on the back seat of a car driven by people like Roddy McDowall. Escaping with Debbie, hiding out with Elizabeth—love was a lot more complicated than I'd believed.

We didn't care where we stayed so long as we were together. This was the first time in my life I had felt so complete, so content. I'd spent my life in motion, continually moving toward something bigger, something better. Finally I felt as if I had arrived. I believed completely that we were meant to be together, that I was the one man in the world who truly understood her, and that we would be together forever. Our romance dominated my life. Being with Elizabeth took precedence over everything, including my career. I think that was the biggest mistake I made in my life, and considering some of the other mistakes I've made, that's quite an admission. But I don't regret a moment of it. From the second I found Elizabeth at her swimming pool and she turned and looked at me, I knew I was going to love her for the rest of my life.

At times I've been asked to explain my incredible attraction to Elizabeth Taylor. But never by someone who knew her. I guess the answer is that she was Elizabeth Taylor. I've never known anyone remotely like her. I'm not sure there ever has been anyone like her. She was a star of screen and life, a force who refused to allow anything, absolutely anything, to get in her way. "Remember, Eddie," she always told me, "when you want something, just scream and yell."

She was smart and funny and beautiful. And sexy. Very, very sexy. Sexually she was every man's dream; she had the face of an angel and the morals of a truck driver. Among those things that she wanted when she wanted it was sex, and I was always happy to play my role. Happy? We couldn't keep our hands off each other. We'd make love three, four, five times a day. Elizabeth was daring, she craved excitement: We'd make love in the swimming pool, on Mexican beaches, under waterfalls, in the back seat of a limousine on the way home from a party. There is nothing more erotic than a moonlit beach and Elizabeth Taylor. We fit together as perfect sexually as we did mentally.

Her figure was three children old by then, but I never noticed any imperfections. I was entranced by her natural beauty. I always felt she was most beautiful in the mornings, before she put on any makeup, when she radiated a different kind of beauty. I loved making love with her in the morning. Her idol was the Italian movie star Anna Magnani, who was known for her earthy sexuality, and Elizabeth was earthy, but she was much prettier than Anna Magnani.

And perhaps most enticing of all, she wanted to be with me as desperately as I wanted to be with her. Elizabeth picked me; without her encouragement I never would have pursued her. Contrary to that beautiful old standard, she made me love her, and I wanted to do it. The only question I've ever had about that was when she decided we would be together. Once that decision was made, she planned our entire relationship. She knew how unhappy I was with Debbie; she knew I was available to her. Elizabeth knew her power over men. She knew Eddie Fisher was not going to be able to resist Elizabeth Taylor. People have also asked why she picked me. There were several reasons for that, I think: I was considered to be a handsome and very successful man; I was the best friend of the man she loved; we were compatible in every way; and when she desperately needed someone I happened to be right there.

She was always in control of our relationship; she always held the power. I didn't care—I was getting what I wanted. I never challenged her. I couldn't challenge her. Elizabeth always had a problem with pills and alcohol, for example, but I overlooked it. Overlooked it? Twice I literally caught her when she passed out cold; she once passed out between words in a conversation. It was like catching a dead person. She was very lucky she hadn't been seriously hurt. Obviously I was very worried about her. Dr. Kennamer suggested I get her to a psychiatrist. Believe me, there was as much chance that I was going to be able to convince Elizabeth to see a psychiatrist as there was of Debbie and I going to Niagara Falls on a second honeymoon. Me, telling someone else to see a psychiatrist. I was really the wrong person to do that. But I had to try. One night we were in our little love nest. We'd made love and we were having a drink and I was reading love poems aloud to her. As I did I started thinking about Dr. Kennemar's advice and said to her, "Elizabeth, what would you think about going to see a psychiatrist?"

As it turned out, not very much. She erupted. She started screaming at me. She was hysterical, maybe she even threw something at me. She got out of bed, totally naked, and ran down the stairs. I ran right after her. She got into her Cadillac and turned on the engine. It was crazy, this hysterical naked woman trying to drive while I ran alongside the car, holding on to her door. I was begging her to stop, telling her, "It's not you, it's me. I'll go to the psychiatrist. I'll go, I'll go, it's me. . . ."

We made up as we always made up: by making love.

There is a price to pay for this kind of love, and I paid it. But it was never a one-sided relationship. Believe me, Elizabeth loved me as completely as I loved her. We vowed to each other that we would never be

apart. That when one of us was working, the other one would not work.
It was a childish pledge, the kind of promise children make in junior
high school, but we meant it—and for a long time we were faithful to
that vow. She trusted me to make professional decisions for her and she
listened to me when I told her what to do. At one point we decided we
would co-produce her movies—I negotiated multi-picture deals for her—
to ensure we would always be together. And she was just as supportive
of my career, attending my nightclub performances, coming to the studio
when I recorded, she was always there for me. Ours was very much a
mutual passion.

We stayed at the house in Beverly Hills as long as possible. I would
have stayed in our little room forever, but we were living under siege.
We were desperate for privacy. This was 1958, so we couldn't live together openly. I rented an apartment for myself on Sunset Boulevard—
I went there for a housewarming party, left in the middle, and never saw
that place again—and a beautiful Spanish villa in Bel Air where I actually lived with Elizabeth. It was owned by actress Linda Christian, who
had lived there with her husband, Tyrone Power. For some reason Tyrone
Power had kept his own small bedroom, but there was no bed in it. I
didn't have my own room. My room was wherever Elizabeth was.

Elizabeth lived in fear that photographers were going to sneak into
the house and take pictures of us making love. I thought she was over-
reacting, that even journalists respected some boundaries of privacy. It
was incredible that after all those years I could still have been that naive.
So we were always very circumspect, even around our own house. Although I thought a lot of it was unnecessary, in retrospect this was nothing more than basic training for what was to come two years later.

I don't really remember how we spent so much time doing nothing,
but the days just sped by. When we went out it was usually to a friend's
house or a restaurant like Chasen's, where our privacy could be protected. We rarely went out in public, I mean, what was Elizabeth going
to do, go to the supermarket? On occasion we'd sneak out to a local
movie theater and sit in the dark touching each other. One weekend I
brought her to Philadelphia to meet my mother. My mother loved her
instantly. They acted like two little old Jewish women. Elizabeth knew
how to charm just about anybody, both men and women. I can close my

Dancing with Joanie Wynne,
my first love.
Grossinger's

Princess Margaret sent me a note before
I went on: "Please don't be frightened. I'll be
leading the applause."

bottom right: Milton Blackstone and me beneath an
ad for one of my shows at the Palladium.
You can see the "die Fis" of "Eddie Fisher."

The posters for one of my Carnegie Hall performances.

Already being upstaged by Carrie

top left: From my time in Korea. The fellow driving the jeep, Art Friedman, was killed the next day.

bottom left: Me with my parents at Grossinger's, for a special sneak preview of the stinker *Bundle of Joy*.

top: That's me with Jack Benny (far left), George Jessel (next to Benny), Frank Sinatra, and George Raft (second from the right), at the Friar's Club.

bottom: Me and Frank.

Me and
Elizabeth
during
happier
times.

bottom:
Some kid,
lounging back-
stage at the
Copacabana,
1947.

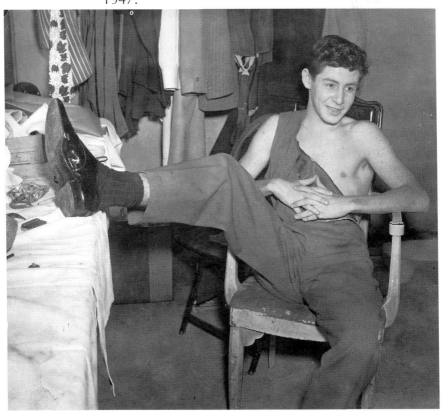

Dinner with Carrie and Paul Simon.
Judie Burstein

eyes and see her sitting on my mother's lap—and she was very skinny at the time! Elizabeth and I went ice-skating that weekend and she fell on the ice and hurt herself. She banged up her knee so badly I had to take her to the hospital.

I spent considerable time buying her presents. Making her happy was what made me happy. I was obsessed with her—I couldn't buy enough for her. I guess that was the Mike in me. I gave her jewels and clothes and furs. How many jewels were enough for the woman I loved? Just a few more than she had. For her twenty-seventh birthday I had a handbag made studded with twenty-seven diamonds spelling out LIZ. I never called her Liz, but even I couldn't afford ELIZABETH. I had designers bring racks of dresses to the house to allow her to choose whatever she wanted. For our engagement I gave her a large diamond ring and a forty-carat diamond bracelet: And in return she gave me a beautiful watch, jeweled cuff links, a jade ring, and, most of all, the pleasure of her company. I always felt I got the best of the deal.

After several months Debbie and I worked out the details of our divorce. Forty years after we broke up, Debbie wrote, "All three of my husbands have taken my money." Forty years later she was still claiming I took her money. Even considering inflation, that's not exactly correct. In our agreement Debbie got the $150,000 house, $40,000 a year in alimony and child support, securities, a $100,000 insurance policy on my life, a trailer, camping equipment, a Jeep, a station wagon, and six life-insurance policies on her life. She even got a Geiger counter, as well as the cash we had on deposit. She also got to keep all her own property, including a home in Palm Springs. Basically, I kept ownership of my companies and music royalties, as well as the two houses I'd bought for my family in Philadelphia. That's how I took her money.

After the divorce hearing, her close friend Camille Williams told reporters, "Debbie was deeply shocked." Deeply shocked at what? It just never ended. Even the settlement wasn't enough for Debbie. She would call me in the middle of a rehearsal and in the most charming way ask for more: "My brother smashed up his station wagon, can I have the station wagon?" Anything, Debbie, anything. I was just so happy to be free. But that's how I took her money.

Debbie had volunteered to raise Carrie and Todd in the Jewish faith.

That was never a subject of negotiation. I didn't ask her to do it, but I thought it was extremely nice of her. I was aware that I had forfeited my right to make that decision by leaving Debbie. But after she married Harry Karl, I went over to see the kids one day—admittedly there weren't too many such days—and she told me she had changed her mind about that because "I don't love you anymore." Now Harry was also Jewish, but he didn't mind that the kids were being raised as Christians. He told me he'd donated $7,500 to the church they attended, explaining, "Would I give anybody seventy-five hundred dollars if they were anti-Semitic?" I had no idea what he was talking about. Anti-Semitic? This was Beverly Hills. In Beverly Hills even the ministers were practically Jewish.

Debbie and I reached our divorce settlement in February, but under California law I had to wait another year before I could remarry. Debbie wanted to hold me to that. "I feel a year is a short time to wait," she said, pointing out, "I was engaged for a year and a half." I had thought that eventually people would get bored reading about us, but that hadn't happened. Instead, everywhere Elizabeth went photographers followed, and everything we did was reported. If we stayed home the press wrote that we were being ostracized by the Hollywood community; if we went out they wrote that we were flaunting our relationship. As Debbie and I once had been the poster couple for wholesome family values, Elizabeth and I might have been pictured on a wanted poster as moral outlaws. There was enormous pressure on us to get married, but legally I couldn't do that. There was one loophole: If I established residence in Nevada by living there for six weeks, with Debbie's permission we could be divorced a second time and Elizabeth and I could be married. I would have divorced Debbie as often as necessary, but for a long time she refused to grant permission. The timing was perfect. The following April I was to begin a six-week engagement at the Tropicana in Las Vegas; if Debbie would consent we could be married then.

Meanwhile Elizabeth had decided she wanted to convert to Judaism. That was not my idea, nor was it, as newspapers reported, a tribute to Mike. In truth, Mike had stopped her from doing it while they were married. It made no difference to me, in fact I didn't think it was a particularly good thing for her to do. I was well aware how much anti-Semitism existed in the world; this would give many of those people who already hated her even more reason to do so. I didn't even know what religion she was converting from. Her mother was a Christian Scientist, a religion that preaches self-healing by mental and spiritual means and forbids practitioners from consulting doctors or using drugs. No doctors? No pills? Well, that was definitely the wrong religion for Elizabeth. She'd married Nicky Hilton in a Catholic church and that marriage had been a failure, so why not try a synagogue? I did think it would be nice for my mother; finally I was marrying a nice Jewish girl, even if that Jewish girl was Elizabeth Taylor.

Her conversion became something for us to do together; go to a screening at Frank's house, play with her children, convert to Judaism. I was her primary teacher. I would read aloud the books she was supposed to read and then I would explain everything I'd read. She really did learn the religious and cultural history of the Jews, the customs and traditions, the reasons for our beliefs. And while at first I hadn't taken the whole thing seriously, as we were doing it I changed my mind; it was thrilling to study the history of the Jews through Elizabeth's eyes. These lessons forced me to remember where I had come from.

In April, just before I was to begin my engagement at the Tropicana, Rabbi Max Nussbaum supervised Elizabeth's conversion to Reform Judaism. Her stunned parents watched the ceremony with about as much enthusiasm as they would have witnessed their house burning down. The newspapers ran the story of her conversion as frontpage news. That was big news: another Jew in Hollywood. One paper explained her conversion by reporting she'd had a nervous breakdown and was locked in a mental hospital. We were so angry we discussed suing that paper for libel—instead we went out for dinner.

Oy, was she a Jew. In my dressing room the night I opened at the Tropicana a reporter overheard me calling her Elisheba. "It's her Hebrew name," I explained. She had chosen Elisheba Rachel as her religious name. Being supportive, Elisheba began singing the first words of an ancient prayer in Hebrew.

When someone congratulated me on my performance I explained, "It's simple. I'm in love."

To which Elish—Elizabeth added, "This is really a *tsimmis*, isn't it?" Challenged to spell it by a dubious reporter, she proudly spelled, *"Tsimmis*, t-s-i-m-m-i-s. It's a tumult, t-u-m-u-l-t."

Like so many other passions in Elizabeth's life, being Jewish didn't really last very long. It was sort of like a test religion. After she'd converted we never went to synagogue and only once did we celebrate the high holidays. And I remember being in Norway several years after we'd divorced and seeing a magazine with her on the cover—wearing a lovely cross.

Officially I was staying at the Tropicana in Las Vegas, but in fact I had rented the Hidden Well Ranch, the Cactus Castle, as it was known, for $500 a week. We stayed there with all of Elizabeth's kids, their pets, her servants, occasional business associates, and some friends. The house was about a half mile from the road, far enough, I thought, to provide us with some privacy. But the ranch was not well-hidden enough, as photographers used long lenses to spy on our every move.

The Tropicana engagement was my first major live appearance since the scandal had become public, and I really did not know how the audience was going to respond to me. Because Elizabeth was going to be there, the media descended on Vegas. As I walked into the hotel on opening night I was very disappointed to see five pickets parading in front carrying signs reading LIZ GO HOME and LIZ LEAVE TOWN. When I confronted them they put down their signs and walked away, one woman explaining she had to take a coffee break, while a man said he had to take a whiskey break.

I was quite nervous when I walked out onstage opening night, until I looked down and saw Elizabeth smiling at me. "I opened here two years ago," I began. "Since then, nothing much has happened." The audience laughed, maybe even a little louder and longer than that joke was worth, but it was their way of letting me know they were with me. This was years before Las Vegas became a theme park with gambling, and the people who came there were pretty sophisticated. The gamblers have always loved me. These were not the type of people who condemned our relationship; they were more likely to be betting whether or not it would last.

Opening night, with Elizabeth sitting directly in front of the stage lovingly looking up at me, I sang standards to her like "Tonight," "It Happens Every Spring," Eddie Cantor's classic "Makin' Whoopie"—which begins "Another bride, another groom. . . ."—and at her request, "To Love and Be Loved."

Following my performance Elizabeth and I met with reporters for the first time. Asked how we felt about the massive amount of criticism we'd received, Elizabeth explained, "We respect public opinion, but you can't live by it. If we lived by it, Eddie and I would have been terribly unhappy through all this turmoil. But I can shamelessly say that we have been terribly happy. I am literally rising above it."

Well, maybe not literally, but we were so happy together it felt like we were walking on air. We would stay up all night, every night, just talking, making love, reading, playing. There was an all-night television talk show on at the time and on occasion we would call the host pretending to be other people and comment on our relationship. Sometimes we supported ourselves, other times we condemned our actions. We thought we were being very clever. We'd finally get to sleep about ten o'clock in the morning because I had to sing in the evening. Elizabeth came to every show, sitting in front of the stage to see me, but mostly to be seen by the audience.

The only problem was her health. Once again, she had to go to the hospital. For several days she ran a very high temperature and finally had to enter Cedars of Lebanon Hospital for minor throat surgery. Her jaw had to be unlocked so her infected throat could be cauterized. It was painful, but several hours after she came out of surgery we were eating takeout chili from Chasen's and washing it down with champagne.

When Debbie returned from Spain, where she had been making a picture accompanied by her friend Camille Williams, a mob of about fifty reporters descended on her. Just about the first question she was asked was, "Will you contest the divorce? America is waiting!"

America was waiting for Eddie Fisher to get married? Fidel Castro had overthrown Batista in Cuba, the Chinese Communists were invading Tibet, and America was waiting for me to get married. Debbie told reporters, "It comes as very much a surprise to me. The position in which I was placed made it necessary to give my consent."

I divorced Debbie and married Elizabeth the day I finished my run at the Tropicana. The divorce took ten minutes and cost ten dollars. I had no cash with me, so I had to borrow the money from Bernie Rich. It was worth every penny of his money. I tried to pay for my marriage license in gambling chips, but the license bureau also insisted on cash.

It was a typical two-rabbi Jewish ceremony. As usual, Elizabeth was late for her own wedding. We invited very few people, among them our parents and some friends. Mike Todd Jr. was my best man. We were married under the *chuppah*, a canopy, and as is traditional, at the end of the ceremony I stomped on a wineglass.

Several hours after the ceremony we flew to Los Angeles, happily singing Jewish folk songs with the other passengers and signing autographs. We were going to honeymoon in Spain, where Elizabeth was to shoot exterior scenes for *Suddenly, Last Summer*, as well as make an unbilled cameo appearance in Mike Todd Jr.'s Smell-O-Vision classic, *Scent of Mystery*. As it turned out, the scent emanating from that film wasn't a mystery.

Producer Sam Spiegel loaned us his yacht to sail the Mediterranean for a week. Our cabin was a replica of Christopher Columbus's cabin aboard the *Santa Maria*. It was awful. Our bed was built into the prow of the ship, and every time it pitched forward we would slide up the bed and when it fell back we would slide down. We had a hard time making love.

We stopped in several ports: Saint Tropez, Portofino, and in Cannes we stayed with Aly Khan and his mistress. Wherever we dropped anchor large crowds of reporters and photographers materialized as if by magic. Of course I sympathized with them, having to traipse all over the Riviera, sitting in cafés, waiting at the beach just in case we docked. For many of them, I suspect, this was the assignment of their lifetime.

We ended up in Torremolinos, Spain, where we were met by Elizabeth's children. I really wanted to impress them, maybe because I felt I was losing my own kids. One Sunday afternoon Elizabeth and I took them to the local bull ring. We were having a wonderful time, right up until the moment they asked for volunteers. This was the afternoon I discovered why there are no great Jewish matadors.

After watching several local men make a few simple passes at young bulls I decided it didn't look that difficult or dangerous. Maybe I'd been sitting in the sun too long, but I found myself asking the kids, "How would you like to see Daddy fight the bull?"

They were kids, what did they know about temporary insanity? "Yes, please, oh yes."

Elizabeth was a bit more sensible, threatening, "You do that, I'll break your fucking head."

In addition to all the normally insane things I've done with my life, on occasion I would do something stupidly insane. Going into a bull ring with a live bull has to be one of the stupidest things I've ever done, although it did enable me to answer that classic musical question, What kind of fool am I? Actually, the matador was supposed to hold the cape and I was supposed to stand close to him as the bull made its pass, but that wasn't good enough for me. I didn't want to share the honor with the matador. I insisted he give me his red cape and stand out of the way. After a brief argument, he saw that I was determined to be a hero, shrugged his shoulders, and moved away.

I held the cape in my hands. I wasn't the slightest bit scared. I confidently snapped the cape through the air several times as if I knew what I was doing. "AAH!" I screamed defiantly, just as I had heard the real matadors do. Then I looked up and saw the bull standing about 100 feet away, pawing the ground, snorting. And suddenly I thought, What the fuck am I doing? The bull lowered his head, maybe there was no steam coming out of his nostrils, but he looked very big; very, very big. It occurred to me right at that moment that the bull wasn't in on the joke. Nobody had cued the bull; all he was seeing was a skinny man standing there holding a bright red cape.

When the bull started running toward me I spread the cape as wide as possible—but this bull didn't seem the slightest bit interested in the cape. Apparently this bull was more attracted to skinny Jewish singers than red capes. He just came right for me. "Aah," I squealed. I was totally paralyzed. I could not move a muscle. I think Elizabeth saw her entire sex life about to disappear.

Until that moment, I don't think I ever truly appreciated how large a bull is up close. And getting closer. Incredibly, the bull pinned me between his horns and with his head pushed me backwards against the wooden barricade. He didn't even break my skin.

I have been lucky all my life, so lucky that I wanted to take another pass at this bull. Lucky, not smart. But I felt I had to try again, because the entire arena was laughing at me. Again the bull pawed the ground as I snapped my cape. Again he charged at me. But this time I stepped out of his way and made a beautiful pass. And as soon as that bull raced by me, I threw the cape into the air and ran out of the ring. It wasn't until I was in the tunnel on the way back to my seat that I started breathing again, and realized what a fool I'd made of myself. Although I was a fool in one big piece.

The only thing that marred our honeymoon was a phone call from Louella Parsons, who asked, "Did you know that your son just had a hernia operation in Palm Springs?" When I told her I knew nothing about it, she admitted, "Debbie called me to try to find you."

Debbie had to call one of the most famous gossip columnists in the world to find me? How about reading any newspaper in America? How about calling my agent, or my business manager, or even my mother? Instead she called a newspaper columnist. And by the time she placed that call the operation was done and Todd was perfectly fine.

There is no way I can defend my actions as a father to Carrie or Todd. I wasn't there, I was never there. When they make the list of the worst fathers, I know my name will be right on the top. But did Debbie really have to contact me that way? It was so typical, so absolutely typical.

Our honeymoon lasted several years. Most couples return from their honeymoon and settle into normal life. But with Elizabeth there was no such thing as normal life. The only thing predictable about our life was that it would be chaos. With Elizabeth, something was always happening, and if it wasn't, she made it happen. If nothing was happening, she would start a fight. Every day was a surprise, and I never knew from day to day what to expect, but I didn't mind that. I loved her, so nothing else mattered.

Suddenly, Last Summer, in which Elizabeth co-starred with Katharine Hepburn and Monty Clift, was directed by Joe Manckiewicz, who loved women as much as I did. And maybe loved more of them. He was in love with Jean Simmons, he was in love with Judy Garland, and while Elizabeth was working with him I heard rumors that he was in love with her. I heard rumors that Elizabeth was having an affair with him. I knew that wasn't true. When Elizabeth was making that movie I was on the set every day and with her every night. We had made a pact never to be apart and I was fulfilling that obligation.

Suddenly, Last Summer was a typical Tennessee Williams story, your basic mix of homosexuality, cannibalism, and pedophilia, with a lobotomy thrown in for drama. Joe Manckiewicz did an incredible job getting that picture made. Satisfying the needs of both Elizabeth and Katharine Hepburn required a magician even more than a director. Acting is a very strange profession for a grown-up, and there is no right or wrong way of doing it. Every actor has his or her own method for giving their best possible performance and it's the director's job to create the environment necessary for them to be able to do their best work. Hepburn and Elizabeth were both brilliant actresses, but they worked quite differently. Hepburn was a disciplined actress, always precisely on time, always well prepared. She had perfected all the nuances of her character before she arrived on the set. Elizabeth was a natural actress who didn't have a wealth of training, so she depended almost completely on her innate ability. She showed up on the set when she got there. Elizabeth and Manckiewicz were always at odds, battling over nothing. But somehow Joe Manckiewicz managed to get great performances out of both his leading ladies. Three years later, in desperation, I would remember that and turn to him for help.

He even got an acceptable performance from Monty Clift, who was continually drunk or stoned. He was a lost little boy, no longer living in this world. But Manckiewicz held it all together.

As Elizabeth had been with me during my six-week engagement at the Tropicana, I stayed with her for the months it took to shoot *Suddenly, Last Summer*. My TV show had been canceled and I had nothing to do except make sure she showed up on the set on time and prepared. Although in reality I was ceding control of my life to Elizabeth, in my mind I believed I was more in control than ever before. I thought I was building a new career for myself as a producer. I'd learned a tremendous amount from Mike when he produced *Around the World in 80 Days*. I kept busy meeting with studio executives to discuss movies Elizabeth might make or I might produce. In fact, my real job was keeping Elizabeth happy. I was confident I could produce major motion pictures involving hundreds of people, but keeping Elizabeth happy, now *that* was a tough job.

My own career was disappearing. My singing, which had once been the thing I lived for, was becoming more of a well-paid hobby. Ironically, I thought the quality of my voice was better than it had ever been. It was richer and deeper, full-bodied. But the quality of my voice no longer mattered to audiences, who came to see me more than hear me. Actually, they came to see me with Elizabeth. Maybe we weren't the most beloved celebrity couple in America, but we certainly were the best known and the most controversial. Elizabeth and I had become a two-act: Her role

was sitting directly in front of the stage looking gorgeous as I sang meaningful love songs to her. And everybody in the audience was in on our
act. In the spring of 1959 I played the Desert Inn in Las Vegas for several
weeks in preparation for a four-week engagement at the Empire Room
in New York's Waldorf-Astoria.

The Empire Room was an important engagement for me. It was my
first major appearance in New York in several years; a lot of columnists
were describing it as my "comeback." It hadn't occurred to me that I'd
been away long enough to have to come back. But my record sales had
fallen drastically, my TV show had been canceled, and I was no longer
making guest appearances on other shows. So maybe it was a comeback.

Opening night was a major event in New York City. The Waldorf had
to squeeze extra tables on the dance floor and people were still turned
away. The waiting line for tables stretched through the lobby almost to
the sidewalk. Elizabeth invited seventy of our closest friends, including
Gloria Vanderbilt, former heavyweight champion Ingemar Johansson,
and Aly Khan. Caviar was piled on the tables. Unfortunately, a group of
fifteen people, headed by a Brooklyn dentist, had seen my first show and
refused to leave. One of them said to Elizabeth, "Listen, lady, we knew
Eddie when he was a waiter at Grossinger's, and our money is as good
as yours." It might have been as good, but I doubt that he had as much
of it. Elizabeth resolved the problem by paying their entire check.

I sang twenty-two songs, ranging from "Tonight" to "Hava Nagilah."
I did a Jolson medley, I sang love songs to Elizabeth, I sang until two in
the morning and still the audience wanted more and more. I received
several standing ovations, Elizabeth claimed she "applauded all the hair-
pins out of my hair," and *Time* magazine decided I was "an undisputed
smash." The first of my many comebacks was a success.

We celebrated our six-month anniversary backstage. I gave her a mink
sweater. "You wear it with slacks or something casual," she decided,
and she gave me diamond-studded cuff links. Then she announced to
the press that she wasn't pregnant.

The only problem was her health. Once again we had to go to the
hospital. If you think you've read that before, you're just beginning to
understand what it was like to be married to Elizabeth. Thanksgiving
afternoon, during the second week of my run at the Waldorf, Elizabeth
collapsed. After suffering with a persistent cough for several weeks, she

started having difficulty breathing. On the advice of the esteemed physician, Dr. Max Jacobson, we rushed her to Columbia-Presbyterian Hospital by ambulance. In the ambulance she was struggling to breathe, but as we approached the hospital she suddenly sat up on the stretcher. It was as if a miracle had taken place. "Help me," she said.

I would have done anything for her.

"Get me my lip gloss," she commanded, and proceeded to put on her makeup. I understood—what woman wants to look bad when she goes into the emergency room?

She was diagnosed with a viral form of double pneumonia, and spent several nights in the hospital sleeping under an oxygen tent. I was very frightened; I was terrified she was going to die. Of course, this was just practice for the crisis that was going to come. I took a room down the hall and lived there between shows. I never stopped worrying. That had become my real area of expertise, worrying about Elizabeth. It was while she was in the hospital that she decided she wanted to have her fallopian tubes untied so that we might have a child together. Lip gloss, another child, whatever she wanted I wanted her to have. The doctor told her, "If you want it, Elizabeth, it will be done." But for some reason it could not be done.

As a direct result of the scandal, the studios were offering Elizabeth more money than any actress had ever been paid. She pleaded with MGM President Sol Siegel to release her from her contract, telling him she needed the money for her children. Siegel replied, "Miss Taylor, all sentiment in this business died a long time ago." Finally, he agreed to release Elizabeth from her contract if she starred in one additional picture for MGM at her old salary of $125,000.

The script they picked for her to do was *Butterfield 8*, just about the most exploitive story they could find. It was the story of a nymphomaniac who falls in love with a married man and almost breaks up his marriage. Hmm, now where did that concept come from? There was a line in the script where this character claims that she is sleeping her way through the alphabet by college—and had worked her way through to Yale. At a climactic moment of the film she has to admit to her mother, "I was the slut of all times." The best thing I can say about the script was it wasn't as bad as *Bundle of Joy*.

MGM warned her that if she refused to do the picture they would suspend her and she would not be able to work for two years. She was outraged. Livid. She hated them for making her play this particular part. Some days she swore she wouldn't do it—and few people swore like Elizabeth—but other days she realized she had no choice. Finally she told the producer, Pando Berman, that she hated the script, that she would be as uncooperative as possible and that the studio would regret forcing her to do it. But she would do it, she said, if they replaced David Janssen, who was cast to play her best friend, with me. The character I was supposed to play was named Eddie, but because I was playing the role they changed his name to Steve. That was about the extent of their creativity.

At home Elizabeth and I referred to the picture as *Butterball 4*. Pando Berman might not have been the worst human being who ever lived, I mean there was Attila the Hun, but even by the standards of Hollywood he was a miserable human being. He hated actors. In fact, he hated everybody except himself. To try to save the script, Elizabeth enlisted friends like Tennessee Williams, Paddy Chayefsky, Christopher Isherwood, Joe Mankiewicz, Truman Capote, and Daniel Taradash to make suggestions and do some rewriting. They'd come to the house at night and work with us. Because the writers' guild was on strike they couldn't claim any credit, so Elizabeth told Berman we were doing the rewriting. The director, Danny Mann, filmed some of these new scenes, including a pretty explicit love scene between Elizabeth and me.

When Elizabeth had been rushed to the hospital in New York City a reporter asked Lenny Gaines if I was actually as upset as I appeared to be. "Absolutely," Lenny replied. "Eddie's not that good an actor."

I think that was pretty accurate. But making love to Elizabeth did not require any acting ability. I had had plenty of practice, but still I insisted on rehearsing. We actually made love on the set; I didn't have an orgasm, but we did everything else. We did it right. For the craft of acting, of course. Knowing the camera was filming us was a tremendous turn-on. We were so happy to be working together that we were giddy, like kids, and having sex on camera was the highlight.

Our love scene ended up on the cutting room floor. It was one of the sexiest scenes ever filmed to that point and Pando Berman insisted it be cut out of his movie. He refused to change one line of his script. "No actors change any script of mine," he said. He had some of the most talented screenwriters in the world working for him—for free—and he rejected them. He just dropped their work in a wastebasket.

The director, Daniel Mann, lost control very early. He tried to deal with Elizabeth as her equal, and that was a big mistake. Mann believed in method acting, in which the performer attempts to become the character. We used to make jokes about that. "Act like a tree—and leave." It's a highly disciplined form and requires a lot of training to make it work. Elizabeth's method was to show up and allow her talent to take over. And me, I just wanted to play with Elizabeth. So there was a lot of conflict on the set. One day, I remember Mann very seriously telling Elizabeth, "Make believe you're fucking this faucet. That's the expression I want."

Elizabeth looked at him like he was insane, then walked off the set.

Elizabeth and I both hated the movie. The only publicity she did for it was to tell reporters, "I think the picture stinks." As for my performance, she gave me a huge statue of the patron saint of actors, St. Genesius, inscribed, *If you win the Academy Award before I do, I'll break your neck.* The reviews were mixed. "Brandy, martinis, and brittle dialogue flow like water," wrote the *New York Times* critic Bosley Crowther. He hated my performance. "Only Eddie Fisher. . .seems like something dragged in from left field. He. . .acts as if he wishes they would all go away and leave him alone." I actually got a good review from the *New York Herald-Tribune*, whose critic wrote, "Eddie Fisher looks surprisingly comfortable in the role." And that critic didn't even see my love scene.

When Elizabeth had converted to Judaism the previous April the Arab world had banned her movies. In response she'd said, "Now that I've taken the Hebrew faith, I won't be able to float down the Nile in a barge— something I always wanted to do." And we all laughed. Elizabeth the queen, floating down the Nile. Who did she think she was, Cleopatra?

CHAPTER SEVEN

For Elizabeth's twenty-seventh birthday I threw a surprise party for her at Kurt Fring's house. I think the biggest surprise was that I managed to get her there only two hours late. After dinner we were all sitting on the living room floor and I stood up to propose a birthday toast. "I didn't know what love really was until I knew Elizabeth," I began, or something like that, and then I proceeded to tell her how much I loved her.

When I finished the room was silent for a moment, then Lana Turner, *Lana Turner*, one of the most beautiful and desirable women in the world, said softly and sadly, "Oh, I wish somebody loved me like that."

I knew that Elizabeth and I had found a very special kind of love, a love that was going to last a lifetime. And at times being with Elizabeth three years did seem like a lifetime. I'd once assumed, naively, that the scandal that had erupted when I left Debbie to marry Elizabeth was the most difficult period I'd ever live through. I lost every bit of privacy. I couldn't walk out of a room without being confronted by a reporter or photographer. But it was nothing really, just a speck compared to what was to happen when Elizabeth starred in the most expensive, most elaborate, most publicized, criticized, and analyzed movie ever made, *Cleopatra*.

I've always believed that the making of this movie would make a much better movie than the movie itself. It changed the lives of just about every person who was associated with it, it destroyed careers and marriages. Even by the most outrageous Hollywood standards it got completely out of control, and it almost bankrupted one of the great Hollywood studios.

So considering all that, I guess it's fair to say this was not one of my best ideas. The whole thing started when the legendary producer Walter Wanger, who was running a studio when they were still making silent pictures, decided to remake the story of Cleopatra. Following the great success of *Ben-Hur*, studios were looking for spectacular stories; they wanted to make "extravaganzas." Particularly if they could make them inexpensively. Cleopatra was a story that had all the elements of great entertainment: love, death, betrayal, and suicide. 20th Century-Fox president Spyros Skouras wanted to make the film with Joan Collins, who was under contract to the studio, as Cleopatra, for $350,000. He suggested filming it on the studio's back lot, using the basic structure from a silent movie version that had starred Theda Bara. Several other actresses were considered for the role, including Brigitte Bardot, Kim Novak, Suzy Parker, Joanne Woodward, Gina Lollobrigida, even Audrey Hepburn, but Wanger insisted that only Elizabeth Taylor could be the Queen of the Nile. Skouras eventually raised the budget to $3 million, and in 1958 that made it an expensive film.

Wanger had sent Elizabeth a rough draft of the script, but she hadn't even read it. The story just didn't interest her. When Elizabeth was shooting *Suddenly, Last Summer* in London, I had nothing to do except be there if she needed me. So I started reading a pile of scripts. Cleopatra was near the top of the pile. The first line of the script read, "On the screen appears her eyes." When I read that, in my mind I visualized Elizabeth's extraordinary violet eyes covering the entire screen. I read five pages. The script was terrible, but I loved that image, "On the screen appears her eyes." Elizabeth was in the bathroom brushing her teeth and I shouted in to her, "Elizabeth, you should do this for a million bucks."

"You're crazy," she said, laughing at my ignorance. Few actors had ever been paid that kind of money. Bill Holden had gotten a million against 10 percent of the gross for *The Bridge on the River Kwai*, but no woman had ever been paid anything close to that. I believed Elizabeth was worth it. I thought she was the only actress capable of bringing the power of Cleopatra to change history to the screen. And I knew Elizabeth as Cleopatra would make the film an event.

When Wanger called us several hours later we told him Elizabeth would do the picture in Europe for $1 million, although payments would be spread over several years for tax purposes. After a brief pause to let that sink in, he said, "I'll get back to you." It seemed like minutes later that he called back—maybe it was two hours—and agreed.

A month later, while I was performing at the Desert Inn, Wanger told Elizabeth that the studio wanted Susan Hayward to play Cleopatra. By then Elizabeth loved the idea of playing a real queen and started crying. "But I want to do it," she said. "Why don't they want me?"

It's the money, Wanger said, the studio wouldn't pay her $1 million. After Elizabeth and I discussed it, she agreed to sign for $750,000 against 10 percent of the gross plus a large expense account and all kinds of perks—we had to have both penthouse suites at the Dorchester in London for the duration of the filming—plus the right to choose her own crew. I don't think I ever knew precisely how much she earned for making the picture, but for our divorce settlement the figure we agreed on was $7 million.

I was paid an additional $125,000, although no one ever told me what my job was. My job description was primarily "Elizabeth's husband." I was to be there just in case she needed me, and to make sure that she got to the set on time and prepared. All Elizabeth had to do to earn her salary was act in the picture. I had to take care of Elizabeth. As it turned out, she had the easier job.

Elizabeth and I were very happy together. We had no real home, living wherever our careers took us. We were like a gypsy caravan. When we had to be somewhere we uprooted her children and all her pets and her secretary, Dick Hanley; her assistants and publicity people and friends; a nurse for the children; hundreds of dresses and pairs of shoes, which were packed in I couldn't even guess how many pieces of luggage, and eventually settled somewhere for the next several months. I bought a lot of houses while we were together. I bought a house in Las Vegas; a magnificent house in Gstaad, Switzerland; a house in Jamaica; and a house in Westchester, New York, but we never really lived in any of them.

From the very beginning everything was wrong with the film. Wanger had been a great producer, but he was an elderly man well past his prime. *Cleopatra* was too much for him at that stage of his career. It really required someone with the vision of a Mike Todd, but the only person with that vision was dead. Skouras was a large, imposing man who was constantly playing with his Greek worry beads—for good reason. Fox was in terrible financial trouble. Television had changed the entertainment industry and the old ways of doing business—the methods that had always worked for Skouras—no longer applied and he didn't know how to change. What I remember most about Skouras is that he kept falling asleep while watching the dailies, the rough footage filmed the day before. It's probably a bad sign when the guy who's putting up the money can't stay awake to watch his movie.

The director was Rouben Mamoulian, who had once been a great director, but he must have been at least seventy-five years old. He had done Garbo's first movie, *Anna Karenina*, he'd directed *Oklahoma!* and *Carousel* on Broadway, revolutionizing the musical theatre, but he was completely wrong for this project.

Peter Finch was cast as Julius Caesar, Stephen Boyd was hired to play Mark Antony, and the budget was raised to $4 million.

The first major mistake they made was deciding to shoot in England. At one point they had intended to make most of the film in Italy, but for financial reasons settled on London. Shooting in England never made any sense, but somehow they had figured out that building massive sets and working a five-day week in London would be cheaper than using some actual Roman backgrounds and working a six-day week in Italy. More importantly, I'd been in England with Elizabeth when she'd made *Suddenly, Last Summer* and I know—oh boy did I know—that the damp weather there was terrible for Elizabeth's health. She'd been sick almost the entire time we had been there. I tried to explain that to them in the nicest way possible, but what does a singer know about the weather? Apparently if you want to know about the weather the right person to ask is a movie producer. Believe me, these people were so busy running around doing everything that nothing got done.

We arrived in London at the end of August 1960, after stopping in Rome to attend the opening ceremonies of the Olympic Games. The one thing that it was impossible to ever forget when you were with Elizabeth Taylor was that you were with Elizabeth Taylor. The world wouldn't let you. Richard Burton once said that he didn't know what fame was until he walked down any street with Elizabeth. Well, he should have been there when she walked into the Olympic stadium. The ceremonies stopped for her. The entire stadium greeted her with a huge ovation. They went wild for her. The years of negative publicity, the accusations of being a home-wrecker, were over. I was so proud to be with her, to be her chosen companion, I didn't even care that behind my back people were starting to refer to me as "Mr. Elizabeth Taylor."

The picture was behind schedule and over budget before it got started. The studio had spent several million dollars constructing elaborate sets, palm trees had been flown in from Hollywood—but the fresh palm fronds had to be shipped from Egypt. They had a problem with seagulls getting in the frame and making too much noise, so someone decided to buy thousands of rotting fish and laid a trail of them to lure the seagulls away from the set. Then serious union problems resulted from Elizabeth's insistence on using her own hairdresser, Sidney Guilaroff, who was not a member of the British hairdressers' union. The union claimed that Elizabeth's insistence on bringing her own hairdresser from America cast aspersions on the ability of British hairdressers and walked off the set, shutting down production for several days until a compromise was reached. And yet all the problems might have been worked out if the weather hadn't gotten bad.

Almost from the day we arrived in London, Elizabeth was sick. She ran a slight fever and none of the doctors we consulted could figure out what was causing it. At first they thought it was a cold, then they decided it was some sort of low-grade viral infection, but no matter what they tried her fever just wouldn't go away. Mamoulian began working around her, shooting scenes with Finch and Boyd or crowd scenes in which she didn't appear. The weather got worse. Elizabeth's health got worse. The picture was falling further behind schedule. She was so sick she couldn't even be fitted for her costumes. And I had absolutely nothing to do but take care of Elizabeth.

The studio dealt with all these problems by deciding to shorten the shooting schedule and lower the budget. I thought I was one of the last completely sane people involved in the whole production—and it was beginning to make me crazy.

By mid-October, for the first time in the year and a half Elizabeth and I had been together, I had to get away from her. I had successfully made the transition from one of the country's most popular singers to Elizabeth's companion and nurse. I was caught in a magnificent trap, and even though I was madly in love with her, it was still a trap. I'd forgotten who I was. Any semblance of the performer I'd been when married to Debbie was gone, long gone. My career had evaporated. The only singing I was doing was around the house.

Elizabeth and I had decided that we would co-produce her pictures after *Cleopatra*. I set up an office in London to look for the right properties. Now I had completely filled Mike's position. We received dozens of scripts for her every day, and most of them were terrible. I got very interested in the story of dancer Isadora Duncan; I was surprised it hadn't been filmed. Her life was a romantic tragedy, just the kind of story Hollywood loves. But as I read more and more about Isadora, it was obvious that the movie would have to feature a lot of dancing. It wasn't the right role for Elizabeth; she could barely walk, she certainly couldn't dance. But she wanted to do it, and if my baby wanted to do it, I wanted her to do it. It was as ridiculous as attempting to film the story of the Queen of the Nile on the Thames.

I'd made a deal to produce four pictures for Warner Brothers. Elizabeth would star in two of them. In October I went back to Hollywood ostensibly to look for properties for Elizabeth, but the truth was I just needed to breathe on my own. She didn't want me to go, she told me I was not living up to our agreement that we would always be together. Later, columnists would write that Elizabeth had begun to realize that our marriage was a mistake, that she had married me in the midst of her despair over Mike's death, but anyone who saw our parting scene would know that was not true. She had a tantrum befitting a queen. She tried all her usual strategies; she cried, she begged, she threatened; and when I walked out the door I felt free, really free for the first time since the day I saw her sitting by her swimming pool. I got as far as the lobby. She had me paged as I left the hotel and swore she would not sleep until she knew that I had landed safely.

I spent three weeks in Los Angeles playing gin, listening to offers, and talking to Elizabeth on the telephone. I wasn't the slightest bit free. We'd speak three, four, five times a day and then again at night. Of course I loved it. I loved being loved by her. Warners gave me an office on the lot—for which they later billed me $60,000—and offered us their best projects. Harold Mirisch wanted Elizabeth to co-star with Paul Newman in *Two for the Seesaw* but he refused to pay her $1 million and wanted her to give 2½ percent of her back-end deal to Paul Newman. He took me into the men's room and told me if I'd settle for $950,000, he'd give me another $50,000 in cash. "Harold," I told him, "Elizabeth won't go for that."

He was shocked—not that I turned down his offer, but that I would tell her about it. "You handle your wife," he said. "I'll handle mine."

I immediately told Elizabeth about this offer. "Tell him to go fuck himself," she said.

I really didn't have the experience to negotiate deals. Milton Blackstone had always done the negotiating for me, but once I realized people were taking me seriously, that I could get away with it, I enjoyed it. I thought it was great. I had always wanted to be in the movies and the fact that I couldn't act hadn't stopped me. I had become a player; I was part of Hollywood royalty. I was having such a good time I didn't even notice that my life was going completely out of control.

Everything was normal when I got back, meaning that Elizabeth was still sick. The picture was now completely shut down. The studio was frantic, but England's best doctors, including Lord Evans, the Queen's physician, had no idea what was causing this fever. I was beginning to have my own theory. I was beginning to wonder if the real cause of her illness was her desire for painkilling pills. She'd be popping pills and drinking most of the day. One Sunday, I remember, I found a pill I'd never seen before on her nightstand. It was round, a little ball of medicine. She was very groggy so I decided to take one of these pills myself. At this time I didn't take drugs—I hadn't even spoken to Max in almost two years. But I took one of the pills and got back into bed. I couldn't stand up until the next morning.

I discovered she was getting prescriptions for sedatives and painkillers from several different doctors. None of the doctors knew about what her other doctors were prescribing, and even she didn't know what she was taking. The combination of the pills and the booze was incredibly dangerous, but there was nothing I could do to stop her. At times I would hide her pills and pretend I didn't know where they were. But I would help her search through the nine bathrooms in our suite. Eventually I just couldn't take it anymore and I'd give them to her. The most I could do was be there in case—just in case.

The situation got progressively worse. Not her illness, that stayed about the same, but her need for the painkillers increased. She was drinking and taking pills and passing out. She was constantly passing out. It was just awful; not awful enough to make me miss my life with Debbie, but awful. I started taking ten milligrams of Librium just to get some sleep, but I never got through a night. Every night she would have some sort of problem and we would call the doctors. They would give her a shot of something and leave. She really knew her medicine. One night she woke up screaming; she couldn't breathe, she couldn't breathe. She was having an attack, which I knew she could bring on anytime she needed a painkiller. When the doctor got there, he tried to give her a placebo. No chance. She knew what he was doing, she knew more about these drugs than the doctors. The doctor gave her several different drugs and she was screaming at him the whole time, "That's the wrong one, you cocksucker, don't try to give me that fucking shit, give me the right one!"

I had taken my Librium for the night, so I sat there with a big smile on my face, watching all this.

I started feeling very sorry for her doctors. It seemed like they had to come to the hotel every night. So I volunteered to give her a shot of morphine if she needed it. If she needed it? She needed it more than she needed a husband. So in a very brief period of time I'd gone from trying to hide her pills to actually giving her the shots. Ah, the things we do for love.

When she woke up the first night I was to play doctor I rolled her over and gave her a shot in her behind. Who needed eight years of medical school? I was trained by Dr. Jacobson. I did the same thing the second night, but this time, while it made her groggy, it didn't knock her out. She asked me to give her a second shot. When I refused she pleaded, then demanded. She was out of control. That was the end of my medical career.

Initially the doctors suspected she was suffering from something they called Malta fever. Who ever heard of Malta fever? Sometimes I thought they would make up diseases for her. Then they decided her fever was being caused by an abscessed tooth. I mean, they didn't know what they were doing. They were to medicine what Skouras and Wanger were to moviemaking. They gave her an anesthetic and knocked her out cold, right on the floor of our suite, and extracted a tooth. Only Elizabeth could turn an abscessed tooth into a medical crisis.

Extracting her tooth did no good at all. Her headaches got worse and she needed large doses of Demerol to fight the pain. She was eating Demerol like candy. She had several doctors writing her prescriptions. When her fever climbed to 103 degrees we called an ambulance and rushed her to the famed London Clinic—one of eleven times she was hospitalized during the three years we were together. The doctors then decided she was suffering from something called meningism, an inflammation of the membrane covering the brain and spinal column. This was a dangerous condition, and her doctors insisted she rest for several months.

Cleopatra was turning out to be the first great disaster picture. After spending three months and more than $5 million, Mamoulian had shot about twelve minutes of film—and not one frame of it was useable. It wasn't his fault. The production was completely out of control. With Elizabeth ordered by her doctors to rest for three months, the studio suspended production. The plan was to resume filming the following February.

The media blamed Elizabeth and printed all types of rumors. They claimed that she was so unhappy with the script that she had faked her illness, they claimed production had been stopped because she was too fat to get into her costumes, they claimed that our marriage was falling apart. They wouldn't leave her alone for an instant.

While I was in Los Angeles a photographer in London actually had climbed down from the roof of the hotel onto a balcony and through a closed curtain shot photographs of Elizabeth dressed in a flimsy gown playing cards with several men. This was supposedly proof that she was cheating on me. When the photograph was printed Elizabeth was more than furious—she was practically out of her skull with anger.

The magazines were worse, if that was possible. It seemed like she was on the cover of every magazine, and every cover line was false or misleading. One magazine claimed in a banner headline, LIZ' CHILDREN WILL BE TAKEN AWAY FROM HER! The story inside explained that one day her children would grow up and lead their own lives. The story behind the headline LIZ HAS A NEW LOVE! revealed that I had changed, I was the "new" Eddie. DOES LIZ HAVE TWO HUSBANDS? pointed out that Liz had continued to wear Mike Todd's ring after we were married. WHAT LIZ WILL TEACH ELVIS ABOUT LOVE! was how to deal with the loss of a parent. WHAT THE KIDNAPPERS DID TO LIZ was to remind her that she had to be a good mother. STEPHEN BOYD HAS SPLIT UP EDDIE AND LIZ claimed that Boyd's leading ladies always fell in love with him and predicted Elizabeth would be the next. These stories were absurd, but instead of laughing at them, as we should have, we decided to take action. We decided to sue several newspapers and magazines for libel. We eventually won a substantial judgment against the *Daily Mail*.

I don't know when it became obvious to me that there was no possible way this film was ever going to get made with Rouben Mamoulian directing it. But it did. One afternoon I had lunch in London with Walter Wanger and several top studio executives. Everyone was trying to figure out how to save the picture. There was never any discussion of replacing Elizabeth. Skouras had proclaimed, "Elizabeth is Cleopatra." There was general agreement that Peter Finch was wonderful but that Stephen Boyd wasn't powerful enough.

Then I had a brainstorm. "The only way you're going to get this picture done," I said, "is to get Joe Mankiewicz." I told them that Mankiewicz knew how to control Elizabeth, that they had had a wonderful working relationship while making *Suddenly, Last Summer*. The more I heard myself talking, the more I became convinced I knew what I was talking about. Rouben Mamoulian was a talented, decent man and I had tremendous respect for him, but this picture wasn't going to get done with him as the director. There was no chance that somebody Elizabeth didn't know could take over and bring everything together. It had to be somebody she respected. And that was Joe Mankiewicz.

There was absolute silence when I finished speaking. It was as if I had said what they had all been thinking: Mamoulian had to go. Then one of the executives asked me, "Will you tell Skouras?"

They brought a phone to the table. After I'd repeated that to Skouras, he said, "Eddie, I will never forget you for this. We'll make a deal with him. And God bless you, you're a wonderful man."

Elizabeth was just as adamant. "Nobody's going to do this picture but Rouben." She was tremendously loyal to anyone to whom she wasn't married. My job was to prepare her for the inevitable transition to Mankiewicz. I didn't tell her, but I knew that the studio was negotiating with him. In addition to a large salary and expense account, they bought his company for $3 million. I made Joe Mankiewicz a rich man.

Every time I mentioned his name to Elizabeth she went into a tirade. "I'm not going to bow down to him!" It's not bowing down, Elizabeth, I explained. "He's not going to tell me . . ." He's a director, Elizabeth. I kept after her, but she resisted. "I don't care if they make a deal with him, I'm not going to . . ." In fact, she insisted she would not work with him right up until the moment he walked into our hotel suite.

"Joe," she said, embracing him.

"Elizabeth," he responded, holding her. I watched this like the proud parent. I'd made a *shidukh*, a match. I felt like I had just set the world on fire.

Mankiewicz began by throwing out everything that had been done, from the costumes to the cast—but not Elizabeth. Elizabeth not only was Cleopatra, but with all the publicity she had become bigger than Cleopatra. Mankiewicz brought with him a whole new concept for the film, telling us, "I'm not interested in making a movie about people eating grapes in reclining positions." He wanted to make the story sexually driven, more of a love story than a big costume epic. "The trouble with George Bernard Shaw's version," he explained, "was that his Cleopatra didn't have much sex."

While Mankiewicz and Lawrence Durrell worked on the new script, Elizabeth and I returned to Los Angeles. While we were there, I remember, we met with director George Stevens, who was producing and directing the story of Jesus Christ, *The Greatest Story Ever Told*. The script was being written by Pulitzer Prize–winning poet Carl Sandburg. Stevens wanted Elizabeth to play Mary Magdalene. Elizabeth as Mary Magdalene? Hollywood casting at its best. Well, they were both in love with a Jew. During a meeting in Palm Springs, George Stevens literally got down on his hands and knees and begged her to accept the role. He got so emotional he started crying. It reminded me of the members of the British Royal Court bowing to the Queen.

On our way back to London we stopped in Munich, Germany. We stayed in a very historic suite; it had been used by Mussolini to entertain Hitler. Elizabeth was still drinking very heavily and popping her pills. I don't think that had anything to do with Hitler. I didn't know how to stop her—nobody could. In London, Dr. Kennamer had told me to speak to her about drinking while taking pills. When I asked him why, as her doctor, he didn't try to stop her, he told me, "Because I don't want her to lose confidence in me."

Sometimes it seemed as though my life has been written by Lewis Carroll.

I loved her, but I finally accepted the fact that I was just about powerless to help her. She'd been getting away with this behavior her entire life. The only chance I had, I knew, was to make a drastic threat. One night in Munich, as we got ready for bed, I exploded in anger. I don't remember what triggered it—it could have been almost anything, the reason didn't matter. The real reason was that I had had enough of the booze and the pills. "That's it," I said. "This is the end. I'm leaving in the morning."

Who knows if I meant it. I doubt I was really capable of leaving her. But I never had the chance to find out. "Oh yeah," she said, "you're leaving in the morning? Well, I'm leaving right now!" She grabbed a bottle of Seconal that was sitting on her night table and poured a handful of pills down her throat.

I tried to stop her from swallowing them. I stuck my hand right into her mouth, right down her throat. She bit me. Then she ran into the bathroom and swallowed I don't know how many more sedatives. I grabbed the bottle out of her hand and threw it on the floor. We were screaming at each other. It was a bitter fight. Finally, she sat down in front of a mirror and calmly started brushing her hair. "Are you crazy?" I yelled at her. "What about the children?"

"You'll take care of the children," she said, as if we were having a rational discussion. Then she started foaming at the mouth. She tried to stand up, her legs buckled, I caught her as she collapsed. I was terrified. I have never been so scared in my life. The love of my life was dying, and it was my fault. I was the one who had tried to stop her from killing herself, and that had made her so angry she had tried to kill herself.

I tried to stay calm, although it's hard to stay calm when foam is coming out of your wife's mouth. I screamed for help. Kurt Frings, who was asleep in another bedroom in the suite, thought he was having a nightmare and leaped out of bed. By then it was probably four o'clock in the morning. After waking up, Kurt took control. He represented several of the top female movie stars, so he had experience in dealing with suicide attempts. We had two things to consider: We had to save her life *and* keep it out of the newspapers. He managed to convince an elderly German doctor—the man had to be close to ninety—to come to the hotel.

Kurt and I were dragging Elizabeth around the room, keeping her awake and on her feet as we had learned from bad movies, when the doctor arrived. She was barely conscious. He gave her an injection of something and made her drink some coffee, then more coffee and we walked her around and around the room. The doctor explained that she would be fine. I gave him about $1,000 and begged him to tell no one about this.

It took her almost a full day to feel well enough to be very angry with me. I did not leave the bedroom until I was sure she was okay. I lay there for a long time wondering if there had been anything else I could have done to get her to stop. I couldn't come up with any alternatives.

When she finally woke up we started fighting again, but this time it ended with both of us apologizing and vowing eternal love for each other. Had this been a real suicide attempt? The attempt was real, but I'm not sure about the intention. She certainly swallowed enough pills to die, but she knew I was right there. She trusted me enough to make a suicide attempt from which only I could save her. But whenever she did something like that, there was always someone there to save her.

Many men gave their hearts to Elizabeth Taylor; I was the only one who gave my appendix. I felt that she was on a path towards complete self-destruction, and I had to do something to save her. So I decided to develop an illness of my own. We were supposed to go to Saint Moritz for a ski holiday, but I just didn't have the heart for it. I told my friend Bob Abrams that I intended to check into the hospital when we got back to London. He was very concerned. "What's wrong with you?" he asked.

"I don't know yet," I admitted. "But I'll think of something before we get there."

The answer was delivered to me by room service: a double order of wiener schnitzel. By the time we got to the airport I had a dose of heartburn. Heart problems, I decided, that was enough to get me into the hospital for a few days. That I had the heart for. And, in fact, I really was having heart problems—the problems with Elizabeth were breaking my heart.

Elizabeth's doctor, Dr. Goldman, met us at Heathrow Airport. "What's the problem, Eddie?" he asked.

I told him I had pains in my chest, but after poking and prodding he insisted the pain was in my stomach. I wanted heart trouble; I didn't want appendix. It's not down there, I told him, it's up here. But Dr. Goldman wanted appendix. I tried to tell him that there was really nothing wrong with me, but he was the doctor. They rushed me to the London Clinic and performed an emergency appendectomy. They removed a perfectly good appendix. Newspapers reported that my frantic wife rushed me to the hospital, where doctors operated with only hours to spare. Before what, I wondered, dinner? Many of the stories concerning my illness wondered what it would do to my "already weakened wife." I couldn't even have my own medical emergency.

Elizabeth was very upset. She didn't like getting up in the morning to go see me in the hospital. They were ready to release me after a couple of days, but I didn't want to leave so quickly. I asked Dr. Goldman if he could find an excuse to keep me there. Finally, we agreed on a heart problem. He told Elizabeth he wanted me to stay in the hospital while he conducted some tests. Elizabeth immediately consulted Dr. Kennamer, who told her from Los Angeles, "He's fine. There's nothing wrong with his heart."

That diagnosis was good enough for Elizabeth. "Please come home," she said to me. "You've been here long enough. The children and I want you to come home." That was the end of my attempt to be sick.

All of this was just a prelude to the crisis that was about to occur. Fox had made plans to resume filming in April. That wasn't the crisis, that was just a silly decision. One night in early March Elizabeth woke up in a cold sweat. She was struggling to breathe, and her heart rate was 225 beats per minute. When the doctor arrived he argued with Elizabeth about the proper treatment. She wanted morphine, but he wanted to give her something less powerful. But he being the doctor and she being the movie star, naturally she won. He gave her the morphine.

None of her doctors seemed to know exactly what was wrong with her, although I've always believed she had overmedicated herself. This is just my opinion. She really did need painkillers; she'd suffered serious back injuries when she'd fallen off a horse filming *National Velvet*, but after a while she needed more and more painkillers just to counter the effects of the painkillers. Whatever the reason, she was seriously ill. She refused to go back to the hospital, so doctors put an oxygen tent over her side of our bed. I was with her almost twenty-four hours a day; I sat in the room reading during the day, just listening to her breathing, and I slept next to her at night. I also hired nurses to be in the suite at all times. Elizabeth never got out of bed. She was treated like a queen. In fact, Lord Evans was able to borrow Queen Elizabeth's personal portable toilet, used when the Queen traveled to third world countries, for her.

After being with her almost every moment for three days, I needed some time to myself. I told one of the nurses to stay with Elizabeth and went into another bedroom to try to get some sleep. In the middle of the night the nurse called me in a panic. "Come quick," she said, "your wife's in a coma."

It was pure luck, or maybe it was fate, that the nurse had been in the room at that time. I don't think I would have noticed the subtle difference in her breathing. I called the Dorchester operator and told her to get help fast. I called Elizabeth's doctors. I didn't know what else to do, I felt completely helpless. Fortunately, there was a bachelor party being held right in the hotel for a medical student and the operator figured that doctors would be there. One of England's top anesthesiologists and resuscitationists came running down the hallway dressed in formal tails. The doctor realized immediately that Elizabeth's lungs were so congested that she was suffocating. He shoved his fingers down her mouth, trying to make her vomit. It didn't work. He started hitting her in the chest, he stuck his fingers in her eyes, he tried everything to get her to respond, but she barely reacted. Elizabeth remembers waking up briefly and telling him, "Why don't you bug off." That sounds like something she might say, but not the way she would have said it. I don't remember her saying anything at all, but I was so frightened she was going to die that I probably wouldn't. It seemed like it took a long time for the ambulance to arrive, though it was only a few minutes.

They strapped Elizabeth on a stretcher and took her downstairs to the ambulance. As we raced through the streets of London at about 100 miles an hour, Dr. Middleton Price stuck a rubber tube down Elizabeth's throat and began mouth-to-mouth resuscitation. He was saving her life. I was going crazy. Everything had happened so quickly, I didn't know what was going on.

The usual mob of photographers and reporters was waiting for us at the London Clinic. Who knows how they got there so quickly. I pushed them out of the way, I tried to stop them from taking pictures. It was absurd: My wife was dying and I was protecting her from the media. They rushed her directly to the operating room. Somebody, I have no idea who, brought me into a little waiting room and left me there.

The first person to arrive at the hospital was Joe Mankiewicz. Within minutes a doctor came in and showed me an X ray of her lungs. They were completely congested, completely filled with mucus. She couldn't breathe. The official diagnosis was double pneumonia. Her condition was extremely critical. He needed my permission to perform a tracheotomy. I didn't even know what that was. He explained, a tracheotomy was a slit in her throat into the trachea that would enable her to breathe. "It'll leave a scar," he said. Without the operation she would be dead within the hour.

I knew what I had to do, I just didn't know how to do it. I was nearly hysterical. I was sure she was dying, the better part of me was dying, and if she died I didn't know how I could live. First Mike, then Elizabeth. Mankiewicz said firmly, "Go ahead and sign it, Eddie."

They performed the operation minutes after I signed the paper. They cut a slit about two inches long and a quarter-inch wide and inserted a respirator tube to force air into her lungs and pump out the thick mucus that was preventing her from breathing. She almost died four or five times on the operating table. This wasn't one of her suicide attempts, this wasn't caused by her pills or too much alcohol, this was a medical crisis. The operation kept her alive, but none of the six doctors in the operating room dared give me a prognosis. I later found out that in America it was initially reported that she had died. Mankiewicz stayed with me through the night, constantly reassuring me that Elizabeth would be fine.

Finally the doctor walked into the waiting room. I was ready for him to tell me she was dead. Instead, he said she had survived the operation. I sat down. Sat down? I practically collapsed. She was in extremely serious condition, he continued, the next few days were going to be critical. Although I didn't think so at the time, it sounded like dialogue from a B-movie. Except it was true. They brought me into the operating room because they thought seeing me might give her strength. But it was important for me to see her too; it gave me strength because I felt like I was dying with her. I was positive I was losing the love of my life.

She was conscious, lying on the operating table. I remember thinking as I looked at her that this was her deathbed. Tubes ran from machines into her ankles and arms. Liquids were flowing in and out of her body. Bandages covered much of the slit in her throat, but part of the incision was visible. She looked so vulnerable, so small, not at all like the powerful woman I knew her to be.

A nurse was holding up a mirror so Elizabeth could see me. She couldn't speak at all, not even a whisper. The nurse handed her a tube of lipstick or some sort of grease pencil and she scribbled on the mirror in large, misshapen letters, "Am I going to die?"

"No," I said, shaking my head. "No, you're gonna be fine."

Then she wrote, "When I can go home? Take me home. I love love you."

I love loved her, too. I didn't leave the hospital for several days as she drifted in and out of a coma. Occasionally I would stand at the window and just stare at the crowds waiting outside the hospital. Hundreds of people stood mostly silently behind police barricades. Some of them lit candles and prayed for her. Others, I don't know what they were doing there. They just had some morbid need to fulfill. I called her parents, who immediately flew to London to be with her. I didn't see the newspapers, so I had no idea that Elizabeth's fight for life had become the most important story in the world. The hospital gave hourly updates about her condition, which instantly became headlines. Two years earlier she had been vilified as the temptress who'd stolen me away from sweet Debbie, but suddenly she was the courageous young woman fighting for her life. It was the ultimate life-and-death drama. Only someone with the talent of Mankiewicz could have written a script like this and gotten away with it. If she lived, it was an excellent career move; of course she did have to live.

None of the attending doctors knew what had caused this to happen. Officially they announced that she was suffering from double pneumonia, but privately one of the doctors told me he thought she'd suffered a respiratory failure brought on by depressant drugs. Her pills. So I thought it was very strange that they continued to treat her with other pills.

For five days she slipped in and out of consciousness. I stayed with her day and night, at least twice during that period if I hadn't been there she would have died. I was her eleventh doctor, continually checking all the machines, all the instruments, watching for any signs of distress. One night her temperature went up to 104 degrees and I started screaming for help. The medicine the nurses needed was locked in a cabinet they couldn't open, so they wrapped her in ice packs and cooled her body with electric fans to force down her temperature. She had needles and tubes stuck in her arms and legs. A tube running directly into the incision in her throat connected her to an electric inhaler to help her breathe. One day I lifted a blanket and discovered that her ankles were swollen several times normal size. The intravenous feeding tubes in her ankles had been incorrectly inserted and her body was filling with blood. Her ankles were bigger than her calves. If I hadn't discovered that she would have died.

One night she suddenly started wheezing. She clutched her throat, unable to breathe. I screamed for help. The doctor rushed into the room and discovered that the new electric inhaler was backfiring into her throat. That too would have killed her.

Nothing her doctors did seemed to be working. I had very little confidence in them. They kept trying different drugs, but none of them seemed to have much of an effect. She woke up one day and wrote down "Make them give me something stronger to sleep. Not like before." She knew exactly what she wanted, but the doctors gave her something else— and she slipped back into the coma. I was spending the little time away from her I had calling doctors all over the world for advice. I figured somebody somewhere must know something. And I was right, everybody did know something, but they all knew something different. Just about every doctor I spoke with gave me some advice, but no two of them gave me the same advice. I heard about a new medicine being tested in America and I had Milton Blackstone get a bottle of it in New Jersey and fly to London to give it to me. Milton also suggested I call Max Jacobson. Milton always had confidence in Max.

Max? Elizabeth was being treated by the finest doctors in London. Max was an alchemist; I could picture him bent over his different-colored bottles mixing his elixirs and chortling. Max didn't seem to live on the same planet as these fancy British doctors. But after five days Elizabeth was still in critical condition, still mostly comatose. So in desperation, I called Max. After I gave him a medical update he sighed and asked, "Did they check her gamma globulin?"

Gamma globulin? Ask me about the arrangement to "Lady in Paris." I had no idea what he was talking about. But incredibly, just as I hung up with him, Dr. Carl Goldman came into my room and told me, "Eddie, we've made a terrible mistake. We forgot to check her gamma globulin." The coincidence was chilling. They immediately injected large doses of gamma globulin into her thighs. Maybe it was a coincidence, maybe it was the medicine Milton flew over from New Jersey, but whatever it was, her condition began improving. She regained consciousness. The inhaler was removed from her throat. A day later she began speaking.

One of the first things she told me was that she had had a near-death experience. Like most people who have an experience like that, she saw God. But Elizabeth had also seen Mike Todd. "I saw God," she whispered. "I touched God's hand and I saw Mike. And Mike told me he loved me. And I love you more than I love God. I love you more than I love my children."

I believe Elizabeth meant it when she said it. She was not a very subtle person; she always said exactly what was on her mind.

I knew for certain she was going to be fine when she started demanding chili from Chasen's and Dom Pérignon champagne. She could barely speak and she was drinking champagne. People around the world were still busy praying for her, and she was drinking. I did everything possible to keep that story out of the papers.

Her doctors insisted she stay in the hospital until she had cut down her dependence on sedatives. So for the next several weeks she held court in her hospital room. Friends like Truman Capote and Tennessee

Williams would keep her amused. When I learned that John Wayne was returning from Africa, where he'd made a picture, I went to the airport to ask him to see her. He was great, he was John Wayne. Before going to the hospital he went to his hotel and put on a clean shirt and suit. I don't remember exactly which country he had been in, but I remember he told me, "The United States ought to own that place."

The incision in Elizabeth's throat had been kept open so doctors could clear the congestion from her lungs. She kept it covered with an English threepence, which enabled her to speak. John Wayne sat on the edge of her bed as they spoke. He was just great with her. But suddenly she gave a loud cough, the coin flew off her open wound, and a big ball of bloody mucus just splattered all over his clean suit and shirt. She was mortified, but he insisted, "It's okay, it's all right. I'm fine."

He stayed only a few minutes more. As soon as he left the room he practically collapsed against the wall. He was in shock. This. . .this death had been spewed all over him. I never had more respect for him than at that moment. When the cameras were rolling, when he was performing for Elizabeth, he had been strong, he'd been John Wayne; but once we were outside he just leaned against the wall for support.

By the end of March she was ready to leave the hospital. The incision had left a long red scar on Elizabeth's throat. The doctors probably could've done a better job hiding it, but she didn't care. She wore it proudly, like a medal. We flew back to New York on a specially equipped airplane. There was no nurse on the plane, so I proudly told reporters, "I'll be her nurse." And why not? That's what I had become. My career? As I also told reporters, "I'm appearing at the London Clinic."

Everywhere we went—when we left the hospital, when we landed in New York, when we landed in Los Angeles—large crowds had turned out to welcome her, to show support for her. Elizabeth's life had all the twists and turns of a great soap-opera plot, but it was bigger and more complicated, and it was real. Sometimes I wondered what she could possibly do for an encore. What more could happen to her?

A month later she won the Academy Award as Best Actress for *Butterfield 8*, the picture she detested. It wasn't so much a victory as a coronation. The motion picture academy honors survivors, and she was the greatest survivor of them all. It seemed obvious to me that they were going to give it to her by acclamation. This was the ultimate climax, the queen rising from her deathbed to receive the love of her court. Shirley MacLaine, nominated for her role in *The Apartment*, said later, "I lost to a tracheotomy." But it made for a legendary story.

Elizabeth wasn't as certain as I was that she was going to win. When they announced her name she screamed, then turned and kissed me. "Take me down the aisle," she said. As the audience cheered for her she walked slowly down the long aisle on her crutches, leaning on me for support. The long, long walk down the aisle. I was so proud of her. I suspected that the academy had intentionally seated us in the middle of the audience rather than near the stage to prolong the drama. After we'd slowly climbed the steps to the stage she said, "Walk me to the podium."

"No kid," I said, "this one you go alone." Ah, they don't write dialogue like that anymore.

This officially made Elizabeth the most valuable movie star in the world. With all the initial problems, then Elizabeth's gallant fight for life, and finally the Oscar, if Fox had ever harbored any doubts about going ahead with *Cleopatra*, they were forgotten. *Cleopatra* was already one of the best-known motion pictures in history, and it hadn't even been made. There was no script, no cast, no one even knew where it would be filmed. Joe Mankiewicz was busy working on the script. Skouras was fighting with the insurance company, who refused to insure Elizabeth again, and trying to decide where to shoot. It definitely would not be in England. "I appreciate what Skouras said, 'No Liz, no *Cleopatra*,' " I told reporters, "but without good weather it will be no Liz."

Skouras decided to make the film in Hollywood, with some exteriors in Rome. The massive sets in England were dismantled without ever having been used, and construction started on new sets in Hollywood. Fox even began digging a small lake on an old western set where the naval battles would be filmed using miniature ships. But before the sets were finished Skouras changed his mind again. *Cleopatra* was going to be made in Rome. Supposedly Fox would save millions of dollars by knocking down the new sets and moving the entire production to Italy. The lake, which had cost $350,000, was filled in and sold to a real estate company.

Peter Finch and Stephen Boyd were paid off, having been paid not to act. I liked Finch, who was paid $150,000 and had been drunk most of the time. I had rarely spoken to Boyd. Both parts had to be recast. When Elizabeth and I were in New York we'd gone to see her good friend Roddy McDowall, who was starring with Rex Harrison in a play called *The Fighting Cock*. Roddy was the cock, but a very tiny one. But that was an appropriate title for "Sexy Rexy" Harrison, as he had a reputation as one of the great ladies' men. At the time he was engaged to actress Rachel Roberts—they married while the picture was being made—and she was wonderful. At the toss of a coin she'd hop up on a table and say, "I'll take any three men now." That was her act. After watching Harrison onstage for about ten minutes, I said to Elizabeth, "There's your Caesar."

Backstage after the show I asked him, "How would you like to play Caesar?"

"Oh," he replied, "do you think that would be a good idea?"

Elizabeth also loved the idea. Skouras did not. We met with him in his suite at the Sherry-Netherland and he showed us the financial reports for all of Rex Harrison's pictures—just about every one of them had lost money. Harrison was a stage star; people just didn't buy tickets to see him in the movies. Elizabeth didn't care about that, she wanted him. She probably didn't know why she wanted him, she just did. And what Elizabeth wanted . . .

Harrison was signed to play Caesar to her Cleopatra. Then I started looking for someone to play Cleopatra's young lover, Mark Antony. Reading the newspaper one afternoon, I saw an ad for a movie. I believe it was *The Robe*, starring the Welsh actor Richard Burton. In that ad he looked a lot like my image of Mark Antony. "Richard Burton," I said, "that's Mark Antony." Now, I remember that Elizabeth and I called several people trying to find Burton, but I'm not sure we ever did. Although we recommended Burton, I can't claim complete credit for his being cast as her lover. Which is sort of like saying I'm not really sure if I bought the knife or the poison.

One role I know for certain I did cast was Cleopatra's dog. I was in my office in Rome when a woman walked in with a gorgeous camel-haired Afghan. Elizabeth loved animals, and I knew how much she'd love a dog like that. "You get me another one just like that one," I told the woman, "and your dog's in the movie." Most people know about the casting couch; this was more of a casting kennel.

Elizabeth was ecstatic when I brought this dog home. She immediately fell in love with him. Until that moment her favorite dog had been a little Yorkshire terrier named Theresa, who slept in her bed. Elizabeth was so crazy about the Afghan that Theresa was temporarily banished from the bedroom, which caused her to have a heart attack. I rushed her to the hospital—by that time I knew how to do this—and the vet saved her life. The Afghan, meanwhile, developed a taste for antique furniture, so we had to muzzle him. That worked for a short time. Elizabeth and I had a Christmas party and our chef had made a large, gorgeous ham. We walked into the dining room and found the Afghan on the table, having chewed through his muzzle and half of the ham. That was the end of her love affair with this dog.

While new sets were being built in Rome and Mankiewicz was working on the script, Elizabeth and I had little to do. So it was time for me to make my next comeback. I don't know precisely when singing had become a sideline to my real job as Elizabeth Taylor's husband, but I hadn't sung professionally in eighteen months. Mel Ferrer, who was married to Audrey Hepburn and so knew exactly what it felt like to be married to Hollywood royalty, worked with me to prepare my new act. I opened at the Desert Inn in Las Vegas for $25,000 a week in May 1961. Every performance was sold out, although certainly many people showed up just to catch a glimpse of Elizabeth. She didn't disappoint them, sitting at the front of the stage for almost every show. I noticed she wasn't there one night, which did not surprise me. I thought she was probably at the house with the children. But in the middle of a song a waitress dropped an entire tray of metal plate warmers. I made a little joke and the waitress replied in a Cockney accent. I recognized the accent, and the waitress. It was Elizabeth, in a pink wig. The audience caught on right away. I asked her to come closer to the stage and as she did she picked up a second tray—then dropped that one too. Eventually she took off her uniform to reveal the beautiful dress she was wearing, and came onstage to help me finish my act. The audience loved me—us.

In vaudeville, acts like Burns and Allen were known as "two-acts," two people working together. While I worked alone, I had become a two-act. Elizabeth's presence was always onstage with me. The audience expected me to talk about her, and when she was in the room I would look lovingly at her as I sang songs like "That Face" and "You Made

Me Love You." I knew that people referred to me behind my back as "Mr. Taylor," and I really didn't mind. I knew the truth. But when our love affair became more important in my act than my music, it did begin to bother me, and at times I found myself protesting to reporters. I remember Joe Hyams did an interview with me in my dressing room after my second show and I told him quite distinctly, "It's been written that she's part of the show and that people come to see Elizabeth rather than hear me sing—"

"That's not true," Elizabeth interrupted.

"I just got through saying you're not part of the act," I said to her, "and here you are right in the middle of it."

"I'll just sit quietly and say nothing," she said.

There was precisely no chance of that. "It's my greatest pleasure to see her in the audience. Even when she's not there I sing all of my songs to her—"

"Especially 'Mack the Knife,' " she interrupted. Offstage, we were definitely a two-act.

This comeback was a huge success. I had offers to play the Palace, Carnegie Hall, the Winter Garden; I even had a serious offer to star in a Broadway musical. Naturally, I turned them down—we had a movie to make in Italy. I did agree to play the Cocoanut Grove in Los Angeles, my first appearance there in seven years, since the night Debbie had been my date for my opening and Pier Angeli had left crying.

I was no longer a nervous young crooner. Instead of bobby-soxers, Hollywood society turned out for my opening; John Wayne, Henry Fonda, Lucy, Groucho, Kirk Douglas, Yul Brenner. . .and Frank Sinatra with the entire Rat Pack. Now they make movies about them and write books about them, but we had to live with them. There were people who wrote that my opening night at the Cocoanut Grove was the beginning of the end of the Rat Pack.

They started heckling me the moment I walked out onstage. They were all drunk. When I started singing "That Face" to Elizabeth, Dean yelled out, "If I were you, I wouldn't be working. I'd be home with her." That's the clean version that was reported. And Dean was my friend. Eventually they took over the stage. There was nothing I could do but go sit down and watch them. They were completely out of control. They started doing imitations, limericks, racial jokes, and drunken songs. Someone took a photograph of me with a bemused smile on my face and it was reported that I was livid with anger. That wasn't true. Elizabeth was, I think, but I wasn't. I was used to their behavior. At times they had been clever and funny, but most of the people in this audience had seen their act many times before. These celebrities had come to see Eddie Fisher sing love songs to Elizabeth Taylor, not a drunken fraternity party, and they started booing them. Believe me, that was a tough act to follow. But I managed to win back the audience, I appealed to their patriotism. I asked them all to stand and join me in singing "God Bless, America" "to show President Kennedy we're behind him."

I had opened at the Cocoanut Grove a week after Elizabeth and I had returned from Russia. We had almost caused an international incident there; not between the United States and the Soviet Union, but rather between America and Italy. Several months earlier the Russian Moiseyev Dance Company had been performing in the United States and we'd been asked to host a party for them. This was at the height of the cold war; both nations were building fallout shelters in preparation for atomic war. But we discovered that when people got together—with great music and dancing and a lot of vodka—the walls of distrust came down. We had such a wonderful time that the party went on for three nights. The first night, I remember, Elizabeth ended up kicking off her shoes and dancing around the restaurant with members of the company to the strains of that classic Russian melody "Hava Nagilah." It was just incredible for me to see my wife dancing so wildly, with such freedom, four months after being critically ill. I wanted the party to go on forever.

I arranged for the Russians to see the movies of their choice the next day, and we partied again that night. Hedda Hopper wrote that we were obviously Communist sympathizers. The smell of the Hollywood blacklist was still in the air, and a lot of people took her seriously. Not us. We were Elizabeth Taylor. We responded by inviting all our fellow Communists: Frank and Sammy and Dean, Tony Curtis and Janet Leigh, Laurence Harvey, to another party at the very capitalistic Escoffier Room atop the Beverly Hilton. That was one of the great nights. I led the dance troupe in several verses of "Moscow Nights," we danced, we drank, we toasted each other, we drank, Janet Leigh and Natalie Wood taught swing dancing to several young members of the company, I sang "Around the World in Eighty Days," and we drank. The newspapers reported the next morning that actor Lawrence Tierney had been arrested for fighting with police officers when he was asked to leave. . .and we drank.

We formed such a warm relationship that we were invited to be part of the American delegation at the Moscow Film Festival the following month. We stopped in Paris on our way to Moscow and I went shopping for Elizabeth at the House of Dior. Yves St. Laurent, then the head of design, personally showed me the entire collection. He didn't try to sell me anything, but I selected ten $5,000 dresses. The man was a great salesman. Elizabeth brought four of these dresses to wear in Moscow. For the opening night reception, held in St. George's Hall inside the Grand Palace at the Kremlin, she decided to wear a short-laced cocktail dress with a wide boat neckline and a wide, bell-shaped skirt. She looked absolutely gorgeous.

We arrived at the reception almost exactly one hour after it had started. For Elizabeth that was just about on time. As we walked down the long red carpet she glanced up and saw Gina Lollobrigida, who was being honored by the festival, also wearing Dior's short-laced cocktail dress with a wide boat neckline and a wide, bell-shaped skirt. Of all the gin joints in the whole world. . .They were wearing exactly the same dress. Gina's sash was red, Elizabeth's was blue; Gina was wearing pearls, Elizabeth was wearing rubies, but otherwise they looked like twins. Even their hair was done the same way.

Elizabeth smiled at Gina. She could have won her second Academy Award for that performance. "How could St. Laurent do that to me?" she hissed. She was beyond furious.

"He wouldn't do that to you," I whispered back. "There's got to be a mistake here." I didn't know what it was, but I knew I was going to find out.

When an American reporter asked Gina what she thought of the mixup, she also smiled and replied, "Oh, it's very nice." Her performance would have earned her at least a nomination. Throughout the night the two of them did everything possible to avoid each other. I didn't know with whom Elizabeth was more angry, Gina Lollobrigida or Yves St. Laurent. Particularly when the *New York Times* ran a photograph on the front page of the two women standing next to each other.

That was not the only reason the reception was memorable. After a classical concert featuring Russian pianist Emil Gilels, the Soviet Army Choir, and several ballerinas, the Russian minister of culture, a beautiful middle-aged woman who was also known to be Khrushchev's mistress, asked me to sing. Few ad libs were better rehearsed. Fortunately, I had my accompanist with me. I was the first American to be invited to sing in the Kremlin since Paul Robeson—the man Eddie Cantor had told me to stay away from. The next day the *Herald-Tribune* headlined, "Eddie Fisher Rocks the Kremlin." I gave them my best Jolson: "Swanee," "April Showers," and finally "Rock-a-bye Your Baby with a Dixie Melody." I had the audience of Russian diplomats and dignitaries on their feet swaying with me.

Every once in a while it was really nice to prove that I still had that sound in my throat.

We stayed in the same hotel room Ambassador Averell Harriman had occupied while in Russia. The first thing we did was search the room for hidden cameras; we suspected they wanted to have pictures of us making love. If they were spying on us, we never caught them. We were driven around the city in what appeared to be the only limousine in Moscow. When we walked, people continually approached us and asked us questions about the United States. But on occasion other people begged me in Yiddish to help them get out of Russia. "You have the power," they told me. We came from completely different cultures, but I felt a bond with these Jews. I told them the truth. I had no power, there was nothing I could do to help them. Nothing.

Before leaving, Elizabeth and I had a private meeting with Premier Nikita Khrushchev. I remembered the last time Elizabeth had been in Moscow, when Mike had tried to rent the Russian army and Khrushchev had refused to meet with him. But Elizabeth was happy to meet him. He invited us to stay a bit longer and tour his nation, but Elizabeth explained that she had to return to America to have plastic surgery to remove the scar on her neck.

Actually Elizabeth couldn't wait to leave. What she most wanted to do was kill St. Laurent. By the time we landed in France she had calmed down. She didn't want to make a scene. She wanted *me* to make a scene. St. Laurent was *très très apologetique*. He was sorry in several languages. Gina Lollabrigida's dressmaker had copied his design, he explained, and there was nothing he could do to prevent it. "I had nothing to do with it," he told me. "It is the last thing I would do." I told him that Elizabeth was so angry it almost *was* the last thing he did. As a gesture of apology he told me to pick out any dress in his entire collection. I selected his most expensive gown. It cost more than $10,000. He never said a word.

Elizabeth was thrilled. She had gotten a free dress from the most famous designer in the world. I was thrilled too. She had gotten a free dress from the most famous designer in the world.

At the end of the summer we sailed for Rome. We took Elizabeth's three children, including Liza Todd, whom I had legally adopted at Elizabeth's insistence several weeks earlier; Dick Hanley; a nurse for the children; four Yorkshire terriers; a Saint Bernard; two Siamese-Persian cats; and I stopped counting at 100 pieces of luggage. She brought 300 dresses and 120 pairs of shoes.

After our marriage broke up there were people who said knowingly that we had been having problems before Burton. The truth is that we were having such terrible problems that Elizabeth wanted us to have a child. Physically, that was impossible for her—her tubes had been tied. So on our way to Rome we decided to adopt a baby. Elizabeth had three children, so why did she want another child? Because Elizabeth always wanted another anything. She always wanted more. Why did she want another child or another dog or another dress? And me, I already had two children, Carrie and Todd, whom I rarely saw, yet I willingly went along with this plan. The answer is, and the answer always has been, because she was Elizabeth and I was madly in love with her.

In a Catholic orphanage in Greece we found the most beautiful baby boy. The nuns agreed we could take him with us—one baby boy to go. They told us to come back the following day. He was to be Alexander Fisher. But that night the nuns found out we were both Jewish and both divorced. The adoption was canceled.

Once again, Elizabeth was devastated. Secretly I was relieved, but she persisted. When Maria Schell, the beautiful German actress, learned that we wanted to adopt another child, she sent us photographs of several German orphans. Elizabeth fell in love with a one-year-old little girl and Maria made all the necessary arrangements. We picked her up in Munich in mid-December and stayed in Maria Schell's guest house, a converted fifteenth-century church, for a week. We named the baby Maria.

At first Maria was silent. She neither cried nor laughed. But for several days Elizabeth rarely put her down. Maria slept in our bed with us. And finally she started smiling, then laughing. It was only when she tried to walk that we realized something was wrong with her. The orphanage officials had assured us she was perfect, but she wasn't. Although we told reporters she had a dislocated hip, in fact her pelvis was deformed. She had to have a series of operations, though by the time she was out of a cast, I was long out of Elizabeth's life.

When we arrived in Rome it appeared that Mankiewicz had finally gotten *Cleopatra* under control. Every possible mistake that could have been made had already been made, all the problems had been solved. From this point on, *Cleopatra* was going to be just like a normal shoot. I actually believed that.

As the world was soon to discover, the serious problems hadn't even begun.

CHAPTER EIGHT

I do an excellent Richard Burton imitation. "*Eee*lizabeth, if you're not careful, I'm going to take him upstairs and I'm going to fuck *heem!*" But apparently it wasn't good enough.

Once again, the production was delayed before it started. The sets weren't built, the costumes weren't made, the script wasn't finished. In fact, nothing at all had been learned from the mistakes made in London. Mankiewicz was in control of the budget and no one was in control of Mankiewicz. And he had decided that this would be the most lavish movie ever filmed. In addition to constructing sixty interior sets on seven large sound stages, thirty outdoor sets were built to re-create ancient Rome. The Roman Forum covered twelve acres and consisted of thirty brick and white Italian marble buildings; the set was larger than the original Forum. When Elizabeth saw this new Forum for the first time she was extremely pleased. "I like it," she said. "I wouldn't change a thing."

The new Alexandria was spread over twenty acres. For the naval battles twenty-eight reed boats were built. An exact duplicate of Cleopatra's barge cost $100,000. One hundred and sixty large statues were constructed, to equip the seven armies and four navies in the script 15,000 historically accurate bows and quivers and 10,000 spears were made. Twenty-six thousand costumes were designed and made, ranging from ornamental horse saddles to a $6,500 gold clasp for Elizabeth.

Every day something else went wrong. In camera shots of the Forum, the upper floor of a large house was visible in the background, so the whole floor had to be dismantled brick-by-brick to be replaced when filming was completed. Construction workers building the foundation for Alexandria at Torre Astura uncovered a World War II minefield; it took them six weeks to defuse hundreds of mines and thousands of rounds of ammunition. Only after the site had been cleared did someone realize that NATO was using a nearby beach for naval target practice; for safety reasons—they were shooting very large shells—no one was permitted on the set on the days they were firing. The Italian circus owner contracted to supply elephants sued Fox for slandering his animals by referring to them as wild. By the time most of these problems had been solved the weather had turned cold and the shooting schedule had to be completely rearranged once again.

The budget continued to escalate. At one point Skouras placed a $10 million cap on the budget—but by the time he did so, substantially more than that had already been spent.

Then Cleopatra met her Mark Antony. And from that moment on, words can't express. . . .

Richard Burton was a well-known and well-respected stage actor when he was cast as Elizabeth's lover. Although actors respected him for his *Hamlet*, the American public knew him as the singing King Arthur in *Camelot*. He certainly wasn't a star. He had a booming, Shakespearean voice; onstage I kind of liked his singsongy quality, but in my home I didn't like anything about him.

I never knew exactly when Elizabeth fell in love with him. Once she claimed it was the first day of filming, when he came to the set so drunk his whole body was shaking and she had to help him lift a cup of coffee to his lips. I could see his appeal; the entire time Elizabeth and I had been together I'd been trying to get her to cut down on her drinking and pills, and no one likes a conscience. So I guess it was liberating for her to meet a man who would match her drink for drink. As she said, for me she used to *kvell* (Yiddish for a warm, loving feeling), but when she met Burton she *cwtched* him (Welsh for embracing someone completely). Of course, for several months I didn't know any of this was going on. I was either at home with the kids and the nurses and the servants and Dr. Kennamar, whom the studio had hired to watch Elizabeth, and my friends Bob Abrams and Bernie Rich, and the dogs and the cats and the reporters, always the reporters, or I was at my office trying to figure out what it was I was supposed to be doing at my office.

In my effort to keep busy I went into the same studio in which Mario Lanza had last recorded and I recorded "Shalom" and "Milk and Honey." The record became a big hit. Elizabeth was with me for the entire session. She sat in the control booth and as I sang to her she practically had an orgasm. We never touched, yet it was an intensely passionate moment.

We lived in what was supposedly a fourteen-room villa—but only if you count a step as a room—about ten miles outside Rome. It sounded like a castle and it was set on eight acres, but in reality it was a terrible place. In addition to the staff we'd brought from America, we had twelve in help. There were always people around. Our life was actually pretty routine when Elizabeth wasn't at the studio. The day would start with breakfast in bed, a light lunch, and then we'd often have dinner in our bedroom. At home Elizabeth would usually be dressed in full-length nightgowns. At night we went out only occasionally because each time we left the villa the paparazzi would mob us. The only thing worse than the mosquitoes in Rome were these photographers. The mosquitoes were a nuisance, but the paparazzi were dangerous.

One night soon after we'd arrived in Rome, Elizabeth accepted the Silver Mask, the Italian equivalent of an Oscar, for her performance in *Suddenly, Last Summer*. The dress she chose to wear had either a very low neckline or a very high waist. Photographs of Elizabeth fully clothed were easily sold around the world, so a picture of her in this sexy, revealing gown was extremely valuable. As we left the dinner the paparazzi descended on us. But this time they didn't just stand back and take pictures, they devoured us. The media had enabled me to become a star, I appreciated that, and I appreciated that they had a job to do, but this was terrifying. They started shoving us, forcing us backwards, blinding us with flashbulbs, and as this pack closed in on us our police guard was overwhelmed. The photographers were out of control—it was a human feeding frenzy. This wasn't a Fellini movie; this was reality.

I saw a limo waiting at the curb. I opened the rear door and pushed Elizabeth inside to safety. I locked the doors. The mob climbed on the car and pounded on the windows. Fortunately, our own car arrived. When our driver pulled alongside, the police held back the crowd long enough for us to slip into our car and be driven away.

So we spent most nights in our villa. But there was one night, one wonderful night, when we went to a beautiful restaurant with Audrey Hepburn, whom I adored, and Mel Ferrer, and Tony Martin and Cyd Charisse. In the middle of the dinner Tony Martin and I started singing loudly, and the fact is that we were great. We thrilled everybody in the restaurant. When we finished they stood and cheered, then passed a plate around and gave us a pile of lira. Tony and I were feeling pretty proud of ourselves; we were basking in that limelight. But a few minutes after we'd sat down, the room shook. Three tenors from the Italian opera were in the room and they started singing an aria. They buried us, they just buried us. They were beyond comparison. It was thrilling to be there.

It reminded me of the day Sinatra was rehearsing at the Radio City Music Hall with Pavarotti. Sinatra sang the first few bars, *"Oh solo mio, la la la la . . ."* and then Pavarotti opened his mouth and sang *"Oh solo mio, boom boom boom boom!"* Sinatra was stunned. Whoever heard a sound like that? He turned to his piano player and asked, "What the fuck was that?"

That's what it was like that night in Rome. What the fuck was that? It was a grand, glorious sound. We should have given them back the plate of money.

The only problem Elizabeth and I had those early days in Rome was that she had started drinking again. At the villa she would have a drink in the morning, four or five glasses of wine at lunch, and who knows how

much for the remainder of the day. For just the two of us and our occasional guests, we spent an average of $450 a week on liquor. Some
weeks we spent as much as $700. And as I discovered, she wasn't just
drinking at home. When she went to the studio, which often wasn't until
midafternoon, she'd take a case of vodka, some tonic, and tomato juice.
I don't know what I thought she was doing with it. But when she was
shooting the famous nude scene in early November, I found out.

Nude? She'd showed more skin at the Italian movie awards, but by
the accepted film standards of the time, this was quite risqué. The nude
scene was my idea—always give the public what they want. It was actually more the suggestion of nudity than actual exposure. The truth was
that she had gained so much weight that her figure was disappearing.
She had no hips at all, no curves where there were supposed to be curves.
Mankiewicz did a masterful job covering her up. The set was closed, and
only a minimal crew, myself, and Roddy McDowall with his camera were
permitted to be there. This was nine o'clock in the morning and as I
waited with her while her hair was being done, her makeup lady arrived
with a bottle of Coke. When I took a sip of it, I was stunned. It wasn't
Coke; it was brandy.

I figured Mankiewicz must have known that she was drinking on the
set. I sat down next to him and told him what I'd discovered. "Come on,
Joe," I said. "Tell me what's going on here."

Mankiewicz took a long, slow drag on his pipe and sighed. "Eddie,"
he replied, "she hasn't the faintest idea what she's doing."

Like the pills, there was nothing I could do to stop her. It would have
been like standing in front of a hurricane. Burton never tried to stop her,
he would just drink with her.

Among all the memories from that time, all the images, all the pain,
there was one day I would never forget. Elizabeth had finally gone back
to work in late September 1961. I went with her to the studio for her first
costume fittings and camera tests. I was standing in the back of a large
set with the makeup people and costume staff when Elizabeth came out
dressed in a golden gown as Cleopatra. The entire set, normally a noisy,
hectic place, suddenly quieted. She wasn't just dressed as Cleopatra,
when she stood in front of the camera she became Cleopatra. The trans-
formation was remarkable. Once more, she took my breath away. I could

feel her strength. My first thought was that after all she had been through, she was finally all right, she had survived. But at the same time I was also very sad. I felt like something profound had ended. My second thought was that I had lost her. I didn't know to whom, or to what, but I knew my job was done. I had helped her live, and she no longer needed me.

On that set, on that day, she was completely within her own environment; the world of make-believe was her real world. I cried. It was as if a great burden had been lifted. It was fly-away time. I stood in the back and I cried.

They had begun shooting before Mankiewicz had finished his script, so everything was just about as disorganized as it had been in England. At times Mankiewicz would finish writing a scene the night before it was shot. Or he would decide he desperately needed a set and it would be built at double time or triple time, then he'd change his mind and shoot somewhere else. Burton worked only one of the first seventeen weeks he was in Rome. Elizabeth had gotten Roddy McDowall a part in the picture, but he worked once the first four months he was there. Carroll O'Connor worked seventeen days in ten months. Hume Cronyn was in Rome four months at $5,000 a week before his first day of work. Even Elizabeth often worked only two or three days a week. It was chaos—but nobody complained because everybody was on the payroll. Everybody was getting paid for not working. The budget just continued to escalate. The situation was so completely out of control that a Fox executive in Hollywood decided he needed to meet with a Fox executive in Rome, at the same time the executive in Rome decided he needed to meet with people in Hollywood. Their planes practically crossed flight paths as they flew in opposite directions.

Often filmmaking is a very intensive process. The film becomes your life, it occupies every minute of the day. When you're not on the set, you're thinking about your role. At least that's what I've been told. But not this time. The principle members of the *Cleopatra* cast had the luxury of being on salary in one of the most romantic cities in the world with very little work to do. Actors and actresses with free time in the heat of making a movie is the perfect environment for romance. Or at least sex.

But I wasn't concerned about my relationship with Elizabeth. We were in love. In everything we did there was complete devotion to each other.

I never sensed any negative feelings from her, although there obviously were some on her part. I believed that, no matter what was happening between other people on the set, we were untouchable.

And I certainly didn't think Richard Burton would come between us. Even if he hadn't destroyed my marriage I would have disliked him. From the first moment I met him, I thought he was an arrogant slob. Elizabeth and I used to make fun of him. We compared him to the great producer of MGM musicals Arthur Freed, about whom it was said he could grow orchids under his fingernails. So one night at a party at Burton's house I went over to him and after looking at his hands I said, "We're wrong, Elizabeth, Richard isn't growing orchids under his fingernails."

It was only after I'd met him that I heard about his reputation for sleeping with all his leading ladies, among them Susan Strasberg, Claire Bloom, and Jean Simmons. His wife, Sybil, was known to be very understanding. Very, very understanding. I didn't know how understanding she could be—he showed up on the set with a very attractive ex-Copa girl named Pat Tunder, to whom he'd apparently promised a role in the picture.

Burton was a handsome man, in a rugged sort of way, but his anger made him ugly. And he was always angry at something, some perceived slight or some insult. He was angry when he was sober, so his drinking just made that worse. I didn't like him, but truthfully, I never blamed him for what happened. I don't think either one of them could help themselves. They were two powerful forces crazed by passion, fueled by alcohol, fighting the world. Who could resist that?

Who knows when their affair started. The timing never mattered to me. I don't think Burton had any concept of who he was getting into. For him it probably started as just another movie-star conquest. Not only was he cheating on his wife, he was also cheating on his Copa girlfriend. I'm sure it was great for his ego. I know how I felt, the kid from the streets of Philly who grew up to marry the queen of the movies; he was the kid from the Welsh coal mines who had grown up to fuck the queen of the movies. Ever the classy gentlemen, I learned later that he once marched into the makeup trailer and pronounced loudly, "I have just fucked Elizabeth Taylor in the backseat of my car!"

I don't think Elizabeth believed her affair with Burton was going to

break up two marriages. I doubt that she ever considered the consequences. As always, she did what she wanted to do when she wanted to
do it. She certainly had started her affair with him when we officially
adopted Maria in January, and if she had thought her relationship with
Burton would break up our marriage I can't believe she would have
signed all the papers.

When I read about people who get hit by trains while walking on the
tracks I wonder how that could happen. I mean, it's a train! How could
they not see or hear it coming? So it doesn't surprise me when people
wonder how I did not see Burton coming. When I first heard the rumor
that Elizabeth and Burton were having an affair, I dismissed it. People
were always spreading rumors about Elizabeth. Supposedly Mankiewicz
had had an affair with her. Rex Harrison was supposedly having an affair
with her. This was very typical of the kind of gossip that is spread on
every movie set. In fact, rather than me worrying whether Elizabeth was
having an affair, she was concerned that *I* was cheating on her.

At a party one night Elizabeth and I met a beautiful young princess
who was married to an Italian movie producer. The next morning I went
shopping for jewelry for Elizabeth's birthday, and I asked the princess
and the wife of humor columnist Art Buchwald to help me make a se-
lection. Elizabeth was still asleep when I got home. When I woke her,
the first thing she said to me was, "She was really beautiful, wasn't she?"
It was more an accusation than a statement. That's the closest Elizabeth
ever came to being jealous. But even the thought that I might cheat on
her was ridiculous. I had as much feeling for that girl as I did for a
bicycle. Why would I want a princess when I had the queen?

It was at a small dinner party at our villa that I first realized that
Elizabeth and Burton had become friendly. In addition to Burton, Kurt
Frings, Bob Abrams, and Robert Wagner were there. All of us had a lot
to drink: vodka before dinner; champagne through dinner; and "Ivan the
Terribles," a mix of vodka, grappa, and ouzo, after dinner. As we downed
Ivan the Terribles in the living room I noticed that Elizabeth and Richard
were sitting together on a small couch, whispering, talking, laughing.
That wasn't unusual for Elizabeth—she often sat like that with friends
like Roddy McDowall, Truman Capote, Monty Clift, and Tennessee
Williams—but I was surprised to see her with Burton. Up until that
night she rarely had said anything positive about him.

Maybe it was the liquor, but as I watched the two of them I felt excluded. Trying to bring them back into the general conversation, I sat down at the piano and started singing. That didn't make Elizabeth very happy. She glared at me as if I were interrupting something and told me to stop. I was pretty angry by that point, so I got up and left the party. Our guests left soon after that. Impossible as it may seem, I still didn't know that train was bearing down on me. It still did not occur to me that Elizabeth was falling in love with Richard. I thought she was simply mad at me for something. Elizabeth and Richard? Richard and Elizabeth? It just wasn't possible.

The next day she didn't even come out of the bedroom. We actively ignored each other. But by the evening everything was forgotten and she was her usual sexy, flirtatious self with me.

Elizabeth did her first scene with Richard Burton on January 22, 1962. Until that time most of her scenes had been with Rex Harrison, but now it was time for Mark Antony to make his entrance. I didn't even bother going to the set that day. Ironically, it was a love scene. "To have waited so long," Cleopatra said softly to Mark Antony, "to know so suddenly. Without you, this is not a world I want to live in."

To which Mark Antony responds, as he embraces her, "Everything that I want to hold or love or have or be is here with me now."

So who knew?

The rumors were getting stronger and stronger. When I walked onto the set I could feel people looking at me, I could hear them lower their voices. But until I was forced to deal with it, I pretended everything was fine. But one night, just as we turned out the lights, the phone rang. It was my friend Bob Abrams. "Hey Eddie," he said. "There's something you really should know. A lot of people are talking about Elizabeth and Burton."

"What do you mean?"

He told me what I probably already knew. After hanging up, I lay silently in the dark, trying to decide if I wanted to face this. Finally I realized I had no choice. "That was Bob Abrams," I told Elizabeth. "Tell me the truth: Is there something going on between you and Burton?"

Elizabeth was always honest, always painfully honest. "Yes," she said.

That train just slammed right into me. I packed a bag and left the villa that night. She did nothing to stop me. I was in a daze, in complete shock. I was Eddie Fisher—women loved me, they didn't cheat on me. I didn't know what to do, I didn't know how to respond. Minutes earlier I had been sharing a warm bed with the woman I loved, then suddenly the world had become a cold, cold place. I felt so alone.

The next day I turned to Joe Mankiewicz for advice. Mankiewicz was one of the very few people in the world I trusted. If anyone knew what was really going on, it was Mankiewicz. I knew he would be honest with me. He didn't know a thing about the affair, he lied to me. I believed him because I wanted to believe him. At that point it didn't occur to me that he was more than $15 million into this picture and probably would have done anything to keep his cast together and sane until it was done. Mankiewicz told me to go back to the villa before Elizabeth charged me with desertion. My wife was having an affair with her leading man and I was deserting her? That was absurd, but it made sense to me. As I drove back there I could hear his voice reverberating in my mind: "Eddie, she hasn't the faintest idea what she's doing."

I didn't know what *I* was doing. I started taking her Percodans just to get me through the days. I remember one day I took a couple of them and looked in the mirror and I couldn't bear to look at myself. When I walked back into the bedroom she said, "Eddie, you look like you have a face full of shit." That was exactly how I felt.

I had no idea what was really going on between them. I thought, I hoped, it might be just a sexual flirtation that would soon end, then we would be back together. I put up with it because I had no choice. As always, she was in complete control. What could I do, threaten to leave her? I didn't think she'd care. She no longer even tried to hide her affection for Burton. Hide it? She flaunted it. "Guess where I was today? Guess who I had a drink with today?" she said one night, then told me, "Well, I had a costume fitting with Irene Sharaff, then I had a drink with Richard." She knew how much she was hurting me, but she just couldn't resist. With all of her charms, with all the wonderful things about her, she was also a bit of a sadist.

My friends wanted me to take action. Leave her, confront her, confront Burton, make a scene. Something, anything. One of them even gave me a gun. Me, with a gun. I don't know what they expected me to do with it. So I carried it around.

The situation was affecting the movie, so Walter Wanger suggested I leave Rome for a little while. For my own good, naturally. I considered going back to New York, but finally decided to go to the house I'd bought in Gstaad, Switzerland. At first Elizabeth thought that was a good idea, but just as quickly changed her mind. She wanted me to stay. "Why should I stay, Elizabeth?" I asked.

"Because I'm having lunch with him," she said. Nothing made any sense to me anymore. "Please don't leave me," she continued. "I have to work with him. And I have to figure out how we're going to do that."

I interpreted that to mean she was going to end their relationship. That was exactly what I wanted her to say. Maybe it was just a ploy to get me to stay, but I believe she meant precisely that when she said it. I agreed to stay with her. When I held her close that night, I actually believed we were going to get through this with our marriage intact.

A few days later Elizabeth and I were picking at dinner—I was too depressed to eat anything, she was too drunk—when Burton called. She took the call in another room, but I heard her speaking as clearly as if I were holding the receiver to my ear. "Oh dahling," she said in the phony British accent she had recently affected, "I'm so sorry. That's bloody awful." When I heard her call him "dahling," my heart just sank. Once more, she took my breath away.

"Richard had a fight with his brother," she said coldly, as if she were talking to a stranger, "Philip hit him across his back with a chair. They X-rayed it. . .and they think it's cancer."

At that moment that story made about as much sense as my whole life. But I was beyond trying to understand; I was simply surviving. What surprised me was that she told it to me so matter-of-factly, as if I were a good friend, like Roddy McDowall, with whom she could share her problems, rather than her husband. "Oh," I said. "I'm so sorry." Truthfully, the only thing I was really sorry about was that his brother hadn't killed him. Actually, it didn't even have to be his brother. I was hoping anybody would kill him. But cancer, that was a hopeful sign.

Apparently his brother had been trying to beat some sense into him. Burton was so bruised he couldn't work the next day. That was the best day I'd had in several weeks. It didn't last long, though. A few nights later Elizabeth brought Burton home with her, or possibly he just came over after dinner. But they were both drunk when he got there. We sat down in the living room and there he played one of the great scenes of his life. He was bold, he was dramatic, forceful—but mostly he was drunk. Many people remember Richard Burton as a great Shakespearean actor with a *deeeeep*, commanding voice. I remember him as a coarse, mean drunk. We sat there opposite each other for six hours, playing out this scene. I don't know how much brandy it's possible to drink, but I know we went through several bottles. I probably drank more that night than ever before in my life, and yet I stayed sober. Ah, the mysteries of love . . .

Elizabeth was in the room with us at the beginning of this confrontation. I have to say this for Burton, he was not given to subtleties. He looked right at her and snarled, "Elizabeth, who do you love? *Whooo do you love?*"

Her friend Tennessee Williams couldn't have written better dialogue. If it hadn't been my life that was being destroyed, I might have even admired his work. Elizabeth. . .oh, Elizabeth. I can't even honestly claim she was torn between the two of us. She looked at me, then at Burton, and said softly to him, "You."

"That's the right answer," he snapped, then added threateningly, "but it wasn't quick enough."

There was nothing for me to say, nothing for me to do. Inside, I was empty. I was running on fumes. Emboldened by her response, Burton picked up a photograph of Elizabeth and Mike Todd. "He didn't know how to use her," he said, like some monster trampling through my life, "and neither do you."

Elizabeth broke down. She started crying hysterically. Burton ignored her, concentrating his bile on me. She ran out of the room, out of the villa. I had no idea where she was going. And I didn't really care.

Burton was relentless. Whatever he was trying to accomplish, this was a bravura performance; sometimes charming, sometimes threatening, he roared and he whispered, he lectured and he questioned, he moved easily from bitter rival to sympathetic friend. And I sat there, listening to every word. Finally, when he paused to sip his brandy, I said evenly, "Why don't you leave her alone, Richard? She's my wife. I love her."

I will never forget his response. "You don't need her anymore," he said with a calculated coldness I'd never seen in him before. "You're a star already. I'm not, not yet. But she's going to make me one. I'm going to use her, that no-talent Hollywood nothing."

Almost every half hour Elizabeth would call us from wherever she was. In an insane world, my wife calling me in our home while I drank brandy with her lover, that somehow seemed perfectly normal. During one of those conversations Burton got angry at her—I don't know what she'd said to him—but he screamed at her, "You fucking sagging-tit, no-talent Hollywood cunt. This man loves you so much, how can you treat him like that? Elizabeth, if you're not careful, I'm going to take him upstairs and *I'm* going to fuck him."

The man was a poet with the English language.

Roddy McDowall and his close friend John Valva carried Burton out of the house about two o'clock in the morning. He'd drunk himself into a stupor. He was blubbering; he couldn't even stand up. I actually believed he had made such a fool of himself that night that even Elizabeth would have to see it. I thought he had destroyed himself with his actions. I told Dick Hanley that Burton had admitted he intended to use her to become a star, and that he had called her a "sagging-tit, no-talent."

Elizabeth was devastated. She locked herself in the apartment Dick Hanley shared with his cousin, refusing to even speak to Burton. I had a glimmer of hope that maybe she had come to her senses. Burton must have felt that too, because he literally kicked down Hanley's front door and confronted her. Not only did he admit that he had said those things, he called her all kinds of other nasty things.

There is a lovely song in *Camelot* in which a confused King Arthur recalls the magician Merlin's advice about "How to Handle a Woman." Believe me, there was nothing a magician could teach Burton about that subject. Rather than hurting Elizabeth, Burton's insults just made him more desirable to her. How to handle Elizabeth? Burton rejected her; when she called him he refused to speak to her or he hung up. He was one of the few people in the world who had any control over her. She needed him desperately. He was the magician who'd cast a spell on her.

Meanwhile, they had scenes together almost every day. The budget of the movie continued to escalate, to over $20 million and rising.

I felt like I was living in an insane asylum. Of course, I knew that I was just as crazy as they were—I'd gone along with it. By this time the media had found out about Elizabeth and Burton and the first headlines appeared. I denied all the stories. I insisted that everything was wonderful between my wife and myself. That was the big headline: LIZ, EDDIE DENY SPLIT.

Meanwhile, I was getting advice from everybody. One day Stewart Granger, who was married to Jean Simmons, came to see me. "You know I had a similar problem with my wife," he said. "Don't do anything— it'll work itself out." Mankiewicz wanted me to stay in the house. Don't leave that house, he told me, don't talk to anybody. Maria Schell insisted, "You belong together, wait until it blows over." My friends urged me to leave Rome, although there was some lobbying for killing Burton. It's Italy, they said, they understand crimes of passion.

Finally, I just couldn't take it anymore. I wasn't quite a completely broken man. I still had hopes that this would all pass, that Elizabeth would realize how much she loved me and I would forgive her and we would make passionate love and all would be forgotten. And I wasn't even on her pills at that point. I finally realized I had to get out of there. I just had to go somewhere, anywhere, it didn't matter. I had to get away from them. I decided to go to New York, where truly sane people like Max were waiting to help me.

But before I left, I decided, I had to speak with Sybil Burton. I don't know why, maybe just to get even with him, to hurt him as he'd hurt me, but I had to speak to her. I don't know what I expected her to tell me. Sybil was not surprised to see me. This was a scene she'd been through before with Burton. "You know they're having an affair," I said to her.

"Yes, of course," she said.

"What are you gonna do about it, Sybil?"

"Nothing," she said. "Richard always comes back to me. He has a love affair with every leading lady, but he always comes back to me. This thing with Elizabeth is over. This isn't any different."

"Oh, it is," I insisted. "You don't know Elizabeth, Sybil. It's not over. And this time he's not coming back." Maybe I tried to explain to her that Elizabeth always gets what she wants, and what she wanted was Sybil's husband; if I didn't say it, I thought it.

I think that Sybil knew this time was different too. Like me, she just didn't want to have to face it. Finally she broke down. She started crying and ran out of the apartment. I should have felt badly for her, but I was beyond feeling very much of anything.

I got in the car with several of my friends and we started driving, toward Milan. Sybil responded to my visit by storming onto the set and confronting Burton. Mankiewicz suspended production for the day, at a cost of $100,000. Good for me.

So much happened so fast that much of it seems like one great blur. The order in which things took place is sometimes confusing. But the one thing of which I am sure is that I loved Elizabeth every minute of this time. No matter what she did to me, how much abuse I took, I never stopped loving her. Not for a minute. I loved her more than I loved myself, and I would have done anything to win her love. Those who have never experienced this kind of love can't possibly understand how I felt, but those who have loved to this depth know completely.

We drove through the day to Florence in the green Rolls-Royce Elizabeth had given me as a token of her love. Almost every time we stopped along the way I called the villa, hoping she would get on the phone and ask me to come back. I was already in the hotel in Florence when I finally reached her at Dick Hanley's apartment. Burton answered the phone, which told me everything I needed to know. "What are you doing there?" I asked.

"I'm with my girl," he said smartly.

"She's not your girl," I corrected him. "She's my wife."

"Well, then I'm with your wife."

Elizabeth got on the phone and started cursing at me for going to see Sybil. She swore at me using British slang. I was a "bloody" something-or-other. She was becoming him.

It was obvious the two of them had been drinking as they plotted revenge. I'd done a terrible thing: I'd fought to keep my wife. Burton got back on the phone. "You spleeeeen," he said, "you nothing . . ." Spleen? What kind of insult was that, a spleen? How could I respond to that, "Who are you calling a spleen"? It was crazy. "You cocksucker," he continued—cocksucker, now there was an insult I knew—"I'm gonna come up there and kill you."

"Don't bother," I told him. "Stay right there. I'm going to kill you." I still had my gun. But they were in Rome and I was calling from Florence. At that distance I had to be some great shot.

I spent the next three days at Lake Como, obsessively calling the house. I couldn't stop myself; I had to speak to her. My excuse was that I was worried about her. Burton was known for hitting women, and I really was afraid he was going to beat her. Is she all right? How is she? If anybody knew how she was, it was me. I'd been with her in a very similar situation.

She was in all her glory was how she was, standing up against the world for the man she loved. Well, at least against me. After three days I began to realize she didn't want to speak to me, so I decided to fly to New York. During a layover in Lisbon I checked into the Ritz and again tried to reach her. I spoke to Mankiewicz several times but he didn't know where she was. In desperation I called Roddy McDowall at the studio. Roddy kept me holding on the phone for several minutes, but he was happy to talk to me, the little—Roddy McDowall, there was another phony. He worshiped Elizabeth; when he lived in Bel Air he would come to the house and literally sit at her feet. I asked him where she was, and he must have been feeling very brave because he told me that everybody was furious because I'd gone to see Sybil. "You didn't act like a man," he said. I didn't act like a man? I had to hear that from this marshmallow? From this hanger-on? I hung up on him.

Later I called the villa again. Dick Hanley got on the phone. Dick was someone I respected; he was as honest as his job allowed him to be. "She's in the hospital, Eddie," he said. "But you don't have to worry. She's fine."

She was in the hospital? That was the best news I'd heard in weeks. Things were getting back to normal. Taking care of her in the hospital, that was my specialty. "I'm coming back," I said.

"You don't have to come. Honestly, she's fine."

Finally I had exactly what I was looking for: an excuse to return to her. I would have flown around the world until she needed me. My conversation with Sybil Burton had paid off. After giving Burton an ultimatum Sybil had packed and flown to New York. Forced to choose between his wife and Elizabeth, Burton had apparently told Elizabeth that their affair was over, then had left for Paris—ostensibly to do a cameo in Darryl Zanuck's film *The Longest Day*—to try to keep his marriage together.

No man had ever left Elizabeth Taylor, now two men had left her within a few days. Supposedly she'd told Walter Wanger that she was terribly confused, that she loved both me and Burton and didn't know what to do. So she did the most natural thing under the circumstances: She took an overdose of sedatives. They had rushed her by ambulance to Salvator Mundi Hospital.

Meanwhile, I was a complete wreck. I was just barely holding myself together. I hadn't slept in days, I hadn't shaved, I just wanted to be left alone. Unfortunately, on the flight back to Rome I ended up sitting next to my friend, His Eminence Francis Cardinal Spellman of New York City's St. Patrick's Cathedral. He didn't know anything about Elizabeth and Burton, so he started telling me how pleased he was that Elizabeth had recovered her health and that we had adopted a little girl. He might have even said he knew we were going to be very happy together. How was I going to respond, "Elizabeth is fine, except for the fact that she's in the hospital because she'd overdosed on sleeping pills that she swallowed when her lover left her"? I just forced a big smile and lied to one of the most important clergymen in the world.

As soon as the media found out she had gone into the hospital the rumors started. Studio publicists insisted she was suffering from a mild dose of food poisoning. "From eating American boiled beans," said Wanger. "Oysters, I believe," said Dr. Pennington, the doctor in charge. "Food poisoning?" asked Dick Hanley, "Where'd that come from? Liz is exhausted." The ambulance medic reported, "Paralysis." *Time* reported that I'd rushed back from "a TV performance in Lisbon," and that "Taylor. . .is merely using the Burton rumors to shield the real truth: that she is mad, mad, mad for her personable director, Joseph L. Mankiewicz."

Mankiewicz responded to that rumor by insisting the real story was that he was having an affair with *Burton*, and then kissed Burton.

Walter Wanger met me at the airport. Dr. Pennington did not want Elizabeth disturbed, so I had to wait seven hours before I was allowed to see her. When he called to tell me I could see her, he suggested, "Be easy with her."

Me be easy with her? What was I going to do, hit her? She was sitting up in her bed when I entered, looking as regal as Cleopatra. As soon as she saw me she started crying, but through her tears greeted me with those beautiful words, "Why did you go to talk to Sybil?"

"Because I love you, Elizabeth," I replied, "and I don't want to lose you." From the expression of satisfaction on her face, I assumed that was the right answer.

She called me at home later that evening to ask me to pick her up at the hospital. "Come in the morning," she told me, "and bring me some clothes, a pair of sunglasses, and a couple of bottles of beer."

Beer? Why not. I would have brought poison if she had asked. She was dressing slowly when I got there, smoking a cigarette. I kissed her as if greeting an old friend and she opened the bottle of beer. It was as if nothing had happened. The episode was over, things were back to normal; she'd just overdosed, tried to kill herself, and she was drinking a bottle of beer. I remember being disgusted. But I'm not sure if I was disgusted at the fact that she was drinking, or that I had accepted her behavior completely.

Perhaps because Elizabeth and I had successfully sued several British newspapers, the Italian papers had not printed any rumors about the affair. But now it was out in the open, now they legally could speculate that her hospitalization had something to do with the stories being whispered all over Rome. The muzzle was off and the press attacked. We left the hospital holding hands. When I saw the cameras I whispered to her, "Smile." In those photographs I look like I'm sneering, but I wasn't. I was trying to project some sort of confident image. This was the first time I'd ever been in a situation like this. I'd never before been rejected by the only woman I'd ever really loved, and I didn't know how to react. I was doing the best I could. The police cleared a path through the media for us and we managed to drive away.

Another mob of paparazzi was waiting for us at the villa. They were clamoring for a photograph of the two of us, proof that we were together. Elizabeth wanted to do it. I refused. I don't know exactly why, but I wouldn't do it. It just seemed too phony to me, too hypocritical. Later, Elizabeth and I took a long walk through the private gardens. And as we did, I couldn't help but remember the stories she'd told me how she secretly romanced Victor Mature while Michael Wilding was in the next room. Now it was my turn. So as we strolled around the garden, I swear I was looking around, trying to figure out how Burton was going to sneak into the house to fuck her. The back way? Up the stairs? Which bedroom?

I had absolutely no illusions that Burton was going to go away and we would be happy ever after. I knew she had already made up her mind. There was nothing I could teach her, show her, give her. Burton had what she wanted: that marvelous voice, his knowledge of acting and his ability to teach her. I also believe she mistook his weaknesses, his alcoholism, his bitterness, and the anger that led to violence, for independence and self-confidence. She thought he was a hero, I knew he was a coward and a user.

Burton had flown back to Rome as soon as he'd learned that Elizabeth had overdosed, but Wanger told him to stay away from the hospital. I think Burton had finally begun to understand the consequences of being with Elizabeth. He had complained when the reporters hounded him in Paris, "It's like fucking Khrushchev. I've had affairs before—how did I know the woman was so fucking famous?"

In a few weeks Burton had been transformed from a well-respected British actor to a world-renowned celebrity—and he loved it. Suddenly he couldn't walk down the street without being recognized. His price to do a picture instantly doubled. But what he didn't yet understand was that he couldn't turn off this fame when it was convenient for him. So when he issued a statement upon his return to Rome claiming the situation "had been distorted out of proportion," the reporters knew immediately that the rumors were true. In the world of Elizabeth, a denial was accepted as a verification.

But I still loved her and I was willing to fight him for her. The scandal grew. The more we denied it, the bigger the headlines around the world. Everything that had happened when I'd left Debbie for Elizabeth was happening again, except this time I was playing a very different role. This time I was the one being left. And this time the scandal was international.

Elizabeth, Burton, and I continued to deny all the rumors, but it was like bare-handedly trying to stop that train that's bearing down on you. Everybody around us was selling stories to newspapers and magazines. Many of the stories that appeared in print were true, although we denied them, but the majority were false, and we denied them, too. Occasionally even I had to laugh at the absurd things that were being printed. Probably the most ridiculous of them all was that Roddy McDowall was having an affair with Sybil Burton. They might just as well have written that

McDowall was having an affair with Richard Burton. In fact, they were living in the same house. The paparazzi dressed up like priests and plumbers and tried to sneak into our villa. One night I turned on the lights in the garden and caught them climbing over the wall on ladders. They came at us like a plague.

With each other, Elizabeth and I pretended that everything was fine between us. But each morning when she went to the studio I wondered if she would be coming home that night. Publicly I continued to deny, deny, deny. "The rumors that our marriage is in trouble are absolutely ridiculous," I told columnist Vernon Scott. "Elizabeth and I are still very much in love. We couldn't be happier than we are this minute. And I mean that with all my heart. We just can't let gossip interfere with the way we feel about one another." I don't know why it was so important to deny the truth. There was little benefit for me. Maybe it was just force of habit, or maybe I was praying that if I said often enough that Elizabeth and I were happy together it just might come true.

To prove my love I hosted a champagne party for her thirtieth birthday in the appropriately named Borgia Room of the exclusive Hostaria dell'Orso. Burton was not among the eighteen invited guests. I wanted to give her something very special, but it was difficult to buy a special gift for Elizabeth because I was always buying her special gifts. As I'd often joked, even something as small as a $50,000 diamond bracelet would make everything wonderful for as long as four or five days. I'd often bought jewelry for her at Bulgari. About a year earlier I'd bought several necklaces and bracelets for her there. The price was $350,000— but I was told that if we took the stones out of the settings when I took them out of the country I wouldn't have to pay taxes on them. Instead an Italian doctor had put them in his medical bag and flown to England. I'd walked into the bedroom and casually tossed them on the bed, Elizabeth had been ecstatic.

For her thirtieth birthday, in addition to a nice ten-carat yellow-diamond ring, I had Bulgari create a gorgeous folding mirror that opened into an emerald-studded snake. On the mirror I had inscribed in my handwriting, *I'll always love you, Eddie.* In fact, I don't know if I gave her these gifts because I was trying to win her back or because I wanted her to have something beautiful to remember me by.

I gave her the ring at the party and I got zip reaction. Nothing. I gave her the mirror in our bedroom, after the party, because the sex was always wonderful after I'd given her a gift.

I knew that night that I had lost her. It wasn't anything she said or the way she acted, but I could feel it. Try to imagine that you're standing in the warm glow of the spotlight, then suddenly the light shifts across the stage, illuminating someone else, leaving you standing alone and ignored in the cold darkness. That begins to describe what I felt like.

I knew it before she did. Elizabeth desperately needed excitement and our relationship had settled into a marriage. Comfort wasn't enough for her. Her love affair with Burton was as forbidden, as scandalous, as our love affair had been. She was addicted to drama, to the fights and making up, to breaking down doors. I knew she couldn't give it up. She did her best to keep up the pretense. She would write me love letters, telling me that she still loved me, leaving them on my pillow at night.

Elizabeth wanted us both, her husband *and* her lover. She didn't want to lose what we had together, but there was no possible way she could have given up what she found with Burton. It was new, and it fulfilled a greater need. He sang a better song. I think the effect Burton had on her was beyond even that of Mike Todd. Her relationship with Mike had been animalistic—she had never met a man like him. It was a great love affair. Mike was very clever, very shrewd, and very strong and possessive. But Burton went far beyond that. Burton was crazy. She needed his approval, as an actress and as a woman, and by withholding it he made her need him desperately. They fought all the time; he beat her, he said terrible things about her, yet somehow he made it work.

Burton wanted the same thing Elizabeth wanted: his marriage and his love affair. I'm sure he never planned to leave Sybil. She permitted him his affairs. I don't even think he intended to give up his Copa girlfriend for Elizabeth—even in the midst of their affair this girl would come to the set every day. He just wanted to get as much out of life as possible. He wanted to control Elizabeth because he knew what it meant to his career.

I was the problem. I think if I had been able to live with this for a while, as Sybil had done for years, our marriage might have survived. But I couldn't, I just couldn't take it. When I went to see Sybil I forced everyone to deal with reality. That's why they were so angry at me.

I understood how Elizabeth and Richard felt about each other. And I knew I couldn't fight their passion. I tried, but I couldn't do it. They couldn't help themselves; they were playing Antony and Cleopatra, they were living their roles. My time was over.

I stayed in Rome with Elizabeth for several weeks after her birthday, wanting to believe her when she told me her affair with Burton was finished. But I didn't believe it for a moment.

When she didn't come home from the studio one night I knew it was time to leave her. It was more than leaving; I was escaping. I was breaking free. It hurt. It hurt terribly. I lay awake most of that night just waiting to hear her come in. She finally arrived very early in the morning. I pretended to be asleep as she undressed and got into bed. Then I rolled over and made love with her for the last time. It was a farewell kiss, the last breath of our romance.

Later, as we laid next to each other I told her I was leaving Rome in the morning, that I'd already made plane reservations. She erupted with anger. I wasn't allowed to leave her. "If you leave me now," she said, "you'll never see me again." What else could she use to threaten me; if I left she'd have an affair with Burton?

That morning I downed at least one Seconal with several drinks and flew back to New York. I don't remember the flight very well. I think I was probably in a mild state of shock. For three years my life had revolved completely around Elizabeth Taylor. Every place I'd gone, everything I'd done, every song I'd sung, had been for her. And suddenly she was gone. I didn't know what to do, I didn't know where to go. I felt incomplete.

I couldn't stop loving her, and needing her. I missed her more than I had ever missed anyone in my life. I couldn't sleep, I couldn't eat, I couldn't sit still, so I did the only thing that made sense at the time. I appeared on the television quiz show *What's My Line* as the mystery guest. The panel, which included gossip columnist Dorothy Kilgallen, who had already written that my marriage was done, put on blindfolds and tried to guess my identity. Many people might think I had to be crazy to agree to do this, and they're probably right. I don't know why I did it, probably to try to convince people that my marriage to Elizabeth was intact and we were deliriously happy together.

Milton convinced me to continue this charade. Sometimes we do things in our lives that we can't completely explain or even understand. But for some reason I felt it was very important to hide the truth from the media. I had absolutely nothing to gain by lying. I was just being Mr. Nice Guy. Maybe because of the movie, maybe because I still couldn't accept it myself, maybe because I was embarrassed and humiliated, or maybe because lying to the media had become a habit. Whatever I did, right or wrong, I did for Elizabeth. Before I'd left Rome she and I had agreed that we would deny all the stories that we had separated. Supposedly I had come to New York on *Cleopatra* business— we were going to produce a line of Cleopatra cosmetics. Sure we were, and the first product was a cover-up. So I went on *What's My Line* and predicted that "Elizabeth Taylor Fisher" would win an Oscar for *Cleopatra.*

I didn't even win the fifty bucks.

I was lost, and Milton Blackstone and Max Jacobson found me. Better I should have wandered in the desert for forty years. I was exhausted and in a severe depression, my dream was lost. I checked into the Pierre and spent most of my time lying on a couch, drinking too much vodka and taking too many Seconals. Max wanted me to stop taking the pills— he wanted me healthy enough to take his shots. To get me away from the media while I got off the Seconals, Max sneaked me into the Gracie Square Hospital, a small private hospital on the Upper East Side, under the name of Edwin Miller. Gracie Square Hospital had both a medical section and a psychiatric section. I was in the medical section. After two days a newspaper reporter found me there and assumed, naturally, that I was in the psychiatric wing. According to various reports, I'd suffered a mental breakdown, I'd had a complete collapse, I'd "cracked up," doctors were considering shock treatment and I was locked in a padded room in a guarded corridor. While Elizabeth had driven me crazy, none of this was true. The only crazy thing I did was listen to Max and Milton. Max and Milton, Milton and Max, my brain trust.

They decided they had to get me out of the hospital. Max gave me a shot of his special mix. In the past he'd only given me a small dose, but this time he gave me the whole shebang. I was sleeping, andinstantly-Iwasawakeanddressedandreadytoleavethehospital! I was flying. That was my very first full dose of methamphetamine, and it woke me up. Woke me up? It shot me through the roof. Within minutes I'd gone from the depths of despair to the heights of elation. They wheeled me out of the hospital around midnight and slipped me into a private ambulance.

Milton, meanwhile, told reporters he'd spoken to me and "I sounded perfectly normal." Normal for what? To prove I was sane, Milton told them I was going to hold a press conference at the Pierre. He told them, not me. I wasn't in any condition to speak with the media. At the appointed time he went downstairs to explain the "misunderstanding," but as soon he saw the mob of reporters and photographers and TV cameras and radio microphones, he immediately turned around and headed for the elevators. The reporters took off after him, literally chasing him through the corridors of the hotel. It was like a scene from a Marx Brothers picture. When the reporters cornered Milton in the banquet manager's office he admitted, "Eddie can't come today because he's resting."

I was being hidden in the home of two of Max's elite patients. This was a married couple and the woman was gorgeous. She was immediately attracted to me. I must have looked really good: I hadn't shaved in several days, my clothes were rumpled; mostly I looked like I was dead. But she would sit on the side of my bed and talk as if we were on a date.

I couldn't stay there. Max and Milton finally convinced me I had to have a press conference to prove that I wasn't locked up in a padded cell. Of course, in the state I was in, holding a press conference was crazy, but I was too crazy trying to prove I was sane that I didn't realize it. I cleaned up, Max gave me a shot, and I walked into the Pierre. It was instant bedlam. Reporters were jammed into the Sapphire Room fighting for position; photographers were climbing on tables. Before the press conference began I'd called Elizabeth on the set. I wanted her to deny the stories too, but she couldn't come to the phone. I was told she would call back.

I'd become a very polished liar. "I foresee a long and happy marriage," I said. "Lots and lots of happiness, misunderstandings, love, consideration." I called the stories of Elizabeth's romance with Burton "preposterous, ridiculous, absolutely false," and promised that she would be calling from Rome to issue a similar statement. I said I thought Burton was "very amusing, pleasant, charming, and a very fine actor." I was doing very well until she returned my call.

I went into the manager's office to speak with her. I didn't know that the manager was allowing some reporters to listen in on an extension. Elizabeth was very abrupt. She said, "I can't go along with the story that you went to New York on *Cleopatra* business."

Go ahead and pound that stake in my heart a little deeper, please. "Why?" I asked.

"I can't tell you, but you'll have to handle it some other way."

Well, I'd said there would be misunderstandings. I had to go back inside and face the media. This was, perhaps, the most humiliating moment of my life. "Elizabeth has no statement to make," I said. Then I tried to explain. "You know, you can ask a woman to do something and she doesn't always do it." But I insisted that "I miss Europe and I miss Elizabeth and blah, blah, blah." The only person I was really kidding was myself, and I knew I was lying.

Finally a reporter asked me about a photograph to be published on the cover of the Italian newspaper *Oggi* that showed Elizabeth kissing Burton. I hadn't known anything about it. "I'd like to see that myself," I replied. Truthfully, that was about the last thing I wanted to see.

The next day Elizabeth and Richard went public, posing arm in arm outside a Rome nightclub in which, according to stories, they had "frolicked to 3 A.M." How dare they frolic in public!

Milton insisted that I continue to be seen around town, claiming it was necessary for my career. The last thing in the world I was concerned about was my career. I had never been more depressed. All the other bad things that had happened in my life seemed as if they were just practice for this. The pain in my heart just wouldn't go away. Oh, it hurt, it hurt so much. I had been rejected and embarrassed by the only woman I'd ever really loved, and I had no idea how to deal with that. My humiliation had been reported on the front page of every newspaper in America, it was broadcast around the world. Eddie Fisher dumped! Every time I left the room I was sure everybody was looking at me and thinking, There goes the greatest loser in the history of the world. I would look at the newspaper photographs of Elizabeth and Burton and I couldn't understand how she could be so happy when I was in such pain. I couldn't get her out of my mind for a second, yet she seemed to have completely forgotten about me. Was I that forgettable? Had our relationship been that terrible?

The Friars were holding a testimonial dinner for Joe E. Lewis and asked me to say a few words. I loved Joe E. Lewis—I would have done anything for him—but I told Max, "I can't. I'm just not in any shape to do it."

"Don't vorry," Max promised. "I put you in shape."

Max loaded a syringe for me and showed me how to give myself an injection. More than anything else at that time I just wanted to be alone, so I went to this dinner in the Grand Ballroom of the Waldorf-Astoria and was seated on the dais in front of two thousand people, next to the great comedian Phil Silvers and the Nobel Peace Prize winner Dr. Ralph Bunche. I felt like everybody was looking at me because, in fact, everybody was looking at me. Dr. Bunche said to me, "I just don't know how you stand all this, it's amazing." How could I respond to that, show him my syringe?

When I felt myself fading I went into the bathroom, locked myself in a stall, and gave myself the shot. If I had been caught it would have been the end of my career, but that didn't even occur to me. Not getting caught shooting up with metamphetamine in the men's room of the Waldorf-Astoria was the best thing that had happened to me in weeks. But I was so far gone that the shot had no effect at all. When I walked out of the bathroom the photographers were lined up to take my picture. Very important: Eddie Fisher goes to the bathroom. I couldn't take it anymore. Instead of going back to the dais I ran through the lobby of the Waldorf, got into a cab, and went back to my cocoon.

The moment I lay down on the sofa, the phone rang. It was Max, "Vhat happened?"

"Nothing happened, Max, I just couldn't do it. I had to get out of there."

"You muss come back and go through vit it. You should do it for yourself. I be right over."

I pleaded with him to leave me alone. "Max, I'm a sick man. I need a rest, I don't need any more excitement, I don't—" He stuck a needle in my arm and whoa. . .I zipped right back over there. On one side of me Phil Silvers was telling burlesque jokes trying to make me laugh; on my other side Ralph Bunche was sympathizing with me. Milton Berle introduced me and I spoke for less than a minute, then returned to the hotel.

Our attorney, Louis Nizer, made the official announcement of our divorce. "Elizabeth and Eddie Fisher announce that they have mutually agreed to part. Divorce proceedings will be instituted soon." If Elizabeth had decided we mutually agreed to part, who was I to argue?

Not only were they frolicking in Rome, they were also "nuzzling." In New York I was struggling to get out of bed every day. Knowing that I had lost her made me love Elizabeth even more intensely. I loved her so much I didn't dare be angry with her. I couldn't think of anything else except Elizabeth. Max got me through the days. Without a shot I couldn't even get out of bed. I had three shots a day, four shots, and that was the only time I felt good. And when I started coming down the depression overwhelmed me, I needed more Max. I didn't realize it at the time, but all I was doing was trading one addiction for another. To salvage some shred of pride at night I went to the theater, to restaurants, I was trying to convince people I was fine. Well, I wasn't fine. I was barely surviving. That's what happens when love casts its beautiful spell.

Many people tried to help me. Sinatra wanted me to stay at his house in Palm Springs, telling me, "Use the house, take my plane, take my boat." And Audrey Hepburn, whom I loved. In Rome one night Elizabeth and I had dinner with Audrey and Mel Ferrer at their house and Audrey told us excitedly that she'd been cast as Eliza Doolittle in the movie version of *My Fair Lady*. As Elizabeth and I went to sleep that night she said, "Get me *My Fair Lady*!"

I didn't believe what I was hearing. I said, "But Elizabeth, we're friends, it's Audrey, I can't. . ."

"Get me *My Fair Lady*," she said firmly. That was one of the very few times I refused to do her bidding. And only because of the way I felt about Audrey. Audrey stayed in the room next to mine at the Pierre and tried to help me get through it. We'd just sit and talk about it and talk and talk about it. There was nothing else that interested me. There was never anything physical between us, but I loved her.

At my request, Maria Schell, who was eight months pregnant, spent three days with Elizabeth. Then she called and told me, "Eddie, you are so lucky, you are so lucky that you're out of that thing. It's pure insanity." Maria Schell was a lovely woman and, more than a year later, we did have a brief affair.

Several months after leaving Rome, I was in the steam room at the Biltmore with Kurt Frings when I saw Mafia boss Frank Costello sitting across the room. Costello had just been released after spending nine months in prison. A lifetime ago, two lifetimes ago, Costello had wanted to manage me. I was sure he'd forgotten. But as we left I got a message. "Mr. Costello would like to see you." Kurt was very excited. When I introduced him to Costello, he said, "I hear you've been on a trip."

Costello laughed. "Eddie," he said in a gruff voice, "I just want to tell you, if there's anything you need, anything, you come to me. I'm at the Waldorf barbershop every morning nine o'clock. I like you, kid. You got a lotta talent."

Given the situation, I interpreted that to mean he was volunteering to take care of Burton for me. Even Kurt asked me, "So why don't you ask him to break Burton's legs?"

Sure, I was going to have Burton's legs broken. His legs weren't the problem. I never took the offer seriously. Maybe I hated Burton, but I understood completely the trap he'd fallen into; more than anyone, I knew how irresistible Elizabeth was.

Leaving Rome wasn't quite the end of my relationship with Elizabeth. As I began to put my life back together I continued to hear the wild stories about them. Apparently the drinking and the pills had gotten out of control. Early in May Elizabeth went into the hospital to recover from bruises and a black eye, which she claimed she'd gotten when her chauffeur stopped suddenly, causing her to fall forward. As *Time* reported, the truth was that Burton had beaten her up. I was told that he'd punched her and kicked her out of a car. She couldn't go in front of the camera for almost three weeks. Then Burton literally added insult to injury by telling journalists emphatically that he had no intention of marrying Elizabeth and, commenting on the fact that his price per picture had doubled, he joked, "Maybe I should give Elizabeth Taylor ten percent." Nice guy.

Two months after that terrible press conference I spoke to Elizabeth again. She called me at the Essex House. When I heard her voice I could barely breathe. All the feelings I was trying desperately to bury overpowered me. I felt like somebody was ripping a bandage off an open wound. I recognized her tone immediately; she was terribly upset about something. I thought, She needs me, she wants me to come back. Actually, she was calling from the chalet I'd bought for us in Gstaad for

$280,000—it's now worth millions—to complain. "Do you know there isn't one single bathtub in this house?"

I didn't know and I didn't care.

She continued, "Could I borrow the set of silverware?" I'd bought four sets for the house.

I'd given her my soul—what did I care about knives and forks? "Keep it all," I told her. We carefully avoided speaking about the only thing that really mattered: our entire life together. But finally I pointed out to her, "You know, you forgot our anniversary."

"No, I didn't," she responded. The next day I received a telegram reminding me that I'd gotten the date wrong. I forgot the day on which I married her? I must have been getting over her. That wasn't easy to do. I was as addicted to Elizabeth as I was to any drug. The withdrawal period was long and very painful. I'd spend hours just thinking about her, missing her, wanting her. I couldn't bear to see happy couples walking hand in hand down the street. Everything reminded me of her. I went to see the movie version of *West Side Story*. I may have even gone with the star, Natalie Wood, and one of the love scenes reminded me so much of myself and Elizabeth that my left arm went numb. I lost all feeling in that arm.

I was very frightened. I went right to Max. Usually I was the king of Max's office. It didn't matter who was there when I walked in—Alan J. Lerner, Zero Mostel—he immediately took me. This time he let me sit in his waiting room for hours. "So? Vat's wrong?" he finally asked. When I told him he sort of shrugged and said, "I mix up something special for you."

He took a little from this bottle, some from that bottle—none of these bottles were labeled but he knew what was in each of them—and filled a syringe. He put the syringe in his mouth and started rolling up my sleeve, and as he did he grabbed my arm and snapped my elbow. Instantly, the pain disappeared. It was completely psychosomatic. The real pain was in my head.

Elizabeth and Burton and *Cleopatra* continued to make headlines. Every photograph of them was like a little jab in my heart. But as the months passed the pain became less and less. At times I would go hours without thinking about Elizabeth. Then a full day. I found that the busier I was, the less I thought about her, so I tried to fill every minute of every day. The scandal hadn't been bad for my career, either. People wanted to see me. Some were curious, others wanted to give me support, and still others just wanted to say they had seen me. Whatever the reason, I was as hot as ever. I was getting $40,000 a week in Vegas, the Latin Casino in Philadelphia paid me $60,000 a week. I was sick, and singing was the best possible medicine for me. Singing and Max's shots.

When I opened at the Desert Inn in June, Elizabeth had sent fifty lavender long-stemmed roses. On occasion we had spoken about the children. I'd even heard rumors that she wanted to reconcile with me. In October, I was playing the Latin Casino, and I was such a big hit that my original run had been extended a fifth week. At about four one morning the phone rang. I had just about reached the point where I had stopped hoping it was Elizabeth every time the phone rang, but this time it really was her. When I heard her voice I was. . .words can't express is what I was. "I want to come home," she said. "I want to come back to you."

In the years I'd known Elizabeth nothing she had ever done had surprised me. I knew she was capable of anything. But this phone call surprised me. I didn't know what to say, I didn't know how to respond. I was so incredibly, unbelievably happy to hear from her. And at the same time I was terrified. Go through it all again?

"Why?" I asked her.

"Because it's right. The children love you, I love you . . ." I just let her talk. I was dizzy. I was flying. She said all the right things: children, marriage, husband, love. Love. Instantly, I was again madly in love with her. Not the Burton/Elizabeth kind of love, this was real, this was Elizabeth and Eddie. I wanted to laugh, I wanted to cry. She told me when she was coming to New York. "I want you to meet me at the airport."

"I can't meet you at the airport." I was falling. "I'm doing a show. You come here."

We spoke for almost an hour. I hung up the phone and took my first deep breath in months. She was coming back to me. She loved me. I was alive again. My brother was living with me at the time, and when I told him about the call he started crying. This was a great victory. We were whole again.

And then, as I sat there, as I started remembering what it was like to be with her, I knew I could never go through it again. The passion, the drama, the chaos; the wondering, the mistrust. I knew I could never again be comfortable with her. Inevitably, the same thing was going to happen again, maybe with Burton, maybe with somebody else, but it would happen. That's who she was. As I thought about it, I realized I didn't like the person I had to be to be with her. I didn't like the compromises I had to make, the little lies I had to accept. I didn't want to be her nurse anymore.

Within half an hour I called Dick Hanley in Switzerland. "I want you to do something for me," I said, explaining what was going on. "Whatever plan Elizabeth tells you we've made, I think you should find a good excuse for her not to come right now. You know what to say."

Elizabeth called me the next day to tell me she wasn't coming. "Something terrible has happened." What was it? "I can't talk about it right now," she answered. Or, as it turned out, ever.

In June 1963, with a publicity kit weighing more than ten pounds and the future of 20th Century-Fox at stake, *Cleopatra* opened. In addition to my marriage and the Burtons' marriage, the film had cost $40 million, more than double the cost of any film ever made. It ran slightly more than four hours, making it the longest film ever released. Each print weighed 600 pounds, making it the heaviest film ever made. After I left Rome, Walter Wanger was fired and sued the studio. Skouras sued Wanger, claiming he had libeled him in a book about the making of the picture. Darryl Zanuck replaced Skouras as president of the studio. And after shooting was complete Zanuck replaced Mankiewicz and then rehired him to edit the film. The studio sued Elizabeth and Burton for $50 million, claiming their "scandalous" conduct had depreciated the value of the film, and cited things like Elizabeth's black eye and the fact that she was often late getting to the set as having helped raise the budget to astronomical proportions.

And I had started it all when I picked the script off a pile and suggested to Elizabeth, "You should do this for a million dollars."

The film that Mankiewicz described as "conceived in emergency, shot in hysteria, and wound up in blind panic" received mixed reviews. The *New York Times* called it "one of the great epic films of our day," while the *Tribune* said it was "at best a major disappointment." *Time* decided that "Burton staggers around looking ghastly and spouting irrelevance, like a man who suddenly realizes he has lost his script. . .and in the big love scenes he seems strangely bored." And while Elizabeth looked wonderful, *Time* said, "When she plays Cleopatra as a political animal she screeches like a ward heeler's wife at a block party."

But Rex Harrison was nominated for an Academy award as Best Actor. Years later, after being sold to television, the film supposedly earned back its cost. But what it cost me I never got back.

I never saw the picture in the theater. The tickets were too expensive. Eventually I did see about half of it on television. Maybe I'm biased, but even I could see the vodka in their performances. But I was supportive, I tried to be the dutiful ex-husband. Based on the dailies I'd seen, I told reporters, "Elizabeth gives the greatest performance of her career. She *is* Cleopatra. And Rex Harrison is magnificent." And Burton? I was asked. "Burton? I didn't notice. Is he in the picture?"

I was the one who was out of the picture. My divorce from Elizabeth took longer than our marriage lasted. There was a substantial amount of money to be divided, as well as interests in our companies and custody of Liza and visitation rights to the other children. The divorce went on for years, and even after Elizabeth and Burton were married in Mexico our divorce fight continued. In many ways it was similar to the fights that occurred when I was trying to divorce Debbie, although in this case I was playing the role of spoiler. Supposedly I was the bad guy standing in the way of these great lovers being together. More than two years after we'd separated, we all happened to be in New York City. Burton was doing *Hamlet* on Broadway. I called them and we agreed to sit down face to face and try to work out our differences.

We met in their suite at the Regency. I was surprised at how the balance of their relationship had changed. Elizabeth was in complete control, Burton had become almost docile and very domesticated. Burton was unusually friendly to me. He asked me where I bought my cigars, and when I told him the Connaught Hotel in London he called and ordered the same cigars. Then he invited me to stand in the wings when he did his *Hamlet*. And meanwhile, as Elizabeth and I were talking, he was performing all my old duties: He was picking up, giving her a pillow, pouring drinks. He had become her nurse. Maybe he was doing *Hamlet* onstage, but in real life he was playing my role.

I laughed, oh how I laughed. She'd won again. We didn't settle the divorce, in fact it continued for several more years, but as I left the hotel I felt a sense of freedom I'd hadn't felt in a long, long time. I still loved my image of her—and I always would—but I was no longer in love with her. It all seemed so long ago. I actually felt a little sorry for Richard Burton. I was free and I knew it—I was free.

Well, except for this little doctor with a thick accent and his magic mixtures.

CHAPTER NINE

When my marriage to Connie Stevens ended in 1968 she wrote me a long letter, which concluded, "I wish you good luck, good health and wealth and happiness in your own time on your terms—I do not wish you love as you wouldn't know what to do with it."

Maybe she was right. The quest for romance has dominated my life. I allowed it to take precedence over my career, the biggest mistake I ever made. And yet—and yet I wouldn't have missed it for the world. I was in love with Elizabeth, madly in love. I once believed that nothing could break us up. The end of our marriage left me with a hole in my heart. I tried very hard to fill that void. I wanted so much to find that feeling again. The fact that the women in my life were exceptionally beautiful did not make it difficult. Maybe I should have realized that it was impossible. No one would ever compare to the image of Elizabeth that is always in my head.

By the time I was thirty-three years old I'd been married to America's sweetheart and America's femme fatale and both marriages had ended in scandal; I'd been one of the most popular singers in America and had given up my career for love; I had fathered two children and adopted two children and rarely saw any of them; I was addicted to methamphetamines and I couldn't sleep at night without a huge dose of Librium. And from all this I had learned one very important lesson: There were no rules for me. I could get away with anything so long as that sound came out of my throat. And even after everything that had happened, I still believed that would be true forever.

In the previous two years I'd released only one record and had worked just seven weeks, yet I was a bigger attraction than ever. The less I worked, the more popular I became. When I'd returned from Rome, Milton had immediately set up an ambitious nightclub schedule that started in Los Angeles and ended in New York. People wanted to see me, he said. He was absolutely right; they wanted to see me, not necessarily hear me.

This time, *this time*, I vowed to treat my career seriously. I realized how lucky I'd been. I'd never had to struggle; I'd always gotten the right breaks at the right time. I'd come very close to throwing it all away. I'd allowed romance to come first with me, maybe even first and second, then the music. That was all going to change. I was going to concentrate on my career. I was going to do all the things I'd neglected to do. But just to be certain, I had Max to help me.

I didn't want to exploit the scandal. But that was almost impossible. In every interview the first questions were always about Elizabeth and *Cleopatra* and Burton. I generally refused to comment on that subject. In fact, sometimes it seemed like I was the only person in America who wasn't talking about Liz and Dick.

Milton got me into the recording studio as quickly as possible. *"Arrivedérci, Roma"* and *"After You've Gone"* became my first hit record in several years. Asked if I'd selected that song to cash in on the headlines, I explained, "That's ridiculous. What did you expect me to sing, 'Take Me Out to the Ball Game?' " My private life was so publicly known that almost every song Milton and I considered seemed to carry a hidden, personal message. Among the songs Milton suggested were "I'm Beginning to See the Light," "Don't Talk about Me When I'm Gone," "Someone Else May Be There When I'm Gone," and "The Thrill Is Gone."

Less than two months after separating from Elizabeth I opened at the Cocoanut Grove in Hollywood. It was like the old days at the Paramount. Opening night they turned away 5,000 people. I got a standing ovation just for showing up. I opened my act by asking, "Well, what's new?" then adding, "A funny thing happened to me on the way to the Forum." I couldn't ignore the subject, so I used it as material. "You all know about *Cleopatra*. They took so long to shoot that picture they could have used the original cast—and I wish they had!" Ba-dum-dum. "Fourteen million for a war scene. A real war doesn't cost that much!" Ba-dum-dum! I opened with a specialty number, titled "Love Is a Lovely Thing, But Don't Let It Get You Down," and finished seventy minutes later with "I'm Sitting on Top of the World." I was a huge hit. Winchell wrote that it was "one of the most exciting and electric premieres in the last 50 years," explaining, "He stopped the show colder than a faithless wife's heart." The Associated Press reported that "Eddie Fisher sang as if a weight had been lifted from his tonsils."

It had. When I'd left Rome one journalist wrote that Elizabeth had "turned away from him in a public gesture of such disdain such as. . . the world had not seen since Emperor Caligula named his horse a proconsul of the Roman Empire." I didn't know how I would recover from that public humiliation. I knew that it would be a long time—a long, long time—before I ever fell in love with another woman. Before I could ever trust another woman.

It took weeks and weeks. Well, at least weeks. I was in my suite at the Pierre Hotel with Lenny Gaines watching the Academy Awards. I was in a complete stupor. It seemed impossible that it had been only a year ago that Elizabeth and I had walked together to the stage to receive her Oscar. If I took a deep breath I could still smell her perfume. I could still feel her warmth as she leaned against me. It had been a glorious night, a night I could never forget. So as I watched all those glamorous, happy couples at the Academy Awards I felt so alone, so depressed, so worthless—and then a young girl named Ann-Margret danced across the screen. Well, maybe life wasn't so terrible after all. Hellooooo, Ann-Margret Olsen.

"That's the girl who's gonna get me out of this," I told Lenny.

"Oh, no," he said. "Here we go again."

Here we went again. Instant magic. The nicest compliment I can pay Ann-Margret is that the contents were every bit as wonderful as the package. She was young and beautiful and just bursting with life. Her smile, the way she moved, her body language was the most expressive I'd ever seen. Every word in that language meant sex. After all the drama with Elizabeth, she was light and free, she was playful, she was exactly what I needed. As I watched her I knew that she could cure my problems. My problems? As I looked at her I thought, She could cure cancer.

I met her the night I opened at the Cocoanut Grove. There was a mob of people in my dressing room after the show and, like a song, I looked across the room and saw her standing there. We started dating almost immediately. Just Ann-Margret and me and her parents. She was an old-fashioned Swedish girl and insisted that her parents chaperone us on our first few dates. I thought it was charming. I invited Ann-Margret and her parents to come to see me perform at Lake Tahoe, much as I had invited Debbie's parents to London, and Elizabeth's parents to Rome. But charming endures only a few dates.

It was obvious she was going to be a big star. She had the talent, the beauty and the intelligence. Everybody loved her. George Burns was crazy about her, but I had a big advantage. As I said in my act, "I'm available. Boy, am I available."

Maybe because of her Swedish background, she had very healthy feelings about sex. She loved life and she loved love. We didn't make love for several dates, but once we started we didn't stop for about a year. She more than lived up to the character she played, the sex-kitten, which I found rarely happens. Many women use sex as a tool or a weapon to attract men or to keep them, but not Ann-Margret. For her, and with her, sex was fun. She seemed to get as much pleasure out of sex as any man.

After finishing my booking at the Cocoanut Grove I opened at the Desert Inn in Las Vegas. Edie Adams, the widow of my friend the brilliant comedian Ernie Kovacs, was working at the Riviera. The widow of a friend? That sounded familiar. She was struggling with her act, so I tried to help her. I made a few suggestions, but all I really did was give her the extra confidence she needed. Eventually our relationship became personal. Edie was a sexy lady who liked to wear a full-length chinchilla fur coat with nothing under it. She was my date for my opening at the Desert Inn. After the show I was in my dressing room—it was a tiny room but I'd forced them to enlarge it and put in a bathroom so I wouldn't have to pee in the sink—when Ann-Margret walked in. She'd flown to Vegas to surprise me. Which she most certainly did. Suddenly the door opened, and Edie Adams was standing there in that fur coat. "Oh," she said, embarrassed, shocked, maybe even a little hurt. "I'll be at the bar."

What could I say to her, "Have you met Ann-Margret?"

Ann-Margret didn't make me forget Elizabeth. No one could do that. My love for Elizabeth was on a different plane; it was real and it was deep and it was lasting. It wasn't something you simply get over. But Ann-Margret took me out of mourning for that relationship. Once I had been in love with being in love, now I was falling in love with sex. Sex *and* my career could both be first.

This was the very beginning of the sexual revolution in America, and perceptions about what was acceptable, about what was right, were changing. And in that sexual revolution, I was a prisoner of war. I was born with a sound in my mouth, but I was also born with an appetite for love. Let the experts explain where it came from. Maybe I was over-compensating for all my childhood insecurities. I don't know. I know it was as much a need as a desire. And women were so easily available to me. How could I resist? How could any man in my situation resist? And why would I want to resist? Women wanted me as much, and sometimes even more than, I wanted them.

My voice enabled me to reach the hearts of my audience, but it also changed me. I loved the sound of my voice, I loved what I heard, and that gave me tremendous self-assurance, incredible confidence. It made me feel attractive.

I was in love with Ann-Margret as much as I was able to be in love with anyone not named Elizabeth Taylor. Our relationship wasn't mo-nogamous. Neither one of us was ready for that, and there were a lot of men pursuing her. Among those men was the President of the United

States, John F. Kennedy. Maybe he didn't sing as well as Richard Burton, but it was quite good for my damaged ego to have the President pursuing my girlfriend.

I had met President Kennedy several times. One morning I had arrived at Max Jacobson's office for my shot and found the place in an uproar. "Come vit me," he ordered. "I haf to see the President." I knew Max had very powerful friends, but the President? That President? It did not strike me as odd or even unusual that several hours later I was sitting outside the Oval Office with Max waiting to see the President of the United States. With Max, anything was possible. Max could make night into day. Max with his filthy fingernails and his magic potions treating the President of the United States? But I never doubted him.

Max told me that photographer Mark Shaw had introduced him to Jacqueline Kennedy, whom he had also treated. Then Jackie convinced Jack that Max could relieve his back pain, and probably anything else that bothered him. Years later Jackie would claim that Jack had brought Max into their lives, but that was not what Max told me.

I'd been Harry Truman's favorite private, I'd sung for Ike, I'd flirted with a princess, but I'd never met anybody like Jack Kennedy. He was the first politician to understand the power of his image, the first show-business President, the only President to give me the monogrammed shirt off his back. While getting a shot one day he took off his shirt—he didn't have to, but he did—and tossed it to me. I put it on—it was about four sizes too big for me. "You don't want that?" he asked me.

"I don't want it? Yeah, I want it." So he gave it to me. I kept it for a long time. The President of the United States gives you the shirt off his back, that means something. But like everything else I once owned, somewhere, sometime, it just seemed to disappear.

I went with Max to the White House several times. On one occasion Kennedy met with Max before confronting Roger Blau, head of U.S. Steel. The President was elated when he came out of the meeting with Blau, and gave much of the credit to Max. So Max became almost indispensable. My friend Max became a White House doctor. Max giving his pick-me-up shots to the President! The people around Kennedy hated Max. They didn't like anything about him, from the way he looked to the way he treated his patient. Bobby Kennedy hated him more than he hated Hoffa. The White House doctors demanded to know what was in the shots he was giving the President, and Max, my little Maxie, refused to tell them. Tell them? He wouldn't even tell *me*. "If I told you," he'd reply when I asked him, "would you know?"

Kennedy protected Max. I heard him tell a subordinate one day, "I don't care if there's panther piss in there, as long as it makes me feel good." Feel good. Feelgood. That's who Max became, Dr. Feelgood. That was the nickname people knew him by: "I'm going to see Dr. Feelgood."

Jackie did not receive shots from Max as often as the President. But once I remember, the night before they were scheduled to leave for Paris, she found out about some of Jack's women and decided she wasn't going with him. She locked herself in the Lincoln Bedroom. Somehow Max ended up begging her to come out. He gave her an injection and she changed her mind.

The President even took Max and his wife, Nina, with him when he went to Vienna for a summit meeting with Russian Premier Nikita Khrushchev. Looking back on it, it's amazing how we all just accepted the fact that the President was taking Dr. Feelgood with him to a meeting that would affect the entire world. The fate of the free world rested on Max's injections. I can still see Max taking a little from this bottle, a little from that one, and pull down your pants, Mr. President.

I first met Jack Kennedy in the midst of my separation from Elizabeth. He knew all about it; he loved celebrity gossip, and wanted to know all the details. "What's new? What's going on?" he'd ask. I used to think he was more interested in gossip than in Russian missiles. Most people are, I've found. The only people who aren't are called Republicans. But I didn't want to discuss Elizabeth and Burton, even with the President of the United States. I think it was pretty obvious that I was in the middle of a serious depression. Eventually Max gave him his shot and we left.

The following October, two weeks before the Cuban missile crisis began, I was in New York to play the Winter Garden. There is no connection. Ann-Margret, who was there with me, was invited to meet President Kennedy in his suite at the Carlyle. Between Burton and Kennedy, by that time I'd had just about enough of Camelot. Apparently Camelot consisted of dating Eddie Fisher's wife or girlfriend. I kept telling Ann-Margret, "It's him or me, it's him or me." Believe me, she was so beautiful, she could have picked Burton.

I took her to the Carlyle in my limo. Of course I trusted Kennedy—

he was the President of the United States—but just to be certain I waited downstairs for her. She was up and back down in fifteen minutes. What could happen in fifteen minutes? It didn't. But it was extremely flattering to me that this beautiful, sexy, young woman had picked me over Jack Kennedy.

Kennedy and I had actually had several things in common in addition to an attraction to Ann-Margret. They were Angie Dickinson, Judith Campbell Exner, and a gorgeous German model named Renata Boeck. Near the end of my relationship with Ann-Margret I'd met Renata at the home of attorney Sidney Korshak, an extremely powerful man few people outside of Los Angeles, Las Vegas, and New York had ever heard of, and we'd started dating. Many of the people I was with at that time were friends of the White House and I was told that Jack Kennedy wanted to meet her. I don't know if they ever met, but he knew I was going out with her.

During the brief period I was dating both Ann-Margret and Renata, I co-produced a birthday party for the President at the Waldorf-Astoria with Alan Jay Lerner. Audrey Hepburn sang, Louis Nizer danced, Sugar Ray Robinson moved the piano. But the highlight was Ann-Margret, who did a provocative dance directly in front of Kennedy. People remember Marilyn Monroe's incredibly suggestive rendition of "Happy Birthday" to him, but Ann-Margret's dance just buried that. She was so bold. Jackie was sitting right next to the President, smiling, but I don't think she meant it. After the show I was standing in the reception line between Audrey Hepburn and attorney Louis Nizer. My good friend, my pal, Jack Kennedy, for whom I'd co-produced this grand show, said a few words to Audrey, said a few words to Nizer, and then walked right past me without a word. Not a word. I was stunned. He didn't even acknowledge my presence. I couldn't believe he would insult me like that in front of all these people. But as he moved down the line he suddenly did a triple take, turned to me with a mischievous smile on his face, and, knowing exactly what I was doing with both Ann-Margret and Renata, asked, "So Eddie, how are you feeling now?"

I dated Ann-Margret for almost a year. I even gave her a little Yorkshire terrier. Jewels and Yorkies, those were my favorite gifts. But eventually she said something terrible to me: "Marriage." Marriage? I was almost four years away from being divorced from Elizabeth. I don't know if Ann-Margret really meant it. We both knew we weren't going to get married; it's possible that was just a nice way of ending our relationship. How else could she do it? Burton was taken. We ended as friends.

I wasn't ready to be serious with anyone. I was still in the process of transforming my nervous breakdown into my lifestyle. But I was surprised to discover that being dumped by Elizabeth had made me an extremely desirable man. I had gained a reputation for being an incredible lover—which is not a terrible reputation to have. And, unlike being a member of a subversive group, it isn't something you need to deny. There were many women like Sue Lyon, the very beautiful little girl who had starred as *Lolita*, who wanted to know if I was a better lover than Burton, so she slept with both of us. She was very upfront about her motives: This wasn't love, this was an experiment. Naturally, I rose to the challenge.

I've often been asked about my secret for attracting beautiful women. My secret was that I had no secret. I just showed up with a clean shirt, a sweet song, and occasionally a small jewel. I treated women nicely. When I was married to Elizabeth I had been completely faithful, but after we parted, the only person to whom I was faithful was myself. I never lied to the women I dated. I didn't promise fidelity and I didn't ask for it.

I often dated more than one woman at a time—although except for that situation with Edie Adams I usually only dated one woman a night. At just about the same time I started dating Ann-Margret, for example, I began seeing dancer Juliet Prowse. I also met her at the Cocoanut Grove. She had one of the most exquisite bodies I'd ever seen, perfect long legs—I mean long, long legs—and the most beautiful complexion. I was immediately attracted to her, but there was a slight problem—she was seeing Sinatra. I called him in London, at Claridge's, and he "granted" me Juliet Prowse. "Go ahead, have a ball." Then he invited me to join him in London when I finished my engagement.

My relationship with Juliet Prowse was perfect. We enjoyed being together, the sex was lovely, and we were both in love with other people. Neither one of us had any expectations beyond that night. She was in love with Sinatra, and in addition to me, she was dating Elvis Presley. I was in love with Elizabeth, and in addition to Juliet and Ann-Margret, I was dating a lot of women. We dated long enough for Winchell to wonder,

"Eddie; Frank; Juliet—New Film Triangle?"

Kurt Frings and I left for London the day after I closed at the Cocoanut Grove. Although Kurt was Elizabeth's agent, in reality he hated her, and we had become closer friends because he thought I felt the same way. "One day we'll get even," he said.

When Kurt and I got to London, Sinatra was trying to organize a new Rat Pack with Yul Brenner, Laurence Harvey, and several other candidates. There were women there—there were always women when Frank was there—and we'd go out, we'd gamble, then return to Sinatra's suite to dance to Frank Sinatra music. And *only* Sinatra music. I liked listening to my own music, but I also enjoyed other singers. When I was with a woman I played Sinatra, a lot of Perry Como, and even Eddy Arnold, who had one song that was just great for sex: "Whatcha Doin' in My World." But at Sinatra's place we danced only to Sinatra. I kept making jokes about that, but nobody listened. They were listening to the Sinatra music.

I knew Sinatra well. When I was just a kid crooning at the Copa and dating Joanie Wynne, Frank had been dating Joanie's roommate. Since then, our careers, and our women, had crossed many times. We were never really close friends, although he always treated me differently than the other singers. I never asked him for anything—he asked me. When he couldn't sing, he'd call me to replace him. "One night," he'd promise, "just for one night." Inevitably I'd be there a week.

While I respected Sinatra for his career and his music—no one will ever compare in any way to what he accomplished as a singer of songs, not Elvis, not the Beatles, certainly not me—I didn't consider him a friend. He knew he was the king and he played that role. I remember him saying, "I'd rather be a don for the Mafia than President of the United States," and that's the way he acted. While at times he was the most gracious, generous person possible, he could also be mean and spiteful and petty. I remember one morning in London when Kurt and I went over to Sinatra's for breakfast. He was with a beautiful woman whose head was covered with a kerchief. Trying to be funny, pretending to be an obedient servant, I bowed and said, "Good morning, Your Highness." I didn't know who she was. We were not introduced. But that afternoon newspapers reported that Princess Alexandra had been with Sinatra. He was livid. He was determined to find out who had betrayed him. It was as if he were starring in a bad gangster movie. He was obsessed with finding the guy who ratted him out. This was the other side of him: the tough guy, the bully. Eventually he told me he'd narrowed it down to two hotel employees. He planned to confront them with his "evidence." Finally, at a party the night before he was scheduled to leave, I said to him, "Leave it alone, Frank. It doesn't make any difference."

He glared at me with those cold blue eyes. "Who the fuck asked you?" Nothing ever came of it, and he left London without uncovering the source of the leak. Who knows what he would have done if he'd found out. Nothing, probably.

Sinatra continually surprised me with his actions. After giving me permission to sleep with Juliet Prowse, for example, practically the first thing he did when he returned to America was call her. "I want to see you right away. I've missed you terribly," he said, and started seeing her again.

I didn't mind. I'd remained completely infatuated with Juliet Prowse right up until the first night I'd slept with her. Then my feelings changed. The sex was wonderful, the sex was always wonderful, but without realizing it, I had become infatuated with the chase. When I was with a woman, the woman I really wanted to be with was the next one. In the language of the politically correct, I had become a serial polygamist.

The women I dated had two things in common: They weren't Elizabeth and they were all beautiful. Renata Boeck was the most beautiful of them all, but I could say that about any one of them. Certainly one of the things that made Renata so attractive to me was the fact that she wasn't available. I had to pursue her, I had to win her. The chase was on.

She had been dating a friend of mine, Bob Evans, for almost a year. I'd first met Bob Evans years earlier, when he'd tried unsuccessfully to steal Joanie Wynne from me. He'd made a fortune in the garment industry, appropriately in women's pants, running a sportswear company called Evan-Picone. I thought he was an amusing guy. He enjoyed playing the role of the aristocratic bachelor; he dressed conservatively and spoke in a very affected manner. It was always "Good evening, gentlemen." And like a lot of people I knew, he desperately wanted to be a star.

Evans had the money, but what he really wanted was the attention and the power—and the beautiful women—that came with fame. But the difference between Evans and almost everyone else is that he actually made it. He sold his company and moved to Hollywood to become an actor. I didn't know he wanted to be an actor. I thought he wanted to sell pants. He befriended the aging actress Norma Shearer, who got him the role of her ex-husband, Irving Thalberg, in *The Man of a Thousand Faces*. She helped him get roles like Ava Gardner's lover in *The Sun Also Rises* and a rich bachelor in *The Best of Everything*. This was Bob Evans, the pants guy, the guy who sent Elizabeth more than 100 pairs of slacks as a present, starring as Ava Gardner's lover. I was very impressed; as an actor he was every bit as talented as I was. When his acting career ended he became a successful movie producer, eventually running Paramount.

I met Renata Boeck at Sidney Korshak's brownstone in New York. Kurt Frings had warned me, "You're going to meet the most beautiful girl you've ever seen in your life." Kurt knew his beautiful women. She was a twenty-two-year-old "cover girl," the term used in those days for "supermodel," and she was gorgeous. Irresistible. The fact that she was Evans' girlfriend didn't stop me from pursuing her—I knew Evans was a player. There were always beautiful women around him, so I didn't think he was any more serious about Renata than he had been about several other women.

I told Evans that I was attracted to her, but he continued to put temptation in my way. I suspect he needed a challenge to spark romance as much as I did. And perhaps he liked the fact that after all the years we'd been friends, the situation was finally reversed: He was with a woman I wanted. So when I was playing the Eden Roc in Miami Beach he brought her with him, and I sang my love songs directly to her. When I was working at the Americana Hotel in New York a month later, on Sundays we would all drive out to the estate of a mutual friend of ours. Evans would play tennis, leaving me alone with Renata. At every opportunity I would ask her out. I really pursued her. I used all my charm. Finally she agreed to have dinner with me.

When Evans found out he called and began threatening me. "You know she belongs to me," he said.

"Nobody belongs to anybody," I told him. Boy, I'd learned that lesson.

"All right," he finally decided. "I challenge you. And may the best man win!" It was such a wonderfully archaic thing to say, and perfectly in character for him. "May the best man win." Even Burton never said that. Once gentlemen had fought over the affections of a lady with pistols at ten paces, or with swords. Our weapons were going to be credit cards, candlelit dinners, and sexual prowess.

Renata and I had dinner in New York. We talked, we laughed, we drank, we fell in love. Love is lovelier. . .the tenth or twentieth time around, but we didn't sleep together that night. Evans was livid. I didn't hear anymore of that "best man" stuff. Instead, he came looking for me at the hotel. He was crazy. He was going to kill her. He was going to kill me. He was going to kill everybody. Imagine what he would have threatened if we had slept together.

When he couldn't find me, he stashed her in an apartment with her two dogs and her blind cat. "You'll never see her again," he told me. "She doesn't love you!"

It seemed to me I'd heard this song before. How could she not love me? We'd already been out once! I knew it was the real thing. Evans agreed to meet me. The two of us would meet on Fifth Avenue at two o'clock in the morning. It was egos at ten paces. I'd never heard of anything so ridiculous, but for the love of a beautiful woman I agreed. The truth is that I was a little apprehensive. Actually I was a lot apprehensive. He felt he had been wronged. To protect myself I had my valet, my friend, Willard Higgins, tag along. His assignment was to stay back about half a block but be ready to assist me if I needed help.

"You know," Evans said when we met, "she's my girl."

"Bob, she's not your girl. You can't hide her. You've got to let her decide."

Finally we agreed that we would send her to Europe, away from both of us, where she could take her time and decide which one of us she wanted to be with. "But no calling her on the telephone," he said, "because I know what you do on the telephone."

Instead of going to Europe, Renata got away from Evans and wound up at Sidney Korshak's house in Los Angeles. She called and told me she wanted to see me. I was opening the new Crystal Room at the Desert Inn and we made plans to meet there. I arrived in Las Vegas three days early to rehearse. The night before I opened she finally called and asked me to come to Los Angeles. The night before I opened? This was my career, I was in the midst of my big comeback. I couldn't possibly get away. How could I fly to Los Angeles to meet a beautiful woman? It was just one rehearsal—I was there that night.

I couldn't resist. That night I made love to her nine times. Nine times! Nine orgasms. I was exhilarated. Exhausted, but exhilarated. I couldn't get enough of her. Nine times. Nine. Nothing like that had ever happened to me before. I didn't think that was possible. It had to be a miracle. So at six o'clock in the morning I called my genius. "Max," I said, "Max, you're not gonna believe this, but I swear it's true. I made love last night nine times. How could that happen?"

Max responded calmly, "Don't expect it to happen all the time."

All the time? Before that it had never happened to me once. Debbie and I. . .well, Elizabeth and I had had an active, lusty sex life. But nine times, never. And the next night it was eight times, then seven, six. Renata came to Vegas with me. She came to every show and sat at a table by herself, and I sang my love songs to her. I was staying in a brand-new penthouse and I didn't want her dogs and cat running around, so I rented a bungalow with a pool for her on a golf course at the Tally Ho Hotel. When the animals started climbing all over me, I rented a second bungalow—with another pool—just for them.

Almost immediately our relationship made gossip-column headlines, EDDIE FISHER'S IN LOVE, wrote Dorothy Kilgallen. Oh, she hated me so much. "What made her switch from Bob to Eddie, although Bob is not only handsomer but richer and more amusing? 'Marriage' is the answer." Marriage? "The crooner has hinted broadly to friends that he intends to make Renata his next bride. . .within three or four months."

Suzy wrote that I was so crazy about Renata that I'd taken up golf and given up gambling. The closest I came to the golf course was her bungalow. She would run around the course in a white bikini. And rather than giving up gambling, Renata and I spent part of every night in the casinos. Since Mike Todd had introduced me to the casinos I'd become a heavy gambler. At the crap tables I'd bet the limit, $7,000 a roll. Renata was what I referred to as my "limited partner." When I won, she got half my earnings; when I lost, she still kept half those earnings. She would bet with the "vigorish," something between ten and twenty-five dollars. She'd win or lose a few bucks but enjoyed the thrill of playing.

And when we got back to her room at night she'd make neat piles of her earnings, which was a bigger thrill. I don't know how much money she had, but there were a lot of piles.

I knew I was in love with her, nine times, when Ann-Margret arrived in town with Elvis and I didn't even try to see her. But as we were gambling one evening, Renata turned to me and asked me for ten dollars to bet. I don't know exactly why that hurt me so much— what was ten dollars to me? I'd happily given her thousands, enough to build a house for her parents in Germany, but all of a sudden I felt like she was using me. In that instant I stopped loving her. I saw her as a very different person. That was it. I didn't want to be with her anymore. We'd been together a long time, more than two months, it was time to end it.

I just stopped talking to her. I'd sit by myself and read. She became hysterical, demanding to know what had happened. I closed my mind is what had happened. But that wasn't the end of our relationship.

She began seeing Jim Aubrey, the "Love Machine," who became the president of CBS. About a year later I was working at Skinny D'Amato's 500 Club in Atlantic City when she slipped a note under my door. It said, "I still love you. Come up to the roof." I met her there and we made love under the overcast sky.

Sometime later we were both in New York and met for dinner. Later we were drinking beer in her apartment and started again. I stopped. "I'll give you a hundred dollars if you let me go pee first." She took the hundred. Ah, the things we still do for love.

This comeback was a tremendous success. I filled every room I played. The offers just poured in. As I told a reporter, "There are enough offers to keep me singing on this planet until I get my first engagement on the moon. I'll sing anyplace, anywhere, at any time." While Elizabeth wasn't in my life, she was still an important part of my act. When I opened at the Winter Garden, Juliet Prowse appeared with me. She did a number in which she sang, "I'm Cleo, the nympho of the Nile." When Elizabeth heard about this she supposedly told reporter Jim Bacon, "Eddie's trying to make people think I'm a nymphomaniac."

To which Bacon also supposedly sighed and replied, "Well, Elizabeth, I've never met a nymphomaniac I didn't like."

Elizabeth and I spent years fighting over the terms of our divorce. She and Burton had a tempestuous marriage. They made several terrible movies together as his career dissipated, and still our divorce wasn't settled. I was beyond caring. I still loved Elizabeth, but the Elizabeth I loved existed only in my memory.

Elizabeth had set me free, which is probably the nicest way of describing the events in Rome, to live every man's fantasy. I had few responsibilities, I had as much money as I needed, I had Max to make me feel good, and I was continually meeting gorgeous women who wanted to be with me. I never stopped to think about what I was doing. If I had, if I had really thought about it, I suspect I would have been absolutely thrilled, and I would have kept doing it. Thank heaven for little girls.

Beautiful women were never more than a phone call away. *Playboy*'s Hugh Hefner and I had become friends, and there were always gorgeous women around him. Once when I was spending a few days at the Waldorf Towers in New York before going to San Juan, for example, he sent over ten girls to entertain me until I left. I met women everywhere, every day. Women of all types and shapes. And I loved them all, until I met the next one.

Three weeks after Louella Parsons reported that Renata Boeck was "the real thing," we were done and I'd met Carol Lynley. Now Carol Lynley was beautiful outside and inside, although admittedly it was the outside in which I was more interested. And Carol Lynley became "the real thing" for several days. And then I met a smart, talented young actress named Stefanie Powers at the Daisy, the hottest club in Beverly Hills.

Carol who? The moment I saw Stefanie it was lust at first sight. She reminded me of a sexy Audrey Hepburn, and I loved Audrey Hepburn. When I took Stefanie with me to Las Vegas, her mother came along to chaperone us. Her mother was also a very attractive woman, so to get her out of the way I fixed her up with Moe Dalitz, the most charming mobster I've ever known. Moe Dalitz was a handsome guy who ran the Desert Inn for the "boys." I never knew what happened between him and Stefanie's mother, but that was the end of our chaperone. At the end of the evening Mrs. Powers would remind me, "Please take care of my little girl." And I always listened to mothers.

I dated Stefanie for several months, but, as always, I continued seeing other women. One night Stefanie and I were in bed and I got a call from

Sandy Grant, Tony Bennett's ex-wife, with whom I'd had a lovely affair. I shouldn't have answered the phone. She started screaming at me, "You should be with me. You belong to me."

"I don't belong to anybody," I said. Maybe Max, but I didn't say that.

When she threatened to commit suicide if I didn't see her, I hung up the phone. Now *that* was a lesson I had learned from Elizabeth. I'd made a pledge: The moment I heard the word *suicide*, I walked.

Stefanie had that same single-minded determination to be a star that I'd seen in so many women. Her career was the focus of her life. So she was always concerned with her weight, always dieting, worrying about every pound. I thought she was becoming obsessive, and we argued about it. She was a beautiful girl, but she insisted on losing weight. "You're getting too thin," I told her. "You don't want to be an Audrey Hepburn."

You don't want to be Audrey Hepburn? Audrey Hepburn was one of the most popular movie stars in the world, an internationally acclaimed actress. What young actress didn't want to be Audrey Hepburn? Eventually I lost interest in Stefanie. My excuse was that she got too thin, that I no longer found her attractive. But I had stayed with her about as long as I was capable of being with any woman. It wasn't the pounds, it was the time.

One night at the Daisy, Stefanie had introduced me to Steve Brandt, who was a press agent for several music groups, including the Mamas and the Papas. Steve didn't appear human; he looked like a living scarecrow. He was flamboyantly gay long before being gay was politically acceptable. The girls liked him because he was a great dancer and they were completely safe with him, and the guys liked him because the girls liked him. Everybody in Hollywood knew him, but he had very few real friends. I was one of the few. I liked him because he was so—vulnerable, maybe. Defensive? I saw something behind the facade he showed to the rest of the world. He let me see aspects of his personality that he hid from everyone else. And he adored me; he worshiped me.

I'd bought a spectacular house in Beverly Hills overlooking Los Angeles, a perfect place to throw parties, and I let him plan these parties and invite the guests. These were his parties. I just played host and paid the bills. There were often several hundred people there, ranging from the biggest stars in Hollywood to hippies who'd just arrived in town.

Steve was constantly trying to prove himself to me. He introduced me to so many beautiful women that I began to refer to him as my procurer. He hated that, hated it. But it was based on fact; it was Steve who introduced me to Sandy Grant and Sue Lyon, Michelle Phillips, Barbara Perkins, Peggy Lipton, every one of them beautiful. He once insisted on betting me that he could introduce me to a new girl every single night of a three-week engagement at the Cocoanut Grove. I thought it was ridiculous—there was something tawdry about it—but he insisted. This was his way of proving himself to me.

So for eighteen nights—I had Mondays off—at the end of the evening he brought a new woman to my dressing room. Mostly starlets, but some of them known actresses. All of them beautiful. Eighteen nights, eighteen women. It was an experiment in sex. I was exhausted, but curious. Some nights I couldn't wait for the door to open to see what he had for me, other nights I was so tired I wanted to lock the door.

And I loved them all. Not just those women, but all of them. That was my problem. Once I started, I just couldn't stop. Couldn't stop? Why would I want to? Why would I not pursue a woman as beautiful as Michelle Phillips? The Mamas and Papas were at the height of their success when I met Michelle Phillips. She was unhappily married to John Phillips. I don't even think they were together at the time. There was a great visceral attraction between us, like sexual magnets. I remember that somebody had recently given me a ring that I loved, but I immediately loved Michelle more, so I gave it to her. Our affair was brief and wonderful.

Almost every affair I had was wonderful—and brief. Too brief for it not to be wonderful. Peggy Lipton, the lovely star of the TV show *Mod Squad*, was one of the very few Jewish girls with whom I had an affair. Not counting Elizabeth, of course. An affair? That sounds so formal. It was a romance, a charming romance. After Peggy Lipton married Quincy Jones, I was always afraid I was going to run into them and he would want to fight me. But by the time I met him, he and Peggy Lipton had divorced and he was married to Nastassja Kinski. "You know, when Peggy was very young . . ." I confessed to him. He knew all about it. We sat and talked for hours, I'd never met anyone who knew the record business better than he did. My conversation with Quincy Jones lasted almost as long as my affair with Peggy Lipton.

Because I so admired Quincy Jones, I had been concerned about his feelings. But generally I believed that all was fair in love and war— although I wasn't too sure about war.

Sinatra and I dated several of the same women. Not at the same time, of course. Well, except for Mia Farrow. Mia Farrow was a beautiful and strange little girl who grew up to become a beautiful and strange woman. I'd never met anyone like her: very smart, very mature; sometimes I thought she was not of this world. She was certainly attractive, but it was probably the fact that she was dating Sinatra that made her so desirable to me. I think one of the reasons she started seeing me was to make him jealous. Sinatra was crazy about her. He was calling constantly, but she didn't want to speak with him. She told me she wasn't going to marry him. I knew Sinatra better than she did. As long as she refused to marry him, they were going to get married. "You watch," I told her. "You're going to marry him."

I remember the night I almost married her. First thing that morning George Hamilton had called and hinted to me that he was in bed with Lynda Bird Johnson, the President's daughter—the hint was that he told me he was in bed, then put her on the phone. That night Mia and I went to his house for dinner, and afterward George and Lynda and Mia and I settled down on couches to watch the appropriately named movie *An Affair to Remember*, but really to make out. Eventually Mia and I left for another party, and then she decided we should drive to Mexico. Drive to Mexico? At that hour driving to Mexico with a beautiful young woman for the night seemed like exactly the right thing to do.

After we crossed the border into Tijuana she had another idea. "Let's get married."

It was obvious she didn't believe in long engagements. Marriage? Like till-death-do-us-part-type marriage? Well, I knew that would affect her relationship with Sinatra. But at that hour, in Mexico with a beautiful young woman, it seemed—totally insane. So naturally I agreed.

There was only one condition. She said, "I have to call Roddy Mc-Dowall and get his permission."

Now, this is what is known as irony. This was Roddy—Elizabeth's close friend, the person who told me I wasn't a man for going to see Sybil—McDowall. After all these years my hatred for Roddy McDowall was finally going to pay off. He would never give Mia permission to marry me. Mia couldn't get Roddy McDowall on the phone, so obviously we couldn't get married. It would be inaccurate to describe my response as "heartbroken." I probably was not even "heart-cracked."

Would I have married her? It would be simple to say no. But considering all the crazy things I've done in my life, the answer is I really don't know. But the only good thing Roddy McDowall ever did for me was not be there.

My entire relationship with Mia lasted little more than a week. One date, she claimed publicly. Like it had no meaning. How could she so easily forget the man she almost married? I must have been in love with her for. . .hours.

Sinatra and I also dated Abbe Lane, the most exotic Jewish girl from Brooklyn ever to become a Latin star. Abbe Lane is in my heart and in my mind. She was discovered by the great Spanish band leader Xavier Cugat, who had the good sense to marry her. I met her in Mexico City, after she had divorced Cugat and been thrown away by Frank, so she was very sad and unprotected. And oh so gorgeous. I was opening a new club and she was scheduled to follow me in, so she came down a week early to rehearse. She'd come into the club every night and I would introduce her, then I would do a little Spanish number and she would come onstage, moving her body like few women have ever moved their bodies. Cugat was no dummy. I couldn't take my eyes off her. I wasn't with anyone and as I watched her shaking that magnificent body, naturally I thought, I've got to get her a Pucci dress.

Pucci made beautiful, sexy dresses and I bought one for her. It looked so divine on her about all I could think of was how beautiful she would look without it. One night after my show we had dinner and for dessert I suggested a moonlight walk in the park. As we strolled in the quiet of a balmy Mexico City evening, I asked sweetly, "Abbe, could you just slip off your dress and keep walking?"

Gracefully, she complied. She was wearing high heels. That was all, just high heels. And she kept walking in the moonlight, glancing occasionally over her shoulder to smile at me. For more than three decades that memory has made me smile. It was a perfect moment, a moment I will never forget.

There were a lot of beautiful women who moved easily between successful men. If a woman was pretty enough or sexy enough, when one relationship ended there was another man around to pick up the pieces, and the checks. Sometimes it seemed like we were all at the same dance, changing partners when the music stopped. For example, Sinatra and I shared Elizabeth, Juliet Prowse, Abbe Lane, Mia Farrow, Kim Novak, and years earlier, the beautiful singer Hope Lange. I wonder, does that make us relatives? And in addition to our mutual attraction to Ann-Margret and Renata Boeck, Jack Kennedy and I both dated Angie Dickinson and Judy Campbell, who later became Judith Campbell Exner.

Kennedy's relationship with Angie Dickinson was well known. It was not a big secret. I met her after his assassination, when we were both campaigning for former press secretary Pierre Salinger, who was running for the Senate. She was smart and beautiful, one of the great women, and totally dedicated to Kennedy's memory. We became friendly in the back seat of a limo. We went back to her house that night. It was practically a shrine to Jack Kennedy. Everything was Kennedy. We sat and we talked and drank and talked, mostly about Kennedy. It was very sad.

The next night we met at my house, because I couldn't imagine making love under that poster of a young, vibrant Jack Kennedy, smiling broadly—although knowing him, I suspect he would have understood. I also suspect he probably did it himself.

My relationship with Judy Campbell lasted considerably longer and was much more complicated and intense. Judith Campbell Exner was the only woman I felt might have been more beautiful than Elizabeth. I met Judy through Sam Giancana, the Mafia boss who ran Chicago. Sam and I became very close friends. He treated me like the Jewish son he never had. I knew who he was, I heard the stories about him, but he never talked to me about singing and I never talked to him about running a criminal organization. To me, he was Sam, a warm, vital, funny man, who just happened to have these big, burly guys hanging around him all the time. One night I was at dinner with Sam and Phyllis McGuire, one of the beautiful McGuire Sisters, and Judy Exner and my man Max, and Sam was complaining about some ailment. Max told him, "I think I can take care of that." Max could cure the world.

Sam was agreeable. "Fine," he said. "You take care of it, that'd be great. But if you don't you may not be around very long." Maybe that wasn't his funniest line.

I met Sam Giancana the night I opened for Sinatra at a mob club outside Chicago called the Villa Venice. This was just after Marilyn Monroe had died and Frank was too upset to work. Sam was introduced to me as Dr. Goldberg, I didn't know who he was, but he didn't strike me as a typical Jewish doctor. As I got to know Sam he often gave me good advice. It was Sam, for example, who warned me that I should never give a woman a gun. Sam was crazy about Phyllis McGuire. Who wouldn't be? She was a great woman. For a brief time Phyllis and I had a music publishing company. We published one song, "I Give Thanks," a religious number. But their affair was tempestuous. "I got her this little Beretta," he told me once, "a gold-plated Beretta to keep in her pocketbook. And wouldn't you know it, a couple of days later she's chasing me down the street with it."

Sam used to talk about Phyllis with the mixture of pride and love that reminded me of Mike describing Elizabeth. He once showed me a scar he had hand on his leg; his battle wound, suffered in the war between the sexes. He told me Phyllis had hit him with a poker and broken his leg. Who knows if that ever happened. The scar was real.

At one point when I was leaving for Vegas to open at Caesar's Palace, Sam told me, "When you see Phyllis, ice her." Now, I knew that was mob slang for killing someone, but I also knew that what Sam meant was that he wanted me to freeze her out, ignore her. I couldn't wait to talk to Phyllis to tell her I wasn't supposed to talk to her. But after my opening show I was in my dressing room and people were pushing their way in, pushing me back against the wall, when through the crowd I saw Phyllis walk in, and across the entire room she yelled to me, "Sam told you to ice me, didn't he?"

Judy Campbell was with Sam the night I met him. Sam loved the beautiful girls, and Judy was one of the most beautiful of them all. Apparently he had asked her to marry him several times. The fact that he was already married and a Catholic didn't seem to bother him. But she said no. Then, later, when she changed her mind and told Sam she was ready to get married, he replied with those two charming little words, "Fuck off."

Judy Campbell got around. For a time she'd dated Sinatra, who introduced her to both John Kennedy and Sam Giancana. Years later she claimed that she had passed messages between the President and Giancana. She never discussed that with me. I certainly don't know for sure, but I doubt it happened. Our relationship went way beyond the secrets stage.

I was immediately attracted to her, but once I found out who Sam was I stayed away from her. It was Sam who pushed us together. When he was busy he would insist that I take her with me to dinners and parties, to Hefner's mansion. On those nights it would be just the three of us, Judy and I and "Big John," the bodyguard Sam had assigned to us. Believe me, I behaved.

My relationship with Judy changed from a friendship to a love affair after Sam turned down her marriage proposal, and she flew to New York with me. Believe me, Burton never intimidated me, Bob Evans didn't scare me, but Sam Giancana? Until I heard directly from Sam that it was all right, there was no way I would have dared have an affair with her.

She wasn't feeling very well when she arrived in New York so I took her with me to see Max. She quickly became addicted to his medicine, which created a bond between us. I bonded easily with a lot of people, except my own children.

I fell madly in love with Judy but neither one of us had any interest in marriage. What finally happened between Judith Campbell and me? The same thing that happened between me and so many other women. I don't know. Time. We ran out of fun. After Elizabeth, I was unable to commit to anyone. In my own mind I truly believed that I was looking for love, instead I found wonderful sex. That's not a complaint, but after a while that wasn't enough for me. But only after a while.

In addition to Ann-Margret and Judy and Angie Dickinson, I knew all the Kennedy women. In my life I've been to the biggest and most elaborate parties and balls, but there was never anything like a Kennedy party, especially when he was there. At a Kennedy party the feeling in the air was that we were at the center of the universe. Anything was possible. Everybody knew about Jack Kennedy's affairs—people used to tell stories about how he sneaked away during his inauguration parties for a real inauguration ball and had almost been caught—but what was not as well known was that the women in his administration also had their affairs. Pat Newcomb, who had handled Marilyn Monroe's public relations and who had represented Elizabeth, was part of the Kennedy crowd and on several occasions she tried to fix me up with some of the Kennedy administration ladies. I didn't want any part of that. I couldn't believe these ladies were propositioning me. I remember being at a party where there had to be a thousand people, including some of the most handsome, successful single men in the country. I was looking around and wondering, With all these guys, what the hell do they want with me?

But the people in the Kennedy administration were all young and attractive and successful. They had enormous power, and with all that came a great sexual appetite. But the only person in the White House with whom I was ever involved was Jackie Kennedy's press secretary, Pamela Turnure. Pat Newcomb introduced us at one of the parties.

She was a terrific damn lady. Although Pam never admitted it to me, I was sure she was one of Jack's girls. Jackie's brother-in-law, Prince Radziwill, told me once that this was the girl Jack Kennedy really should have married.

My usual pattern was to meet a woman, fall immediately and madly in love with her, and rush into an affair, which ended almost as fast as it had started. But with Pam Turnure it was different. There was very little immediate attraction; it was only as I got to know her that I became attracted to her. Unlike most of the women in my life, she had a quiet sexuality. She was cool and sophisticated, very controlled. But beyond that facade lay a very passionate woman.

One night, I remember, she came with the brother-in-law prince to a recording session. "I'm going to record just for you," I told her. That was my gift to her, my music. That and some jewelry, some clothing, and several other things. I'm not sure I ever knew what the prince was a prince of, but after the session he was so enamored of my music that he wanted to become my new manager. For 5 percent of my earnings he offered me $5 million up front. I think he was as serious as anyone who had as much to drink as he did could be, but I didn't even consider the offer.

Pam was with me at the Copa the night Sammy Davis Jr. opened, and Elizabeth and Richard Burton showed up. This was only a few days after I'd met with them at the Regency to discuss our divorce, but it was the first time the three of us had been in the same room in public since I'd left Rome. I didn't know they were going to be there. I'm not sure what I would have done if I had. I like to believe I would have gone anyway. They marched in fashionably late, about fifteen minutes after the show had begun. I thought that was a bit much—I'd gotten there only ten minutes after the show had started. Pam and I were sitting on the balcony with Walter Wanger, next to Jennie Grossinger and Mike Todd Jr. The balcony was the best place to sit in that room. That's where Frank Costello used to sit. Waiters set up a ringside table for Elizabeth and Richard in my line of vision to the stage. I couldn't watch Sammy Davis without seeing them. Knowing that everybody in the room was watching to see if I was watching them, I spent a lot of time actively not watching them. I was whispering to Pam or Walter or examining my glass of Coke. I'm not sure I'd ever carefully examined the fine masonry of the rear wall of the Copa until that night.

It was an uncomfortable situation made even more difficult by my friend, my pal, Sammy Davis, who treated them as if they were royalty. Throughout his entire act he spoke directly to them, and when he wasn't talking to them he was talking about them. I was so shocked that Sammy would embarrass me like that that I didn't even have time to think about them.

During the evening a man I didn't know whispered to me that Dr. Goldberg needed to see me. I slipped out of the room and a limo took me to a nearby Italian restaurant, where Sam was waiting. Instead of staying there, I brought him back to the Copa and sat him next to Pam. Sam was. . .Sam. If you didn't know who or what he was you'd think he was just another extremely powerful man. Sam exuded strength and confidence. He immediately started flirting with Pam. "You know," he told her, "there are the good guys and the bad guys in the world and a nice young lady like you should be careful about who you're with." The joke was that he was warning her about me.

Pam was with the President and Jackie on that fatal trip to Dallas. He was assassinated on a Friday, November 22, 1963. Jack Kennedy and Pam had arranged an appointment for me with Vice-President Lyndon Johnson for the following Monday to discuss an effort I was leading to change our national anthem from "The Star-Spangled Banner," which is very difficult to sing, to "America the Beautiful." Obviously that meeting never took place.

On the flight back to the Washington after the murder, Pam told me, Jackie Kennedy told her, "Lyndon Johnson did it." Words I'll never forget.

Of all the women I was with after Elizabeth, Pam Turnure was the one my friends thought I should marry. Jennie Grossinger loved her. And maybe I would've, but Pam did the one thing I really couldn't handle: She fell in love with me. She was willing to sacrifice her career to be with me. I needed an independent woman, a woman who could live happily without me. But after we fell in love she started canceling her own plans so we could be together. That was the wrong thing to do if you wanted to be with me. Most of my relationships ended in some sort of friendly fashion, but not this one.

One night Pam had too much to drink. We argued about something and she warned me that if we didn't stay together she was going to commit suicide. That was the wrong thing to say to me. I walked out angrily. I wasn't doing such a great job being responsible for my own life, and I had no intention of being responsible for hers. The next morning, when I walked into the living room at the Pierre, every gift I'd ever given her was lying on the couch. I never saw her again.

I know it seems like my life consisted of a seemingly endless succession of beautiful women—because it did. It was so easy for me to meet almost any woman who attracted me. One night, for example, I saw an absolutely beautiful starlet on the *Tonight Show*. I got her phone number from Johnny Carson and called her. I was planning a trip to Vietnam to entertain the troops and invited her to go with me. Now that's about as good an opening line as you're going to find. And it was legitimate. I meant it. A few days later we were in bed in my hotel suite. It was that easy for me.

A lot of men hung around with me not because of my scintillating personality, but rather because there were always extra women. That was my reputation: Eddie, women. That's not bragging, that's reporting. I had campaigned heavily for Lyndon Johnson in 1964 and after the election I was the first person he called to invite to his ranch for the celebratory party. He even sent the presidential helicopter to pick me up in Austin. It was a huge barbecue, and I sang for him. I was so proud, me and my friend, the President. When I finished singing, Jack Valenti, LBJ's friend and close aide, sat down next to me. And after a few moments of small talk he asked, "Eddie, what about getting some of your castaways for the old man?"

The President of the United States wanted me to find women for him?

I didn't know whether to be honored or insulted. Instead I just laughed, pretending that I thought Valenti was kidding.

About the only thing that prevented me from pursuing a woman was a wedding ring. I knew what it felt like to learn your wife was cheating on you. Oh boy, did I know that one. With all the beautiful single women in the world, I didn't want to do to someone else what Burton had done to me. There were only two exceptions: Michelle Phillips, and Nathalie Delon, the wife of actor Alain Delon, with whom I fell madly in love.

At that time, Alain Delon was the leading romantic star in the French film industry. Kurt Frings was his manager, so I'd known him for several years. In fact, I'd hosted the party for him when he'd arrived in America. One night Alain invited Dean Martin and me to play gin with him and his wife, Nathalie, whom I'd never met. When Dean and I walked into their rented house Nathalie and I took one look at each other—and immediately she ordered her large German shepherd, "Kill." Dean and I ran into the bathroom and locked the door. I learned something very important that night: I was much faster than Dean. I mean, it was crazy. Hysterically funny and crazy.

Nathalie was almost as beautiful as Alain was handsome. She was extraordinarily beautiful. She reminded me of a very pretty Julie Christie; Alain was maybe the most gorgeous man in the history of the world. Together they were the most magnificent-looking couple I'd ever seen. The night was wonderful. Alain spoke some English, Nathalie spoke almost none, but somehow we all managed to communicate.

I became very close friends with both Alain and Nathalie. We went to the best clubs and the most chic parties together. Sometimes I'd be with a date, but most of the time I was alone. Nathalie would often come to my house for a sauna with her beautiful girlfriend after they'd been horseback riding. In fact, she wanted me to have sex with her friend. She loved to play with other people's lives, but I wasn't interested. I was certainly attracted to Nathalie, but I wouldn't touch her. I wouldn't go near her. Not only wouldn't I do that to a friend, I couldn't believe she would be the slightest bit interested in me. Not while she was married to Alain Delon.

I knew that Alain was not faithful to her. He was always prowling for women, and with his looks and that devastating French accent he never had to look very hard. It was strange to me that he would spend so much time looking for beautiful women when he already was with the most beautiful one of all. But he told me once, "I need to have at least six woman. I can't be with one woman." As a couple they acted more like brother and sister than husband and wife. It seemed like they were constantly fighting, and I rarely saw any displays of affection between them. But I wasn't exactly the expert on what constitutes a good marriage.

I guess I was a bit surprised when Kurt told me that Nathalie had something to tell me, that she needed to speak with me alone. I didn't even try to guess what she wanted. We were friends, so it could have been about a thousand different things. My house was very special, very warm. It felt like it grew naturally out of the ground. It was almost completely enclosed by glass walls, but when I pressed a button in my bedroom a long door slid closed to provide privacy. So one afternoon I walked through the living room, through the bedroom out to the pool, where Nathalie was waiting for me. I kissed her on both cheeks, being so continental, and she said quite unexpectedly in her thick accent, "I must tell you that I am in love with you."

Just like that. "I am in love with you." Sometimes, there are no words, but sometimes a few words are everything. I didn't know how to react. More than anything else I was embarrassed. There are some women in this world who understand passion, who know exactly what to say or how to say it in a way that will destroy a man. Nathalie was one of those women. Those few words, and the matter-of-fact expression on her face, just put me away.

After everything I'd been through, I didn't think there was too much that could shock me. This? This shocked me. I didn't kiss her; I didn't dare touch her. This was my friend's wife. From that moment on we were wildly in love, although we resisted making love. We began spending time together. We went to see Alain's movie *Purple Noon* together. We went to see *Doctor Zhivago* together, and she became the Lara of my life. She would leave notes for me: "I love you, Lara." Alain would find the notes and ask, "What is Lara? What is this?"

Nothing. Is nothing.

Nothing? For me it was something. We'd spend time together at Dean Martin's house. We'd go to the Daisy. This was a love affair, but we just didn't make love.

Just as it was with Elizabeth, not having sex was far more erotic than sleeping together. I was planning to go to Vietnam with comedian Buddy Hackett and I decided to fly to Las Vegas to spend time with him. Nathalie insisted on going with me. Alain didn't mind at all. I suspect he was pleased to have the freedom. I brought a woman with me, for appearances and maybe even to protect me from myself, as well as Joey Foreman and his wife, who was also French. I booked three suites at the Sahara.

The second night we were there we all went to the Sands to see Dean Martin's show. Afterwards he joined us in the lounge. Dean had had his usual few drinks, like a camel at an oasis, and came on strong to Nathalie. "Heh, why donnne you and I go way for a weekend?" She pushed him away. It was so obvious we were in love that hiding it from Dean was imposs. . .well, maybe we could hide it from Dean. When Dean was drinking seriously you could hide a building from him. So Dean didn't see anything.

We stayed in separate rooms, but throughout the night she called, asking me to come to her room. "I can't, Nathalie," I told her. And I didn't. Imagine, me resisting a beautiful woman. That does take some imagination. But it is absolutely true. We returned to Los Angeles still without having even kissed seriously.

That year I attended the Academy Awards with Barbara Perkins, a raving beauty with long, coal-black hair. After the ceremonies we attended the board of governors' dinner. The lights in the ballroom were seductively low, but for some reason I turned around—and Nathalie was walking into the room by herself. Almost as if I were in a trance, I got up from our table and walked across the room. We embraced and kissed. We didn't care who saw us. Without so much as an apology to Barbara Perkins, I left the party with Nathalie.

We went to a quiet restaurant in Santa Monica, La Scala, where we could be alone—to wait for Alain to join us. We just sat there staring at each other. The fact that she spoke very little English never mattered. We communicated. We had long, beautiful wordless conversations. It was crazy. It was such a wild love affair. All that was missing was the sex.

I was scheduled to open at the Fountainbleau in Miami Beach the following week. It was actually a relief to be leaving her. I didn't think I could stay away from her much longer. And then Alain and Nathalie decided they would come with me to Florida. "You sure?" I asked.

"Oh yes," Alain said happily, *"mais oui."*

The three of us shared the two-bedroom Frank Sinatra Suite at the Fountainbleau. Bob Evans was also at my opening show, and years later he wrote that I played my whole show to Nathalie. That wasn't true, but I certainly featured her. I certainly was singing to her. I loved having the woman I loved in the audience when I performed. I always gave a wonderful show; if you listened carefully, you could hear the love in my voice.

After my second night Alain told us that he had to return to Los Angeles for an interview to promote his new picture. I really didn't want him to go. As long as he was there, I knew I could resist her. Nathalie and I both tried to talk him out of it, but he was insistent. When he left we interpreted that as his acceptance of our relationship, although I suspected he was really going back to meet another woman. But the situation was so obvious—we were all sharing a suite—that he might just as well have asked me to make love to his wife.

He told us he would return the next day, but he never came back. We spent nine days together, and for nine days we were inseparable. Day and night. She was a wonderful, wonderful lover and a delicious play-mate. She loved living dangerously; we spent days playing on powerful water scooters, driving right toward each other and turning away only at the last moment. When it's quiet, I can still hear her laughing.

We were like children who had discovered sex. We were on fire. After we had made love for the first time, we were lying in bed, our hearts were crashing, and she told me she felt, *"Bien baisé,"* "well kissed." Well kissed. With just a few words, she could send me flying. That may be the sweetest compliment I've ever been given.

When we returned to Los Angeles, Alain was at the airport to meet us. Nothing was said about what had happened, but he knew. And I think he was ambivalent about it. He'd set up the situation, but I suspect it bothered him more than he'd anticipated. After that he made certain Nathalie and I would not be alone.

I was crazy about her. The fact that we couldn't be together made her even more desirable. But for the next several weeks, while Alain finished his work in Hollywood, the three of us pretended nothing had changed. When they returned to Paris I drove them to the airport. We all cried as we parted, but for very different reasons. I watched her get on that plane believing she was out of my life forever, and maybe I felt a tinge of relief.

She began calling me from Paris, Saint-Tropez, Rome, day and night. She was the aggressor and I was the happiest victim in the history of the world. We'd speak on the phone for hours—and she couldn't speak English. We were making love on the phone. Oh, she had such a beautiful voice, an arrogant snarl, and the sexiest laugh I'd ever heard. And she sent me the sweetest love letters and nude pictures of herself. My love for her grew the longer we were apart. She was the perfect woman for me, a complete fantasy figure.

Several weeks later I was in New York preparing to open at the Persian Room in the Plaza. The afternoon before I opened I was deep in the middle of a rehearsal. My sister Miriam was in the audience, sitting with Mike Connolly, a columnist from the *Hollywood Reporter*. In the middle of one of my songs I saw a white shape moving across the room. I could just barely make out a person wearing what appeared to be a white leather suit. I stopped singing and walked out into the audience. Nathalie had come back to me. We kissed as if this were the conclusion of a great movie.

If it was a total shock to me, I can just imagine what it did to Alain Delon. Bob Evans claimed that he had been on a plane with Alain, and Alain had told him that he was furious that his wife had left him, that he couldn't believe that a small peon like me could steal a woman from Alain Delon. I didn't steal her; she declared her love for me.

She stayed in my suite with me. I was kind of nervous before my opening because this was New York City; I was singing some new songs, and the woman I loved would be there. I left before she was dressed. I remember waiting in a small mirrored dressing room to be introduced, then walking out to a tremendous ovation. The Persian Room had no stage; we performed from the floor. Nathalie was sitting ringside, alone, her back to me, wearing a dress that was cut down to. . .to. . .it had no back at all. I played my whole show to her back. She barely acknowledged my presence. That dress, that French fuck-you attitude. I just ate it up. She made me dizzy.

Nathalie and I spent every minute of the next week together in New York City. It was almost as if I had found Elizabeth again. That feeling of doing something so wonderfully illicit just thrilled me. We walked down Fifth Avenue, kissing in front of the Plaza in exactly the same place Elizabeth and I had once kissed. We made love all night as Elizabeth and I had once made love. It was perfect, perfect.

So perfect it couldn't possibly last. Finally Alain called. He and Nathalie had a screaming argument. She kept screaming, "Oh, my God! Oh, my God!" When I spoke to him he explained very calmly that Nathalie must return to him. It wasn't that he was so madly in love with her, I realized, when he told me, "If she does not come back it would ruin my career."

I guess he meant that it would not enhance his reputation as France's most romantic leading man to have his wife leave him for a peon. As a Frenchman, it was his job to do the leaving. I told him I couldn't force Nathalie to do something she did not want to do.

"You said once you would do anything for me," he replied. "Now pull her by the hair, put her on the plane."

"Oh, Alain," I said, "that's not the way to do it. Let her decide when to come back."

Nathalie and I both knew she had to return to France. When she'd left her first husband to marry Alain, she'd lost custody of her child; if she left Alain she certainly would lose custody of their son, Alexander. And given my track record for long-term relationships, I probably wasn't a real good gamble. We spent our last night together planning ways we would be together in the future, but I think both of us knew that was impossible.

I took her to the airport the next day. Shakespeare was wrong. Parting was not sweet sorrow, just very painful. After that we spoke on the phone for hours and hours and hours, but I never saw her again. I drove home that afternoon feeling almost as bad as I'd felt when leaving Elizabeth. Once again a woman I loved was leaving me. My heart had sunk so low. I was lovesick, depressed. I knew it would be a long time, maybe forever, before I gave my heart to another woman. I just didn't think I could stand the pain.

And as I walked through the lobby of the Plaza I bumped into Connie

Stevens. She was in New York doing a show with Jerry Lewis. I invited her for a drink. That night we slept together for the first time.

Nathalie was right: in my life I have been so well kissed.

CHAPTER TEN

This is an excerpt from a song written by my youngest daughter with Connie Stevens, Tricia Leigh. The song is titled "Try:"

> The emptiness of wanting you
> Was in everything I touch
> The gentle strength I thought,
> Could come only from you
> Child love I never knew
>
> It's time I closed my eyes and
> Didn't have to make believe
> He's here after all these years

To kiss away the tears I've cried
Oh, Daddy, don't you go

I held on to what I wanted
to see
Even when you gave up on
knowing me
But now I've found the gift
You've given me
The sadness from your soul
Is now my poetry

The primary thing that Connie Stevens and I had in common when we met is that neither one of us ever intended to get married again. She was in the middle of obtaining a Mexican divorce, and the process was so difficult that she told me, "The most I'm going to do is have a three-month relationship with a man." Finally, the woman of my dreams.

I didn't want to marry her, she didn't want to marry me, it was obvious we were meant for each other. How could we not get married? I'd first met Connie when she appeared on *Hollywood Palace,* a TV variety show I hosted one week. She was a beautiful girl, a beautiful face. I'd called her for a date but she was leaving for a tour of Japan. We agreed to get together when she returned, and then we just bumped into each other in New York. After meeting in the lobby of the Plaza we went into their restaurant, had a shrimp cocktail and a few drinks, and spent most of the next two years together.

Concetta Rosalie Ann Ingolia was half Irish and half Sicilian, so she was born with beauty, passion, and a wild temper. She'd made a few movies but was best known for playing Cricket, the adorable girl singer on the detective series *Hawaiian Eye*. I had just put Nathalie, the woman I loved, on a plane to Paris when Connie and I met. I was feeling miserable, but I took one look at Connie and thought, This is just what I need right now. She was even more desirable to me than Max.

Connie made me love her. Literally. When we were living together she would wake me up in the middle of the night for sex. And contrary to the lyrics of that famous song, I did want to do it. Sex was the one thing we always did extremely well together. When I look back on our relationship I don't really remember too much of what we did or where we went, I know there were a lot of parties, but most of all I remember the sex. That was unforgettable. We were so good together sexually, it was all the rest of the time we had problems.

As much as we loved each other, we could never put two good days together. I don't believe in astrology, but we're both Leos, so together we are fire and fire. The same passion that made the sex so good made our arguments so bad. We never should have married; if we hadn't married we would have been together longer. I think it was getting married that broke us up.

I'd never met anyone like Connie. While she loved having a good time, she also worked harder at her career than anyone I'd ever known, including Debbie. And while she was an exceptionally smart business-woman—she understood the value of money in a way I had never learned—she was not particularly well educated. I remember walking into the kitchen one afternoon while she was having a conversation with her best friend about religion and I said something about Jesus Christ. "Eddie, that's not fair," Connie complained. "You read books."

Several years ago Connie and I appeared together on Geraldo Rivera's program. When he asked Connie about my drug use, she told him, "I never knew Eddie was on drugs."

I thought that was an incredibly nice thing for her to say. We were living in the same house and I was about as high as I could be and she didn't happen to notice that I was using drugs? We smoked the same marijuana. Of course Connie knew what I was doing, but she was on her own "bicycle," as I referred to it—she was into diet pills. She loved the black beauties. They were like speed; they gave her what might chari-tably be termed an extremely high activity level. I always wondered how she could work so hard, how she could accomplish so much. Then I took a couple of these pills to see what it felt like. It felt like crap is what it felt like. It was a horrible experience. I didn't know what the hell hit me. I thought, She's on these things? No wonder she can't get off that bicycle.

I tried to convince her to stop taking these pills. Imagine that, me telling someone else to stop using drugs. What could I tell her, my drug supplier doesn't think they're healthy? She couldn't stop any more than

I could live without Max's shots. These pills were a sure thing for her; she depended on them when she needed that extra boost. And her use of them was not the slightest bit comparable to the way Elizabeth used drugs.

I loved Connie too much to marry her. I was good at singing songs, not being a good husband. But when she was offered the title role in Neil Simon's *Star-Spangled Girl* with Tony Perkins on Broadway, I realized how much a part of my life she had become. I wanted to be with her. So I rented a penthouse apartment in New York and flew there as often as possible. The show was a rare Simon failure, but not because of Connie. She was terrific and the audience loved her. I wanted her to quit; I didn't think starring in a bad show was particularly good for her career, but she insisted on fulfilling her obligations.

It was only when it became obvious that she was pregnant that she abruptly left the show. Singing I know about, romancing women I know about, but having babies? My job when my children were born was to stand by and faint at the proper time. So when Connie got pregnant we decided to have the baby. I didn't really know what to do. I didn't want to get married, yet I didn't like the idea of having a child out of wedlock. So I compromised. I did nothing.

Connie wanted to get married. That "three months with a man" decision had been long forgotten. We were living in my house, maybe the most perfect house in Hollywood, but months before we'd agreed to have this baby she had been pressuring me to buy a new house. "This is not a house to raise children," she'd insisted.

Children? "Listen," I'd promised, "when we get to that part, I'll buy a house."

She'd taken me to look at a property once owned by William Randolph Hearst. It was just a wall and some acreage, but the realtor claimed it was a bargain at $350,000. The only thing I ever knew that was a bargain at $350,000 was $500,000. Shaking my head in disbelief, I said, "I'm not buying a wall for that kind of money." We had another one of our big arguments about that.

I didn't think Connie knew the first thing about buying a house. I was the expert. I'd bought houses all over the world. And eventually all of the them had become worth millions more than I'd paid for them. Of course, by that time I'd sold them for a lot less. But Connie loved houses; she was a collector and loved collecting small things, like small properties. Connie knew so little about houses, in fact, that the best she could do was become wealthy from her real estate. She lived with the girls in Sonja Henie's sweet twenty-seven-room home on 2 ½ acres of Holmby Hills. If she had known any less about real estate she might have owned Holmby Hills.

I couldn't do nothing forever when Connie got pregnant. She was starring on Broadway and her costumes were getting tighter and tighter. So I decided the best thing to do was next to nothing. I decided we should get engaged. I think we were both surprised when I gave her an engagement ring. It was a late-night recording session. She wasn't feeling very well. She had a sore throat and was lying on a couch. I walked over to her and casually slipped a nine-carat marquise diamond ring on her finger. She was stunned. If she hadn't already been lying down, she would have fallen down.

Even if we had wanted to, we couldn't have gotten married right away. Legally we were both still married. Connie's Mexican divorce would not become final for several months, and as part of my attempt to retrieve some of my property from my marriage to Elizabeth, I was contesting the validity of her Mexican divorce. It would have been difficult for me to claim I was still legally married to Elizabeth if I married Connie.

When it became public that Connie was having my baby and we weren't married I got all the blame. I was the one who took advantage of her. This was in 1967, in terms of morality about a century ago, and long, long before having a child without being married was considered acceptable behavior. Once again I was in the center of a scandal. The *Los Angeles Times* reported "the latest sport at cocktail parties is exchanging Eddie Fisher jokes." For example, "The deejays are giving great play to Eddie Fisher's recording of 'Call Me Irresponsible.' " *Silver Screen* told readers, "What Liz Knows about Eddie as a Lover that Connie Found Out Too Late" was that I made a better lover than a husband.

Once again, I was under tremendous pressure to do the right thing. Unfortunately, the right thing for the public was the wrong thing for me and Connie. I loved her very much. For our first-month anniversary I gave her a simple diamond bracelet with 162 small stones; for Valentine's Day I gave her a $6,600 evening bag initialed C. F., for Connie Fisher, but I just couldn't give her a wedding ring. Publicly we insisted that we would get married as soon as our divorces were final.

Joely, named not after Al Jolson but rather an Americanization of the French word *jolie*, "pretty," which she certainly was, was born on October 29, 1967, in Burbank, California. I was playing the second night of an engagement at the Frontier Hotel in Las Vegas. My press agent "admitted" that I'd told him Connie and I had been secretly married the previous March in Puerto Rico, while my divorce lawyer, Greg Bautzer, insisted, "It's impossible. He's still married to Elizabeth Taylor." When reporters pressed me to see our marriage license, I asked, "Have you ever shown your marriage license to anyone? Of course you haven't. So why should I be different? It's nobody's business but Connie's and mine."

Many men have pretended they weren't married; I was in the odd situation of having to pretend I *was* married. Claiming I was married to Connie definitely damaged my claim that I was still legally married to Elizabeth. Depending on which story people believed, I was not married, I was married to either Elizabeth or Connie, or I was married to both of them. But when Elizabeth finally agreed to pay me a $500,000 settlement rather than the $1 million I felt belonged to me, we settled. My marriage to Elizabeth Taylor was legally ended, which meant there was no legal reason not to marry Connie. Eventually I realized I had no choice; Connie and I had to be married. For Joely, for our careers, for the wonderful sex. And at times I even had hopes it might work.

People tried to talk me out of it. When Jim Aubrey heard that I was going to marry Connie, he spent days looking all over New York for me. Finally he sat me down and told me, "You can't do this. Don't do this." Jim was a very savvy man, a powerful man in the entertainment industry. He made all the sense in the world, but all the sense in the world goes out the window when you're stuck on a pussycat.

Comedian Buddy Hackett, with whom I'd been working, volunteered to host our wedding at his home in Fort Lee, New Jersey. I had accepted the reality of the situation right up until the day of the wedding. Connie's family was there, my family was there, the caterer was there—and I just couldn't do it. It wasn't that I didn't want to marry Connie; I didn't want to marry anybody. Our wedding party instead became an engagement party, although we were celebrating an engagement that probably would never lead to marriage. It was a terrible day. I felt awful for Connie and embarrassed for myself, but I believed I was doing the right thing.

Several weeks later I returned to the Fountainbleau, the first time I'd been back since being there with Nathalie. Connie was in Los Angeles with the baby. Frank Sinatra was to appear there right after me, so he came down early and we ended up spending a lot of time together. He had the flu and kept throwing up. Frank had married Mia Farrow and they were in the midst of their own problems. Frank and I spent hours discussing his relationship with Mia and my relationship with Connie.

Finally he told me, "You have to live up to your moral obligation." That was a legitimate flow of Republican words and he wasn't even a Republican yet. This from the same man who once said he'd rather be a don in the Mafia than the President of the United States. And yet, I listened to him. I listened to him because he had this sound in his throat and that made him smart. Use my plane, he offered, get married.

Does this begin to sound like a marriage made in heaven? Connie met me in Miami but she didn't want to take Sinatra's plane to Puerto Rico. She'd had a nightmare, she explained, in which the plane had crashed into the ocean. Connie believed in that stuff. She'd often had psychics at the house, which drove me crazy. I used to tape these silly women in an effort to make Connie understand that their premonitions were nonsense. We fought about that, too. Connie's nightmare about the plane crashing made me feel a little uneasy, but I convinced her to ignore it.

A few minutes after takeoff a warning light started flashing in the cockpit and the pilots called on the intercom and asked me to come forward. There was something wrong with the landing gear, they explained. We had to return to Miami. When I told this to Connie she leaned back in her seat and stretched out her arms as if she were on a cross. Her nightmare seemed to be coming true. We were flying over water in a damaged airplane. Connie was too sacred to gloat, and I certainly was too scared to apologize. I'd never been completely comfortable on an airplane, even before Mike had died in the crash. As we landed I saw ambulances and fire engines racing alongside. The plane lurched across the runway. The front landing gear had cracked, but somehow the pilots retained control and brought the plane to a safe stop.

I insisted we take the next commercial flight to San Juan, probably based as much on my belief that if Connie didn't get right back on an airplane she might be too afraid to fly again as my feeling that if we didn't married right away I might be too afraid to try again.

We were married by the mayor of San Juan in her office. I'll never forget her words to us just before the wedding in Spanglish: "Now children, don't fight . . ." We started arguing when we landed in Puerto Rico and, basically, didn't stop until we separated and divorced. We fought about the same things other people fight about. Sex, for example. Before we were married we couldn't get enough of each other, after we were married I still wanted to make love all the time. I was incredibly attracted to her, but she seemed to lose interest. Our foreplay was foreshortened.

We fought about everything. We fought about her pills, and we fought about her career. Connie insisted on appearing on television game shows. Maybe I was being a bit of an elitist, but my previous wife had starred in the most extravagant and expensive motion picture ever produced, and it bothered me that Connie was appearing on shows that gave away refrigerators. I didn't think these shows were prestigious enough for her. I didn't think they helped create the proper image for her. But she insisted on doing them.

I don't think I ever cheated on Connie, but it does get a little confusing trying to remember exactly when we were married or separated or divorced. There were other women. It was while I was with Connie that I somehow managed to fit in Kim Novak.

I knew Kim Novak had a crush on me. It seems so long ago that I'm connected to it only by a wonderful memory, but I still enjoy the thought: Kim Novak had a crush on me. She had told several people that her three favorite men were Aly Khan, Cary Grant, and Eddie Fisher. Poor Cary. First Elizabeth had turned down his invitation to drop LSD with him and now Kim Novak considered me equally desirable. I was very flattered to be included in any group with Cary Grant; whatever his sexual proclivity, he was a real man. Not Aly Khan, he was just a large spoiled child, if he didn't get to dance with the prettiest girl in the room he'd sit by himself and pout.

Kim Novak began pursuing me while I was married to Elizabeth. We'd never met, but she called me at a party at Betty Bacall's house to tell me that she missed me, that she wanted to know how I was. How was I? I was married. At that time I had no interest in meeting her. Kim Novak was the only woman ever to approach me while I was with Elizabeth, and she was not the slightest bit intimidated by her.

When I was attempting to produce the motion-picture version of *Paint Your Wagon* I wanted Kim Novak for the female lead, the role of a wife shared by Clint Eastwood and Lee Marvin. The part was eventually played by Jean Seberg. I wanted Kim Novak because I thought she was right for the role, but also because I knew she was interested in me. Kim wanted the role. She needed a hit picture and thought this would be it. Dorothea MacElroy, a wonderful woman who owned the Westbury Hotel and published a fan magazine, arranged for us to meet in an apartment in Los Angeles.

Dorothy introduced us, then left. Kim and I didn't say another word. We were all over each other. She was wearing a simple dress with nothing on underneath. She was statuesque, tall and sculpted, with an absolutely gorgeous face; she was a Venus, a goddess. She was even more beautiful in person than on the screen. As we made love I realized that this was the single greatest introduction of my life. It was much more memorable than a handshake.

I thought that was going to be the start of a real romance. On occasion she would fly down to Los Angeles from her home in Big Sur and we would get together. I was sure she was going to do the movie, but Josh Logan, who'd directed her in *Picnic*, and Alan Jay Lerner, who eventually ended up producing the film, didn't want her. Not at all. When it became obvious that she wasn't going to get the part I felt very bad. I felt as though I'd misled her. Obviously if I had really cared for her that wouldn't have mattered, but it did matter to me and I didn't see her again.

If Connie did not know about Kim Novak, she certainly suspected I was seeing other women. By June 1968 it was obvious to both of us that our marriage was a mistake, and we were spending much of our time apart. Once again I was working at the Frontier, and Connie had heard rumors that I was seeing other women so she flew to Las Vegas to surprise me. At that time new owners were renovating the hotel and my dressing room consisted of two big trailers put together. I was staying there with five dogs, five puppies all named Sam after Sam Giancana. The truth is that I was seeing other women, but not the precise moment Connie showed up.

When Connie arrived there were about a dozen men hanging around my dressing trailers. She was all ready to catch me with another woman, and maybe she was even angrier when she failed to do so. But she was livid. Absolutely livid. She started screaming at me and I responded in the most antagonistic way: I didn't fight back. She was prepared for a big fight and I was completely passive. Nothing is more infuriating than your opponent doing nothing. Finally she got so angry she picked up a shot glass and threw it at me. It smashed against the wall. "No, Connie," I explained calmly, "if you want to hit me, you have to throw it over here."

Some women can't take a little joke. That was the start of our biggest fight. By the time I returned to Los Angeles I'd stopped wearing my wedding ring. In anger I'd bent it out of shape and hung it on the staff of an Italian flag that flew over our bedroom fireplace. When Connie discovered I'd taken off my ring she was ready to blow up the house. "Don't get so excited," I told her. "It's somewhere in this room." She searched all over for the ring, and she didn't think it was as amusing as I did. By the time I showed her where it was she was totally out of control. She picked up the phone and told me, "I'm checking you into a hotel. I want you out of here."

Who into where? I reminded her that it was still my house and that I had absolutely no intention of leaving. Finally I was beginning to show my anger, but even that didn't make her happy. She went into the living room to use the phone near another fireplace, and made a hotel reservation for herself and Joely. I was trying to calm her down. "Come on, Connie, you know that's not . . ."

I followed her into the living room. As I got close to her she picked up a fireplace poker. "Now what is that for?" I asked.

"For protection."

"From me? Are you kidding?" Our marriage had been ending since the moment we got married, before we got married, but this was the night it actually happened. This was the night we separated. Probably the only thing that prevented us from getting divorced was the fact that Connie had gotten pregnant again. That and the fact that we still loved each other. Connie started looking for another house. By the time gossip columnist Harrison Carroll revealed, "Forget those rumors that Connie Stevens and Eddie Fisher aren't married. They definitely are. Eddie even is seen wearing a gold wedding band," we were apart.

A month after that fight Connie was making her Las Vegas debut at the Flamingo, a job that I got for her. Onstage Connie used to introduce me as the greatest man who ever walked into her life, the man who taught her everything she knew about show business, at which I would smile shyly. It was sweet. Connie was sweet, but those statements were about as true as the gossip columns' claim that I made love to Elizabeth twelve times a day. Connie had celebrity talent. She was pleasant to look at and did several things well, but she didn't really excel at anything. Onstage, I mean. And she didn't have to because people simply wanted to see the Cricket they'd fallen in love with on television.

I used to watch her rehearsals and make suggestions. I'd give her long notes. Don't try to be a singer, I told her, just carry a bubble. Like a lot of actors, she could carry a tune, but a great singer she wasn't. Do a happy tune, I suggested, do a sad song, but don't try to be Barbra Streisand, because you're not Barbra Streisand. I tried to teach her but she never listened to me and the result was a very successful act. Connie has always known her strengths.

But her opening night was a disaster. She had spent so much time in rehearsal teaching the kids in her act their parts that she'd neglected to learn her own. The audience didn't care; they probably didn't even notice it. They got to see what they wanted, but Connie was devastated. Between shows she locked herself in the bathroom and wouldn't come out. "It's opening night," I was shouting to her. "The first show doesn't matter. That's a rehearsal. It's the second show that counts." That was the major contribution I made to Connie's act—getting her out of the bathroom.

While she was at the Flamingo I was working directly across the street at Caesar's. I had just signed what was to be the last big deal of my career—though I certainly didn't know it—a three-year contract with Caesar's to play six weeks a year at $60,000 a week. Connie and I took a wonderful photograph of the two of us hugging each other in the middle of the strip, looking very much in love. It was a good thing it was a photograph rather than a movie, because by that point we wouldn't have been able to sustain our happiness more than a few frames.

It wasn't Connie's fault our marriage didn't work, but who else could I blame? Debbie? Burton? Myself? Max and all the pushers who came after him? Connie was easiest. In my life I have done both dumb things and colossally dumb things. This was one of the real big ones. I don't know why I did this, maybe to get Connie out of my system, maybe because I just needed to demonstrate that I'd regained my independence, maybe because I was running out of fantasies or maybe just because I could. I invited five women to come with me to Vegas and put each of them in a separate room on the same floor. None of them knew the other girls were there. Connie didn't know any of them were there. My plan was to sleep with each one of them without any of others finding out. I planned my strategy carefully. Believe me, Rommel didn't organize his strategy any more carefully than I planned this.

Rommel had his whole army. All I had was me. The plan was a good one, but my libido refused to cooperate. There was a song in my heart, and that's where it stayed. Whether it was the meth or anxiety, who knows, I couldn't—nothing happened. Late in the evening Connie caught me lying on a bed—by myself, in my valet Willard's room, reading a book. "What's up?" would have been the appropriate thing for her to say, to which I could have replied honestly, "Absolutely nothing." Instead she snapped at me, "Where have you been? I've been looking all over for you."

"I'm right here, Connie," I said, or something equally inane, "as you can see. Reading a book."

Connie once told a television interviewer that she'd divorced me when she discovered I was using drugs. That was probably about as accurate as Connie's accusation in her first divorce that her husband used "abusive and vulgar language." What brought our marriage to a legal end was another woman. I don't think Connie ever knew about Kim Novak, or the five girls at Caesar's, or even the former *Playboy* Playmate of the Year, but she certainly couldn't miss the naked twenty-year-old Scandinavian student.

I met Eda Bjorn Hansen at a dinner party at my house. The doorbell rang and Sam Presley, a friend visiting from Las Vegas, answered it and announced in his loud southern accent, "Oh, this one we're going to fight over."

She had come to the United States to further her education. Which she did, but probably not in the way she had anticipated. I fell in love with her in about thirty seconds. Rather than registering for college she stayed with me. We were in bed one morning when Willard woke us to warn me that Connie was on her way up with Joely. Eda jumped out of bed and ran out the back door to hide. Seconds later Connie walked in with the baby in her arms. I didn't even have a book to hide behind. Connie was in midsentence when she saw Eda, totally naked, by the pool. Always the pool; Debbie and I had escaped reporters by sneaking out through the pool, I'd fallen in love with Elizabeth as she sat by her pool, and now Connie had discovered my naked girlfriend hiding by the pool. Connie started screaming at me. Willard took Joely from her and we went at it. I think Connie went after me with her shoe. But she started breaking things, throwing things around, ripping pictures off the wall. She loosed every bit of that Irish-Sicilian temper. "That blonde" she kept calling Eda. I didn't think that was an appropriate moment to point out to her that Eda had black hair.

That day I learned another important lesson: People who live in glass houses better have good hiding places. Our marriage was finished. Our second child, Tricia Leigh, was born the day after Christmas. Four months later her mother and I filed for our divorce.

This was going to be the nicest divorce I'd ever had. There was no bitterness, no problem with the financial arrangement, just two people who loved each other getting divorced. Ours was going to be a model divorce. But the night before we were supposed to be in court the judge called. "Connie is not going to show up in court tomorrow. You'd better do something."

Apparently Connie's lawyer had informed the judge that his client wanted a postponement. This was a very powerful judge and he was doing us a favor by presiding over our divorce. I didn't want to get angry with Connie on the eve of our divorce, but I had to convince her to be there.

What could I say to her? If you really love me you'll divorce me? I called her and she suggested I come to her house and have dinner with the kids. My girlfriend was very upset that I was seeing my wife, but I really had no choice. After dinner we played with our children, and when they went to bed, we went to bed. We made love until six o'clock in the morning. It was completely insane. At six o'clock I said, "I've got to go home to get ready for court. I'll see you there at nine."

She arrived about ten minutes after nine. During a break in the proceeding she whispered to me, "I don't think we should be doing this. I still love you."

"We have to, Connie," I said. "I'm crazy." Maybe that was the sanest thing I ever said to her. And she knew me well enough not to be able to deny it.

Our divorce has been very successful. We've always gotten along very well; in 1986 we even did a show together for producer Frank Kenley, titled "An Evening to Remember." Connie did as much as she could to compensate for my absence in our children's lives by being a big, loving presence. She never made the kids feel that an important part of their lives was missing. When Joely was married she asked me to walk her halfway down the aisle, "because that's traditional," and wanted Connie to give her away, "because she's earned that right." As I completed my part in the ceremony Connie leaned over, right in front of Joely, and said, "Thank you for giving me the greatest gifts of my life," and kissed me. Now that's a happy divorce.

I had been telling Connie the truth about one thing. I *was* crazy. I just didn't realize it. As long as I had people like Max around, with whom to compare myself, I was sane. There was a meth to my madness. Although I wouldn't admit it, I had become a drug addict. During the 1950s and early sixties I'd taken Max Jacobson's magic medicine any chance that I got, but I hadn't become addicted to him until I returned from the craziness in Rome hooked on vodka and Seconal. To get me off them, Max began pumping speed into my body in larger doses than I'd ever had before. Withdrawal from Seconal is supposed to be extremely difficult, but Max got me through it without any discomfort. Of course, I was so high on speed that I didn't sleep for a week. And when it was done, I'd replaced one addiction with another.

I believed I was in good hands and I was feeling good. Good? I was feeling terrific. I only needed one big shot a day, maybe two; it was only later that I'd need three or four shots a day to function. In fact, I felt so good that I began skipping appointments with Max, instead taking long steam baths with Kurt Frings. Max would be furious with me, and warn me that I was sick and needed his medicine. I didn't know I was addicted. None of Max's patients did. Back then, if you were getting medication from a doctor you just assumed he knew what he was doing. And when a doctor tells you very professionally, "I vant to see you tomorrow," or

"I see you later today," you follow his instructions. I did, we all did. I think we would have followed Max anywhere. His patients worshipped Max Jacobson. He was shooting the stars. He was Dr. Feelgood, Dr. Miracle, Dr. Needles. There were many imitators, but he was the original, the one and only.

Before people became addicted to the needle, to the drug, we first became addicted to Max. Max, Max, Max. I believed he was a genius. I didn't know that he was going to be a killer. I didn't know that he was destroying lives. All I saw was the good he did. He was helping humanity. He was helping the President of the United States. Max made his patients feel better, and if after seeing him we didn't feel good, we'd go back and he'd make us feel better. If a dose wasn't correct, like any responsible physician he'd adjust it. Max cared about his patients; he wasn't a one-shot doctor. Even a responsible doctor like Rex Kennamer, who despised Max, admitted to me once that Max was a chemical genius.

I saw the evidence. One night before a performance of his show *A Funny Thing Happened on the Way to the Forum*, Zero Mostel had an adverse reaction to a shot and collapsed. I was in the theater and I ran backstage. He was lying on the floor, breathing heavily, sweating profusely. I felt his pulse, his heart was racing. He was scared he was going to die—we were both scared. I sat next to him, holding his hand and talking to him, telling him everything was going to be all right as soon as Max got there. If you believed in Max, as we both did, you knew that was true. Max finally got there and gave Zero another shot that calmed him down. We thought Max had saved Zero's life, we didn't focus on the fact that Max's first shot had put him on the floor.

Max truly believed he could fix any medical problem with his chemicals. I was with him at the airport when we ran into the Yankees' Mickey Mantle, who was struggling with severe knee problems. "I can fix it," he insisted, giving Mantle a shot of cortisone in his knee.

One night in Puerto Rico, Max and I were with Harry Belafonte, who had lost sight in one eye. I was finishing an engagement at the El San Juan and Harry was following me in. We had been friends for years. Early in our careers we used to hang out in Greenwich Village with Dean Martin, Merv Griffin, and Jerry Lewis. Belafonte wasn't one of Max's patients, but that night Max tried to convince him that with just one shot he could restore sight to his eye. Harry didn't take him seriously; the best eye doctors in the world had told him the problem was incurable. "Let me try," Max pleaded.

"You can't, Max," I insisted. "The cornea's gone. It can't be fixed."

Max persisted and finally Harry agreed. I guess he figured what harm could Max do—well, he didn't know Max. This is how crazy we all were. The best eye doctors in the world could not restore Belafonte's sight, yet we let this man convince us that he could perform miracles. When Max's first attempt failed he simply mixed up a batch of something else and gave Belafonte a second shot. The results were no better. Max finally gave up, but offered to give Harry another shot before his show that night.

It was Harry's opening night. The moment he walked out onstage I recognized all the signs of someone who was overmedicated. He was hyperactive, sweating right through his clothes, even his normally impeccable timing was off. His performance was a disaster; Max had destroyed him. Afterwards I went to his suite; he was furious. Out of control. Jumping up on the beds, trying to get Bobby Kennedy, the attorney general of the United States, on the phone. "I'm gonna stop him, Eddie," he promised. "I'm going to get his license taken away."

When I saw Max later he asked, "How is he? Does he want to see me?"

I thought, yeah, he wants to see you in jail is how he wants to see you. "Not right now, Max," I said. "I don't think right now is a good time."

Even now, even knowing the damage Max did, I still don't believe he intended to hurt anyone. He believed completely in what he was doing. He was his number-one patient; he always experimented on himself before treating other people. He probably took a hundred times more of his chemicals than he gave to anyone else. And I saw the good he did for people.

He treated everyone the same. He was an equal-opportunity destroyer. The most powerful, most important and wealthiest people in America would show up in Max's office and sit there meekly waiting, sometimes for hours, for their appointments. They paid him a fortune. But on Thursday nights he treated multiple sclerosis patients for free; they would come into his office all bent over and his shots would provide some temporary relief. They, too, thought he was god.

There were some people who tried to warn me about Max. Rex Kennemar told me he was a dangerous man. My regular physician, "Wild Bill" Hitsig, one of the great doctors in the world—he was Nehru's doctor—told me, "Eddie, that man is putting poison in your system. It's dirt. It's shit."

Max's lovely wife, Nina, who knew him best of all, suggested several times that I find a more conventional doctor. But all I saw was the good he was doing for people. With Max, I believed, anything was possible. We know so much more now about the effects of these chemicals that it's sometimes difficult to remember how little we knew then. Nobody knew how dangerous those drugs could be, all we saw were the results. How could anything that made me feel so good be bad? So I believed that he could fix Mickey Mantle's knee, Harry Belafonte's eyes, and if you didn't have a heart, Max could make one for you. I was Max's biggest supporter. My solution to every conceivable medical problem was simply, "You've got to go see Max." I arranged appointments so my friends could see him and still make the opening of their Broadway show or nightclub performance. I used to spend my days at his office talking to patients on the phone. I entertained people in his waiting room. I would go with him to his filthy laboratory in a shack on Long Island and help him cook his chemicals and I would go with him to the White House. The first time he was to see President Kennedy he fell asleep in the bathtub trying to shave. I wound up shaving him in the bathtub. "I love Eddie like my own son," Max once told a reporter, and I was proud of the fact that I was just about his only patient who didn't have to wait hours to see him.

All of Max's regular patients, people like me and Alan Jay Lerner and Mark Shaw, knew Max had some problems, but we believed he had discovered something that eventually was going to prove very important. Many of us tried to get him associated with legitimate medical facilities, and when the AMA and the FDA investigated him, we protected him. Oh, we protected him, I couldn't stop protecting him. Many years after I'd stopped seeing Max, Jack Kelly, a deputy commissioner of narcotics and dangerous drugs who had become a good friend, told me, "They finally got Max's license. They looked in his files and they found all these deaths there."

I knew that couldn't be true. Max never kept files. "What deaths?" I said. "One death." I saw several people have adverse reactions to a shot—Alan Lerner, Johnny Mathis, Anthony Quinn—but I only saw one person die.

One day, returning from a trip to Los Angeles, I went directly to Max's office for a shot. I strolled into the office to find the place in turmoil. A man I'd never seen before was lying on the examining table, barely conscious. Max was in a mild panic. He was talking loudly to the patient in German, trying to keep him awake. Max ordered me to give him coffee, and I spent the next twelve hours in the office force-feeding coffee into this man as Max tried to remember what shots he had given him. I don't think I realized how serious it was; I'd seen Max perform too many miracles to even think this patient was actually going to die. The patient went into a coma and Max tried desperately to revive him. He was sticking needles everywhere in his body, trying to get some response. I couldn't believe this was happening. How could this stranger do this to Max? Finally, when Max realized this man wasn't going to survive, he told me, "Leave the room now." I felt terrible for Max, but I also appreciated the fact that he didn't want me involved. I don't remember if it even occurred to me that Max had killed this patient.

The patient's family tried to bring charges against Max. Milton, Alan Lerner, Mark Shaw, and I rallied his supporters to pay for his defense. The court eventually dismissed the charges.

I didn't think of myself as a drug addict. Not yet. To me, a drug addict was someone who used real drugs like marijuana or cocaine. The first time I tried marijuana, for example, I was really scared. This was in the early 1960s and I'd heard so much about it, I'd heard it was nice and peaceful, that I decided it was time to try it myself. So I called Dean Martin and asked if he would send me over "one marijuana cigarette." Instead he sent me a huge bag, several years' supply. I smoked one thin joint and it had no effect on me at all. None. So I put the bag away. Then I got in my car and started driving down the mountain. About halfway down I panicked. I began thinking, Maybe I didn't hide it well enough; the maid's definitely going to find it; or the cook's going to find it. And when they do they're going to call the police. And the police will come to my house and arrest me. Within minutes I had convinced myself I was going to jail. I turned the car around and raced back to the house before the entire Los Angeles Police Department arrived. It took me a long time to hide that bag; every place I considered seemed obvious to me. Finally I found a place and secreted it there, still completely convinced that the marijuana had not affected me at all.

As far as I was concerned that was my introduction to real drugs. Dean Martin was my pusher. The pills that Elizabeth had taken, the Seconal that I had taken, that was medicine. Max's chemicals, that was a doctor administering treatment. But marijuana? I couldn't believe I'd actually handled an illegal drug myself.

Although I didn't realize it at the time, Jack Kennedy's assassination was the beginning of the end of my relationship with Max. In November 1963, I was living in an apartment in the Waldorf Towers. I was taking a shower when Bob Abrams burst into the bathroom to tell me Kennedy had been shot. I was—there were no words. I ran right out of the bathroom and turned on the television. They had not yet announced that Kennedy was dead. I felt a very personal involvement. It wasn't just the President who had been shot, it was Jack, with whom I'd shared so much. I called Max, who told me, "He's dead." No one outside Parkland Memorial Hospital knew how badly the President had been wounded. Max knew. And if Max said it, I believed it. Max had an intuition, he could tell a person's temperature and blood pressure just by looking at them. Max often amazed me.

Kennedy's death changed Max. Or maybe it changed the way I looked at him. But after that it seemed like he got more and more out of control. I'd always accepted a little craziness as an aspect of his genius. For a time, I remember, he experimented with magnets. After studying magnetism he insisted his chemicals had to run over magnets. He even attached small magnets to his syringes. Not only did I accept that, I bought him a magnet factory. But after November 1963, his extremes got more extreme. It was as if Dr. Frankenstein had turned into his monster.

I had tried to quit Max before. Years earlier, before I was really hooked, I hadn't seen him in a while and I wasn't feeling well. I was staying at the Del Monico and called Dr. Hitsig. "Wild Bill" Hitsig was the antithesis of Max Jacobson. He was a brilliant doctor who had worked in Africa with Albert Schweitzer. He looked like a god, he drove around

New York City in a Rolls-Royce convertible, his office was immaculate, and he was the only doctor I'd ever known whose bedside manner was better than Max's. He knew what Max was doing and told me, "I can help you with it, but it's going to take some time. I'm going to give you something to sleep." He also noticed that my blood pressure was a little high and gave me an intramuscular shot to lower it.

I got out of bed the next morning—and fell on my face. I had to crawl to the bathroom to pee. Dr. Hitsig rushed to the hotel. As it turned out, the medication he'd given me had brought my blood pressure down—way, way down. And kept it dangerously low. I had to be supported just to sit up. I'd never had a problem like that with Max. I went right back to him.

Max had taught me how to inject myself in my buttocks. It was literally a pain in the ass, but well worth it. I had become totally dependent on Max's medicine. I needed two or three shots just to get through the day. I needed another shot before every show. When I was making my come-back after separating from Elizabeth, for example, I was performing at the Latin Casino in Philadelphia. It was a homecoming for me—the Latin Casino was filled with 2,100 people including my family and friends—but Max was late arriving and I didn't dare go on without my boost. So I waited. My opening act, comedienne Totie Fields, went through all her material. But Max still hadn't gotten there. An hour passed. The audience, my family and friends, was very impatient. Max arrived two hours late.

He did something that night I had never heard of before. In addition to my regular shot, he put a needle into his own vein and drew some blood—then injected it in my buttocks. The feeling was. . .I can't explain it.   I was high, but in complete control. I was euphoric, but strangely calm. I felt capable of conquering the world. I went out onstage prepared to kill. These were my people; they loved me. But when I walked out they started hissing and booing. I felt like I was being booed in my bedroom.

Still, I refused to believe that I was hooked. I ignored the facts that my performances were erratic, that I forgot lyrics or stayed onstage much too long. I ignored the fact that on occasion my hands would shake uncontrollably, that I had no appetite or that I had to take other medi-cines to get to sleep at night. I ignored the fact that as the meth wore off my personality changed, and I became irritable, rude, and nasty. I was Eddie Fisher, the boy with the golden sound in my throat. I was a superstar before that term was being used, I was just too important to be an addict. I just needed Max's shots to help me accomplish all my responsibilities.

I didn't decide to break with Max. I didn't suddenly have some epiphany that he was destroying my life. It just happened. I was working at the Diplomat Hotel in Miami Beach and I wasn't feeling very well, so I called him and he flew down almost immediately. I think he gave me a shot, but it didn't really help. I still felt terrible. As he prepared another shot he ordered me to pull up my shirt. My shirt? "What are you doing, Max?" I asked.

"Pull up your shirt," he repeated. He was going to give me a shot in my solar plexus, right in the middle of my chest. "Come, come," he insisted.

On occasion I'd seen him give other patients a shot in their chests, which seemed to take effect very quickly, but he'd always given me my shots in my arms or buttocks. I didn't like the idea of an injection so close to my heart. "No way, Max," I said. "Nobody's gonna give me a shot right there."

That was it. I had insulted him. Doubted him. He quickly repacked his black bag and left angrily. That was the reason our friendship ended. And I felt very good about it. I felt that way for at least three or four minutes. And then I realized my connection was gone and I had only a small supply of meth and syringes. That's when I started panicking. I wouldn't call Max. I refused to humble myself to him—so instead I called his son, Dr. Tommy Jacobson. I'd known Tommy almost as long as I'd known his father. He practiced in Los Angeles, about as far away from his father as he could get both geographically and medically. While he lacked his father's eccentric genius, he was a serious and excellent physician. He treated methamphetamine as a serious drug, and did not dispense it with the recklessness of his father. I'd often gone to him for my shots in Los Angeles, in fact for a time I practically supported him. So when I called him he flew to Miami to take care of me. When I was in California I saw him every other day. And once again I could reassure myself that I was receiving responsible medical treatment from a doctor.

I allowed Max to inject me one more time several months later. I had been invited to open the 1964 Democratic Convention in Atlantic City by singing "America the Beautiful." I was appearing at Skinny D'Amato's 500 Club when the Democrats began arriving. One afternoon I got a call from Max, complaining that the whole town was barricaded and the police wouldn't let him through. I didn't know what he was doing there and I didn't ask, but I couldn't turn him down. I made some calls and the next thing I knew he was walking into my dressing room. For the first time in years I thought about not taking a shot. I thought about it, but immediately rejected the thought. My dressing room was filled with people but Max didn't care. He opened his black bag and right in front of all them he dumped his bottles on the table and said, "I give you good treatment." I remember looking at him and being repulsed. After eleven years, he disgusted me. I was embarrassed by his presence. But I figured, Ah, what's one more shot.

I don't know what his problem was that night, but he couldn't find a vein in my arm. "Don't look," he said, which is always a bad thing to hear from your doctor. I don't know how many times he stuck me, but he really messed me up.

My performance that night was terrible and I blamed it on him. Not on the fact that my drug addiction was destroying my career and my life, but on Max because he couldn't make me feel as good as he once did. I couldn't wait for him to leave. That was the last treatment I ever got from Max Jacobson.

But it was not the last time I saw him. It's still the same old story— a case of do or die. I wanted Max, not Max's miracle medicines, out of my life. Another former patient of Max's, a horror of a human being, whom I shall call Kenny Hubard, apparently had stolen Max's formula. He was a monster. Several weeks after I'd met him at a party he showed up in my dressing room at the Frontier Hotel with a suitcase full of everything I needed to get high. "Take whatever you need," he told me. "It's on me." With that, Kenny Hubard became my connection.

I began injecting myself. Hubard supplied the drugs, I bought the syringes from Schwab's Drugstore. Before every performance and two or three additional times every day I'd go somewhere private and, just like any junkie, stick a needle in a vein. At night, to get to sleep, I'd take a Seconal. The more meth I took to bring me up during the day, the more Seconal I needed to take me down at night. I wasn't on a roller coaster;

I was on a pogo stick.

After becoming dependent on Hubard, I began doing favors for him. I brought him with me to parties, I let him travel with me, and I introduced him to many people, including Barbra Streisand. I took him to the set of *Hello, Dolly!* and as I spoke with director Ernie Lehman, I looked over and was surprised to see that Hubard was talking with Barbra. Later that afternoon he told me, "Barbra and I are going to have dinner."

Barbra Streisand have dinner with Kenny Hubard? I couldn't believe she had agreed to meet this guy. But just in case I was wrong, I advised him, "Just take it easy. Don't hit her right away." He wrote her a single-spaced three-page, rambling letter mentioning a long list of celebrities to whom I'd introduced him. I told him not to send it, and I don't know if he did. I know that he never again met with Barbra.

Another little favor Hubard wanted me to do was smuggle drugs into the country for him. I was doing a three-month tour of the Far East and he wanted me to stop off in the Golden Triangle, one of the largest drug-producing regions in the world, to pick up "crystals." He knew how easily I could get through customs. I didn't know if "crystals" meant heroin or cocaine, but I was still sane enough to refuse, telling him, "You're out of your fucking mind."

Hubard surrounded himself with strange characters. Not me, of course. Them. There were always girls around who would do just about anything for drugs. And it was through Hubard that I met people like Gen. Curtis LeMay, the ultra–right winger who had once been head of the Strategic Air Command and had considered running for president. I took my son Todd to LeMay's house in Bel Air one day and the general showed us his medal room. That impressed Todd more than anything I ever did with him. The thing I remember most about LeMay is that one day I mentioned to him that I was going over to Bobby Kennedy's house, to which he replied, "What do you want to go over there for? They're going to kill him." I never asked who the "they" were. I just dismissed that statement as an impossibility.

For almost five years, as my career spiraled downward, when I wasn't in the spotlight I was living in the shadows with people like Kenny Hubard. Although his drugs were "free," in return I gave him a small fortune to "invest" for me. Almost every penny of these "investments" was lost. I saw him for the last time when he called me in a panic; he'd overdosed and needed help. I took him to the hospital and then, at his request, called Max. Hubard insisted that only Max could save his life. I called Max, I called other people involved with Hubard, and, that done, rid myself of Kenny Hubard.

I didn't need Max or Hubard. What I needed was drugs and for that I had a man I'll refer to as Sam Quinn. Quinn was a hustler, supposedly a self-made millionaire who had endless stories and access to everything I needed. Quinn was so depraved he made Hubard look almost normal. These were my friends. The first decade of my career had taken me from the streets of Philly to the White House; during the second decade I went from the White House to the outhouse.

Quinn had a seemingly endless supply of meth, more than enough to keep me happy. And it was taking more and more of it to keep me happy. I couldn't go a day without shooting up and, one shot or ten shots, it just didn't give me the lift I needed. The engine wasn't working anymore. I didn't particularly like Quinn, but as I got to know him I liked him even less. But I needed him. As with Hubard, I never paid him, but I did give him money to invest for me. At one point, when I really needed some cash, I asked him to return at least a portion of $100,000 I'd given him to invest. Instead of the money, he gave me three bottles of meth.

I didn't trust Quinn at all. Maybe I was paranoid, or maybe I was crazy, but I knew I wasn't as crazy as Quinn. Rather than injecting myself with whatever was in those bottles, I had the contents analyzed. When I got the results back I called my old pal Max, who was in California staying with Quinn at the home of the nutritionist Gaylord Hauser. Hauser wasn't there; he wasn't involved in this at all. I'd also stayed there on occasion. One of those occasions was to help Quinn mix batches of meth and fill 100-cc. bottles with it.

I was living at the Beverly Hills Hotel and Max came right over. He hadn't changed at all. He immediately offered to give me a shot. "Read this," I said, handing him the laboratory analysis. "This is what your friend Quinn gave me."

As Max read the report the color drained out of his face. He sort of collapsed into a chair. "Oh God," he said. "What have I done?"

The bottles had been filled with cyanide. Had I injected myself, I would have died within minutes. Maybe I was paranoid, but I was also alive. It was time to start cleaning up my life.

It was too late to clean up my act. I'd met Quinn through Hubard, I'd met Hubard through Max, and I'd met Max because I'd lost my voice trying to do five shows a day at the Paramount when I'd come out of the army. I needed the drugs to perform, in the end the drugs prevented me from performing. I had come full circle.

It's too simple to claim that drugs destroyed my career. I took the drugs. I was responsible. I made the choice. I've spent time with baseball Hall of Famer Ted Williams, arguably the greatest natural hitter who ever lived. John Wayne used to say that Ted Williams was the man he wanted to be. The basis of Williams's success, he explained, was gaining control of his talent with discipline, discipline, discipline, and practice, practice, practice. I never really gained control of what I was given. What little discipline I once might have exercised was overwhelmed by my drug use. And practice? I rehearsed, I sang, I recorded, but I didn't practice.

Frank was the chairman of the board; I could have been at least the CEO. But I was too lazy, too interested in other things. Sinatra made it look easy, Bing made it look easy, Perry Como made it look easy. It took them a lot of hard work to make it look so easy. Singing is hard work. It's getting involved in what you do. Hit records are fine and I certainly had my share of them—more than my share. But it was all bubble-gum music, and it lost its taste pretty fast. I was so busy making hit records that I forgot that the most important aspect of a singer's career is recording a catalog of songs that will live forever. A comedian has to renew his material continually. An actor has to have the right roles. But for longevity a singer has to have a repertoire. A singer has to record the standards and the Broadway hits, he has to find his own way of interpreting the great songs. He has to put his sound on a broad body of work. I was too lazy, too busy being a star, to pay attention to the importance of the music. "Oh! My Papa" just never became a standard.

Few singers ever had as many opportunities as I did. I successfully made the very difficult transition from teen idol to star. Even though I rarely performed during the three years I was with Elizabeth, when I returned from Rome I was as big a star as I'd ever been. I sang for the presidents; I was asked to sing "The Star-Spangled Banner" or "America the Beautiful" at the beginning of the Olympics, the World Series, and heavyweight championship fights; and I was one of the biggest draws in Vegas. The boys loved me because the big gamblers loved me, and I loved everything about Vegas.

I didn't want the days—really the nights—to end. I loved the extraordinary feeling I got when I walked into a casino with a beautiful woman on my arm. I loved the sounds, the smell, the action, the excitement, but most of all I loved the attention. In Las Vegas I was an important person. I could make things happen. You need five suites on a Saturday night? Only five? In Vegas, I was a king.

By 1965 I was among the highest-paid nightclub performers in the country. I was still such a big star that my good friends in Vegas wanted to give me a hotel. Give me! Moe Dalitz, who ran the Desert Inn, loved me. He was like a father to me—as long as I was at the Desert Inn.

But the day I signed with the Riveria was the day he stopped talking to me. When I opened at the Riveria they threw a big party for me, and Sidney Korshak forced Moe to come and shake my hand in public. But Moe didn't love me anymore. Moe Dalitz eventually left Vegas and helped build La Costa. La Costa is a club near San Diego that owns about thirty square miles of extremely valuable California property. If Moe and I had stayed friends, I would have had a piece of that.

Korshak wanted to give me the Riviera. All I had to do was work there exclusively. But I turned him down, telling him, "I want a newer hotel." I had an opportunity to buy the Landmark for $250,000. I thought, $250,000 for that piece of crap? I almost laughed. Eventually Howard Hughes paid $13 million for it. I even had permission to build a new hotel on the strip, with help, of course.

When I was working at the Desert Inn I met with a man named Billy Weinberger, who told me, "We're building a new hotel and we want to give you fifty percent of it." In return I would perform there permanently and would use my influence to attract other major stars.

That sounded interesting. "What's it going to be called?" I asked.

"Caesar's Palace."

I laughed. "Let me get this right. You're building a hotel in Las Vegas, Nevada, and you're calling it Caesar's Palace?" I said, "Billy, I love you, but that's the worst name for a place I've ever heard." I turned him down. Now I probably wouldn't actually have owned half of Caesar's Palace, but I definitely would have had points; I would have had a nice piece of it. This was a legitimate offer—my name and my ability to book the biggest stars into the hotel had incredible value. I would have seen the money. But Caesar's Palace? Believe me, I'd already have enough trouble in Caesar's palaces in England and Rome. I'd had enough Caesar and Cleopatra and Mark Antony for my lifetime. How much would my share be worth today? In May 1999, Caesar's Palace was sold to Hilton for three billion dollars. I still believed there would be always be another offer. I still didn't realize I was singing the wrong tune.

While performing in England in the late 1950s I had become friendly with a Jewish song plugger, a man who eventually left the music business to open a very exclusive whorehouse. I went there one night for dinner. At one point he asked me, "Have you heard the new noise?" I didn't know what he was talking about. "A group of boys up in Liverpool," he explained. "They're making a stir." That's how I first heard about the Beatles.

I wasn't interested in some new noise. The only thing I understood was Eddie Fisher in the middle of success. He played their record for me in my dressing room at the Palladium and I thought it was a bunch of dumb noise, just a craze, the newest bobby-soxer attraction. I certainly didn't even suspect that this dumb noise would change the music business. Of course, I'm also the expert who turned down a piece of Caesar's Palace because I didn't like the name.

The song plugger recognized the future of the music business—and was smart enough to take his money and open a whorehouse. This was the beginning of the era of sex, drugs, and rock and roll. Unfortunately, I only had two out of the three. The audience for the kind of music I sang was dwindling. That sound that came out of my throat was no longer as popular as it had once been. The kids who were buying records wanted the Beatles and the Stones, all the other British groups, and Elvis. The radio stations concentrated on rock, and it became very difficult to get any radio play for a new record. All the "pop" singers struggled, all of them. Even Sinatra had difficulty selling records.

I hadn't had a hit record in several years. Some of the songs I recorded were very good, but without proper promotion, without someone pushing disc jockeys to play my music, my records had no chance to succeed. In 1966 I recorded an album entitled *Games That Lovers Play* featuring a single by that same name, for RCA. It was the first record I'd made for them in several years. It was arranged and produced by the great Nelson Riddle, and they put all their substantial promotional power behind it. Just like the old days I toured the country, appearing on any radio or television program that would have me, meeting with program managers and journalists, trying as hard as I could to sell my record. I called Johnny Carson and told him, "I want to do your show—"

"Sure," he said.

"Twice." I flew to New York and did the show two nights in a row. It was a gimmick, but it was so successful that producer Freddy deCordova asked me to "come back tomorrow." I came back tomorrow for five days. They couldn't get rid of me. When I walked out onstage in the middle of the show for the fourth time, Johnny spritzed. All I had to do was ask innocently, "Have I told you about my new record?" and he was gone.

The record sold 150,000 copies in ten days, a big number at that time. The publicity campaign was so successful that *Time* did a piece called "How to Make a Hit Record."

I had one more hit single, "People Like You," which also became an album, but that was my last hit. Hey man, I was hip, I wore a Nehru jacket and love beads, but my original audience had matured and my music didn't interest teenagers. I recorded one more album, *You Ain't Heard Nothin' Yet*, on which I sang most of Jolson's greatest songs. It was a good album but it didn't sell. I blamed RCA for its failure to promote the album and ended my relationship with them. That decision wasn't quite as bad as turning down an interest in Caesar's Palace, but for a singer having difficulty selling records it was disastrous. The Jolson album was the last original record I ever released. In my career I had had more consecutive hit records than any singer in history, and my recording career was finished.

In 1966 Buddy Hackett and I decided to work together. The crooner and the comedian. I thought the chemistry between us would be very good. And I was right. We did a cross-country tour that began in Detroit and ended on Broadway with a six-week engagement at the Palace Theater. I liked playing the Winter Garden, Jolson's theater, but I loved the Palace. It had an intimacy that larger theaters lacked, and it had its grand history. I think the first time I played the Palace I followed Judy Garland, who had tried to burn it down on closing night. Judy had suffered through an unhappy engagement and she was drinking too much and fighting with her husband, Sid Luft, so she started a fire in her dressing room. She was going to burn down the theater. It was a serious fire and could have put her in jail, but she had tremendous power. I dressed in the charcoal room.

I loved Judy. Figuratively and, for a brief time, literally. Years earlier we had been in love for several nights. I wanted to follow in her footsteps. The sad thing is that I almost did.

Buddy Hackett was as crude as any person I'd ever known, right up there with Debbie, but the act we did together was pretty strong. I would introduce him offstage, claiming, "I've known Milton Berle, George Burns, Jack Benny, Charlie Chaplin"—I really laid it on—"W. C. Fields, and now I'd like to introduce to you a guy who's going to prove to you that he's the funniest guy who ever lived." And as I said it I could almost hear Joe E. Lewis promising, "Here's a kid who's gonna cut 'em all!"

Hackett could be wonderful onstage, but too often he didn't know when to stop. He would do anything, say anything, for a laugh. The worst moment of my entire professional career took place with him at the Palace. At the end of the show we would do eight minutes onstage together, but if it was working we'd stretch it to fifteen minutes, twenty minutes. He would sit on the edge of the stage, the spotlight on him, and from the audience I would sing lovingly to him "That Face." Buddy had a fleshy baby face and he'd mug his way through the song. He was brilliant. He was also a wonderful ad-libber. I remember one night when I finished that song I told him, "Buddy, sing this next song with me. Just follow me."

To which he replied, "There were a lot of times in my life I would have loved to follow you."

That night at the Palace we were on fire. We were killing. His ad libs were brilliant—"Eddie, how many houses did you give away?"—and I was singing very well. It was a memorable night. We didn't want to end the show. It got to be 11:20, which is very late, and two little old ladies sitting in the front row got up and started walking out. Buddy stopped, looked right at them and said, "You Jew bastards, where you going?"

I tried to stop him. "Buddy," I said, "maybe they got to catch a train."

He said, "I hope they arrive in a casket."

The audience was stunned. I was embarrassed. With that one line he destroyed the euphoria of the entire evening. But that was Buddy Hackett. I just never knew what was going to come out of his mouth next.

By the end of this tour we were not getting along at all. We were very different people—speed and alcohol just don't mix. I was shooting my meth and he was drinking his vodka and gin. I admit he did try to teach me how to drink! Me, drink? That would interfere with my bad habits.

Almost every night after our show he would come into my dressing room bellowing, "Where are the broads?" He always wanted to know the secret of my success with the girls. In his case it was simple: My big secret was that I wasn't Buddy Hackett.

My career wasn't exactly coming to an end. I was still earning a tremendous amount of money from royalties and working in clubs, but certainly I was no longer as popular as I'd been. My shows no longer sold out. My records didn't sell as well. And while I refused to accept it, the meth affected my performance. At times I forgot the lyrics to songs I'd been singing my entire career, I missed band cues, I became erratic and unpredictable. I canceled engagements, I missed shows, and I showed up late. When I did perform I was often very sloppy. Joe E. Lewis used to say, "Some people drink to forget, I drink to remember." I understood exactly what he meant.

Money I could always make. Just not enough of it to support the scale on which I insisted on living. I'd never really cared about money, and when you earn as much of it as I did you can afford not to care about it. I was making more than a million dollars a year in 1952! I liked giving away my money; I cultivated the image I'd learned from Mike Todd. I gave away jewelry and cars, I bought houses, I spent fortunes on women and drugs. I was just as addicted to spending money as I was to the women and speed. My lawyer admired my Bentley convertible, so I gave it to him. When I left Rome I left my Rolls-Royce convertible in the street. Elizabeth got the ski house. Of course, the primary difference between Mike and me was that the money I was spending was my own.

Even when I started washing out, I was still playing Eddie Fisher. During a tour of the Far East in 1969, for example, long after I could afford it, I bought 145 silk suits, 185 silk shirts, and 50 pairs of silk pajamas. I couldn't wear 145 suits in my lifetime, but it was only money.

I was every bit as good a businessman as I was a parent. I never paid any attention to business, and the money rolled in like I was living downhill from a bank. In addition to the offers to own a Vegas hotel, I passed up many opportunities. Once, for example, I leased a ninety-nine-acre ranch in Pacific Palisades that had belonged to Irving Thalberg and Norma Shearer. I lived there for a year, I even put in a pool. I could have bought it for a song. Literally, one hit record would have paid for the whole thing. It's difficult to imagine how many billions of dollars ninety-nine acres in Pacific Palisades that stretched from Sunset down to the ocean is worth today. But my dog, Admiral Jr., an AKC champion five consecutive years, got out the front gate onto Sunset Boulevard and was killed. So I didn't buy it.

By 1969 I was in serious trouble. I still had that sound in my throat, but it was more gold-plated than pure gold. I couldn't fill the large show-rooms anymore. My Las Vegas contract was abruptly canceled. The word was around that I had become "difficult" to work with, and since I was no longer a major draw there were no other offers. I didn't know what to do so I did my usual: nothing. "Now we're getting a new 'image' of Eddie Fisher," wrote Hollywood gossip columnist Dorothy Manners. "Eddie the recluse. He seldom ventures out of the house, plays records and reads morning, noon and night, dines alone and is skipping all his favorite haunts. He's even given up his card games and trips to the race-track.. . .One of his friends returned my call and said, 'He just wants to be alone, at least for the time being.' "

Does that sound like the portrait of a drug addict? It wasn't completely true, but it was close. I was rarely alone. Almost always there was a woman with me. Even if, for the first time in my life, sometimes I paid them to be there. I found that prostitutes turned out to cost me a lot less than many of the women I'd dated. Often I didn't even have sex with them; we just sat and talked through the night. Eventually I began making videos of them, talking. That's what my life had come to, paying prostitutes—to talk.

I knew I was in serious emotional and financial trouble, but I didn't know how to get out of it. The person I'd once relied on, Milton Blackstone, was as bad as I was about handling life and money—he threw away more money than I did, if that was possible. I'd learned long ago that I could no longer depend on him for anything.

In August 1970, at the advice of a friend of mine, a judge, I declared bankruptcy in San Juan, Puerto Rico. I did it because I didn't know what

I was doing. It was an incredibly stupid thing to do. I declared that I was indebted for $900,000, $700,000 of which consisted of potential losses in two lawsuits that had not yet gone to trial, and had assets of only $40,000. The truth is I had plenty of money. In fact, I took considerably more than that in cash and gave it to a good friend to keep safely in a little box for me.

I filed in Puerto Rico because I hoped to keep it secret. I had been spending a lot of time in the islands. Whenever possible I'd run to Jamaica, I'd run to Puerto Rico, to Acapulco. I was running away from life, from the darkness I was in. It didn't matter how bright the lights were when I was onstage, all I was seeing was the blackness. But any chance of keeping the news that I'd filed for bankruptcy out of the media disappeared when I was detained at the San Juan airport for bringing drugs into the country.

I'd visited Puerto Rico numerous times without ever being stopped at customs. The agents recognized me and waved me through. Not this time. This time they pulled me from the line and searched my luggage. They knew exactly what they were looking for; I'd been set up. I never discovered who had informed customs agents I would be carrying a bottle of meth.

I was taken into a small, brightly lit room and ordered to strip. I couldn't believe it. Didn't they know who I was? I was too embarrassed, too humiliated, to be angry. I stood there naked, doing my best to cover my genitals with my hands, in a daze.

I was released and ordered to remain in the country. The headlines were even worse than I had feared. Not only FISHER FILES FOR BANKRUPTCY but SINGER SUSPECTED OF CARRYING DRUGS. The most awful part of it, much more painful than the public humiliation, was the fact that I was trapped in San Juan without access to drugs. I had to go through withdrawal cold turkey. No speed to pick me up, no Seconal to bring me down. I couldn't eat or sleep, I was dizzy, anxious, and my entire body ached. Eventually I got a note from my doctor, Tommy Jacobson, explaining exactly what drugs I was carrying and the medical reasons I had them in my possession. I was permitted to return to Jamaica.

It was hard for me to accept what was happening: I had been stripped in customs, I'd gone through withdrawal cold turkey, I'd declared bankruptcy, the big casinos in Vegas and the hotels in Miami wouldn't hire me, and my third marriage had failed. I really believed that things couldn't get any worse.

But I didn't even get that one right.

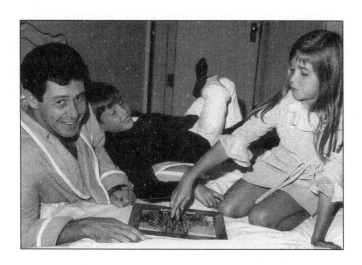

CHAPTER ELEVEN

It seemed like everything I'd done in my life had led up to Chapter 11.
Everything was falling apart for me. I desperately needed time to reor-
ganize. I knew what my problems were, though I didn't have the slightest
idea how to solve them. I knew I had to get off the methamphetamines.
In addition to destroying my life, after so many years, speed had little
impact on me. I couldn't get the same response. So I finally got off speed
the hardest way possible: I started injecting cocaine.

I was in San Juan early in 1973 and somehow I ran out of speed. A
friend of mine, supposedly a friend, introduced me to a member of the
Puerto Rican Senate who understood my problem. "What you must do,"
explained this senator, "is change your habit." With that, he lifted up
his pant leg and pulled a syringe filled with liquid cocaine out of his
boot. He injected it directly into a vein in my arm. I figured I'd have to

wait a little while bef—Wrong again. The effect was almost instantaneous. It was a jolt. Boom! Suddenly I was flying like I had never flown before. Within seconds I was off speed and I had a brand-new bad habit.

A warm wave of pure pleasure flowed through my body. As soon as the wave receded I wanted to feel it again. And again. That's how quickly and how easily I became hooked. I'm completely aware of what drugs did to my life, but the truth is that people don't take drugs because they make them feel bad. The high I got from cocaine was incredible.

The second time I shot it into my muscle it made me feel wonderful. The third time it made me feel good. The fourth time fine. That's how addiction works. It's never quite as good as it was, and you keep shooting trying to get back to that first perfect high.

Compared to speed, which brought me up then dumped me down, cocaine made me feel euphoric. Cocaine made me understand how bad meth had been for me. I continued to believe I was in control. That I still had some choice. I was hooked. I still wouldn't admit it, but I was a junkie. I returned to Los Angeles and read everything I could find about cocaine. I knew everything but I understood nothing. During the next several months I spent several hundred thousand dollars on cocaine and bought 10,000 Seconal pills at a dollar each.

To pay for my new habit I accepted just about every job I was offered. And even then there weren't too many offers. I'd worked my way down from the largest showrooms in Vegas to small clubs and hotels. As my habit increased rapidly from a few shots of coke a day to up to twenty— that's twenty little jabs of coke directly into my system—my performances grew progressively worse. Within months of discovering cocaine I was so high day and night that I could barely speak a coherent sentence, much less do my act. It was either quit cocaine or quit performing.

So much for my career.

I was scared. I knew what was happening but I couldn't stop it. In fact, the only way I could deal with my fear that I had become a drug addict was to use more coke. There were still women in my life, there were always women. The woman with whom I was living at this time— she was not in show business—loved coke as much as I did. Maybe more. In fact, we used to refer to ourselves as "the Cocaines." That was supposed to be funny.

The difference between us was that she preferred to snort it rather than injecting it. Not me. I refused to put it up my nose. In fact, when I saw anyone except her snorting cocaine, I thought it was disgusting. I refused to do it because the nose is connected to the throat and I didn't want to destroy my vocal cords. Eventually, though, I had to stop injecting myself intravenously because I'd run out of veins. I'd stuck so many needles in my veins that they were ready to collapse. My options were to give up coke or learn how to snort it. So much for my career.

My friend Jack Kelly, a deputy commissioner of narcotics, knew exactly what I was doing, knew exactly what everybody was doing. Elvis, Andy Williams, me, everybody. But until I asked him for help he never said a word. I was living with Mrs. Cocaine in a rented house in Bel Air. Hired guards protected our privacy so no one could see what we were doing. Jack was at the house one afternoon to confront a con man trying to beat me out of several thousand dollars. After Jack had settled that problem I got the courage to ask him, "How bad off am I?"

He didn't hesitate. "I give you six months." Before I could reply he continued, "No, wait. . .C'mere." He took me by the arm and put me directly in front of a mirror. "I give you three months."

I'd been addicted to coke for almost a year. That was the day I started quitting. Jack Kelly sent me to a police department doctor. When I asked this doctor about a program that would enable me to withdraw from cocaine, he said bluntly, "You don't need a program. Just quit. You just have to have the willpower to do it and you'll do it."

I began my own little program by flushing about $25,000 worth of cocaine down the toilet. Then I went to Jamaica, where I stayed with my great friend Ernie Smat. Ernie, who had turned his small water-sports business into a large fortune, found a doctor who would prescribe the medication I needed to get through the worst symptoms of cocaine and Seconal withdrawal. I was determined to beat my addiction. It turned out to be a bit more difficult than I had imagined. In fact, it almost killed me to save my life.

I tried to do too much too fast. My whole system collapsed. I started trembling, my body was soaked with sweat, I couldn't think, I couldn't control my body. I. . .something. . .where was. . .finally I fell into a coma. And unlike Elizabeth, not only didn't I see God, I didn't even get to see Mike Todd. Instead I awoke several days later in a bed in a native hospital in a small town. I didn't know where I was or how I'd gotten there. I had no memory of collapsing or being rushed to this hospital. But apparently doctors there had saved my life.

Ernie arranged for me to be transported by military helicopter to a more modern hospital in Kingston, where a group of young doctors insisted on injecting me with vitamins. I felt like a guinea pig. I hated it there, but my condition improved enough for me to return to Los Angeles about a week later.

During the thirty years I'd been using drugs I'd always believed I was making the choice, that I was in control and could stop whenever I made that decision. So it was difficult for me to accept the fact that that wasn't true. After almost dying in Jamaica, I kicked my cocaine habit—but only by returning to meth. I was back where I'd started, only now I was getting desperate to find a way out.

I was willing to try anything; I just didn't want it to be too inconvenient. Coincidentally, Eda, my former girlfriend, called to tell me her mother was in Los Angeles and wanted to meet me.

I told her I'd be delighted to see her mother and, incidentally, "You're going to save my life." I'd been told that there were clinics in Europe that catered specifically to wealthy people trying to kick a drug habit. Supposedly these places put their patients to sleep for seven days, feeding them intravenously, and when they woke up, they were clean. Eda knew a lot of wealthy Europeans, so I thought if anyone could find the right clinic for me, she would be that person.

At Eda's request I moved out of my house into an apartment she shared with five other young actresses. The last thing I was interested in was meeting another woman; I needed to kick my habit. For the first time in my life women weren't important. I was sleeping on the couch and I woke up one morning and Miss Universe was cooking breakfast for me. Literally, Miss Universe. I liked her immediately, although that's probably not much of a surprise. Miss Universe and I became close friends. She wasn't much of a cook, but when you're Miss Universe you could burn water and nobody would care. Care? Who would notice? She had just arrived in America so I took a little time out from trying to save my life to have a brief affair with her. Then I introduced her to Jim Aubrey.

Eda and I flew to Switzerland. The "sleep cure" turned out to be a myth, but she found another hospital that supposedly had an extremely high cure rate. Unfortunately, people had to really be sick to get into this hospital. Eda convinced the administrator to meet me to see if I qualified. "If you're out of bed and okay," Eda told me, "they won't let you in"—this was the first time I'd ever heard of auditioning for a hospital—"so you have to put on an act."

This was the finest performance of my career. Of course with my acting career, that didn't require very much. When the administrator arrived I ran around the hotel suite screaming, "Where are my pills, I'm going crazy." I yelled, "I want my drugs!" I shouted, I slammed doors. I acted like I was completely crazy. I qualified.

I assumed this place was a country club for wealthy people with a problem. It never occurred to me that it actually treated crazy people. The first morning I was there attendants attached sensors to my head and conducted all types of tests. At lunch, when I saw my fellow patients, they all looked like they were crazy. They looked like a group of killers. This place wasn't for me. I only had a drug problem; I hadn't killed anybody yet. Later I discovered I had checked into a psychiatric hospital for the criminally insane. They were killers.

"I've got to get out of here," I told Eda when she came to see me. "This is the wrong place for me." We immediately made arrangements to leave.

Doctors came into my private room and tried to convince me to stay. "We can help you," I was told.

They didn't understand me at all. I didn't want to be sane, I just wanted to get off drugs. After searching for another place where I could get the proper treatment, Eda found a weight-reduction clinic in Zurich that had a withdrawal program.

The Bircher-Benner Clinic was heaven for the wealthy. People came from around the world and waited months to get in. Typical of the people who came there was my friend the emerald king. Every summer he'd live on his yacht and gain twenty pounds, and every fall he would come to the clinic to lose it. It was the healthiest place I'd ever been. They grew all their own vegetables. Mueslix originated there. My treatment began with the most thorough physical examination of my life. Doctors put pipes into, up and down every orifice in my body. Everything in my stomach was tested. My eating behavior was carefully monitored. Finally I was put on a strict diet and given medication to reduce withdrawal symptoms.

The program worked well for me. I completed withdrawal and gained twenty pounds. I may have been the only person in the history of the weight-reduction clinic to successfully gain weight.

I returned to Los Angeles as healthy as I'd been in more than a decade. I was determined to stay clean, to resume my career, to regain control of my life. I'm clean, I thought, I'll start all over. The problem was that I had no program to follow. No rules. I wasn't smart enough or strong enough to stay away completely. I was an addictive personality in search of an addiction.

I had no one to help me. Almost everyone on whom I had once depended was gone. The last time I saw Max was at his wedding in 1973. But it wasn't really Max, just what was left of a crazy genius. His own drugs had destroyed him. At the wedding reception his wife, a nurse from his office, had to feed him. And then she took him into a private room and gave him a dose of his own medicine. In 1975 New York State took away his license to practice medicine. Although many people wanted him prosecuted, he ended up working quietly in the back room of another doctor's office for about three years. He died in 1978; he had become his last victim.

Milton stayed loyal to Max until Max died, even after he had lost his license. My relationship with Milton ended bitterly. To the surprise of everyone who knew Milton, when he was fifty-eight years old he married for the first time. His wife was a lovely woman, but Milton's erratic lifestyle was too much for her. Within a year they separated and Milton asked me to help them get back together. I think that sums up Milton's condition at the time. He was so out of it he asked *me* for marital advice! I did speak to his wife for him—and I had as much success with her as I had with Debbie, Elizabeth, and Connie. The marriage lasted about a year.

Milton had built two things in his life: Grossinger's and Eddie Fisher. When my wonderful, beloved Jennie Grossinger died in 1972, her son, Paul, who'd been running the hotel for several years, gained complete control. At Paul Grossinger's urging, we offered Milton a small salary to advise us both. "I don't need your charity," Milton angrily replied, turning us down. He wanted complete control of Grossinger's

I owed my past success to Milton and Max, and I couldn't get free of them. I had deep emotional and legal connections to Milton. Years earlier we'd signed a fifty-fifty agreement, and while he'd rarely taken his entire share, we were still equal partners. After bitter negotiations, some of it handled by United States Senator Jacob Javits, we finally settled our financial differences. Our relationship ended in a series of bitter lawsuits and fights. After we'd reached an agreement to dissolve our partnership, he insisted I had tricked him into signing. The lawsuits went on longer than my divorces. After all those years, after everything we'd been through, I heard myself yelling at him.

But that wasn't really Milton, not the brilliant Milton Blackstone who had built my career. This was what was left of that Milton after years of drug and alcohol abuse. The man who had once negotiated some of the largest contracts in show business, who had run one of the greatest resort hotels in America, who built successful corporations, was no longer capable of handling his own finances. His two brothers took control. I heard terrible stories, awful stories, that Milton was living on the streets, surviving on handouts. But there was nothing I could do to help him. I couldn't even help myself.

Max had treated the President of the United States, Milton had built an empire and Sam Giancana had been the Godfather. He had run Chicago. He had been one of the most powerful members of organized crime in America. His mistake had been enjoying life too much. He loved the spotlight almost as much as I did. That's acceptable for a crooner, but not for a Godfather. He was the subject of too much publicity. While a lot of men in his business had their careers end abruptly, Sam was permitted to "retire" to Mexico, where he maintained several homes, including a luxurious penthouse suite in Mexico City. Supposedly he was laundering mob money, but I never knew what was reality with Sam.

Sam and I were from very different families, but I loved him like a brother. I was in awe of him; I found him fascinating. Sinatra always wanted to be a tough guy. I didn't; I just liked hanging around with tough guys. When I was working in Mexico City, Sam arrived unexpectedly and stayed with me for three weeks, sleeping in a small room in my suite. He hinted that he was in some sort of danger. "You don't answer the phone," he told me. "Don't answer the door. I'll take care of everything." Was he ever really in danger? When I was with Sam I was always aware the threat was there, but he acted so confident he made me feel safe.

Till the end he was always trying to impress me. I remember playing gin with him one night; I won a couple of thousand dollars and he took out a check and signed it and said, "Fill it for any amount and it's as good as the wheat in Texas."

"You cocksucker," I replied. That was me, the Jewish tough guy. "You can't buy me. I'll slit your throat from ear to ear and throw you right over that balcony."

"Piano, piano," he said in Italian. "Take it easy, Eddie. Forget about it." Yeah, I'm sure he was quaking in his loafers.

Whatever deal Sam had made, he was not supposed to return to the United States, but on occasion I would get a message that Dr. Goldberg wanted to see me and we would meet for dinner. One afternoon the comedian Guy Marx called and told me, "You gotta come to dinner tonight"—I didn't want to go to dinner—"because Sheila's going to be there."

It was Sam. When I walked into the restaurant he was sitting with his back to the window. I'd read enough books about gangsters to know that that was either foolish or arrogant. "Sam," I asked, "how come you're sitting with your back to the window?"

"Well," he said, "you're going up to Vegas to do your show. I'm going to Washington to do my show." He was going to testify before a government committee. Although he said nothing to me, he knew the penalty for speaking to the wrong people. That was the last time I had any contact with him. Not too long after that he returned to Chicago and was killed. He was shot in the mouth seven times.

Max, Milton, Sam. . .I even lost my flamboyant friend Steve Brandt. Steve lived in his own hell. For years he had been threatening to commit suicide. He had even attempted suicide on several occasions. He'd called me at 4 A.M. once to say good-bye, to tell me he was going to kill himself. I alerted the Los Angeles Police Department, who rushed to his house and saved him. But the fact that people knew he'd even failed at suicide mortified him. Several weeks later he checked into the Chelsea Hotel in New York City and swallowed a bottle of sleeping pills. This time there was no one to save him.

One by one the men who had been important in my life were disappearing. In 1972 my father had a stroke and was put on life support. That was just like my father. I was struggling to save my own life and he had to go and have a stroke. I didn't know what to do. I wanted to

love him, I'd always wanted to love him, he just never let me. The closest
we came to ever finding peace with each other was in 1964. I was singing
at the 500 Club and he came to see me. The moment he walked into my
dressing room it was obvious he was very sick. He was pale and drawn.
I took him to California to see Rex Kennemar. A day later he was in the
hospital having a kidney removed.

I don't remember the words we said to each other, but both of us were
crying. We embraced, that I'll never forget because it happened so rarely
in my life, and I must have told him I loved him. I'm sure I did.

I commuted every day from Las Vegas to see him. I thought we'd
finally made peace with each other. But we hadn't. My father wasn't
capable of having a real relationship with his sons. He was always doing
something or saying something to destroy any relationship we might have
had. When I divorced Connie, for example, he called and complained,
"What happened to you, Sonny Boy? You could have been a pillar in
your community." I hung up on him.

When I think of my father I recall mostly unpleasant times. I remember him fighting constantly with my mother and my brothers. I remember
him coming into my dressing room after I'd done a great show. I'd killed,
I'd stood the audience on their heads, and I'd be soaking wet with per-
spiration. Just once I wanted to hear him tell me I was better than Jolson,
I wanted to hear him tell me he was proud of me, but he was incapable
of that. Instead he would say sarcastically, "You're a regular comedian."
That was his line, you're a regular comedian.

As my father lay dying in the hospital I was immobilized, caught
somewhere between love and anger. I thought about the times we'd spent
together. The joy on his face the night we went to the fights with Edward
G. Robinson, and the two of them spent the night conversing in Yiddish.
The night I introduced him to Joe Louis. The night he sat with Connie
at the Empire Room and from the stage I asked him, "What do you think
of her, Daddy?"

And he replied, beaming, "Sonny Boy, I've loved them all."

Oh, mein papa, to me you were so difficult. I called the hospital in
the middle of the night and screamed at them not to turn off his life-
support machine. I don't know what I thought I was going to do. By the
time I got to Philadelphia he was dead. I arrived at his funeral just before

they closed the casket. I didn't want to look at him, but one of my brothers pushed me forward. He looked so small to have caused so much pain.

I was more alone than I'd ever been in my life. And my career was—well, my career wasn't. I had taken success for granted for so long that I didn't know how to deal with failure. I was no longer in demand and I had no one to advise me. Now my entire career had become one long comeback attempt. Unexpectedly, of all the performers I thought were my friends, of all the people I'd worked with, it was Buddy Hackett who gave me a real chance. He offered me an opportunity to work with him in 1975. I was very grateful. I took full advantage of what was possibly my last chance to save my career and I worked as hard as I could. And I did it sober. I worked without my usual boost. It wasn't like the old days—because in the old days I needed meth to perform. Instead I got that energy from the audience. Buddy Hackett and I were so successful that the Riveria booked me at $30,000 a week.

An addictive personality can become addicted to almost anything. Sometime during this period I started taking tranquilizers, mostly Valium, but also several other pills. Of course I wasn't addicted to these pills, I just used them on a daily basis to regulate my moods. Doctors prescribed them, I took them.

I worked again with Buddy Hackett in the spring of 1976. We did capacity business at the Sahara. He was the featured attraction, but I got a great response. I was starting to regain my confidence, and for me being too confident was a dangerous thing.

In the fall I again worked at the Sahara with Buddy, but this time business was poor. There were probably a lot of reasons for that, but Buddy blamed me. Our personal relationship, which had never been great, deteriorated even further. I knew he disliked cigar smoke so I started smoking cigars in my dressing room just to keep him out. I didn't actually smoke them, I'd just puff the smoke into the air.

Behind my back he began making arrangements to replace me; all he needed was a good excuse. When my voice cracked during a performance he came onstage and suggested, "Hey Eddie, maybe you should go back to that doctor who helped you last time." It was a nasty remark. One afternoon he came to my suite to deliver a beautiful watch and belt he'd bought for my forty-eighth birthday. When he walked in the room he noticed a bottle of Tylenol next to my bed. "Ha!" he said. "You're on drugs again." I knew Buddy's sense of humor. I didn't think that remark was funny, but I knew it was meant as a joke.

The watch was inscribed *To Eddie: Fuck you on your birthday.* That wasn't meant as a joke. But I needed him, I needed the job, so I swallowed my pride. I thanked him and put on the watch.

Between shows that night the hotel's entertainment director fired me. He mumbled something about Buddy making demands and promising me two dates later in the year, but I didn't pay much attention. In my career I'd missed shows, I'd given bad performances, I'd even been so stoned I couldn't remember lyrics, but I'd never been fired. And firing me between shows was unusually cruel. There was nothing I could do but accept it as gracefully as possible. "It's okay," I said weakly, or something like that, and then went out and gave a good performance.

I was taking off my shirt in my dressing room when I heard Buddy Hackett tell the audience, "He's going to see a doctor."

I don't know what got into me. I was completely sober, but I exploded. I just couldn't take any more crap from him. I went back onstage and we got in an argument. The audience was stunned. This was an incredibly self-destructive thing for me to do, but I just couldn't help myself. I'm a self-destructive person. I read the inscription to the audience, then threw the watch and belt at him and walked offstage and out of my career.

Literally minutes later the phone rang in my dressing room. Word of the fight had spread so rapidly that comedian Shecky Greene was calling from Lake Tahoe. Shecky was one of the wildest men I'd ever known. When he drank he actually climbed the walls and when he lost his temper. . .well, I did see him turn over a crap table one night. I'd worked with him many times and we really liked each other. Shecky and Buddy were very competitive, so I could almost hear the smile on Shecky's face that night when he said, "I'll bet you wish you were up here in Tahoe with me."

Well, at least the newspapers were writing about me again. They reported that I had stormed onto the stage half-naked, cursed irrationally at Hackett, and proceeded to strip. The hotels could have accepted that—even if it were true—if I could still draw people into the casinos. But once I stopped selling tickets I lost the right to be difficult. The hotels wanted nothing to do with me.

I'd gone decades without having to stand in a single line. Stores would open or close at my convenience. I walked into theaters and championship fights without a ticket. I could make a phone call and have airplanes wait for me. Now I had to learn how to lead a normal life.

Less than two years later I was doing one-night stands in civic auditoriums as the star attraction of Roy Radin's Vaudeville Revue, or, as Tiny Tim referred to it, "The cavalcade of has-beens." This was the bottom rung of show business—and I was the master of ceremonies. The nicest thing I can say about Roy Radin is that he was sleaziest person I'd ever known. He was guzzling cocaine. Along with producing the show he was making big coke deals. What a long journey it had been from Mike Todd to Roy Radin.

Years later the police would find Radin's body decaying in the Mojave Desert. He'd been shot in the back of the head. I don't believe his murder was ever solved, but he was involved in so many bad deals there must have been many suspects.

I was grateful for the job. In addition to myself and Tiny Tim, among the featured performers were Georgie Jessel; Donald O'Connor; Frankie Fontaine as "Crazy Guggenheim"; Jackie Vernon, who once remarked, "I'm a household word now, but garbage is also a household word"; an Elvis impersonator; Danny and the Juniors; Ronnie and the Ronettes; Meatloaf; and Earth, Wind and Fire—although Fire didn't show up. We'd travel by bus mostly to suburban auditoriums and draw capacity crowds every show.

I remember telling a reporter from the *New York Times*, "The applause is better than the money. It really is." But believe me, I wasn't working for the applause. This was about the only job with serious money I could get and I took it.

Most of the people on the tour were in the same situation as me, thankful for any job. As Jessel said, "I'd like to retire, but if I did, I'd have to eat my newspaper clippings." Jessel had become a caricature of himself, wearing a military uniform and medals. He would wake me at seven-thirty in the morning to complain if I'd failed to mention when introducing him that he'd been named Toastmaster General of the United States by five presidents. Donald O'Connor was a terrible alcoholic. He was whacked out of his mind most of the time. He didn't dance, he'd just go onstage and fake a little soft-shoe for five minutes. But these audiences weren't there to judge talent; they had come to see in the flesh the people with whom they'd grown up. As long as I sounded more like Eddie Fisher than the Elvis impersonator sounded like Elvis, they were thrilled.

I accepted it. I didn't stop planning another comeback, or believing that with the right producer, the right arranger, the right manager, I could do it.

I'd lost so many of the people on whom I'd once relied. I was struggling to retain some semblance of a career, but, incredibly, the women were still there. Lovely women drifted through my life, several of them staying with me for long periods of time before the inevitable breakup. I may have even married for the fourth time—though I was never quite sure about the legality of that one. It happened in a small town in Baja, California. She was a beautiful woman, a former contestant in the Miss World contest about half my age, and one romantic evening, at the urging of friends, we held an impromptu ceremony under the stars. The man who married us had been ordained by mail order and, after the fortune I'd spent in jewels for other women, I slipped a cigar band on her finger.

The wedding was legal enough for us. Naturally I had to buy another house. Appropriately, the house I bought in the town of Palmdale was about 1,000 yards from the San Andreas Fault. It was the perfect metaphor for my whole life: Now I actually was living on shaky ground.

We tried living a simple life away from Los Angeles. The simple life got me so depressed I became addicted to tranquilizers. Eventually I checked into a local motel with a private nurse for two weeks and kicked that habit. I was clean—well, except for my little addiction to Valium.

She wanted to be a singer and an actress, but her real talent was being beautiful. My daughter Carrie always referred to her as "tits and ass." If we actually were married, it lasted only five months. At the advice of my lawyer we were legally divorced, which put me in the odd situation of divorcing a woman to whom I may not ever have been married. I was unable to sell the house; it was just too expensive for a house so close to an earthquake fault line. The buyer had to be someone unusually foolish with his money—and I had already bought the house. I just stopped making mortgage payments and lost it.

I needed to be with a woman as much as I needed my drugs. I never lost my love for love. The right woman for me was always the next one. The more unavailable a woman was, the more attractive she was to me.

I remember meeting a beautiful woman a few weeks before she was leaving California to marry a billionaire. Her packed trunks were in her living room ready to be shipped. She was marrying a billionaire—you can't find a woman much more unavailable than that. So I began my pursuit. I called her incessantly, asking her not to get married. I was working at the Latin Casino in Cherry Hill, New Jersey, and I got her on the phone and let her listen to my whole show, an hour and a half on the phone. All my romancing experience went into that project. Finally I talked her out of it. She picked the singer over the billionaire.

We went to Aspen, we went to Las Vegas, and then we went to Jamaica. As much as anything in my life, I loved being in love in Jamaica. We spent three perfect weeks together and then I realized she was an alcoholic. She drank every night. I became disenchanted with her. As quickly as it had started, it was over. I took her back to California and eventually she married her billionaire.

I don't know why the sight of a drunken woman disgusted me. Certainly I wasn't turned off by a woman who used drugs. I fell deeply in love with another woman who snorted cocaine. She was a flower child, but that flower that she loved most of all was the coca leaf. I didn't care, I still loved her. Drug addiction I understood. When we first got together I wasn't using cocaine, although I would buy it for her. A year later I started doing it with her. Once more, I was addicted to coke—but at least I wasn't an alcoholic!

One of the reasons I loved this woman so much is that she introduced me to other women. Among the few sexual fantasies I'd never fulfilled was being with two women at the same time. I'd always boasted I was a one-woman man—one woman at a time. But one afternoon she introduced me to a beautiful young woman whom she described as bisexual. We had drinks. We had dinner. We had a ménage à trois.

Suddenly it wasn't enough for me to have one great woman. I wanted to have two. It was so new, so exciting, and the cocaine made it even more exhilarating. I've been addicted to everything, and I became addicted to that. I would never have done it in the past. I wouldn't have dared. In my mind I was still the Coca-Cola Kid, the boy America loved, and having sex with two women didn't fit that image. Maybe it was my sense of moral guilt that made it so ecstatic, or just maybe it was the ecstasy that made me so guilty. Whatever it was, once I experienced it

I wanted to do it all the time.

Unfortunately, while I was deeply in love with my girlfriend, I also became infatuated with the other woman. That was the beginning of the end of my relationship with my girlfriend. I begged her to stay, which was another reason she had to leave; I was weak and she didn't like weak men. After we separated, the other woman came with me to Atlantic City, where I was working. In the middle of the night the phone rang. It was my former girlfriend and she was furious. "How dare you!" she screamed.

Me? Dare? She'd split up with me! After all those years women still amazed and confused me. Which is probably why they still thrilled me. I was as addicted to women as I was to any drug at any time. They played a significant role in my downfall—but finally it was a woman who rescued me. I've been married five times, if you count my beauty queen, but I've really only had one wife. Her name is Betty Lin. It would be a few more years until I found her, or she found me, and before then I had still farther to fall.

It was a long slide down. Ironically, among the very few people who were there to break my fall were my four children, Carrie and Todd, Joely and Tricia. I was not the father of any year. I was their father only biologically, and I'll live forever with a deep guilt about that. When they were growing up I wasn't there and that's a reality I can't escape. But I always loved them, each of them—I just didn't know how to be their father.

Debbie seems to enjoy describing how Carrie would stand by the window waiting for me to pick her up, only to be disappointed when I never arrived. Or how she would sign my name to Carrie and Todd's Christmas presents so they would believe I remembered. Sometimes I hate it when people tell the truth about me. Those are incredibly painful images, but if Debbie's purpose is to make me feel bad about that she's much too late. I know what I did—or rather didn't do—and I've spent my life feeling guilty about it.

Debbie once said that the best thing about me was my sperm. As far as our relationship was concerned she's probably right. I gave my children my genes, but I had nothing to do with raising them. The four of them are very different from each other, but each of them is very talented.

I inherited my parenting skills from my father. The difference between us was that he was there and too often I would wish he would disappear, while I was basically nonexistent and my kids wanted me there. At times I didn't see my children for years. I was the ice cream man of their childhood, a stranger who would show up once in a while and play with them and give them gifts. I wasn't there often enough, or long enough, to have the right to reprimand them, to be a parent. I can't explain why. There were no obvious reasons. Maybe I was too self-involved, too selfish. But there was never a day, never a second, that I didn't love them. I made several attempts to be my children's father, but they all failed.

I can't blame Debbie for my failure as a parent, but she did make it difficult for me to see Carrie and Todd. On those few occasions when I asked to see them there would always be some kind of problem; she'd be taking them out of town or have some reason why it wasn't convenient. She imbedded in their minds that I was a monster. One of the reasons I found it so difficult to visit my children was Debbie's presence. After being with the kids she'd invite me to stay for dinner and—I just couldn't do that. I hated it. I hated the phoniness of the situation.

I don't think Debbie wanted me to have a relationship with our children. She's tried all her life to come between Carrie and Todd and me. When I returned from Rome one of the first things I did was visit my kids. I was desperate to win their affection so I took Todd to Uncle Bernie's Toy Menagerie and bought him the most expensive toy in the store, a $600 child's car. It had a little motor and actually could be driven. Now, these kids had just about everything a child could have; their rooms were filled with possessions. Todd had more trains than Lionel, his walls were covered with his collection of arrows from every Indian tribe in America. But Debbie was angry when I bought him that car. "You're spoiling him," she said accusingly. One toy, I'm spoiling him.

Once I went to see Debbie and the kids perform at the Sahara. After the show I went backstage and she made sure I knew where the battle lines had been drawn. "I know you have part of Carrie's heart," she said bitterly, "but Todd is mine. He's all mine."

In 1979 Carrie was living in New York and invited me to stay with her. "You and me can start over," she said, adding, "and when you come, bring me the head of Beverly Hills." How could I turn down an invitation to meet my daughter? But very late one night the doorman rang from downstairs. I was alone. Debbie was there with a friend of hers. They walked into the apartment holding wineglasses. Debbie tried to be friendly, so I knew she must have had a lot to drink. Finally she took out her checkbook and told me, "I've got a blank check here. Fill it in. I want you to stay away from Carrie." Ladies and gentlemen, tonight the role of Sam Giancana will be played by Miss Debbie Reynolds. I started laughing. It was like a mob hit from two drunken ladies. If I had known she was so willing to pay me to stay away from Carrie maybe I wouldn't have done it for free for so many years.

I couldn't get them out of there fast enough. Maybe Debbie thought she was protecting Carrie from me, but Carrie was twenty-two years old; she didn't need any protecting. Carrie dazzles me. A journalist once said to me, "You must be very proud of Carrie."

Proud isn't even in the ballpark. "It goes well beyond that," I replied.

Carrie once told me, "I had no father. I had no mother. I raised myself and I think I did a hell of a job." And she was absolutely right. Carrie is perhaps the most unusual person I know. There are so many sides to her personality. She can be incredibly tough when she feels she has to protect herself, much tougher than I could ever be, but her essence is that of the girl next door.

The first time I saw her onstage was at the London Palladium with Debbie. Debbie brought out Carrie and Todd in costume and the three of them did a number together. Cute. But I never thought she would be an actress. To celebrate Carrie's sixteenth birthday I'd taken her to San Francisco for a few days. She was still a little girl. Less than a year later she called me bursting with excitement to tell me she'd gotten a role in a movie. I was thrilled for her. I assumed it was some sort of young adult film. Maybe the type of sweet film Debbie made at the beginning of her career.

The movie was *Shampoo*. She played a teenager who propositions Warren Beatty with the line, "You wanna fuck?" I don't remember Debbie having any similar lines in *Bundle of Joy*.

Two years later Carrie created the role of Princess Leia in *Star Wars* and became a movie star. Who knew? I can't even begin to describe the array of emotions I was feeling as I watched her on the screen.

I didn't really know what to expect when I arrived in New York to stay with her. Penny Marshall was with Carrie when I got there. Penny opened the door with a familiar line, "Hi. You wanna fuck?" I didn't know what to expect, but it was obviously going to be more than I expected. Carrie has a lust for living and loving that permeates her life. Whatever she does, she does with all her passion, whether it's writing a screenplay or a book, bringing up her little girl, or arguing with me.

After all those years of not being part of my life, she forced me into her life. It wasn't a typical father-daughter relationship—it was much too late for that to happen—and sometimes it was difficult to determine exactly which one of us was the parent. I certainly couldn't give her advice. I am smart enough to be able to recognize the fact that she is smarter than I am.

I've never tried to make up to her for my absence during her childhood. I can't undo what's done. And real emotional damage was done. "My father was extremely unavailable," she once said, "and that has affected how I relate to men. I don't trust them." She had a long and often difficult relationship with Paul Simon. At one point when they were fighting she sent me as her emissary to try to patch things up. I'd never met him and she gave me strict instructions about what to say and what to do. Paul and I met at the Beverly Wilshire Hotel and got along very well. "I don't know how to handle her," he admitted.

Oh, did I understand that. "Who told you to fall in love with an actress?" I asked.

Carrie kept calling me to find out what was going on. "What's happening?" She wanted to know. "What's he saying?" Finally she couldn't wait any longer. When she walked in we practically melted in each other's arms. I hugged her and kissed her. To which Paul Simon said, somewhat surprised, "Hey, you guys really love each other."

Think he was surprised? I guess I did a fine job getting them back together. Their marriage lasted slightly less than a year. Paul was a very competitive person. I think he had a difficult time dealing with her success. She went to most of his recording sessions, and these sessions can be long and tedious, so one night she brought a book with her. When he saw her reading he went crazy. How did she dare read a book when he was working? Carrie told me that he actually wanted her to quit show business. Hey, I'd warned him just as Marlene had warned me: Don't fall in love with an actress.

After divorcing Paul Simon, Carrie fell in love with a talent agent named Bryan Lourd and they had my granddaughter. "You weren't a great father," Carrie said after the baby was born. "I'm going to give you a chance to be a grandfather." My granddaughter's name is Catherine Fisher Lourd. Carrie wanted her to bear my mother's name, but everyone calls her Billy. Billy is a beautiful little girl and Carrie dotes on her. For a while I was terrific at this grandfather game, but then I started flunking that one, too.

I admired Bryan. He's a very calm and quiet man and sometimes he seemed like the eye in the center of a hurricane. I'd never seen such a good father—he was almost as good a parent as Carrie. And I was kind of jealous because my role as a grandparent got smaller.

Maybe the only thing I could have taught Carrie was that sometimes relationships end. That's another of my areas of expertise: ending relationships. Carrie suffered through a very difficult period when she and Bryan split up. She was in terrible shape, she lost a lot of weight, she didn't sleep very much—typical Fisher withdrawal. It was the only time in either of our lives that she needed me and I actually was there. It was my shining moment. I was living in San Francisco but I flew to Los Angeles several times to be there for her.

When she recovered she wrote me a note. I've had notes from presidents, notes from royalty, even notes from Sinatra, but nothing to compare to this. "For my daddy," she wrote. "Oh my daddy. You were/are a real life bona fide father this year to me, for which I will be grateful to you all my life. I needed you, in particular you, and you came through for me in a way I will never forget.. . .Maybe that's what all this pain was for, the pleasure of having you near. I love you."

My daughter did not get her writing ability from me. From me she got a lovely singing voice, though only her friends know what a nice voice she has. On occasion when she was growing up, she would come onstage with me and we would put our heads together and sing "If I Loved You." She made a record with Paul Simon. I suspect she sounded so good on that record that he didn't want her to sing anymore.

What Carrie did with her talent dazzled me, but as a person she's much more impressive than that. She inherited the talent genes from both of her parents, but the rest of it is pure Carrie. I remember going to Billy's third birthday party and being surprised to see Bryan sitting there on the grass with them after everything they'd been through. I didn't expect to see him there and I was proud of her because it didn't have to be that way. But she worked it out. She put her child before her own feelings, something I was never able to do. Carrie works on her life in a way I never could. In my life I allowed things to happen to me. I flowed along with my life as if I were on a raft on a river, going wherever the currents took me. Carrie navigates through her life.

I have great respect for Carrie. Even when we don't agree with each other, I always respect her. There are times we don't get along at all. Sometimes we fight and she yells at me. So after all these years I guess we've finally managed to have a normal relationship.

When I returned to the United States after separating from Elizabeth, I was pretty much a stranger to my children. I spent a day with Todd and at one point Todd and I went to the men's room. As we were standing next to each other Todd looked at me and informed me, "Carrie's is bigger than yours!" Maybe he was right.

Carrie and Todd are very different people. Debbie may have believed "Todd is all mine," but it was never true. Todd is one of the nicest people I've ever known. He is simply a very sweet human being. Unlike his parents or his sister, he has never wanted to be in show business. He performed with Debbie for a brief time, playing a little banjo and singing, and he hated it. He was good, and he sounded very much like me, but it was not what he wanted to do. For a time Todd wanted to be a preacher.

None of my children are Jewish. Their mothers aren't, so they aren't. They were all raised in the church. Joely and Tricia even attended Catholic schools, although eventually they left. When Todd was in his late teens he became a born-again Christian. He was introduced to it by Debby Boone. He knew the Bible completely; he could speak about it for hours at a time. At one time he even produced his own religious TV program, *Nightlight*, on which he tried to deliver a spiritual message with humor. Even though I'm not a religious person, I loved his enthusiasm for it and his strength of character.

And unlike so many other people, he has always practiced what he preached. When I was in a hospital trying to withdraw from Valium, Todd came to visit almost every day. I was in the psychiatric ward, a place where some patients had to be restrained. I didn't think I belonged there with all those crazy people. Not me. Todd brought me clothes to wear. Wild stuff, but still more fashionable than a straitjacket. And we'd sit and talk.

When it was time for me to leave, he invited me to stay with him at his house in Beverly Hills. This was my opportunity to meet my son. I stayed with him for three glorious months. I saw a lot of myself in him, but not the self-destructive parts. He took care of me, he couldn't do enough to please me. He wanted me to become a born-again Christian with him, but I told him I couldn't let Sammy Davis Jr. be a better Jew than me. No, I didn't say that. I explained that I had been born Jewish and intended to die Jewish. Although I wasn't in a real hurry to do so.

Todd has always had an incredible ability to work with his hands. That skill he did not inherit from me. That he learned from his grandfather, Ray Reynolds, who was always fixing and building. When Todd was young I installed a built-in state-of-the-art sound system in my house. My walls sounded like Jolson. That was one of the few times he ever visited me in my own home and he was fascinated by it. He listened, he just listened. Sometime later he called and said, "Dad, come over to the house. I want you to hear something." It wasn't very often that he asked me to do something—in fact, it was never—so I ran over there. He took me into a screening room and proudly put on a tape. He had built his own speakers, and they were better than mine.

Eventually he studied electronic engineering at UCLA and architecture at Brigham Young. By the time he was twenty years old he could build and assemble electronic equipment so complex that I couldn't even figure out how to turn it on. He constructed a mobile recording studio, which he rented to movie and record companies.

When Debbie opened a hotel and museum in Las Vegas, Todd began working with her. He designed the showroom, booked the shows, and helped run the whole place until it closed. On occasion, Todd has tried to forge peace between me and his mother. He wanted me to perform at his mother's hotel, but that was something I knew I couldn't handle. But he manages to have some sort of sense of humor about my relationship with Debbie. When he asked me to appear at the hotel I said, "Sure, I'll do the show. Then maybe Debbie and I will have another baby."

"Don't worry about that," Todd explained. "She's had a hysterectomy."

Debbie and I have waged an armed peace since our divorce. In the ensuing years, we've seen each other many times at public events or because of our kids. I went to her hotel in Vegas several times to visit Todd and saw her show. The last time I did that she sang a song for me; I don't remember what it was, but it definitely was not a love song, and when she finished she kissed me. As I've said, Debbie always put on a good show.

We've never had a civil conversation. It just doesn't happen. But I can remember only once that we spoke about what happened between us. That was many years ago. "Why did you have to marry Elizabeth?" she asked. "Why didn't you just fuck her like everybody else? I would have waited for you."

While Debbie never missed an opportunity to remind Carrie and Todd that I had left them, Connie was just the opposite. Connie has always been fair, always trying to encourage a relationship between Joely and Tricia and me. The girls have every bit as much right as Carrie and Todd to feel that I neglected them, abandoned them, but they don't. Both of the girls are so good to me after me being so nothing to them. With both of them it was always "I love you, Dad," without hesitation.

One night when Joely was visiting with Betty and me in San Francisco she put on a tape of a song Tricia had written for me, and sang with the recording. It was "Try," and as I listened to her sing I wondered why, why I hadn't been there for them, and I felt very grateful they had decided they wanted me to be in their lives.

> And I forgive you, never
> Holding me before you'd leave
> But I held myself up and
> Daddy now I believe
> We can let go of the past
> And all the things we should have done
> To set me free, and maybe I
> Can learn to truly love someone.
>
> Your eyes told me what was in your head
> I took from your hand the words you never said
> The child is gone, that moment passed us by. I'll carry
>   you
> With me for the rest of my life.

I'll get by, those tears will dry
I know you love me, but I wish you would try
I wish you would try to show me, try.

When Joely was sixteen years old she decided to stay with me in New York for almost two weeks. I was the perfect father for a teenaged girl in New York—I let her do anything she wanted to do. She'd stay out at clubs till 4 A.M. and I'd be there to greet her pleasantly when she came home. But there were also the nights when we just stayed home together watching TV, or playing my music, or tapes she'd made and getting to know each other.

Joely describes our present relationship as a combination of angry days when she feels "Fuck you," sad days when she realizes "there's no turning back," and great days on which I'm her hero "because you survived." I think Joely understood—maybe all of the kids did—that it was hard for me to be their parent because I was so busy being a child myself.

From me Joely got her playfulness, her sense of humor, her big singing voice, and her bottom lip. From Connie she got her endless drive, her quest to succeed, her self-confidence, and her values. Like her mother she's an incredibly hard worker—and admittedly "a great spender."

When Tricia and Joely were studying together in Italy a woman kept calling Tricia *farfalla*, "the butterfly," because she landed somewhere briefly and then again took off in flight, then landed again and again, with no permanent place. Well, we know what Tricia inherited from her father. I remember when she was about twelve we were having lunch together in the garden of the Beverly Hills Hotel, and I looked at her and told her, as every father tells his daughter, "You're going to be a star."

After thinking about that for a moment, she wrote down something on her pad and handed it to me. It read *Tricia Leigh, a star to be!*

A star to be. I think that accurately describes both of the girls. They were born to be in show business. The very first time Joely sang in public the audience gave her a standing ovation—and she was addicted. She has a great sound, a big, rich voice. But one night I was watching her co-starring with Ellen DeGeneres on *Ellen*, and I was amazed at her innate comic ability. That she certainly did not inherit from me. I don't want to say I was a bit stiff when I tried to do comedy on television, but

I used to get fan mail from mannequins. Da-dum bump! But Joely has impeccable comic timing.

Tricia is my baby. It's difficult for me to look at her and accept the fact that she's a grown woman. When she was twenty-one she made a big pop hit, "Empty Beach." I went to see her perform it at the Palladium in New York. Backstage, before the show, she was incredibly calm. I was much more nervous than she was. But when she went onstage and I saw all these boys trying to grab at her, I became really frightened for her. How could they do that to my baby? But she handled it very professionally.

As the girls have gotten older, I've spent more time with them than I did when they were kids. Anything is more than nothing. Whenever we're together we have a wonderful time. The love is there, right out in front, but the time hasn't been put in. Tricia said to me once, "Dad, I don't care how many hit records you've had. I don't care who you are or what you've done. I just want to be with my daddy." I was embarrassed that she had to say that to me. I should have been saying it to her.

There was one night, one beautiful night, that I will never forget. When Betty Linn and her son, the brilliant and innovative "Dr. Winkie," as he's known, opened Mercury Rising, the best restaurant in San Francisco, Connie, Joely, and Tricia came up for a pre-opening party. During the evening I stood up in front and sang "Lady of Spain." And as I was singing Joely and Tricia came up and stood on either side of me and began singing backup. The Fabulous Fishers. The joy I was feeling is almost indescribable. For me, it was a new high. If anyone figured out a way to bottle that feeling I'd be the first person in line. And I hate standing in lines!

One reason I've been able to establish relationships with my children is the persistence of my wife, Betty Lin. Betty is the most extraordinary woman, a person who leaves only joy in her wake. If there is anyone who doesn't like her, there is something terribly wrong with them. To have met Betty at this time in my life is a miracle.

In the mid-1980s I did ten one-nighters in northern California, concluding the tour at the Paramount Theater in Oakland. I had been asked to greet the friend of a close friend of mine after the show. But when I walked out of my dressing room I saw a beautiful blonde wearing a full-length sable coat, standing alone. Sirens, bells, whistles, my entire inner alert system went off. "Holy mackeral," I said. "Who belongs to that?"

Reno Alonzo was his name. And he was the friend of the friend. Reno was a dashing man who had done very well in the antiques business and real estate. Eventually he became one of my closest friends. Along the way he saved my life.

On the journey down it's difficult to know exactly when you've reached bottom. Just when you think things can't get any worse, you get surprised. But when I met Reno I was near the bottom. I was back on cocaine and I wasn't working very much. My life was being chipped away a little bit at a time. I'd put many of my mementos in storage and when I failed to pay the storage fee it was all sold at auction; all my awards and photographs and albums, gifts I'd been given, a thousand pieces of my life, sold to the highest bidder. Whatever was left was taken by the women in my life at that time. Even my memories were being lost.

I had moved to New York City in the early 1980s. There was nothing left for me in L.A. After living with Carrie for several months I rented an apartment on East Ninety-third Street. I'd come almost full circle, from barely surviving in Philadelphia to barely surviving in New York. I accepted every offer I received. I played colleges, I played park band shells in the summer, I played benefits for bizarre diseases, and I played really seedy clubs. I was terribly embarrassed to have to work in some of these places. I just hoped that no one I knew would find that I was reduced to this level. I didn't want any of my friends to see me. It was very, very tough. It's tough just to remember it. My childhood dreams had become adult nightmares. But I kept going. I had no choice; I needed the money. I was just hanging on. I was working my way *up* to just being broke.

I couldn't believe this was happening to me. How could I possibly have fallen from such heights to such depths? On my really good days the best I felt was terribly depressed. On the bad days I could barely get out of bed. When I performed I no longer even cared if the audience liked me. Applaud, cheer, boo, it made no difference to me. As long as the check was good. Once I had loved the nights, I never wanted the nights to end, now I was dreading them. Maybe the worst night of all was a benefit I worked in the Catskills—by that time the Catskills were almost as dead as my career. I had a new hearing aid. And that night the audience was wild about me. It had been years since I'd heard such a roar, such incredible cheering. It felt. . .*wonderful*. They love me, I thought. They don't want me to leave. While the other performers on the bill waited backstage I stayed on and on and sang some more. I wouldn't leave the stage. Finally, they had to take me off. They had to come out and get me—and that's when I found out that my new hearing aid was broken. Every sound was being magnified many, many times. It had been my hearing aid that didn't want me to leave.

I could barely afford to pay my rent. The apartment on Ninety-third Street was furnished in flea market nouveau. The sofa was falling apart, I had no blanket on the bed, I had two knives, two forks, two spoons, two pots, and dozens of cans of tuna fish. I'd pretty much given up. I was lost.

I had been living in New York for almost eight years. Living? Surviving. Reno had come to New York to see me but I'd been avoiding him. I was too embarrassed to let anyone know where or how I was living. Finally he just showed up at my apartment and started ringing the buzzer. Eventually I let him in; I didn't have the energy to keep him out.

When he walked in I was sitting on the floor, the few photographs I had left were strewn on the floor around me. I was just sitting there, looking at those beautiful pictures of a handsome young man with Prince Rainier and Grace Kelly, with Princess Margaret, with Jack Kennedy and Lyndon Johnson and Sinatra and Dean and Como and Elizabeth— sitting there looking at the wreckage of my life.

Reno picked me up and helped me put my life back together. He brought me back to San Francisco and I lived with him for several months. When I was finally ready to return to New York he threw a small going-away party for me at Trader Vic's. Among the invited guests was a very pretty Chinese woman, Betty Lin, whom Reno insisted sit next to me. She spent most of the party taking pictures with an unusual camera; instead of ordinary photographs it produced still pictures that could be shown on a television monitor. I'd never seen anything like it, and when I admired it she gave it to me.

The next day, before I left for New York, I stopped by her apartment to pick up additional film for this camera. That was my excuse, at least. She served shrimp and Dom Pérignon. I didn't drink any champagne; I was only a drug addict. A Swedish photographer who was at the apartment took a photograph of Betty and me leaning over a balcony railing.

Betty was wearing a lovely Chinese silk kimono. As I stood close to her that old feeling started stirring inside me. I could feel it growing, like an engine warming up. As soon as I got back to New York, I started calling her every day. We became friends on the phone, and then I convinced her to visit me in New York.

From the first moment I met her, she fascinated me. She'd built a small business into one of the biggest printing companies in San Francisco. And she did it without losing her grace and kindness along the way. Betty was the exception to every rule about women I'd ever learned. She never has a negative thought; ironically, my wife, the woman I love, is one of the biggest Debbie Reynolds fans in the world. When I tell her about Debbie she just waves me away, she pays no attention to me. The God in whom I don't believe has some sense of humor.

Betty and I are a perfect match. She is an incredibly giving person, and I need an incredibly giving person. When she is with someone she likes, which is most of the time, her entire being lights up. She is caring and loving not only with me, but I'm the prime beneficiary. I've had women in love with me before, but there was always a certain selfishness that went along with that. Not with Betty. Betty has always been there for me and never expects anything in return. She does things because she believes they are the right things to do, not for any personal gain. I've spent a lifetime with another kind of woman—not to mention any names, of course. I've never experienced this kind of love before. This is it, this is the kind of love I'd believed my mother and father had when I was a child. This is what love was supposed to be.

I've never made it easy for her. In reality I've never made it easy for anyone in my life. When I met Betty she was an absolute straight arrow. No one in her family drank or smoked or had ever used drugs. She certainly didn't recognize my drug addiction. When it came to drugs she made a terrible mistake: She believed me. She kept asking me if I was using drugs and I kept smiling my most charming smile and lying. I told her, just as I told Phil Donahue on his show, "I don't know how to use Tylenol." While she never understood why I locked myself in the bathroom, or why strange people delivered packages to me, she believed me.

In April 1990, I performed at a charity concert in Orlando, Florida, to raise money for Snowbabies, an organization established by my friend Dr. Irving Kolin, to help babies born to cocaine-addicted mothers. The concert took place during a convention of doctors and psychiatrists who dealt primarily with cocaine addicts.

Well, they certainly picked the appropriate performer. I went on late in the evening. I was so high on coke that I had difficulty walking a straight line as I performed. Personally, I thought it went very well; I was sure I'd fooled them once again. At the end of the evening they gave me a beautiful bust of a Snowbaby and I stood in the spotlight, loaded to the gills, feeling like a complete hypocrite.

The next morning Dr. Kolin's wife, Shelly, took me out for breakfast while Irving Kolin informed Betty that I was a drug addict, and that if I didn't do something about it immediately I'd be dead within months.

Apparently I hadn't fooled him quite as much as I had believed.

When Betty and I returned to San Francisco she called the Betty Ford Center in Rancho Mirage, California. That was the only drug program she knew about. They agreed to accept me—but only if I called them myself. This was still long before we were married, so confronting me with this was a brave thing for her to do. In a loving, nonaccusational way she asked, "How would you like to go to the Betty Ford Center?"

I was ready for it. Before this I wouldn't have listened to anyone else because in my own mind I was a god. I'd been given the most extraordinary life. But as I'd stood there at the Snowbabies concert listening to Dr. Kolin praise me, I'd felt like such an incredible hypocrite. I knew I had to change. I don't know if I believed the Betty Ford Center was my last hope, but I knew I didn't have too many chances left.

The program at Betty Ford is a bit like basic training, but without the comforts. Their object is to bring you down to your lowest level, to force you to lay it all out, because that's the only way you're going to get out of the cell into which you've locked yourself. I went in there knowing I was very special, I was what was left of Eddie Fisher. It didn't take me long to realize that while every person in there had arrived on different ships, we were all in the same boat. It didn't matter if you were a prostitute or a pop singer, the problem was exactly the same. But because I'd breathed rarified air it took me a little while to accept the fact that I was in the gutter.

I tried to be Eddie Fisher at Betty Ford. I even brought my music with me. I tried to sing. But my counselor, George Vandal, wouldn't let me be Eddie Fisher. He didn't want to hear me sing, he didn't even want to know about my life with Cleopatra. He gave me no special treatment. He had one objective: drumming reality into my head.

Part of the process of breaking down resistance is having to perform menial tasks, the kind of jobs that most people who can afford the center never do. I did things at Betty Ford I'd never done before in my life. The first week I waited on tables, the second week I was in garbage disposal, the third week I was on laundry detail—I was better at garbage than laundry and I was poor at garbage—so a lot of clothing came out of my wash with new and highly unique colors. I had to do my own vacuuming. Every day that I was there was difficult, but each day was just a little better than the day before.

I thought my story was unique, until I heard other people talk about their lives. There are meetings every day and in those meetings everybody dies a little. There was the elegant seventy-five-year-old former Ziegfeld girl who would drive from liquor store to liquor store, buying only one bottle at each store because she didn't want anyone to know how much she was drinking. There was the Vietnam veteran who resisted the program for a long time, only to break down in tears one day and admit that he'd stolen morphine from wounded soldiers and used it to feed his own drug habit. What was the tragedy in my life? Marrying Debbie? Hardly. Life got put in perspective pretty rapidly down there.

I don't remember how long it was before I was permitted to use the telephone, but Betty was the first person I called. "Betty," I told her, "in the middle drawer in your bedroom is an envelope with cocaine in it. I want you to open it up and throw it down the toilet." Ah, they're playing that same old song again. . .but this time I meant it.

This time it was Betty who resisted. By this time she'd learned a bit about drugs. "Oh no, Eddie," she said. "It's worth thousands of dollars."

"Down the toilet," I insisted, and she did it.

Patients are not supposed to have sex at the center, but. . .some addictions I couldn't give up. Betty would visit me for four hours on Sunday afternoons and as I waited for her I was as excited as a little kid about to have his first sexual experience. Just holding her hand sent a surge of sexual energy through my body. We were not supposed to bring anyone to our rooms. We couldn't get there fast enough. No one ever disturbed us.

I was supposed to be there for four weeks, twenty-eight days. As I approached my final few days I began getting very excited about leaving. But on my twenty-seventh day my counselor called me into his office and said, "Eddie, I'd like you to stay two more weeks."

My heart fell right into my stomach. We had a long discussion. He gave me a pep talk, telling me how well I was doing, but all I could think about was getting out of there. As soon as possible, I called Betty and said, "They want me to stay two more weeks."

I don't think Betty quite understood what I was saying. "Oh Eddie, that's wonderful. They love you."

"It's not that. They want me to stay because they think I need more treatment." I told her, "I can't do it. I'm breaking out of here."

Without hesitation, she said, "Don't go without me. Wait for me." She didn't question me, she didn't try to dissuade me. She just didn't want me to go without her.

We weren't exactly Bonnie and Clyde. There were no walls to climb over. I just got into the "getaway car" and we drove to the airport. It was only when I got on the plane that I got frightened. Not of getting caught, but rather being out on my own. Inside the center I felt a great sense of security. It was safe there. Now I was on my own.

One of the first people I heard from when I got home was Donald O'Connor. I hadn't seen him or spoken to him in years. The last time I'd seen him he'd been so drunk he could barely dance a straight line. I thought he was calling me for help; in fact, he was calling me to offer help. He had been clean and sober for years. Eventually we met at Jerry Lewis's muscular dystrophy telethon, and when I looked at him I saw a saint. He was a completely different human being.

I left the Betty Ford Center with the tools I needed to overcome my addiction. The other places I'd tried had provided no direction, no indoctrination, no information about what I had been doing and what I needed to do. At Betty Ford they pound the tools into you. The only thing I could not do was follow the twelve-step program, which includes giving yourself over to God. I couldn't do that. God and I hadn't been on speaking terms in a long time. But I found a sponsor, a man named David Smith who was always there to help me. David Smith is one of the foremost authorities on drug addiction in America. He's the founder and director of the Haight-Ashbury medical clinic. He took me to the first of many Alcoholics or Narcotics Anonymous meetings; and I had

Betty.

I attended the meetings every day, sometimes twice a day, for more than three years. I never enjoyed these meetings; I could never forget that I was there because I had a disease. But at these meetings I found the support I needed. It took me a long time to get up and speak and when I did I told them I didn't believe in God. The other people there were supportive. They told me it was all right, but it really wasn't and I knew it. Eventually I stopped attending the meetings.

I never relapsed. On April 17, 1953, at the Paramount Theater, Max Jacobson gave me my first shot. It took me thirty-seven years to get over it. But finally, finally, I was free. On a television program Betty was asked how she knew that I was no longer using drugs. "Oh, that's easy," she explained with a smile. "He doesn't lock the bathroom door anymore."

Betty and I married in 1993. We live in San Francisco and occasionally I sing for friends or at a party. And when I sing, that sound, that sound that made everything possible, is still there. Not as strong as it once was, not as rich, but still that recognizable sound.

In 1989 I was asked to play the lead in the touring company of the musical *La Cage Aux Folles*. The role is a gay man, and when they first offered it to me I laughed. I laughed in a very deep voice. If I played this character, I thought, Mike Todd or Sam Giancana would be turning over—on the other hand it is a wonderful role. I saw both Van Johnson and Gene Barry playing the lead. Finally, I hired an acting coach and I started working on it. I got close, but I just couldn't do it. I'd spent so much of my life being a ladies' man that I just wasn't able to play a men's man. I just couldn't do it.

I don't regret that decision, but that's probably one of the few things in my life that I don't regret. I have so many regrets, so many. I've made so many mistakes in my life. With all the experience I had, with all the opportunities I was given, I will never understand why I continued to make such terrible mistakes with my life, or why I made the same mistakes over and over. I'm bewildered about that. I think I just didn't know how not to. At times I tried to take control, but I never did. I never could. I had everything, everything, and I blew it all. I loved all the wrong things: the drugs, gambling, and, most of all, the women.

For better or worse. . .oh, if I never hear those words again. For better or worse, I've spent my life in the pursuit of women. And I suspect I know as much about women as any man. But if there was one lesson I've learned, it's that a man will never be able to understand what a woman wants, when she wants it, how she wants it, or who she wants it with. My mother was ninety years old when she died in 1991, having lived long enough to see me at the top and bottom of my career and my life. All she ever wanted for me was to be happy. She had loved all the women in my life, I'd thought. But in 1986, in response to a question about my problems, she said, "Whatever happened to him, she [Elizabeth Taylor] did it to him. She made him suffer so much. When Elizabeth meets a man, she takes him and squeezes the life out of him. He loved her, but I don't think Elizabeth Taylor knows what love is . . ."

Maybe she was right. I loved Elizabeth in a way I've never loved another woman. It was a perfect time in my life. And, when you look at photographs of her, I don't think she was ever more beautiful. I want to be objective about it, but in pictures taken when we were together she seems so young and radiant. After that came Burton and more alcohol and more pills and more men and more marriages and somehow she seemed to become a caricature of herself. She was no longer attacking life like the person I had known, but rather playing the role of the woman who had once been Elizabeth Taylor.

I saw her for the last time in New York in the late 1970s. At Sardi's restaurant. I looked up from my table and there she was, sitting nearby. We smiled at each other, warmly, I think, and certainly without any rancor. By that time we'd both been through so much and so many. I sent a bottle of Dom Pérignon to her table. She raised her glass and mouthed the words *Mazel tov*. That was us, two old Jews getting together.

I went over to her table and we had a brief, pleasant conversation about nothing. I think what surprised me most about my reaction was the complete absence of any emotion. This was the woman I had once loved as deeply as it is possible to love another person. Years earlier just seeing across a room would have set my heart on fire. But this time it caused me to wonder, What was it all about? All that pain. Maybe Connie was right about me when she wrote, "I do not wish you love as you wouldn't know what to do with it."

As I left the restaurant I again stopped at her table. She looked up at me and said softly, "Shalom, Eddie."

"Shalom, Elizabeth," I responded. That was the last time we saw each other.

I've lived a most extraordinary and public life. I grew up in a house where nine people had to use the same bathwater and the toilet could be flushed only once, and I became one of the most popular singers in the world. I've lived among a cast of legendary characters. I've known presidents and mobsters, I've trained with Rocky Marciano, Joe Di-Maggio was my friend, and I've loved the most beautiful and celebrated women. I've played the greatest theaters in the world, I've performed for ten thousand audiences. Once there was a time when every person in America knew who I was. And when I think about it all, about my rise to stardom and my loves and my failures, about the scandals that created headlines around the world, about Cantor and Jennie Grossinger, about Debbie and Elizabeth and Connie and Nathalie and Ann-Margret bursting with life, about how different it all would have turned out if only Mike had not gotten on that airplane, about Max with his infernal needles and Jack Kennedy and Sam and Sinatra and Dean, about the thousand nights of pleasure and the thousand nights of drug-addicted hell, when I think about it all I realized that from the very beginning my mother was absolutely right: Words can't express.

INDEX

20th Century-Fox, 170, 172, 182, 189, 204, 229

ABC radio network (Blue Network), 19

Abrams, Bob, 182, 201, 206-207, 285

Adams, Edie, 58, 94, 236-237, 241

Adler, Dick, 66

Adler, Stella, 60, 126

Alberghetti, Anna Maria, 50

Alexandra, Princess, 243

Allen, Steve, 131, 150

Alonzo, Reno, 325-326

Ameche, Don, 50-51

Anderson, Michael, 115

Angeli, Pier, 73

Ann-Margret, 16, 55, 58, 235-242, 247

Armstrong, Louis, 79

Around the World in 80 Days (film), 105, 111, 113-118, 127-129, 132

Arthur Godfrey's Talent Scouts, 8, 10

Aubrey, Jim, 247, 272

Bacall, Betty, 274

Bacon, Jim, 247-248

Bacon, Mike, 133

Baker, Josephine, 61

Ball, Lucille, 60, 192

Bardot, Brigitte, 170

Bautzer, Greg, 272

Beatty, Warren, 139

Beaverbrook, Lord, 128

Belafonte, Harry, 281-282

Bennett, Tony, 54

Benny, Jack, 36, 73, 133

Berle, Milton, 37, 76, 224

Berlin, Irving, 53, 69, 92

Berman, Pando, 166-167

Betty Ford Center, Rancho Mirage, 328-330

Bircher-Benner Clinic, 305-306

Blackstone, Milton, 22-23, 28, 31-33, 35-38, 40-43, 47, 50-51, 60, 67-68, 79-80, 85-88, 90, 110,

Blackstone, Milton (*continued*)
    131, 175, 187, 220-224, 234-235, 284, 297, 306-307
Blau, Roger, 238
Blondell, Joan, 30, 110
Bloom, Claire, 205
Bluebird Records, RCA Victor, 35-36
Boeck, Renata, 240, 243-248
Bogart, Humphrey, 80
Boone, Debby 320
Boyd, Stephen, 172-173, 178, 189-190
Boyer, Charles, 114
Brando, Marlon, 61, 90
Brandt, Steve, 249-250, 308
Brandwynne, Nat, 58
Brenner, Yul, 192, 242
Brooks, Richard, 133
Brown's Hotel, 23
Buddy Morrow Orchestra, 20-21
Bunche, Dr. Ralph, 224
Bundle of Joy (film), 91-92, 116
Burns, George, 36, 236
Burton, Richard, 123, 126-127, 149, 173, 190, 199-201, 203-220, 223, 226-228, 230-231, 234, 241, 248, 256-257, 332
Burton, Sybil, 205, 212-215, 217, 219
Butterfield 8 (film), 125, 165-167, 188-189

Cahn, Sammy, 16, 69, 133
Calhoun, Rory, 95
Cane, Marvin, 80
Cantinflas, 128
Cantor, Eddie, 9, 10, 19-20, 32-36, 41, 58-59, 80, 84, 145
Cantor, Ida, 19, 33, 84
Capote, Truman, 166, 187, 206
Cappucine, 139
Carnegie Hall, New York, 43
Carroll, Harrison, 277
Carson, Johnny, 258, 294
Caruso, Enrico, 7
Cassidy, Jack, 30
Castellano, Angelina,17
Cat on a Hot Tin Roof (film), 133, 136, 141, 151
Catered Affair, The (film), 88, 94
CBS, 89, 113, 130, 247
Chandler, Jeff, 71
Chandler, Otis, 114
Charisse, Cyd, 202
Charles, Ezzard, 79

Chayefsky, Paddy, 166
Chester, Julie, 69
Chesterfield Show (radio show), 18-19
Chesterfield Supper Club (TV show), 105, 113, 116, 163
Christian, Linda, 154
Clarke, Buddy, 28-29
Cleopatra (film), 2, 123, 170-179, 189-191, 197, 199-205, 207-209, 221, 223, 227, 229-230, 234-235
Cliburn, Van, 89, 142-143
Clift, Montgomery, 117, 125-125, 162-163, 206
Coca-Cola Kid, 25, 51, 314
Cocoanut Grove, Los Angeles, 72-73, 84, 192-193, 235-236, 241, 250
Cohn, Art, 133
Coke Time (TV show), 50-53, 62, 69, 88
Cole, Nat King, 54, 115
Coleman, Ronald, 114
Colgate Comedy Hour, 41
Coliseum, Chicago, 35
Collins, Joan, 61, 170
Colony, New York, 145
Columbia Records, 29
Como, Perry, 18-19, 54, 69, 90, 131
Connolly, Mike, 263
Cooper, Gary, 94, 106
Copacabana nightclub, 21-22, 26-28, 56-57, 242, 256-257
Costello, Frank, 27-28, 35, 226
Coward, Noel, 63, 65, 114
Cowen, Warren, 133
Crawford, Joan, 59
Cronyn, Hume, 204
Crosby, Bing, 36, 54, 102-104, 115
Crosby, Dennis, 104
Crosby, Gary, 102
Crowther, Bosley, 167
Cugat, Xavier, 252
Curtis, Tony, 94, 193

D'Amato, Skinny, 247, 288
Dalitz, Moe, 248, 292
Damone, Vic, 27, 54
Danny and the Juniors, 312
Davis, Bette, 88, 94
Davis, Glenn, 60
Davis, Joan, 33
Davis, Sammy, Jr., 137, 193, 256-257
Dawes, Skipper, 5-6, 11-20, 22-23, 27-28
deCordova, Freddy, 294

DeGeneres, Ellen, 323
Delon, Nathalie and Alain, 259-265, 268
DeMarco Sisters, 38
DeMille, Cecil B., 48
Dempsey, Jack, 61
Dickinson, Angie, 16, 240, 253
Dietrich, Marlene, 15-16, 65-69, 112, 114
DiMaggio, Joe, 80
Disney, Walt, 86
Donahue, Phil, 327
Dorsey, Tommy, 56
Douglas, Kirk, 64, 133, 192
Downey, Morton, 51-52, 85
Dozier, Bill, 92
Duchin, Eddy, 27
Durante, Jimmy, 131
Durrell, Lawrence, 179

Earth, Wind and Fire, 312
Eastwood, Clint, 275
Eddie Ashman Band, 26
Eden Roc, Miami Beach, 244
Edwards, Sonny (aka Eddie Fisher), 13
Eisenhower, Dwight D. "Ike," 2, 25, 69
Elizabeth, Queen, 52, 80, 183
Entratter, Jack, 27
Estess, Elaine Grossinger, 31, 86
Evans, Bob, 243-245, 262-263
Evans, George, 28
Evans, Lord, 175, 183
Exner, Judith Campbell, 16, 240, 253-255

Farrow, Mia, 251, 273
Ferrer, Mel, 191, 202, 225
Fields, Totie, 286
Finch, Peter, 172-173, 178, 189-190
Fisher, Betty Lin, 67, 315, 322, 327-331
Fisher, Carrie (daughter), 81-83, 89, 93-94, 101, 108, 155-156, 162, 301, 313, 315-320
Fisher, Eileen (sister), 3
Fisher, Joe (father), 3-5, 9, 11-13, 40-41, 308-310, 316
Fisher, Joely (daughter), 127, 267, 272, 279-280, 315, 320, 322-325
Fisher, Maria (daughter), 196-197, 206
Fisher, Miriam (sister), 7, 263
Fisher, Mrs. (mother), 3, 5-9, 12, 30-32, 40-41, 67, 81-82, 93, 154-155
Fisher, Sol (brother), 5
Fisher, Todd Emanuel (son), 83, 93, 106, 129, 155-156, 162, 289, 301, 315-317, 320-322

Fisher, Tricia Leigh (daughter), 267-268, 315, 320, 322-325
Fisher's Delicatessen, 4
Fitzgerald, Ella, 54
Fonda, Henry, 192
Fontaine, Frankie, 312
Ford, Glenn, 151
Foreman, Joey, 12, 15-17, 32, 74, 92, 95, 146, 261
Freed, Arthur, 205
Frings, Kurt, 133, 151, 169, 181, 206, 226, 242, 244, 259-261, 280

Gabor, Zsa Zsa, 59
Gaines, Lenny, 95-96, 130, 166, 235-236
Gardner, Ava, 114, 139
Garfield, John, 32
Garland, Judy, 94, 162, 294-295
Giancana, Sam,16, 253-255, 257, 275, 307-308
Gielgud, John, 129
Gilels, Emil, 194
Gleason, Jackie, 27, 61, 102, 131
Gobel, George, 95, 131
Godfrey, Arthur, 10
Goldman, Dr. Carl, 182, 187
Goldwyn, Sam, 94
Graham, Sheila, 85
Granger, Stewart, 212
Grant, Cary, 144-145, 274
Grant, Johnny, 72
Grant, Sandy, 249-250
Greatest Story Ever Told, The (film), 179-180
Green, Johnny, 27
Greene, Shecky, 311
Griffin, Merv, 117
Grossinger, Elaine. *See* Estess, Elaine Grossinger
Grossinger, Harry, 31
Grossinger, Jennie, 10, 23, 31-33, 86, 145, 257-258, 306
Grossinger, Paul, 306
Grossinger's Hotel, 10, 23, 26, 31-33, 36-37, 57, 86, 145, 306
Guilaroff, Sidney, 136, 173

Hackett, Buddy, 261, 272, 294-296, 310-311
Hamilton, George, 251
Hammerstein, Oscar, 69
Hanley, Dick, 135-136, 171, 196, 211, 213-215, 229
Hansen, Eda Bjorn, 278-279, 304-305
Hardwicke, Sir Cedric, 130
Hargitay, Mickey, 64

Harriman, Averell, 195

Harrison, Rex, 190, 206-207, 230

Harvey, Laurence, 193, 242

Hauser, Gaylord, 290

Hayward, Susan, 171

Hearst, William Randolph, 270

Hefner, Hugh, 248, 255

Hendricks, Wanda, 60

Henie, Sonja, 271

Hepburn, Audrey, 170, 191, 202, 225, 240, 248-249

Hepburn, Katharine, 162-163

Hilton, Nicky, 117, 123, 157

Hitsig, "Wild Bill," 283, 285-286

Holden, William, 94, 106, 139, 171

Holingworth, Marion, 16

Hollywood Palace (TV show), 268

Hope, Bob, 36, 131

Hopper, Hedda, 118, 149, 193

Hubard, Kenny, 288-291

Hudson, Rock, 125-126

Hughes, Howard, 60, 91, 116, 134, 292

Huston, John, 115, 132

Isherwood, Christopher, 166

Jacobson, Dr. Max, 48-49, 54-55, 80, 86, 137, 165, 175-176, 187, 221-222, 224-225, 227, 234, 238-239, 246, 253-256, 280-291, 306

Jacobson, Dr. Tommy, 287, 298

Janssen, David, 166

Javits, Jacob, 307

Jeffries, Herb, 28

Jessel, Georgie, 84, 93, 135, 312

Johansson, Ingemar, 164

Johnson, Jeanette, 87, 106-107

Johnson, Lynda Bird, 251

Johnson, Lyndon, 257-259

Jolson, Al, 2, 9, 19, 26

Jones, Quincy, 250-251

Junior Music Hall (radio show), 13

Karl, Harry, 97, 100, 156

Kaye, Danny, 56, 107

Keaton, Buster, 114

Kelly, Gene, 70

Kelly, Jack, 283-284, 303

Kenley, Frank, 280

Kennedy, Bobby, 289

Kennedy, Jackie, 150, 238-240, 257-258

Kennedy, John "Jack," 2, 16, 49, 238-240, 253, 255-258, 283, 285

Kennemar, Rex, 134-136, 153, 180, 182, 201, 281, 283, 309

Keyes, Evelyn, 73, 111, 118-119

Khan, Aly, 127, 129, 160, 164, 274

Kilgallen, Dorothy, 33-34, 220, 246

Kinski, Nastassja, 250

Kolin, Dr. Irving and Shelly, 328

Korean War, 41-47, 61-62, 70, 85

Korshak, Sidney, 240, 244-245, 292

Kostelanetz, André, 79

Kovacs, Ernie, 94

Krushchev, Nikita, 195, 239

La Cage Aux Folles (show), 331

La Costa, San Diego, 292

Lamarr, Hedy, 60

Lane, Abbe, 16, 252-253

Lang, Hope, 253

La Rosa, Julius, 34

Lavi, Dalia, 107

Lee, Gypsy Rose, 11

Lee, Peggy, 79

Leigh, Janet, 94, 193

Leigh, Vivien, 128

LeMay, Gen. Curtis, 289

Leonard, Jackie, 76

Lerner, Alan Jay, 48, 240, 275, 283-284

Lewis, Jerry, 73, 94, 104, 265

Lewis, Joe E., 26-27, 76, 133, 223-224, 296

Lipton, Peggy, 250-251

Loew, Arthur, Jr., 136

Logan, Josh, 275

Lollobrigida, Gina, 170, 194

Longest Day, The (film), 214

Louis, Joe, 43, 309

Lourd, Bryan, 319-320

Lourd, Catherine Fisher (granddaughter), 319

Lynley, Carol, 248

Lyon, Sue, 16, 241, 250

Lyons, Leonard, 22, 65-66, 145

McDonald, Marie, 97

McDowall, Roddy, 117, 151, 190, 203-204, 206, 209, 211, 214, 217-218, 251-252

MacElroy, Dorothea, 275

McGuire, Phyllis, 253-254

MacLaine, Shirley, 114-115, 189

Magic Lady Supper Club, The (radio show), 12-13, 16

Magnani, Anna, 152

Mahoney, Jim, 133

Mamoulian, Rouben, 171, 173, 177-179

Mangel, Manny, 21

Mankiewicz, Joe, 133, 162-163, 166, 178-179, 184-
      186, 189, 191, 197, 199, 203-204, 206, 208, 212-
      215, 229

Mann, Danny, 166-167

Manners, Dorothy, 297

Mansfield, Jayne, 64

Mantle, Mickey, 281

Marciano, Rocky, 2, 68, 79

Margaret, Princess, 52-53, 73

Marlin Sisters, 29

Marshall, Penny, 318

Martin, Dean, 61, 64, 89, 90, 95, 104, 131, 150, 192-
      193, 259, 261, 285

Martin, Hugh, 48

Martin, Tony, 202

Marvin, Lee, 275

Marx, Groucho, 192

Marx, Guy, 308

Mathis, Johnny, 126, 284

Mature, Victor, 126, 216

Mayer, Louis B., 77

Meatloaf, 312

Merman, Ethel, 94

MGM, 71-73, 75, 77, 91, 117, 119, 133, 165, 205

Miller, Bill, 37, 66

Mirisch, Harold, 113, 121, 175

Moiseyev Dance Company, 193

Monroe, Marilyn, 63-64, 80, 114-115, 254, 256

Moore, Terry, 60

Morgan, Jane, 62-64, 99

Morrow, Buddy, 20-21

Mortimer, Lee, 37

Mostel, Zero, 48, 281

Munchausen, Baron, 100

Murray, Jan, 56

Murrow, Edward R., 112, 114

Music Corporation of America (MCA), 50, 90, 131

National Velvet (film), 183

Newcomb, Pat, 256

Newman, Paul, 175

Nightlight (TV show), 320

Niven, David, 106, 114, 118

Nizer, Louis, 225, 240

Novak, Kim, 15, 170, 274-275

Nussbaum, Rabbi Max, 157

O'Brian, Jack, 51, 85, 150

O'Brien,Margaret, 89

O'Connor, Carroll, 204

O'Connor, Donald, 70, 312, 330

Oberon, Merle, 16

Olander, Joan. See Van Doren, Mamie

Olivier, Laurence, 128

Orpheum, Los Angeles, 36, 58

Paint Your Wagon, 90, 275

Paley, Bill, 113

Parker, Suzy, 170, 246

Parsons, Louella, 75, 162, 248

Pasternak, Joe, 71-72

Pavarotti, Luciano, 202

Perkins, Barbara, 250, 261

Perkins, Tony, 270

Pershing, Gen. John J., 43

Philip, Prince, 80

Phillips, Michelle, 16, 250, 259

Piaf, Edith, 59

Picasso, Pablo, 132

Pons, Lily, 79

Porter, Cole, 69

Powell, Dick, 110

Powell, Eleanor, 30

Power, Tyrone, 154

Powers, Stephanie, 16, 248-249

Presley, Elvis, 105, 242, 247, 303

Presley, Sam, 278

Price, Dr. Middleton, 184

Prime Time Junior Music Hall (radio show), 17-18

Proser, Monte, 21-22, 26, 28, 38, 61

Prowse, Juliet, 241-244, 247

Quinn, Anthony, 284

Quinn, Sam, 290-291

Radin, Roy, 312

Radziwill, Prince, 256

Ray, Johnnie, 34

RCA, 35-36, 41, 44, 54, 113, 293-294

Red Garters (film), 71

Respectful Prostitute, The (play), 58-59

Reynolds, Debbie, 10, 15, 25, 31, 55, 59, 70-80, 81-
      108, 118-120, 122-124, 128-130, 132, 134, 137,
      140-151, 169, 176, 315-317, 320-322

Reynolds, Maxene, 71-72, 74, 78, 82, 85-86, 95, 97-98

Reynolds, Ray, 77, 82, 98, 321

Rich, Bernie, 12, 32, 95, 159, 201

Richardson, Ralph, 129

Riddle, Nelson, 294

Riva, Maria, 67

Rivera, Geraldo, 269

RKO, 91-93

Robbins, Freddie, 37

Roberts, Rachel, 190

Robeson, Paul, 34

Robinson, Edward G., 62, 309

Robinson, Jackie, 93-94

Robinson, Sugar Ray, 240

Rodgers, Richard, 69

Ronnie & Ray, 26

Ronnie and the Ronettes, 312

Rooney, Annie, 26

Rooney, Mickey, 132

Ross, Barney, 22

Ross, Jerry, 66

Roth, Philip, 70-71

Roy Radin's Vaudeville Revue, 312

Rudin, Mickey, 108

Russ Case Orchestra, 38

Sacks, Lester, 20

Sacks, Manny, 29, 54, 65, 69, 113, 129

Sahara, 310, 316

Saint, Eva Marie, 145

Salinger, Pierre, 253

Sandburg, Carl, 180

Sarnoff, David, 113

Schell, Maria, 196, 212, 225

Schulberg, Budd, 90

Schwartz, Ida, 11-12

Scott, Vernon, 133, 218

Sharaff, Irene, 208

Shaw, Artie, 98

Shaw, Mark, 238, 283

Shean, Pat, 102-104

Shearer, Norma, 89, 244, 297

Shore, Dinah, 16, 28, 64-65, 73, 131

Shore, Dinah, 28

Siegel, Sol, 165

Silver Mask award, 201-202

Silvers, Phil, 224

Simmons, Jean, 162, 205, 212

Simon, Neil, 270

Simon, Paul, 81, 318-319

Sinatra, Frank, 2, 11, 27-28, 54, 64, 80, 89-90, 101, 104, 114, 115, 125, 139, 150, 192-193, 202, 225, 241-243, 251-255, 273, 307

Singin' in the Rain (film), 70, 77

Skouras, Spyros, 170, 172, 179, 189-190, 200, 229

Smat, Ernie, 303-304

Smell-O-Vision, 111, 160

Smith, David, 330-331

Snowbabies, 328

Sobel, Louis, 22, 37

Spellman, Francis Cardinal, 68, 215

Spiegel, Sam, 160

St. Laurent, Yves, 194-196

Stafford, Jo, 28

Star Wars (film), 89, 317

Stein, Julie, 16, 69

Stevens, Connie, 15, 55, 127, 233, 265, 267-280, 309, 322-324, 332

Stevens, George, 115, 179-180

Stevenson, Adlai, 65-66

Strasberg, Lee, 60

Strasberg, Susan, 205

Streisand, Barbra, 289

Suarez, Olga, 26

Suddenly, Last Summer (film), 126, 160, 162-163, 170, 172, 178, 201

Sullivan, Ed, 38, 79, 131

Talber, Richard, 67

Tammy (film), 105

Taradash, Daniel, 166

Taylor, Elizabeth, 2, 5, 10, 15-16, 31, 55, 61, 63-64, 67, 83-84, 94, 99, 102, 105-106, 109, 242 , 332-333

divorce from Fisher, 247-248, 256-257, 271-272

marriage to Eddie Fisher, 139-167, 169-197, 199-231, 233-234, 241

marriage to Mike Todd, 114, 117-130, 132-137

Teen Time (radio show), 13, 17

Teller, Edward, 69-70

Texaco Star Theater, The (TV show), 37

Thalberg, Irving, 89, 244, 297

Thomas Junior High School, 11

Thomas, Danny, 37-38, 90

Thomas, Lowell, 132

Tierney, Lawrence, 193

Tiny Tim, 312

Toast of the Town, The (TV show), 38, 131

Todd, Elizabeth Frances "Liza," 129, 140-141, 196, 230

Todd, Mike, 29-30, 73-74, 80, 94, 101, 105-106, 109-137, 156, 187, 210

Todd, Mike, Jr., 114, 135-136, 160, 257

Todd-AO, 114, 119-120, 132
Truman, Bess, 44, 88
Truman, Harry, 2, 34, 44-45, 88
Truman, Margaret, 34, 44, 66, 88
Tunder, Pat, 205
Turner, Lana, 169
Turnure, Pam, 16, 256-258

Valenti, Jack, 258-259
Valva, John, 211
Van Doren, Mamie (aka Joan Olander), 15, 61-62, 67
Vandal, George, 328-329
Vanderbilt, Gloria, 164
Ventura, Charlie, 21
Vernon, Jackie, 312
Villa Venice, Chicago, 254

Wagner, Robert, 74, 139, 206
Waitkus, Eddie, 56
Wanger, Walter, 170-172, 178, 209, 215, 217, 229, 257
Warner, Jack, 94
Warner Brothers, 76-77, 174-175
Warren, Fran, 37
Warren, Honey, 66, 88
Wasserman, Lew, 90
Wayne, John, 125, 188, 192

Weil, Al, 79
Weinberger, Billy, 292
Werblin, Sonny, 50
WFIL (radio station), Philadelphia, 11-19
What's My Line (TV show), 220-221
When I Grow Up (radio show), 11
White, George, 112
Whiteman, Paul, 23
Wilder, Billy, 115
Wilding, Michael, 117-121, 125-126, 128-129, 216
Williams, Andy, 303
Williams, Camille, 147-148, 155, 159
Williams, Ted, 291
Williams, Tennessee, 166, 187-188, 206
Wilson, Earl, 37
Winchell, Walter, 22, 38, 116, 145, 235, 242
Winters, Shelley, 23, 118-119
Wood, Natalie, 139, 193, 227
Woodruff, Bob, 51
Woodward, Joanne, 170
Wyler, William, 115
Wynne, Joanie, 56-58, 74, 242-243

Young, Walter, 110

Zanuck, Darryl, 113, 214, 229
Zinnemann, Fred, 115